BEYOND BABEL

Society of Biblical Literature

Resources for Biblical Study

Steven L. McKenzie
Editor

Number 42

BEYOND BABEL
A Handbook for Biblical Hebrew and Related Languages

BEYOND BABEL

A Handbook for Biblical Hebrew
and Related Languages

Edited by
John Kaltner and Steven L. McKenzie

Society of Biblical Literature
Atlanta

BEYOND BABEL

A Handbook for Biblical Hebrew and Related Languages

Library of Congress Cataloging-in-Publication Data

Beyond Babel : a handbook for biblical Hebrew and related languages / edited by Steven McKenzie & John Kaltner.
     p. cm. — (Resources for biblical study ; no. 42)
   ISBN 1-58983-035-0
   1. Middle Eastern philology. 2. Semitic philology. 3. Middle East—Languages—Grammar, Comparative. 4. Middle Eastern literature—Relation to the Old Testament 5. Bible. O.T.—Criticism, interpretation, etc. I. McKenzie, Steven L., 1953- II. Kaltner, John, 1954- III. Series.
   PJ25 .B54 2002b
   492—dc21   2002011759

10 09 08 07 06 05 04 03 02   5 4 3 2 1

Printed in the United States of America
on acid-free paper

CONTENTS

PREFACE

The intent behind this book is to provide a general orientation to the languages of importance for the study of the Hebrew Bible for readers who have not had detailed exposure to those languages. We hope that the book will be particularly useful to students who are just beginning their academic careers in the study of the Hebrew Bible. But it should also find an audience among those who have not had detailed exposure to one or more of the languages discussed here and who would like to cultivate at least a rudimentary acquaintance with it or them. The chapters do presuppose familiarity with biblical Hebrew, although we have included a chapter on biblical and inscriptional Hebrew that situates this material within its broader linguistic context. Indeed, many readers may find it helpful to begin with this chapter before moving to less-familiar territory.

The languages treated here are those that, in our estimation, are the most significant for the study of the Hebrew Bible for purposes of comparative grammar and lexicography or for comparative history and literature, or both. Other languages might have been included. We considered including a chapter on Sumerian but ultimately decided that, given our readership, the linguistic and literary connections with the Hebrew Bible were not strong enough to warrant a separate chapter. Greek literature is increasingly cited in recent Hebrew Bible scholarship for its comparative value. However, we deemed it most appropriate to reserve it—along with other languages that are especially important in textual criticism (Syriac included)—for treatment in a potential companion volume dealing with the New Testament. Failing such a volume, and granted a second chance (or edition) of the present work, the addition of Greek and Sumerian, and possibly other languages, may be appropriate.

As authors for each chapter we sought specialists with proven records of publication in the language that is the subject of the chapter. We were most gratified by the gracious acceptance of those whom we contacted and are deeply grateful for their generosity and excellent work. In an effort to provide consistency between chapters, we proposed a three-part format for authors to follow: an overview of the language, its significance for the study of the Bible, and ancient sources and modern resources for study of the language and its literature. It will be immediately evident that this format is less suitable for some languages included in this volume than for others. Again we are most grateful to the contributors both for their adherence to the format where possible and for their creativity in adapting it to the needs of their subject languages.

Finally, we are grateful to the Society of Biblical Literature for publishing this volume in the Society of Biblical Literature Resources for Biblical Study series, to Rex Matthews and Leigh Andersen for shepherding it especially through the transition process from Scholars Press to SBL, and to Bob Buller for his copy editing and typesetting. We are particularly delighted that a simultaneous hardback edition published by Brill will make this volume easily available to a European readership.

ABBREVIATIONS

GENERAL

acc.	accusative
Akk	Akkadian
BH	biblical Hebrew
C	consonant
CA	Classical Arabic
com.	common
fem.	feminine
gen.	genitive
Heb.	Hebrew
LBH	Late Biblical Hebrew
LXX	Septuagint
MA	Middle Arabic
masc.	masculine
MH	Mishnaic Hebrew
MT	Masoretic Text
NH	New Hittite
nom.	nominative
NS	New Script
OH	Old Hittite
OS	Old Script
OSA	Old South Arabian
PBEH	postbiblical epigraphic Hebrew
PBH	postbiblical Hebrew
PIE	(Proto) Indo-European
pl.	plural
PN	personal name
PS	Proto-Semitic
SBH	Standard Biblical Hebrew
sg.	singular
V	vowel

PRIMARY SOURCES

Ant.	Josephus, *Jewish Antiquities*
b.	Babylonian Talmud
B. Bat.	*Baba Batra*

B. Qam.	*Baba Qamma*
Ber.	*Berakot*
Bik.	*Bikkurim*
ʿEd.	*ʿEduyyot*
Giṭ.	*Giṭṭin*
Soṭ.	*Soṭah*
Gen. Rab.	*Genesis Rabbah*
m.	Mishnah
Sanh.	*Sanhedrin*
t.	Tosefta
y.	Jerusalem Talmud

SECONDARY SOURCES

ÄAT	Ägypten und Altes Testament
ABD	*Anchor Bible Dictionary.* Edited by D. N. Freedman. 6 vols. New York: Doubleday, 1992.
AcOr	*Acta orientalia*
ADPV	Abhandlungen des deutschen Palästinavereins
AfO	*Archiv für Orientforschung*
AfOB	Archiv für Orientforschung: Beiheft
AION	*Annali dell'Istituto Orientale di Napoli*
AJSL	*American Journal of Semitic Languages and Literature*
ANET	*Ancient Near Eastern Texts Relating to the Old Testament.* Edited by J. B. Pritchard. 3d ed. Princeton, N.J.: Princeton University Press, 1969.
AnOr	Analecta orientalia
AnSt	*Anatolian Studies*
AOAT	Alter Orient und Altes Testament
AoF	*Altorientalische Forschungen*
AOS	American Oriental Series
ArOr	*Archiv Orientální*
AUSS	*Andrews University Seminary Studies*
BA	*Biblical Archaeologist*
BaghM	*Baghdader Mitteilungen*
BAR	*Biblical Archaeology Review*
BASOR	*Bulletin of the American Schools of Oriental Research*
BDB	Brown, F., S. R. Driver, and C. A. Briggs, *A Hebrew and English Lexicon of the Old Testament.* Oxford: Oxford University Press, 1907.
BHS	*Biblia Hebraica Stuttgartensia.* Edited by K. Elliger and W. Rudolph. Stuttgart: Deutsche Bibelgesellschaft, 1983.
Bib	*Biblica*

BJS	Brown Judaic Studies
BO	*Bibliotheca orientalis*
BZAW	Beihefte zur Zeitschrift für die alttestamentliche Wissenschaft
CAT	*The Cuneiform Alphabetic Texts from Ugarit, Ras Ibn Hani and Other Places.* Edited by M. Dietrich, O. Loretz, and J. Sanmartín. Münster: Ugarit-Verlag, 1995.
CBQ	*Catholic Biblical Quarterly*
CBQMS	Catholic Biblical Quarterly Monograph Series
CHD	*The Hittite Dictionary of the Oriental Institute of the University of Chicago.* Edited by Harry A. Hoffner Jr. and Hans G. Güterbock. Chicago: Oriental Institute, 1980–.
CIS	*Corpus inscriptionum semiticarum*
CTH	*Catalogue des textes hittites*
CTA	*Corpus des tablettes en cunéiformes alphabétiques découvertes à Ras Shamra-Ugarit de 1929 à 1939.* Edited by A. Herdner. Mission de Ras Shamra 10. Paris: Imprimerie Nationale, 1963.
DBSup	*Dictionaire de la Bible: Supplément.* Edited by L. Pirot and A. Robert. Paris: Letouzey & Aneg, 1928–.
EncJud	*Encyclopaedia Judaica.* 16 vols. Jerusalem: Keter, 1972.
ER	*The Encyclopedia of Religion.* Edited by M. Eliade. 16 vols. New York: Macmillan, 1987.
ErIsr	*Eretz-Israel*
EVO	*Egitto e Vicino Oriente*
FAT	Forschungen zum Alten Testament
GKC	*Gesenius' Hebrew Grammar.* Edited by E. Kautzsch. Translated by A. E. Cowley. 2d ed. Oxford: Oxford University Press, 1910.
GM	*Göttinger Miszellen*
HALOT	Koehler, Ludwig, Walter Baumgartner, and J. J. Stamm. *The Hebrew and Aramaic Lexicon of the Old Testament.* Translated and edited under the supervision of M. E. J. Richardson. 5 vols. Leiden: Brill, 1994–2000.
HO	Handbuch der Orientalistik
HSM	Harvard Semitic Monographs
HSS	Harvard Semitic Studies
HUCA	*Hebrew Union College Annual*
HZL	*Hethitisches Zeichenlexikon: Inventar und Interpretation der Keilschriftzeichen aus den Boğasköy-Texten.* Christel Rüster and Erich Neu. Studien zu den Boğasköy-Texten 2. Wiesbaden: Harrassowitz, 1989.
IEJ	*Israel Exploration Journal*

IOS	Israel Oriental Society
JANESCU	*Journal of the Ancient Near Eastern Society of Columbia University*
JAOS	*Journal of the American Oriental Society*
JBL	*Journal of Biblical Literature*
JCS	*Journal of Cuneiform Studies*
JDS	Judean Desert Studies
JEA	*Journal of Egyptian Archaeology*
JEOL	*Jaarbericht van het Voorasziatisch-Egyptisch Gezelschap (Genootshhap) Ex oriente lux*
JFSR	*Journal of Feminist Studies in Religion*
JHNES	Johns Hopkins Near Eastern Studies
JNES	*Journal of Near Eastern Studies*
JQR	*Jewish Quarterly Review*
JSOTSup	Journal for the Study of the Old Testament: Supplement Series
JSS	*Journal of Semitic Studies*
JTS	*Journal of Theological Studies*
KAI	*Kanaanäische und aramäische Inschriften.* H. Donner and W. Röllig. 2d ed. Wiesbaden: Harrassowitz, 1966–1969.
KBo	*Keilschrifttexte aus Boghazköi*
KTU	*Die keilalphabetischen Texte aus Ugarit.* Edited by M. Dietrich, O. Loretz, and J. Sanmartín. AOAT 24/1. Neukirchen-Vluyn: Neukirchener Verlag, 1976.
KUB	*Keilschrifturkunden aus Boghazköi*
LÄ	*Lexikon der Ägyptologie.* Edited by W. Helck, E.Otto, and W. Westendorf. Wiesbaden: Harrassowitz, 1972–.
LCL	Loeb Classical Library
Lg	*Language*
MDAI	*Mitteilungen des Deutschen archäologischen Instituts*
Mus	*Muséon:Revue d'études orientales*
NAWG	Nachrichten (von) der Akademie der Wissenschaften in Göttingen
NRSV	New Revised Standard Version
OBO	Orbis biblicus et orientalis
OLA	Orientalia lovaniensia analecta
OLP	*Orientalia loaniensia periodica*
Or	*Orientalia* (NS)
OrAnt	*Oriens antiquus*
PEQ	*Palestine Exploration Quarterly*
PL	Patrologia latina [= Patrologiae cursus completus: Series latina]. Edited by J.-P. Migne. 217 vols. Paris: Migne, 1844–1864.
RA	*Revue d'assyriologie et d'archéologie orientale*

RdÉ	*Revue d'Égyptologie*
REg	*Revue d'égyptologie*
RHA	*Revue hittite et asiatique*
RSF	*Rivista di studi fenici*
RSV	Revised Standard Version
SAOC	Studies in Ancient Oriental Civilizations
SBLABS	Society of Biblical Literature Archaeology and Biblical Studies
SBLDS	Society of Biblical Literature Dissertation Series
SBLMasS	Society of Biblical Literature Masoretic Studies
SBLRBS	Society of Biblical Literature Resources for Biblical Study
SBLWAW	Society of Biblical Literature Writings from the Ancient World
ScrHier	Scripta hierosolymitana
SEL	*Studi epigrafici e linguistici*
Sem	*Semitica*
SMEA	*Studi Micenei ed Egeo-Anatolici*
SPAW	*Sitzungsberichte der preussischen Akademie der Wissenschaften*
SubBi	Subsidia biblica
TA	*Tel Aviv*
TynBul	*Tyndale Bulletin*
UF	*Ugarit-Forschungen*
UT	*Ugaritic Textbook.* C. H. Gordon. AnOr 38. Rome: Pontifical Biblical Institute, 1965.
VT	*Vetus Testamentum*
ZA	*Zeitschrift für Assyriologie*
ZAH	*Zeitschrift für Althebräistik*
ZÄS	*Zeitschrift für ägyptische Sprache und Altertum*
ZAW	*Zeitschrift für die alttestamentliche Wissenschaft*
ZDMG	*Zeitschrift der deutschen morgenländischen Gesellschaft*
ZDPV	*Zeitschrift des Deutschen Palästina-Vereins*
ZfE	*Zeitschrift für Ethnologie*
ZPE	*Zeitschrift für Papyrologie und Epigraphik*

INTRODUCTION

John Huehnergard

1. THE STUDY OF NEAR EASTERN LANGUAGES IN BIBLICAL SCHOLARSHIP

In their quest to understand the text of the Hebrew Bible, students and scholars have for centuries turned to other Near Eastern languages. Already in the Middle Ages, Jewish exegetes and grammarians compared obscure Hebrew words and roots with similar forms in the Arabic spoken in their surroundings and with Aramaic forms with which they were familiar. The rise of critical biblical scholarship in Europe some two centuries ago coincided roughly with the beginnings of comparative and historical linguistics; although the latter was founded on the basis of the Indo-European languages, its methods were soon also applied to the Semitic languages, and comparative-historical Semitic linguistics has served as one of the principal tools for elucidating the biblical text and its language ever since.

There are two fundamental reasons for the biblical scholar to study other languages of the Near East in addition to Hebrew. The more obvious is that such study enables the scholar to read texts produced by ancient Israel's neighbors in the original tongues. The chapters on the individual languages that follow survey the major types of texts that form the basis of our understanding of the history and culture of the biblical world. The relevance of a given language to biblical study naturally depends on a number of factors, many of them nonlinguistic, but all languages attested in the biblical region and period (and in earlier periods) are of interest because the texts recorded in them document the biblical world; here, among others, we may mention Akkadian (and, to a lesser extent, since it is much earlier, Sumerian), Ugaritic, Phoenician, Moabite, Ammonite, Edomite, early and imperial Aramaic, Egyptian, and Hittite. Texts that document the early history of Judaism and Chrisitianity are preserved in Hebrew and (various forms of) Aramaic, Greek, and Latin, but also in less-commonly studied languages such as Coptic and classical Ethiopic (Geʿez). For text-critical work, scholars refer to early versions of the biblical text in Greek, Aramaic (Targumic and Syriac), Latin, Coptic, Ethiopic, and other languages.

1

The second, less obvious, reason to study other languages is that such study can shed considerable light on the grammar and vocabulary of biblical Hebrew itself and thus on the biblical text proper. Although classical Hebrew has never ceased to be an object of study, the fact remains that it has long been a dead language (i.e., a language that no one has learned as a first language), a language of texts only, and so it must be learned and explained with the tools of philology (the study of texts). (In this, biblical Hebrew is similar to Latin, classical Greek, and classical forms of Aramaic and Ethiopic, all of which have been the subject of a continuous tradition of study, and unlike, say, Akkadian, Egyptian, and Ugaritic, languages that had been completely forgotten and that had to be recovered or reconstructed *in toto* when they were rediscovered.) There are other, related difficulties in the study of biblical Hebrew, including (1) the relatively small size of the corpus of biblical Hebrew (so that many words that may have been quite common in the spoken language appear only sporadically and are consequently difficult to interpret with confidence);[1] (2) the presence in the corpus of diverse genres, including poetry, narrative prose, aphorisms, and the like; (3) the long chronological span covered by the corpus, nearly a millennium, during which time the spoken language undoubtedly underwent at least some change; (4) the likely existence in the corpus of diverse dialects in addition to the standard Jerusalem literary dialect in which most of the text was written. The study of other languages and of other forms of Hebrew (especially Mishnaic, for which see the chapter on postbiblical Hebrew) provides an awareness of these problems and, sometimes, solutions, as is also abundantly illustrated in each of the subsequent chapters of this book.

2. OVERVIEW OF THE SEMITIC LANGUAGE FAMILY

Hebrew is a member of the Semitic language family. Other members of the family that are described in detail in the present volume are Akkadian, Ugaritic, Phoenician, Moabite, Ammonite, Edomite, Aramaic, and Arabic. Still other Semitic languages are Eblaite, a cuneiform language, closely related to Akkadian, attested in third-millennium texts from the city of Ebla (in present-day Syria); the various Old (or Epigraphic) South Arabian languages, which are attested from the eighth century B.C.E. until the sixth century C.E. (these languages—Sabaic, Minaic or Madhabic, Qatabanic, and

---

[1] In its size the corpus of biblical Hebrew is roughly similar to those of Ugaritic or the Old South Arabian languages, and considerably smaller than, for example, those of classical Arabic, Ethiopic, Syriac, Akkadian, or Egyptian—huge corpora that allow for greater confidence in interpreting both grammar and lexicon.

Hadramitic—are sometimes referred to collectively as Ṣayhadic); the Ethiopian Semitic languages, including classical Ethiopic or Geʿez (from the fourth century C.E.) and a large number of modern languages, such as Amharic, Tigrinya, Tigre, Gurage, and Harari; and the Modern South Arabian languages—Mehri, Jibbali, Soqotri, and others—spoken in Yemen and Oman and not written down before modern times.

The Semitic family itself is part of a still larger linguistic group, called Afro-Asiatic (formerly called Hamito-Semitic). Other members of the Afro-Asiatic phylum are ancient Egyptian; the Berber languages of North Africa; the Cushitic and Omotic languages of Ethiopia, Somalia, and neighboring countries; and the vast family of Chadic languages in central and western sub-Saharan Africa. The fact that most of these branches, with the notable exception of Egyptian, are not attested before the modern period makes comparison with the Semitic branch difficult, and comparative linguistic work on Afro-Asiatic as a whole is still in its early stages.

Which of the Semitic languages are more closely related to one another—that is, the internal classification or subgrouping of the family—is a much-debated topic. It is an important issue, however, because greater closeness implies a more recently shared common ancestor. What follows is a summary of one plausible subgrouping of the Semitic language family. Most scholars are agreed on a primary division, based on the form of the perfective verb, into East Semitic, which comprises only Akkadian and Eblaite, and West Semitic, which includes the rest of the languages. West Semitic in turn is further subdivided into the Modern South Arabian branch, the Ethiopian branch, and a third branch called Central Semitic. The latter comprises the Old South Arabian languages,[2] Arabic, and the Northwest Semitic languages. The Northwest Semitic subbranch includes Ugaritic, Aramaic, and the Canaanite languages, which are Phoenician (and Punic), Moabite, Ammonite, Edomite, and, finally, Hebrew. According to this classification, therefore, Hebrew's closest relatives, the languages with which it most recently shared a common ancestor, are, first, the other Canaanite languages (note that in Isa 19:18 Hebrew is called שְׂפַת כְּנַעַן "the language

---

[2] Until recently, Old South Arabian has been grouped with Modern South Arabian and with Ethiopian Semitic. See, however, Norbert Nebes, "Zur Form der Imperfektbasis des unvermehrten Grundstammes im Altsüdarabischen," in *Semitische Studien unter besonderer Berücksichtigung der Südsemitistik* (vol. 1 of *Festschrift Ewald Wagner zum 65. Geburtstag;* ed. W. Heinrichs and G. Schoeler; Beirut and Stuttgart: Steiner, 1994), 59–81; Victor Porkhomovsky, "Modern South Arabian Languages from a Semitic and Hamito-Semitic Perspective," *Proceedings of the Seminar for Arabian Studies* 27 (1997): 219–23; and Rainer Voigt, "The Classification of Central Semitic," *JSS* 32 (1987): 1–21.

of Canaan"), followed by the remaining Northwest Semitic languages (essentially, Aramaic and Ugaritic), and then Arabic and the Old South Arabian languages.

Common Semitic

West Semitic   East Semitic

Central Semitic

Northwest Semitic   Eblaite   Akkadian

Ugaritic   Canaanite   Aramaic   Arabic   Old South   Modern South   Ethiopian
                                                         Arabian   Arabian

In addition to factors of genetic proximity, account must also be taken of cultural and historical considerations. For example, for much of the second millennium B.C.E., and into the first, Akkadian was a lingua franca throughout the Near East, that is, a language used for communication among peoples speaking different languages, and there are as a result a significant number of Akkadian loanwords—borrowings—in Hebrew, such as מֶכֶס "tax" and מִסְכְּנוֹת "storehouses."[3] Similarly, Aramaic served as a lingua franca for most of the first millennium, and the influence of Aramaic on Hebrew as a result of the pervasiveness of the former is considerable, in both vocabulary and grammar.[4]

3. SCRIPTS AND TRANSLITERATION

A writing system must be carefully distinguished from the language or languages recorded in it. In particular it should be noted that a given script may be used for the writing of a number of languages, which need not be related. Cuneiform, for example, was first used to write Sumerian, which is not related to any other known language, and then to write Akkadian, a Semitic language, and then to write the Indo-European Hittite language and several other unrelated ancient Near Eastern languages (such as Hur-

---

[3] See Paul V. Mankowski, *Akkadian Loanwords in Biblical Hebrew* (HSS 47; Winona Lake, Ind.: Eisenbrauns, 2000).

[4] M. Wagner, *Die lexikalischen und grammatikalischen Aramaismen im alttestamentlichen Hebräisch* (BZAW 96; Berlin: de Gruyter, 1966).

rian and Elamite). Similarly, the Arabic script is also used to write modern Persian, an Indo-European language. Less commonly, a single language, or variant dialects of a single language, may be written in more than one script. The Anatolian language called Luwian, for example, is attested both in Mesopotamian cuneiform and in an indigenous hieroglyphic script. Maltese, a form of Arabic, is written in the Latin alphabet, like English. In the Middle Ages, Jews in Arabic-speaking countries would write the Arabic that they spoke in Hebrew letters (Judeo-Arabic).

No writing system records every significant feature of a language. Different systems are more successful in noting some features, less successful in others. The early Phoenician alphabet, for example, presumably recorded each of the consonants of the language discretely but gave no indication of the vowels. Phoenician had fewer consonants than ancient Hebrew, and when speakers of Hebrew borrowed the Phoenician alphabet they had to press at least one symbol into service to represent more than one sound, namely, שׂ for what the Masoretes later differentiated as שׂ *ś* and שׁ *š* (there were probably a few other such double-duty letters in early Hebrew; see below and the article in this volume on biblical Hebrew). In Mesopotamian cuneiform, on the other hand, vowel quality (and sometimes, but not regularly, vowel quantity) was indicated, but the system was not well adapted for the clear differentiation of series of homorganic consonants (i.e., consonants pronounced at the same place in the mouth, such as the labials, voiced *b* and voiceless *p;* thus, the syllables *ab* and *ap* were always written with the same sign).

Both because of the inadequacies of native writing systems and because of their diversity, scholars find it useful to transliterate the various languages into a common system. This allows the details of the phonology and grammar of individual forms to be represented clearly, and it also greatly facilitates the comparison of forms across languages. The linguistic similarity of Hebrew שָׁמַע, Syriac ܫܡܥ, Arabic سَمِعَ, and Ethiopic ሰምዐ, all meaning "he heard," is obviously much more transparent when those forms are transliterated, respectively, as *šāmaʿ, šmaʿ, samiʿa,* and *samʿa.* Western scholars specializing in the study of the Semitic languages have long used a relatively uniform system for transliterating the sounds into the Latin alphabet, using special diacritics for sounds that are not represented by Latin letters. (Diacritics are marks added to a letter to denote a special phonetic value, like the ˜ in Spanish *ñ* for [ny].) Some of the diacritics have different values in other philological traditions, however (such as Slavic philology, Sanskrit philology). Since 1886, therefore, the International Phonetic Association has promoted the use of a "universally agreed system of notation for the sounds" of all of the world's languages, called the International Phonetic Alphabet (IPA), a system that is now widely used for publications in linguistics.[5] Philologists, however, including Semitists, generally continue to use the traditional transliteration systems of their fields. The main features of the traditional Semitistic system are as follows; the corresponding IPA symbols are also noted, in square brackets:

(1) א and its counterparts in the other Semitic languages are represented by ʾ (in the IPA this is extended with a "tail", [ʔ]), and ע by ʿ (IPA [ʕ]). (א and ע may also be represented by single close-quote and open-quote marks, i.e., ' and ʿ, respectively.) Hebrew ע reflects the merger of two distinct Semitic consonants (which remain distinct, for example, in Ugaritic and Arabic; see below, section 5), the voiced pharyngeal fricative ʿ and a voiced velar fricative, which is transliterated by Semitists as ġ or ǧ (in IPA, this is [ɣ]).

(2) An underdot denotes the "emphatic" consonants, as in ṭ for ט and ṣ for צ; for ק and its counterparts in other Semitic languages, ḳ was used by some scholars in the nineteenth and early twentieth centuries, but this was generally replaced by q; some present-day scholars, however, persuasively argue for a return to the use of ḳ for most of the Semitic languages. (The IPA representation of these consonants depends on their actual pronunciation in the various Semitic languages. In the modern Ethiopian Semitic languages, they are glottalic, thus IPA [tʼ] for the consonant that corresponds to Hebrew ט; in Arabic, they are pharyngealized, e.g., IPA [tˤ].)

(3) An underdot is also used in ḥ for ח. As we will see below (section 4, end), Hebrew ח, like ע, reflects the merger of two originally distinct Semitic consonants (which also remain distinct in Ugaritic and Arabic), the voiceless pharyngeal fricative ḥ (IPA [ħ]) and a voiceless velar fricative, which is transliterated by Semitists as ḫ (i.e., a "hooked h"; in IPA, this is [x]).

(4) The sound "sh" denoted, for example, by Hebrew שׁ, is traditionally transliterated by š (i.e., s with a "wedge" or "hachek"; in IPA, the symbol for "sh" is [ʃ]). The Semitistic transliteration of Hebrew שׂ is ś (i.e., s with acute). (Traditionally, שׂ is pronounced the same as ס, IPA [s]; the probable ancient pronunciation of שׂ is a voiceless lateral fricative, IPA [ɬ].)

(5) The spirantized variants of the bgdkpt consonants are frequently not indicated specially in transliteration; if notation of the spirantization is important, however, this may be done with underlining (or, in the case of g and p, an overline instead), as in kāṯaḇ for כָּתַב.

(6) For Proto-Semitic and for some of the Semitic languages, short vowels are written with no diacritic (thus, a, i, u), while long vowels are

[5] See International Phonetic Association, *Handbook of the International Phonetic Association: A Guide to the Use of the International Phonetic Alphabet* (Cambridge: Cambridge University Press, 1999).

indicated with a mark called a macron ($\bar{a}$, $\bar{\imath}$, $\bar{u}$). (In the IPA system, length is generally indicated by the symbol [ː] or by a colon, [:]; thus Arabic *kātibun* "scribe" would be IPA [kaːtibun]. The length symbol is also used for long or geminated ["doubled"] consonants, thus גִּדֵּל, traditionally *gid-dal*, IPA [gidːal].) For the transliteration of the Hebrew vowels, see the chapter, "Hebrew (Biblical and Epigraphic)."

4. PRINCIPLES AND METHODS OF HISTORICAL AND COMPARATIVE LINGUISTICS

Historical linguistics is the study of how languages change over time. That all languages do change over time is well known; we have only to look at a page of Shakespeare, Chaucer, or Beowulf to see that English has undergone considerable change in just a few centuries. Biblical Hebrew was written over a period of nearly a millennium, and the Masoretic system of vowels and accents was added nearly a millennium later still; in all of this time it is impossible that Hebrew, which was not immune from normal linguistic processes, would not have undergone some development. (See the chapter on biblical Hebrew for more discussion of this topic.) When speakers of a language become separated into two or more groups, for reasons of politics, geography, or climate change, the speech patterns of the separate groups will change in different ways; eventually, if contact between the groups is sufficiently weak, the variant speech patterns, which we call dialects at first, will eventually become unintelligible from one group to the other, and distinct languages will have emerged. These languages are said to be genetically related to one another because they share a common ancestor. Comparative linguistics is the study of the relationships among related languages and between such languages and their common ancestor. Frequently, especially in the case of incompletely attested languages, the study of languages in the same family will clarify aspects of the grammar and vocabulary that would otherwise remain obscure.

One of the main engines driving language change is *sound change.* For a variety of reasons, speakers do not pronounce their language in exactly the same way as those from whom they learned it. One of the most important—and surprising—aspects of sound change is that it is *regular* and can be described by *rules*. As an example, consider forms of biblical Hebrew such as *kesep* "silver," *kaspî* "my silver," and *ᶜebed* "servant," *ᶜabdî* "my servant"; compare those with Akkadian *kaspum* "silver," *kaspī* "my silver," and Arabic *ᶜabdun* "servant," *ᶜabdī* "my servant," which suggest that the original bases of these words were **kasp-* and **ᶜabd-* (an asterisk, *, is used to indicate a form that has been reconstructed for the common ancestral language, or protolanguage). The Hebrew "segholate" forms *kesep* and *ᶜebed* show two phonological developments: the change of the original vowel **a* between the first and second consonants to *e*, and the insertion (anaptyxis) of a vowel *e* between the second and third consonant. These developments may be written as rules, as follows:

(1) *a* > *e* / C_CC# (that is, "*a* becomes [>] *e* in the following environment [/]: after a consonant and before two consonants at the end of a word [the underline _ indicates the position of the sound in question; # indicates a morpheme or word boundary]"; thus, e.g., **kasp* > **kesp*, **ᶜabd* > **ᶜebd*)

(2) ø > *e* / C_C# (that is, "nothing/zero becomes *e* [or, *e* is inserted] between two consonants at the end of a word"; thus, **kesp* > *kesep*, **ᶜebd* > *ᶜebed;* note that these two rules operate sequentially, rule 2 operating on the result of rule 1).[6]

As noted earlier, sound rules are regular; that is, they operate without exceptions. Thus, any base inherited into Hebrew with the form *CaCC* is expected, when it has no suffix, to become *CeCeC.* When we do find exceptions, such as **bayt-* > *bayit* "house" or **baᶜl-* > *baᶜal* "lord" (rather than the forms that our rules would generate, ***beyet* and ***beᶜel* [a double asterisk, **, indicates an impossible or ungrammatical form]), we must rewrite our rules more precisely to take account of additional features of the consonants involved, such as whether any of them are glides (*w* and *y*) or gutturals. The regularity of sound change is a fundamental hypothesis of historical linguistics.

The other main factor in language change is *analogy,* which is change on the basis of a model or pattern. Analogy is responsible, for example, for the nonstandard English form *brang* instead of *brought;* it occurs because a speaker (unconsciously) makes an analogy such as the following: *sing* : *sang* :: *bring* : *X* (that is, "*sing* is to *sang* as *bring* is to …"; *X* denotes the new form created by the analogy). In such an analogy both form and meaning must correspond; in the example just given, a single sound (*i* versus *a*) differentiates the present and past forms on the left of the proportion, and so the similarly shaped present form *bring* on the right of the proportion is changed analogously to create a new past tense *brang* (instead of the inherited, or learned, form *brought*). An example of the working of analogy in Hebrew is the form of the second-person plural of the perfect with a pronominal suffix, as in *heᶜĕlîtūnû* "you brought us up" (Num 20:5; 21:5); there is no regular sound rule in Hebrew phonology according to which the final *-em* of, for example, *heᶜĕlîtem* "you brought up" changes to *-ū-* when a pronominal suffix is appended. Rather, the form

---

[6] A third sound change is spirantization, which applies after rule 2: *kesep* is pronounced *kesep̄*, *ᶜebed* is pronounced *ᶜeḇed*.

heʿĕlîtūnû is the result of an analogy between the third-person masculine singular and plural forms with a suffix, on the one hand, and the corresponding second-person masculine singular and plural forms; it may be represented as follows, using a sound verb to show the forms more clearly:

$$\check{s}\partial m\bar{a}r\bar{a}n\hat{u} : \check{s}\partial m\bar{a}r\bar{u}n\hat{u} :: \check{s}\partial m\bar{a}rt\bar{a}n\hat{u} : X = \check{s}\partial m\bar{a}rt\bar{u}n\hat{u},$$

in which the simple change of *ā* to *ū* that characterizes the change of singular to plural in the third-person forms on the left is extended to the second-person forms on the right.

A subcategory of analogical change is *leveling,* by which a paradigm is made more uniform. An example in English is the generalization of /s/ to mark the plural, where once there were several ways in which plurals were formed (preserved vestigially in forms such as *oxen* and *geese*). An example in Hebrew is found in some verb paradigms: in the perfect conjugation of *ḥāpēṣ* "to delight in," many of the forms have *pataḥ* rather than *ṣērê* in the second syllable, the result of a sound rule (called Philippi's Law: a stressed **i* becomes *ṣērê, ē,* when in an originally open syllable, but *pataḥ, a,* in an originally closed syllable; thus **ḥapíθa > ḥāpēṣ,* but **ḥapíθta > ḥāpaṣtā*); but in some verbs that had **í* in the second syllable originally, the third-person masculine singular also has *pataḥ* rather than the expected *ṣērê,* as the result of leveling, for example, in *qārab* "he approached" (rather than **qārēb;* the expected *ē* appears in the pausal form *qārēbâ* "she approached" [Zeph 3:2]). The same leveling is responsible for the examples of third masculine singular *piʿel* perfects with *pataḥ* in the second syllable, such as *giddal* "he made great" (Josh 4:14). Unlike sound change, analogical change (including leveling) is not regular and predictable; the mere availability of an analogy does not always trigger a new development. Thus, for example, we find *ḥāpēṣ* (Gen 34:19) rather than ***ḥāpaṣ* and the expected *giddēl* (Isa 49:21) as well as *giddal.*

A third type of linguistic change is *semantic change.* The meanings of words frequently change over time, and many examples could be cited from many languages. A well-known English example is the verb *prevent,* which used to mean "come before," as in the KJV translation of *ûbabbōqer tǝpillātî tǝqaddǝmekkā* in Ps 88:13 (MT 88:14): "in the morning shall my prayer prevent thee." In Hebrew we note, for example, that the particle *ʾăbāl* means something like "truly" in early biblical texts, while in later texts it tends to mean "but, however";[7] we may also note the expansion of meaning of the preposition *ʿal* over the course of time, at the expense of

---

[7] Robert Polzin, *Late Biblical Hebrew: Toward an Historical Typology of Biblical Hebrew Prose* (HSM 12; Missoula, Mont.: Scholars Press, 1976), 124–25.

ʾel, which becomes less common.[8] It is necessary to consider the possibility of semantic change when comparing potentially cognate words in
related languages (for "cognate," see further below); for example, while
Hebrew *hālak* means "to go," the Arabic cognate *halaka* has come to
mean "to perish."

One of the methods used to establish earlier stages of a language is
internal reconstruction, in which alternations within an individual language are investigated in an effort to recover an earlier stage of that
language. It is internal reconstruction, for example, that suggests that the
vowel alternation in the second syllable of *hāpēṣ~hāpaṣtā* is the result
of a sound change that has obscured an earlier, more consistent paradigm, *hapíθ(a)~hapíθta*. As another example, consider the forms
luqqah "he was taken" (Gen 3:23) and *yuqqah* "it will be taken" (Gen
18:4); the former has the form of a *puʿal* perfect, the latter of a *hopʿal*
imperfect (jussive), yet, as common as this root is in biblical Hebrew,
there are no attested *piʿel* or *hipʿil* forms that correspond to them; nor
are there any *puʿal* imperfects or *hopʿal* perfects of this verb. This
unusual distribution has suggested to scholars that the forms *luqqah* and
yuqqah may in fact not be *puʿal* and *hopʿal* but rather vestiges of an old
qal passive conjugation that was, perhaps, no longer recognized as such
by the Masoretes.

In *comparative reconstruction,* as the name suggests, cognate forms
of related languages are compared in an attempt to get at an earlier stage.
Cognates are forms, such as Hebrew *kesep* and Akkadian *kaspum* (see
above), that exhibit a similar form and meaning and that can be shown
to share a common ancestor. Hebrew *kesep* and Akkadian *kaspum* clearly
have similar meanings, and their root consonants, *k-s-p,* are identical. Let
us now consider Hebrew *patah* and Akkadian *pete,* both of which are
imperatives meaning "open!"; the forms seem to be cognate (they are
similar in form and meaning), but here Akkadian is lacking the third root
consonant of the Hebrew form. A similar correspondence is shown by
other pairs, such as Hebrew *hămôr* and Akkadian *imērum* "donkey," and
Hebrew *zebah* "sacrifice" and Akkadian *zíbum* "food-offering." In these
word sets we see an apparently regular correspondence of Hebrew *h* and
the lack of a consonant in Akkadian. But in other instances, Hebrew *h*
corresponds to Akkadian *h:* Hebrew *hāmēš* and Akkadian *hamiš* "five";
Hebrew *ʾāh* and Akkadian *ahum* "brother"; Hebrew *mōah* "marrow" and

---

8 Avi Hurvitz, *The Transition Period in Biblical Hebrew: A Study in Post Exilic
Hebrew and Its Implications for the Dating of Psalms* (Hebrew) (Jerusalem: Bialik
Institute, 1972), 22 and n. 25; Mark F. Rooker, *Biblical Hebrew in Transition: The
Language of the Book of Ezekiel* (JSOTSup 90; Worcester: Sheffield, 1990), 127–31.

Akkadian *muḫḫum* "skull." When we consider the Arabic cognates to these words, we find that Arabic exhibits two distinct consonants: *iftaḥ* "open!," *ḥimārun* "donkey," *ðibḥun* "blood sacrifice," but *ḫamsun* "five," *ʾaḫun* "brother," *muḫḫun* "brain." There is no obvious sound change to account for an earlier *ḥ* or *ḫ* splitting into two distinct consonants in Arabic and at the same time being either lost or preserved in the same roots in Akkadian. It is much more likely that Arabic in this instance preserves the original situation and that earlier Semitic, like Arabic, had two distinct consonants, *ḥ* and *ḫ;* the first of these was lost in Akkadian and the second preserved, whereas in Hebrew the two merged into a single consonant, *ḥ*.[9] The merger of *ḥ* and *ḫ* in biblical Hebrew accounts for the existence of a number of homophonic roots whose meanings are unrelated to one another, such as *ptḥ* "to open" (originally **ptḥ*) and "to engrave" (originally **ptḫ*). As another example of comparative reconstruction we may consider the verb *hištaḥăwâ* "to bow down"; in most Hebrew dictionaries until recently, the root of this verb was given as *šḥḥ,* as in BDB (p. 1005), where the forms of the verb are said to exhibit an unusual *hitpaʿlel* conjugation. But when we find in Ugaritic a causative conjugation with prefix *š,* a corresponding passive/reflexive with prefix *št,* and an obvious cognate of this particular verb, imperfective *yštḥwy* "he will bow down," we rightly conclude that the forms of Hebrew *hištaḥăwâ* likewise derive from a root *ḥwy/ḥwḥ* in a vestigial early Semitic *hištapʿal* conjugation.[10]

5. SOME COMMON FEATURES OF THE SEMITIC LANGUAGES

While even a summary of comparative Semitic grammar is not possible here, a few examples of common features found across the languages in the areas of phonology, morphology, and syntax will, it is hoped, illustrate the range of such data available to the student of Hebrew who is interested in this field of study.

5.1. PHONOLOGY

Proto-Semitic (PS), the ancestral language from which all of the attested Semitic languages descend, had twenty-nine consonants (all of which remain distinct in the Old South Arabian languages). In biblical Hebrew, which had only twenty-three consonants, some of the original

---

[9] In fact, certain types of evidence suggest that the distinction between *ḥ* and *ḫ* was preserved in Hebrew for much of the biblical period. See the discussion in the chapter, "Hebrew (Biblical and Epigraphic)."

[10] See *HALOT,* 1:295–96.

Semitic consonants had obviously merged; one Hebrew consonant, **צ** *ṣ*, reflects three PS consonants: *^{t}ṣ, *$ś$, *$θ$; four other Hebrew consonants each reflect two distinct PS consonants, namely, **ז** *z*, from PS *$ð$ and *^dz; **ח** *ḥ*, from PS *$ḥ$ and *$ḫ$; **ע** *ʿ* from PS *$ʿ$ and *$ġ$; **ש** *š*, from PS *s and *$θ$. The following chart lists all of the Hebrew consonants and their PS ancestors, as well as the reflexes of the PS consonants in some of the other major Semitic languages (a slash, /, indicates an alternative reflex: e.g., PS *$θ$ appears in Ugaritic sometimes as *ẓ*, sometimes as *ġ*; parentheses enclose alternative transliterations: e.g., Ugaritic *ð* is also transliterated *ḏ*).

Proto-Semitic	Hebrew	Aramaic (Syriac)	Ugaritic	Arabic	Old South Arabian	Ethiopic (Geʿez)	Akkadian
*ʾ	ʾ	ʾ	ʾ	ʾ	ʾ	ʾ	ʾ/–
*b	b	b	b	b	b	b	b
*g	g	g	g	j	g	g	g
*d	d	d	d	d	d	d	d
*h	h	h	h	h	h	h	ʾ/–
*w	w	w	w	w	w	w	w/–
*ð	z	d	d/ð (ḏ)	ð (ḏ)	ð (ḏ)	z	z
*^{d}z	z	z	z	z	z	z	z
*ḥ	ḥ	ḥ	ḥ	ḥ	ḥ	ḥ	ʾ/–
*ḫ	ḫ	ḥ	ḫ	ḫ	ḫ	ḫ	ḫ
*ṭ	ṭ	ṭ	ṭ	ṭ	ṭ	ṭ	ṭ
*y	y	y	y	y	y	y	y/–
*k	k	k	k	k	k	k	k
*l	l	l	l	l	l	l	l
*m	m	m	m	m	m	m	m
*n	n	n	n	n	n	n	n
*^{t}s	s	s	s	s	s³ (ś)	s	s
*ʿ	ʿ	ʿ	ʿ	ʿ	ʿ	ʿ	ʾ/–
*ġ	ʿ	ʿ	ġ	ġ	ġ	ʿ	ʾ/–
*p	p	p	p	f	f	f	p
*^{t}ṣ	ṣ	ṣ	ṣ	ṣ	ṣ	ṣ	ṣ
*ṣ́	ṣ	ʿ	ṣ	ḍ	ḍ	ś (ḍ)	ṣ
*θ̣	ṣ	ṭ	z/ġ	ẓ	ẓ	ṣ	ṣ
*q (ḳ)	q (ḳ)	q (ḳ)	q (ḳ)	q	q (ḳ)	q (ḳ)	q (ḳ)
*r	r	r	r	r	r	r	r
*ś	ś	s	š	š	s² (š)	ś (š)	š
*s	š	š	š	s	s¹ (s)	s	š
*θ	š	t	θ (ṯ)	θ (ṯ)	θ (ṯ)	s	š
*t	t	t	t	t	t	t	t

It was noted above that sound changes are regular. The correspondences given above, therefore, are also regular, since they reflect sound changes (mergers) that have occurred in the various languages over time. Thus, for example, *ś* in a Hebrew root *must* correspond with *š*, and only *š*, in a potentially cognate Arabic root. A *ṣ* in a Hebrew root may correspond to *ẓ* in a potentially cognate Arabic root, but if the proposed root is also attested in Aramaic, the latter must have *ṭ* in the same slot for all three to be a valid cognate set.

For Proto-Semitic three short vowels and three corresponding long vowels may be reconstructed: *a, i, u, ā, ī, ū*. This simple system remains essentially unchanged in classical Arabic, but in most of the other languages for which we have evidence of the vowel system, including biblical Hebrew, significant developments have occurred, too extensive and complex to be entered into here.

5.2. MORPHOLOGY

5.2.1. NOUNS

All of the Semitic languages exhibit two genders, masculine and feminine, and nearly all nouns are construed as one or the other; the feminine is usually marked by an ending *-t* or *-at* (the ending *-t* is present in forms such as *delet* "door" < *dal-t;* the ending *-at* is still present in Hebrew in construct forms such as *malkat* "queen of" but otherwise has become *-â,* as in *malkâ*). As in Hebrew, three numbers may be reconstructed for Proto-Semitic: singular, dual, and plural; the evidence of some of the languages suggests that the dual was originally more widespread than it is in Hebrew; that is, it was used for "two" of anything, not merely for the parts of the body and certain fixed expressions.

Several of the Semitic languages, such as Akkadian, classical Arabic, and Ugaritic, exhibit a threefold case system, each of the cases marked, on singular nouns, by one of the short vowels after the base: *-u* for nominative, *-i* for genitive (used after constructs and after prepositions), *-a* for accusative (for the direct object and in various adverbial uses). In Hebrew as well as in other languages (such as Aramaic, modern Arabic dialects, and late dialects of Akkadian), the case system has disappeared, leaving very little trace (except as connecting vowels before some of the pronominal suffixes, as in *malkēk* "your [fs] king," from the originally genitive *malk-i-ki;* and *malkô/malkōh* "his king," from the originally nominative *malk-u-hu*).

5.2.2. PERSONAL PRONOUNS

As in Hebrew, other Semitic languages exhibit both independent personal pronouns (such as *ʾānōkî, hîʾ*) and enclitic forms that are suffixed to prepositions and nouns (indicating possession) and to verbs (indicating objects). The fourfold distinction of number and gender in the second-person forms (ms, fs, mp, fp) is also found throughout the Semitic family.

5.2.3. VERBS

The verbal system is the most complicated part of the morphology of any Semitic language. The Hebrew distinction between suffix conjugation ("perfect") and prefix conjugation ("imperfect") forms is found in all of the West Semitic languages (whereas in Akkadian, the form that corresponds in its shape to the West Semitic suffix conjugation is essentially a conjugated adjective, an old feature that can also still be seen in certain Hebrew stative verbs, such as *zāqēn* "he is old"). Internal reconstruction within Hebrew suggests that the prefix conjugation may reflect more than one earlier form: for example, *yāqûm* "he will arise" and *yibneh* "he will build" versus *yāqōm/wayyāqom* "may he arise/and he arose" and *yiben/wayyiben* "may he build/and he built." Comparison with other languages, especially Arabic, Ugaritic, and evidence in the Amarna Canaanite texts, confirms this, showing that imperfective forms such as *yāqûm* derive from earlier forms with a final *-u* (**yaqūmu*), while the jussive and "*waw*-consecutive" forms *yāqōm* and *wayyāqom* originally had no final vowel (**yaqum*). By the same token *yiktōb* "he will write" and *yiktōb* "may he write" derive from two distinct paradigms originally, the former from an imperfective form **yaktubu* and the latter from a perfective form **yaktub*. What we think of as the "*waw*-conversive" or "*waw*-consecutive" of the "imperfect," as in *wayyiktōb* "and he wrote," likewise in fact reflects the old perfective form **yaktub* (which is also why, in verbs that have a distinct form of the jussive, the jussive and the "*waw*-consecutive" form are essentially the same).

Hebrew exhibits a considerable number of verbal roots with phonological peculiarities, such as verbs I–*n,* verbs I–guttural, verbs I–*y,* and geminate verbs. Comparative evidence indicates that, apart from roots with *w* and *y,* especially as the middle radical ("hollow verbs"), these root types can be reconstructed as regular in Proto-Semitic.

The derived conjugations of Hebrew also reflect a common Semitic inheritance. In the following chart, for reference, are names, terms, or sigla for some of the derived conjugations of the other major languages. (In Arabic philology, the conjugations are called "measures" or "forms" and referred to by numbers, as in "second form" [= II]. The Ethiopic and Akkadian derived conjugations are denoted in some works by a numerical system, in other works by letters that convey a significant feature: G for [German] *Grundstamm* ["basic stem"], D for doubled middle radical; C for causative [in Ethiopic]; N for prefixed *n* and Š for prefixed *š* [in Akkadian]. The form corresponding to the *nipʿal* has been lost in Aramaic and in Ethiopic.)

Hebrew	Aramaic	Arabic	Ethiopic	Akkadian
qal	pə'al	I	G or I,1	G or I/1
nip'al	—	VII	—	N or IV/1
pi'el	pa'el	II	D or I,2	D or II/1
hip'il	'ap'el	IV	CG or II,1	Š or III/1
hitpa'el	'etpa'al	V	Dt or III,2	Dt or II/2

Forms corresponding to the *pu'al* and *hop'al* (and to the *qal* passive) are attested in early Aramaic inscriptions and in Arabic. Other conjugations are found in some of the languages: just as the *hitpa'el* corresponds to the *pi'el*, many of the languages have a *t*-form corresponding to the G or *qal* (Aramaic *'etpə'el*, Arabic form VIII, Ethiopic Gt or III,1, Akkadian Gt or I/2; rare Hebrew vestiges of this conjugation are found in forms such as *yitpāqēd* in Judg 21:9; *hitpāqədû* in Judg 20:15, 17); Arabic and Ethiopic exhibit a conjugation with a lengthened vowel in the first syllable (*kātaba;* Arabic form III, Ethiopic L or I,3), which has been compared by some scholars with Hebrew forms such as *rōmēm* "to exalt" and *šōrēš* "to take root."

5.3. SYNTAX

Biblical Hebrew is a verb-first language; the normative word order is verb-subject-object. This is also true of classical Arabic, classical Ethiopic, and the earliest Aramaic texts, and it is probably the original common Semitic word order as well. The verb-final order of Akkadian is undoubtedly the result of Sumerian influence.

The distinctive construct chain so common in biblical Hebrew is also found in all other ancient Semitic languages. But the extensive phonological changes undergone by Hebrew construct forms as the result of the loss of stress (as in *bərākâ~birkat* "blessing [of]") do not occur in most of the other languages; in classical Arabic, for example, there is simply the loss of a final *n* that appears on nonconstruct forms: *baytun* "house," *baytu malikin* "king's house."

6. RESOURCES

The works cited in this section are listed in the subsequent bibliography. There are a great many introductory books on comparative and historical linguistics; among the best of those published recently are those by Arlotto, Bynon, Campbell, Crowley, Fox, Hock and Joseph, Lehmann, McMahon, and Sihler.

The standard reference work for the comparative grammar of the Semitic languages was written by Carl Brockelmann nearly a century ago; although naturally outdated in some respects, it remains indispensible despite the appearance of a more recent reference work by Lipiński, which also contains much useful information but is somewhat idiosyncratic. Another early work, which introduces both Proto-Semitic and most of the individual languages, with text samples, is that of Bergsträsser, which was published in an English translation by Daniels with updated notes and bibliography and with an appendix on Semitic scripts. A still-useful introduction to comparative Semitic studies is a volume written by a number of leading experts and edited by Moscati. Another introduction, both to Semitic linguistics and to comparative-historical linguistics more generally, complete with a good number of exercises for the student, is that of Bennett. A survey of all of the Semitic languages, both ancient and modern, by leading scholars, is the 1997 work by Hetzron; Izre'el's 2002 book is a collection of articles on the "state of the art" in Semitic linguistics at the turn of the century. Two recent German works on comparative and historical Semitic linguistics are by Kienast and Stempel, and a recent Italian volume is that of Garbini and Durand.

A monumental historical grammar of biblical Hebrew was published by Bauer and Leander in 1922. Although some of their underlying assumptions are no longer held to be valid by most scholars, this volume presents an enormous amount of information. A collection of articles on various aspects of the field of linguistics with reference to biblical Hebrew was edited by Bodine in 1992.

There is no complete comparative dictionary of the Semitic languages, although two series are in the process of being published. The first is the *Dictionnaire des racines sémitiques ou attestées dans les langues sémitiques* edited by Cohen, which arranges roots according to the order of the Hebrew alphabet. As of 2001, eight fascicles covering roots beginning ʾ through *z* have appeared. The second is the *Semitic Etymological Dictionary,* edited by Militarev and Kogan, which will be a series of volumes covering various semantic fields, the first of which, *Anatomy of Man and Animals,* appeared in 2000.

An overview of the Afro-Asiatic languages and of comparative Afro-Asiatic grammar was presented by Diakonoff in 1988. A recently published Afro-Asiatic dictionary by Orel and Stolbova has been much criticized in reviews.

7. BIBLIOGRAPHY

Arlotto, Anthony. *Introduction to Historical Linguistics*. Boston: Houghton Mifflin, 1972. Repr., Washington: American University, 1981.

Bauer, Hans, and Pontus Leander. *Historische Grammatik der hebräischen Sprache des Alten Testaments*. Halle: Niemeyer, 1922.

Bennett, Patrick R. *Comparative Semitic Linguistics: A Manual*. Winona Lake, Ind.: Eisenbrauns, 1998.

Bergsträsser, Gotthelf. *Einführung in die semitischen Sprachen: Sprach-proben und grammatische Skizzen.* Munich: Max Hueber, 1928. Translated with notes, bibliography, and an appendix on the scripts by Peter T. Daniels as *Introduction to the Semitic Languages: Text Specimens and Grammatical Sketches.* Winona Lake, Ind.: Eisen-brauns, 1983.

Bodine, Walter, ed. *Linguistics and Biblical Hebrew.* Winona Lake, Ind.: Eisenbrauns, 1992.

Brockelmann, Carl. *Grundriss der vergleichenden Grammatik der semitis-chen Sprachen.* 2 vol. Berlin: von Reuther, 1908–1913.

Bynon, Theodora. *Historical Linguistics.* Cambridge: Cambridge University Press, 1977.

Campbell, Lyle. *Historical Linguistics: An Introduction.* Edinburgh: Edin-burgh University Press, 1998; Cambridge, Mass.: MIT Press, 1999.

Cohen, David. *Dictionnaire des racines sémitiques ou attestées dans les langues sémitiques.* The Hague: Mouton; Leuven: Peters, 1970–.

Crowley, Terry. *An Introduction to Historical Linguistics.* 3d ed. Oxford: Oxford University Press, 1998.

Diakonoff, Igor M. *Afrasian Languages.* Moscow: Nauka, 1988.

Fox, Anthony. *Linguistic Reconstruction: An Introduction to Theory and Method.* Oxford: Oxford University Press, 1995.

Garbini, Giovanni, and Olivier Durand. *Introduzione alle lingue semitiche.* Studia sul Vicino Oriente antico 2. Brescia: Paideia, 1994.

Hetzron, Robert, ed. *The Semitic Languages.* London: Routledge, 1997.

Hock, Hans Henrich. *Principles of Historical Linguistics.* 2d ed. Berlin: Mou-ton de Gruyter, 1991.

Hock, Hans Henrich, and Brian D. Joseph. *Language History, Language Change, and Language Relationship: An Introduction to Historical and Comparative Linguistics.* Berlin: Mouton de Gruyter, 1996.

Hurvitz, Avi. *The Transition Period in Biblical Hebrew: A Study in Post Exilic Hebrew and Its Implications for the Dating of Psalms.* (Hebrew) Jerusalem: Bialik Institute, 1972.

International Phonetic Association. *Handbook of the International Pho-netic Association: A Guide to the Use of the International Phonetic Alphabet.* Cambridge: Cambridge University Press, 1999.

Izre'el, Shlomo, ed. *Semitic Linguistics: The State of the Art at the Turn of the Twenty-First Century.* IOS 20. Winona Lake, Ind.: Eisenbrauns, 2002.

Kienast, Burchart. *Historische semitische Sprachwissenschaft.* Wiesbaden: Harrassowitz, 2001.

Lehmann, Winfred P. *Historical Linguistics: An Introduction.* 3d ed. New York: Holt, Rinehart & Winston, 1992.

Lipiński, Edward. *Semitic Languages: Outline of a Comparative Grammar.* OLA 80. Leuven: Peeters/Departement Oosterse Studies, 1997.

Mankowski, Paul V. *Akkadian Loanwords in Biblical Hebrew.* HSS 47. Winona Lake, Ind.: Eisenbrauns, 2000.

McMahon, April M. S. *Understanding Language Change.* Cambridge: Cambridge University Press, 1994.

Militarev, Alexander, and Leonid Kogan. *Semitic Etymological Dictionary.* Vol. 1: *Anatomy of Man and Animals.* AOAT 278/1. Münster: Ugarit, 2000.

Moscati, Sabatino, ed. *An Introduction to the Comparative Grammar of the Semitic Languages: Phonology and Morphology.* Wiesbaden: Harrassowitz, 1964.

Nebes, Norbert. "Zur Form der Imperfektbasis des unvermehrten Grundstammes im Altsüdarabischen." Pp. 59–81 in *Semitische Studien unter besonderer Berücksichtigung der Südsemitistik.* Vol. 1 of *Festschrift Ewald Wagner zum 65. Geburtstag.* Edited by W. Heinrichs and G. Schoeler. Beirut and Stuttgart: Steiner, 1994.

Orel, Vladimir E., and Olga V. Stolbova. *Hamito-Semitic Etymological Dictionary: Materials for a Reconstruction.* Leiden: Brill, 1995.

Polzin, Robert. *Late Biblical Hebrew: Toward an Historical Typology of Biblical Hebrew Prose.* HSM 12. Missoula, Mont.: Scholars Press, 1976.

Porkhomovsky, Victor. "Modern South Arabian Languages from a Semitic and Hamito-Semitic Perspective." *Proceedings of the Seminar for Arabian Studies* 27 (1997): 219–23.

Rooker, Mark F. *Biblical Hebrew in Transition: The Language of the Book of Ezekiel.* JSOTSup 90. Worcester: Sheffield, 1990.

Sihler, Andrew L. *Language History: An Introduction.* Amsterdam and Philadelphia: John Benjamins, 2000.

Stempel, Reinhard. *Abriß einer historischen Grammatik der semitischen Sprachen.* Nordostafrikanisch/Westasiatische Studien 3. Frankfurt am Main: Peter Lang, 1999.

Voigt, Rainer. "The Classification of Central Semitic." *JSS* 32 (1987): 1–21.

Wagner, M. *Die lexikalischen und grammatikalischen Aramaismen im alttestamentlichen Hebräisch.* BZAW 96. Berlin: de Gruyter, 1966.

AKKADIAN

David Marcus

1. THE LANGUAGE

Akkadian (Akk) was the language of ancient Mesopotamia (modern Iraq) and was used for over two and a half thousand years from 2600 B.C.E. until the middle of the first century of the current era. In the later part of the second millennium, Akk became the lingua franca of the region and was used as such in the Persian Empire. Akkadian derives its name from the city of Akkad, the seat of a Semitic-speaking dynasty in southern Mesopotamia in the mid-third millennium B.C.E., and the name *Akkadian* is now used as a term for all of its dialects.

1.1. HISTORY

The chief dialects of Akk, corresponding to the geographical regions of north and south Mesopotamia, are Assyrian and Babylonian. These can be subdivided chronologically into: Old Assyrian (1950–1750 B.C.E.), Middle Assyrian (1500–1000 B.C.E.), and Neo-Assyrian (1000–600 B.C.E.); Old Babylonian (1950–1600 B.C.E.), Middle-Babylonian (1600–1000 B.C.E.), Neo-Babylonian (1000–600 B.C.E.), and Late-Babylonian (600 BCE–50 C.E.). The classical language is generally held to be that of the Old Babylonian period, and the later literary language (which tended to imitate Old Babylonian) is termed Standard Babylonian (*jungbabylonisch* by German scholars). In addition to these major dialects, the prevalence of Akk in surrounding areas of Mesopotamia led to the development of regional dialects such as those at Mari (eighteenth century), Ugarit (fifteenth to fourteenth centuries), and Tel el-Amarna (fourteenth century). Akkadian has been found in nearly every major archaeological site of the Near East from Iran to Egypt, and about half a million documents written in Akk have now come to light.[1]

---

[1] For additional background material on Akkadian, see Richard Caplice, "Akkadian," *ABD* 4:170–73; Jerrold S. Cooper, "Sumerian and Akkadian," in *The World's Writing Systems* (ed. P. T. Daniels and W. Bright; Oxford: Oxford University Press, 1996), 37–57.

The earliest discovery of Akk documents in the modern period was by European travelers in the seventeenth and eighteenth centuries of our era. However, the first major finds came in the first half of the nineteenth century at sites such as Mosul (Nineveh), Calah (Nimrud), Khorsabad, and Babylon by competing European (British, French, and German) archaeologists. The search for Akk material was intensified because of the enormous public interest in possible biblical connections. In 1872 George Smith identified part of an Akk flood story paralleling that of the biblical story, and this led the *Daily Telegraph* to sponsor him to go to Nineveh to find the other parts of the flood story. Incredibly, one week after he began work at Nineveh he had the extraordinary good fortune to find a fragment containing the missing lines.

Since Akk is written in cuneiform, a logo-syllabic language (see below), the decipherment was accomplished only through the help of parallel texts. The primary breakthrough came with the discovery and publication of the trilingual inscription at Bisutun by H. C. Rawlinson in 1845. This was an inscription in honor of Darius written in Old Persian, Elamite, and Akk. Scholars working on the inscription were able to compare the Akk text with that of the Old Persian and Elamite. This eventually led to a full decipherment by scholars such as G. F. Grotefend of Germany, J. Oppert of France, E. Hincks of Ireland and W. H. Fox Talbot, E. Norris, and Rawlinson of England. After a public test by the Royal Asiatic Society, where four scholars worked independently on deciphering a freshly discovered cuneiform inscription, the decipherment was declared complete. The largest collection of Akk material found was in the library of King Ashurbanipal (seventh century B.C.E.) and written in the Neo-Assyrian script. Consequently, that dialect (Assyrian) gave its name to the field (Assyriology), and the Neo-Assyrian script is the one still most often used in teaching manuals and sign lists.[2]

1.2. WRITING SYSTEM

Akkadian is written in cuneiform, a type of writing formed by impressing a stylus on wet clay. The resulting wedge-shaped indentations are what gave rise to the term "cuneiform," from Latin *cuneus* "wedge." Akkadian employs a logo-syllabic script that consists of a combination of logograms (see below) and syllables. Syllables can be of three types: (1) a vowel (*a,*

---

[2] For more details on the early discoveries and the decipherment of Akkadian, see E. A. Wallis Budge, *The Rise and Progress of Assyriology* (London: Martin Hopkinson, 1925); Johannes Friedrich, *Extinct Languages* (New York: Philosophical Library, 1957); Samuel Noah Kramer, *The Sumerians: Their History, Culture, and Character* (Chicago: University of Chicago Press, 1963), 7–19.

e, i, u); (2) a consonant plus a vowel or a vowel plus a consonant (*da, ab, nu, un*); (3) a consonant plus a vowel plus a consonant (*dan, pal, bir*). Thus, without stressing the vowels, a word such as *dannum* could be written as *dan-num, dan-nu-um, da-an-num,* or *da-an-nu-um.* Cuneiform signs have undergone significant evolution in different time periods. They are organized in sign lists according to standard conventions so that signs made up of one horizontal wedge come first, then signs made up of two horizontal wedges, then angular, triangular, and vertical signs.[3]

Homophonous signs are signs that represent the same sound. For example, there are two signs in Akk to represent the sounds *ur, su,* and *ša.* To distinguish them, signs are numbered according to their frequency. A sign that most frequently has a certain value does not have any special indication; for example, the sign that represents the most frequent value of *u* is represented simply as *u.* The sign that represents the next most frequent value of *u* is represented by *u* with an acute mark (*ú*). A third sign also having the value *u* is indicated with a grave mark (*ù*). Should there be a fourth or more signs having the same values, these are indicated by Arabic numerals attached in subscript (e.g., the fourth value of *u* is indicated as u_4).

A polyphonous sign is one that represents a number of different values. For example, the sign *be* can represent *bat* and *til;* the sign *ur* can represent *lik* and *taš;* and the sign *ud* can represent *per* and *tam.* Polyphony arises because in many cases, in addition to its own equivalents, Akk has preserved the original Sumerian values of the cuneiform signs.

Sample Text: Law One of the Code of Hammurabi (= CH)

Transliteration: *šum-ma a-wi-lum a-wi-lam ú-ub-bi-ir-ma ne-er-tam e-li-šu id-di-ma la uk-ti-in-šu mu-ub-bi-ir-šu id-da-ak*
Normalization: *šumma awīlum awīlam ubbîrma nērtam elîšu iddīma lā uktînšu mubbiršu iddâk*
Translation: "If a man accuses (another) man and has brought against him a charge of murder, but has not convicted him, his accuser shall be executed."

Akkadian is traditionally cited by transliteration, presenting the cuneiform signs in their Latin equivalents (e.g., *bi, dan*). In many syllables there is no distinction between voiced, voiceless, and emphatic consonants so that a sign such as *AZ* serves for *az, as,* and, *aṣ,* or a sign such

---

[3] On the evolution and shape of the cuneiform signs, see René Labat, *Manuel d'épigraphie Akkadienne* (rev. and corr. by Florence Malbran-Labat; Paris: Librairie Orientaliste Paul Geuthner, 1976); Wolfram von Soden and Wolfgang Röllig, *Das akkadische Syllabar* (3d rev. and enl. ed.; AnOr 42; Rome: Pontifical Biblical Institute, 1976); Cooper, "Sumerian and Akkadian," 37–57.

as *IG* serves for *ig, ik,* and *iq.* But only one of these values may be selected for the transliteration. Likewise, many signs ending in *e* can also designate *i* (e.g., *de* and *di, ke* and *ki*), but only one value can be chosen for the transliteration.

Normalization is the putting together of the transliterated syllables to make Akk words in accordance with the rules of Akk grammar. Thus the syllables *a-wi-lum* are normalized as *awīlum* ("a man"), and *id-da-ak* is normalized as *iddâk* ("he shall be executed"). In this stage the transliterated consonants are always indicated but the vowels coalesce. Thus the word *mu-ub-bi-ir-šu* is normalized *mubbiršu* ("his accuser"), since all the consonants are written but only one *u* and *i* vowel.

Interpretation of the signs is assisted by the fact that the scribes practiced vowel and consonant harmony so that there is agreement in normalization between the final vowel or consonant of one sign and the initial vowel or consonant of the following sign. For example, in the word *id-di-ma* from the text above the first cuneiform sign has the values *id, it,* and *iṭ.* The sign that follows it can be read *di* or *ṭi* but not *ti,* which is represented by a different sign. Consonantal harmony necessitates that the reading be either *id-di* or *iṭ-ṭi* (not *id-ṭi* or *iṭ-di*), and lexical considerations point to *id-di* to be the correct reading. Similarly, in the word *ne-er-tam* the second cuneiform sign could be read *er* or *ir,* but the sign that precedes it can only be read *ne* (and not *ni,* which is represented by a different sign), so the correct reading is *er.* Where the principle of harmony leads to more than one possibility, knowledge of the grammar and lexicon determines the correct reading (as with *id-di-ma* above). It has been shown that a combination of three signs in cuneiform could theoretically have over five thousand possible readings, but phonological, morphological, and lexical clues lead to only one correct reading.[4]

A logogram is the term used to describe a Sumerian word that is borrowed into Akk. It is represented by one sign in the case of a simple logogram or by two in the case of a composite logogram. A logogram indicates meaning rather than a syllable or a sound.[5] Thus the logogram É indicates the word for house (Akk *bītum*) not the syllable *é,* and the logogram GAL indicates the word for "big" (Akk *rabûm*) and not the syllable *gal.* When read together as a composite logogram, the two signs É.GAL

---

[4] Erica Reiner, "Akkadian," in *Linguistics in South West Asian and North Africa* (ed. T. A. Sebeok; Current Trends in Linguistics 6; The Hague: Mouton, 1970), 293–94.

[5] Peter T. Daniels, "Semitic Scripts," in *Introduction to the Semitic Languages: Text Specimens and Grammatical Sketches* (ed. G. Bergsträsser; trans. P. T. Daniels; Winona Lake, Ind.: Eisenbrauns, 1983), 251.

represent not the syllables *é-gal* but the word "temple" or "palace" (Akk *ēkallum* [lit. "big house"] = Hebrew *hêkāl*). Logograms tend to be used mostly for common nouns such as "king," "field," "silver," and "barley" and are recognizable in a cuneiform text usually because a syllabic reading of the sign makes no sense in context. In addition, cuneiform scribes often add signs that act as logogram identifiers. Thus some logograms are preceded by determinatives that indicate into which class the following logogram belongs. For example, the determinative GIŠ "wood" is placed before words indicating trees or items made of wood, and the determinative DINGIR "god" is placed before names of gods. Occasionally, phonetic complements (syllabic signs) are added after logograms to indicate that the logogram should have the same ending as the phonetic complement. For example, if the logogram GAL is followed by the syllabic sign *ti* (GAL-*ti*), the syllable *ti* serves as a phonetic complement and indicates that the Akk word *rabûm* "great" should be normalized with an ending of *ti,* for example, as *rabîti* (feminine singular genitive).

Akkadian belongs to the Semitic family of languages whose chief characteristic is that nearly all verbs and nouns can be traced to an original triliteral root. Although written in cuneiform, Akk has retained the standard Semitic consonants, including ḫ (Heb. *ḫêt*), ṭ (*ṭêt*), ṣ (*ṣādê*), and š (*šîn*). It has an *ʾālep* that can represent an etymological *ʾālep* (e.g., *abum* "father" = Heb. *ʾāb; agārum* "to hire" = Heb. *ʾāgar*) or a glottal stop between vowels (e.g., *šeʾum* "grain"). Some Akk consonants undergo assimilation before other consonants. Here are three examples: (1) the letter *n* at the end of a syllable assimilates to the following consonant (e.g., *indin* > *iddin* "he gave"; like Hebrew *yintēn* > *yittēn*); (2) a *t*-infix (see below) in verbs with initial ṣ, ṭ, or *z* will produce the following changes ṣt > ṣṣ (*iṣtabat* > *iṣṣabat*), ṭt > ṭṭ (*iṭtarad* > *iṭṭarad*), zt > zz (*iztakar* > *izzakar*); (3) when a sibilant or a dental precedes the third-person suffixes (*šu* or *šunu*), both the sibilant or dental and the š of the suffix will assimilate to *s* (*bitšu* > *bissu* "his house").

Over the course of time, the language lost the Semitic laryngeals (Hebrew *hê, ḫêt,* and *ʿayin*), though reflections of these lost laryngeals are visible in the later language. Thus the presence of the *e* vowel is often a clue that an original laryngeal has dropped out. For example, Akk *ezēbum* "to leave" corresponds to Hebrew *ʿāzab* and Akk *enûm* "to change" corresponds to late Hebrew *ʿānâ*. In addition to the *e* vowel, Akk has the standard three Semitic vowels of *a, i,* and *u,* which can be short or long depending on the grammar and the lexicon. In transliteration, short vowels have no special identifying mark (e.g., *abnum* "stone" = Heb. *ʾeben; ilum* "god" = Heb. *ʾēl*), but long vowels are identified either by a macron (*ā*) or by a circumflex (*â*). Vowel length is determined by the grammar and lexicon, while the circumflex is mainly used for vowels that have contracted together (e.g., *banûm* < *banāʾum* "to build"; *iddâk* < *iddāʾak* "he shall be executed").

1.3. GRAMMATICAL FEATURES

The Akk noun has two genders (masculine and feminine), three numbers (singular, plural, and dual) and three cases (nominative, accusative, and genitive). Masculine nouns have no special identifying sign, but feminine nouns, other than being naturally female (e.g., *ūmum* "mother" = Heb. *ʾēm*), often possess a *-t* or *-at* ending (*awatum* "word"; *daltum* "door" [= Heb. *delet*]; *išātum* "fire" [= Heb. *ʾēš*]). Akkadian does not indicate definiteness in its nouns (this is a West Semitic feature only attested after 1200 B.C.E.) so that a word such as *bēlum* "lord" (= Heb. *baʿal*) can mean "a lord" or "the lord." In Old Babylonian ([OB] our paradigm dialect) the singular noun (and both the singular and plural feminine) is characterized by mimation, an *m* occurring after the case vowel. This mimation will drop out in later dialects (e.g., OB *šarrum,* Neo-Assyrian *šarru*). The plural of a noun is indicated by a lengthening of the ultimate vowel in masculine nouns and of penultimate vowels in feminine nouns: *bēlum* "lord," *bēlū* "lords"; *bēltum* "lady," *bēlētum* "ladies." The dual number is far more widespread in Akk than in Hebrew and is morphologically distinguished from the plural, as seen, for example, with *īnum* "an eye" (= Heb. *ʿayin*), *īnū* "eyes," *īnā* "two eyes." Duals are used for nouns such as *rīšā* "two heads," originally referring to the tops of the two towers in a fortress or city gate (Ps 24:7), and *kišādā* "two necks," originally referring to two necks or two banks of a river.

Akkadian has retained the three classical Semitic case endings, remnants of which have survived in Hebrew.[6] There are three distinctive case endings in the singular (nominative *u,* accusative *a,* and genitive *i*). The nominative is used when the noun is the subject of a sentence, and the accusative is used when the noun is the object of a verb, as in the phrase "if a man accuses (another) man" (CH §1) *šumma awīlum awīlam ubbir.* The genitive is used when the noun is preceded by a preposition, such as *ina bītim* ("in the house"), and in the construct state (see below). In the plural there are only two case endings. One is used for the nominative (*ū* for masculine nouns [*šarrū* "kings"] and *ātum* for feminine nouns [*šarrātum* "queens"]) and one for the accusative and genitive (*ī* for masculine nouns [*šarrī*] and *ātim* for fem nouns [*šarrātim*]).

When a noun precedes another one in the genitive case (e.g., "hand of the king"), it is in the construct state and may have a genitive ending

---

[6] Bruce K. Waltke and M. O'Connor, *An Introduction to Biblical Hebrew Syntax* (Winona Lake, Ind.: Eisenbrauns, 1990), §8.2.

(*qāti šarrim*). At times, it may lose its case endings and form a special construct form, as in *qāt šarrim* (cf. Hebrew *yad hammelek*). In this construction the two words make up a compound idea "the king's hand." Some nouns regularly drop their case endings in the construct (e.g., *bēl* "lord of," *dīn* "case of"). Others, especially plurals, regularly use the genitive (e.g., *abi* "father of," *šarrī* "kings of"), and some nouns have special forms for the construct (e.g., *šar* "king of," *arad* "slave of," and *uzun* "ear of").

The adjective normally follows the noun and agrees with it in number, gender, and case, such as *šarrum dannum* "a strong king," *šarrātim dannātim* "strong queens." The formation of the adjective is similar to that of the noun except that in the masculine plural the forms are not like the noun *ū* and *ī,* but rather *ūtum* and *ūtim.* Consequently, the phrase "strong kings" is *šarrū dannūtum* in the nominative and *šarrī dannūtim* in the accusative/genitive.

Most Akk nouns are formed from verbal roots according to established patterns. For example, the classical *nomen agentis* forms (those denoting a profession) are represented by participle formations (*nādinum* "a seller" [Heb. *nôtēn*], *mupparisum,* and *mušaprisum*) and by the characteristic *qattālum* form (*dayyānum* "a judge" [= Heb. *dayyān*]). Abstract nouns are formed by the addition of the ending *ūtum* (Hebrew *-ût*) to a noun, such as *šarrum* "king" (= Heb. *melek*), *šarrūtum* "kingship" (= Heb. *mālkût*).[7]

The form of the Akk independent pronoun depends on its case in the sentence. Thus the pronoun "I" has three forms: nominative *anāku;* genitive/accusative *yâti;* and dative *yâši.* Pronominal suffixes may be attached to nouns, verbs, and prepositions. A striking difference between Akk and Hebrew is the fact that Akk uses forms with *š* for the third person (*šû* "he," *šî* "she," *šunu* "they"), whereas Hebrew uses forms with *hê* (*hû'* "he," *hî'* "she," *hēm* "they"). There is a correlation between these third-person pronouns and the initial consonant of the causative conjugations in both languages.[8] The pronoun *ša* (= Hebrew *še*) is used as a relative pronoun or as a genitive indicator expressing "the one of" or "that of," such as in *ša ēkallim* "of the palace." In some dialects *ša* is declined and has a plural (*šût*). When used as a relative pronoun *ša* must be followed by a verb with a special "subjunctive" ending *u* (see below).

The Akk demonstrative "this" is *annûm* (= Heb. *hinnēh*) and is declined as an adjective (masculine *annûm* [plural *annûtum*], feminine *annītum* [plural *annâtum*]). The interrogative pronouns are: *mannum* "who" (= Heb. *mî*), *mīnum* "what" (= Heb. *mah*), *ayyûm* "which" (= Heb.

---

[7] Paul Joüon, *A Grammar of Biblical Hebrew* (trans. and rev. T. Muraoka; 2 vols.; SubBi 14/1–2; Rome: Biblical Institute Press, 1991), 88Mj.

[8] Ibid., 93cN.

ʾayyēh). The indefinites are *mammam, manama* "whoever," *mimma* "whatever," and *ayyumma* "whichever."

Traditionally, Akk grammarians have used the paradigm form of the root *prs* "to cut" to describe the Akk verb, and it is customary in Akk dictionaries to list verbs by their infinitive forms, so *prs* is listed under *parāsum*. Akkadian has two prefix forms (*iprus* and *iparras*) and one suffix form (*paris*). In general, *iprus* represents past time and corresponds to a preterite; *iparras* represents the present/future, though it can also express incomplete or habitual action in past time. The suffix form *paris* is often called a stative because it represents a state of being (e.g., *kabit* "it/he is/was heavy" [cf. Heb. *kābēd*]). The genesis of the Hebrew suffix conjugation is clearly recognizable in the Akk stative,[9] which has been thought by some to help elucidate the origin of the Hebrew *waw*-consecutive.[10] The paradigm of the verb in the I-conjugation (= Heb *qal*) is as follows.

Singular	Preterite	Present/Future	Stative
3d masculine	*iprus*	*iparras*	*paris*
3d feminine	*iprus*	*iparras*	*parsat*
2d masculine	*taprus*	*taparras*	*parsāta*
2d feminine	*taprusī*	*taparrasī*	*parsāti*
1st common	*aprus*	*aparras*	*parsāku*
Plural			
3d masculine	*iprusū*	*iparrasū*	*parsū*
3d feminine	*iprusā*	*iparrasā*	*parsā*
2d masculine	*taprusā*	*taparrasā*	*parsātunu*
2d feminine	*taprusā*	*taparrasā*	*parsātina*
1st common	*niprus*	*niparras*	*parsānu*

Akkadian has four conjugations, which are designated either by Roman numerals (I, II, III, IV) or by their essential characteristics, G (= *Grund* "basic"), D (= *Doppel* "double"), Š, and N (the letters *š* and *n* being their characteristic features). The I-conjugation expresses the basic meaning of the verb and corresponds with the Hebrew *qal*. The II-conjugation modifies the meanings of the I-conjugation in a variety of ways and corresponds with the Hebrew *piʿel*. The main function of the II-conjugation is to make verbs factitive (< Latin *factitare* "to do often, to practice, to declare [someone] to be"). For example, *lamādum* in the I-conjugation means "to learn," in the II-conjugation (*lummudum*) "to teach"; *mašālum* in the I-conjugation

---

[9] Ibid., 42aN.

[10] Waltke and O'Connor, *Biblical Hebrew Syntax,* §29.4.

means to "to be equal," in the II-conjugation (*muššulum*) "to make equal."[11] The III-conjugation is mostly causative and corresponds with the Hebrew *hip'il* (e.g., *maqātum* "to fall," *šumqutum* "to cause to fall"). The IV-conjugation corresponds with the Hebrew *nip'al* and serves as a passive for the I-conjugation (e.g., *dâkum* "to kill," *iddâk* "he shall be executed").

Akkadian also modifies its verb by means of infixes (*t*-infix and *tan*-infix). The *t*-infix has reflexive or reciprocal (expressing mutual relation) meaning, such as *išriq* "he stole," *ištariq* "he stole for himself." In some dialects the *t*-infix expresses the past tense. The *tan*-infix gives the root an iterative (frequentative) or habitual connotation, such as *kašādum* "to arrive," *iktaššad* "he used to arrive"; *šakānum* "to put," *ištanakkan* "he will continually put." Relics of these infixes have been shown to occur in biblical Hebrew.[12] For example, the iterative aspect of the *tan*-infix is found in forms such as *mithallēk* "walking around" (Gen 3:8) and *mištā'ēh* "gazing fixedly" (Gen 24:21) so that a case can be made that some *hitpa'el* forms should be treated as if they were infixed *tan* forms.

Akkadian uses a verbal suffix *am,* called the ventive, which gives verbs a dative or special lexical meaning (*išruk* "he gave," *išrukam* "he gave to me"; *illik* "he went," *illikam* "he came" [lit. "he went here"]). Much more common is use of a *u* vowel added to a verb in a subordinate clause ("the king who came" *šarrum ša illiku*). This *u* vowel is traditionally termed the "subjunctive," though its function is completely unlike that found in Indo-European languages, where the subjunctive expresses a thought or wish. There are no parallels to these usages of the ventive or subjunctive in Hebrew.

Unlike Hebrew, which has an infinitive absolute and an infinitive construct, Akk has only one infinitive form (*parāsum* in the I-conjugation). The infinitive can be declined like a noun (*parāsum, parāsam, parāsim*), so, for instance, after a preposition the infinitive will appear in the genitive case (*ana kašādim* "to arrive"). As in Hebrew, the infinitive with a preposition serves as a temporal clause. For example, the preposition *ina* ("in") with the infinitive *kašādum* "to arrive" and the suffix *šu* "he/him" (*ina kašādīšu*) has the meaning "when he arrived."

The precative (or jussive) expresses a wish or desire and is formed by the particle *lū* followed by the *iprus* form (e.g., *lū taprus* "may you cut"). In some cases (first-person singular and third-person singular and plural), *lū* is joined to the *iprus* form, as in *luprus* "let me cut," *liprus* "may he cut." Its parallel in Hebrew is the conditional particle *lû*.[13]

---

[11] For the Hebrew parallels to these forms see ibid., §§21.2.2; 24.2.

[12] Ibid., §26.1.2b.

[13] Ibid., §§38.2e; 40.2.2d.

In common with other Semitic languages, Akk uses a verb with a cognate accusative, that is, a noun derived from the same root, such as in *dīnam idīn* (cf. Heb *zābaḥ zebaḥ* "he made a sacrifice"). A noticeable syntactic difference between Akk and Hebrew (and other West Semitic languages) is the placement of the verb in a sentence. Whereas in Hebrew the verb precedes the object, in Akk (under Sumerian influence) the object precedes the verb (*šumma awīlum awīlam ubbir* "if a man accuses [another] man"). Thus, when occasionally a verb occurs at the end of a sentence in Hebrew, it may represent influence of Akk legal style.[14] We see an example of this in Lev 19:8: *wəʾōkəlāyw ʿăwōnô yiśśāʾ* "and he who eats of it shall bear his guilt."

2. SIGNIFICANCE FOR THE BIBLE

From the time of George Smith and his identification of the Akk flood story, Akk literature has been accorded special consideration for the light it can shed on the Hebrew Bible. Some early scholars overemphasized the biblical comparisons and the primacy of the Akk literature, and there still exists a scholarly debate regarding the scope of such comparisons. But there can be no doubt that an informed comparison (and contrasting) of Akk literature with biblical literature is today a sine qua non in biblical studies. Because of the overwhelming amount of the material, its relevance for biblical studies is best considered from the point of view of genre. In this essay, we shall briefly demonstrate how Akk assists in elucidating the Hebrew Bible by looking at a number of examples in the areas of language, literature, history, law, prophecy, and wisdom.[15]

2.1. LANGUAGE

In the preceding section we have already outlined how knowledge of Akk helps in clarifying biblical Hebrew grammar in such areas as

---

[14] Joüon, *Grammar of Biblical Hebrew,* 155oc.

[15] On the relationship between the Akk material and the biblical literature, see Jacob J. Finkelstein, "Bible and Babel: A Comparative Study of the Hebrew and Babylonian Religious Spirit," *Commentary* 26 (1958): 431–44; H. W. F. Saggs, *Assyriology and the Study of the Old Testament* (Cardiff: University of Wales Press, 1969); William W. Hallo, *The Book of the People* (BJS 225; Atlanta: Scholars Press, 1991); Peter Machinist, "The Question of Distinctiveness in Ancient Israel: An Essay," in *Ah, Assyria ... Studies in Assyrian History and Ancient Near Eastern Historiography Presented to Hayim Tadmor* (ed. Mordechai Cogan and Israel Eph'al; Jerusalem: Magnes, 1991), 196–212; repr., *Essential Papers on Israel and the Ancient Near East* (ed. Frederick E. Greenspahn; New York: New York University Press, 1991), 69–102.

morphology and syntax. Study of other dialects such as those at Ugarit and Amarna are even more instructive for the early history of the Hebrew language.[16] In this section, we will point out areas where Akk can help elucidate the history and meaning of Hebrew words.

2.1.1. SUMERIAN LOANWORDS

Akkadian provides information on Sumerian loanwords that have entered Hebrew either via Aramaic or directly from Akk. Such loanwords into Hebrew include *hêkāl* "temple" from Sumerian É.GAL "big house" and Akk *ēkallum* "palace, temple"; *malāḥ* "sailor" from Sumerian MÁ.LAḪ₄ "one who leads the boat" via Akk *malāḫum* "sailor"; and *ʾikkār* "farmer" from Sumerian ENGAR via Akk *ikkarum* "plowman."[17]

2.1.2. NEW MEANINGS

Because of its extensive lexical stock, Akk is often able to elucidate hitherto unknown Hebrew words or provide a new homonym for an otherwise well-attested Hebrew root. An example of the former is the phrase *ʾet rōbaʿ* in the verse *mî mānâ ʿăpar yaʿăqōb ûmispār ʾet rōbaʿ yiśrāʾēl* (Num 23:10). This verse was translated in the RSV as "Who can count the dust of Jacob, or number the fourth part of Israel?" with the phrase *ʾet rōbaʿ* rendered as "the fourth part." In the NRSV translation of the text, this phrase evidently has been equated with Akk *tarbuʿum/turbium* "dust," establishing a parallel with the Hebrew word *ʿāpār* ("dust"): "Who can count the dust of Jacob, or number the dust-cloud of Israel?" Examples of new homonyms proposed for Hebrew in light of Akk cognate evidence are Hebrew *šāmar* II = Akk *šamārum* "to rage," and Hebrew *nāṭar* II = Akk *naṭārum* "to rage." These meanings influence the interpretation of Jer 3:5 (*hăyinṭōr ləʿôlām ʾim yišmōr lāneṣaḥ*), which up to quite recently was usually translated, "Will he nurse a grudge forever, retain his anger always?" With the new homonyms in mind, the verse can now be translated "Does one hate for all time? Does one rage forever?"[18]

---

[16] For information on these two dialects, see John Huehnergard, *The Akkadian of Ugarit* (HSS 34; Atlanta: Scholars Press, 1989); and Anson F. Rainey, *Canaanite in the Amarna Tablets: A Linguistic Analysis of the Mixed Dialect Used by the Scribes from Canaan* (Leiden: Brill, 1996).

[17] On Akkadian loanwords in Hebrew, see Paul V. Mankowski, *Akkadian Loanwords in Biblical Hebrew* (HSS 47; Winona Lake, Ind.: Eisenbrauns, 2000).

[18] For other examples of newly recovered Hebrew words, see Harold R. Cohen, *Biblical Hapax Legomena in the Light of Akkadian and Ugaritic* (SBLDS 37; Missoula, Mont.: Scholars Press, 1978).

2.1.3. CULTURAL CONCEPTS

Akkadian words can also elucidate cultural concepts that have been taken over by Israel. For example, the Akk *kurībum* helps clarify the meaning of the biblical *kərûbîm* "cherubim." The cherubim in the ancient Near East were winged creatures, half man and half beast, and they had the duty of protecting sacred regions. This fits the understanding of the biblical cherubim who, after Adam's eviction, were assigned to protect the garden of Eden (Gen 3:24) and of the two golden cherubim with outstretched wings that overshadowed the ark in the wilderness (Exod 25:18-20). The winged cherubim are also said to accompany God from place to place (Ps 18:11).[19] Another example of an Akk word clarifying a biblical context is seen in the reference to the women of Jerusalem weeping over the death of Tammuz in Ezek 8:14. Tammuz was the hero of numerous literary compositions in both Sumerian and Akk. There were songs of love and hymns of joy about his marriage and laments and dirges about his death. One of the months of the Jewish calendar (Tammuz) bears his name to this day.

2.2. LITERATURE

There are a number of myths and epics written in Akk that have been used to elucidate the background of biblical stories. In this section we briefly survey two famous stories that have evident parallels with biblical narratives, the Akk creation story and the Akk flood story.

2.2.1. THE CREATION STORY

The Akk work known as *Enuma Elish* (so named from the opening Akk words, "when on high") has often been thought to have a number of parallels with the biblical creation story in Gen 1. Some of the parallels noted are: (1) both stories refer to a watery chaos that was separated into heaven and earth; (2) both accounts describe the creation of the firmament by a division of primeval waters; (3) both stories refer to the existence of light before the creation of the luminous bodies; and (4) both narratives agree as to the order of creation as being first light, then sky, earth, seas, sun, moon, stars, fish, and, finally, humans.

Notwithstanding these parallels, *Enuma Elish* displays some obvious differences with the biblical account. Genesis is monotheistic, whereas *Enuma Elish* is polytheistic. In *Enuma Elish* the genesis of the world is connected with the genesis of the gods and with the hostilities among

---

[19] For illustrations, see James B. Pritchard, ed., *The Ancient Near East: An Anthology of Texts and Pictures* (3d ed.; Princeton, N.J.: Princeton University Press, 1971), nos. 90, 126, 163, 165.

them. Different parts of the universe are identified with certain deities in
Enuma Elish (e.g., Shamash "the sun," Tiamat "the deep water," Sin "the
moon," and Anu "the sky"). In *Enuma Elish* there is no creation of plants
and animal life or of birds, reptiles, or fish. A major feature in *Enuma Elish*
to which much space is given is the building and dedication of a temple
complex and a long hymn in honor of Marduk, the chief god of Babylon.
Nothing like this is to be found in the Gen 1 account that concludes with
the creation of the Sabbath. Because of these differences, some scholars
believe that *Enuma Elish* should more properly be compared, not with the
creation account, but with other parts of the Bible. For example, the major
battle of Marduk (the storm god) with Tiamat (the sea) evokes parallels of
God battling the Sea (Isa 51:9-10; Job 9:13-14). Similarly, the elevation of
Marduk and the building of his great temple in Babylon appears to parallel the exaltation of Yahweh in the Song of the Sea (Exod 15) and the
subsequent erection of the tabernacle in the wilderness.[20]

2.2.2. THE FLOOD STORY

As noted earlier, it was the comparison of the Akk flood story with its
biblical counterpart that generated much excitement and interest for the
fledgling science of Assyriology in the mid-nineteenth century. Though
other flood stories have now come to light, particularly in the Old Babylonian Atrahasis Epic, the most celebrated Akk flood story is that found in
the eleventh tablet of the Epic of Gilgamesh (= Gilg XI). Some of the major
parallels are mentioned below.[21]

(1) The building of an ark. Gen 6:14: "Make for yourself an ark of gopher
wood." Gilg XI:24: "Tear down (this) house, build a ship!"
(2) Placing of animals in the ark. Gen 6:19–20: "And of all that lives, of all
flesh, you shall take two of each into the ark." Gilg XI:27: "Aboard the
ship take thou the seed of all living things."
(3) Entry into the ark. Gen 7:7–9: "Noah, with his sons, his wife, and his
sons' wives, went into the ark.... of the clean animals, of the unclean animals, of the birds, and of everything that creeps on the ground, two of

[20] Further discussion of these parallels can be found in Thomas W. Mann, *Divine
Presence and Guidance in Israelite Traditions: The Typology of Exaltation* (JHNES
9; Baltimore: Johns Hopkins University Press, 1977); Victor Hurowitz, *I Have Built
You an Exalted House: Temple Building in the Bible in the Light of Mesopotamian
and Northwest Semitic Writings* (JSOTSup 115; Sheffield: Sheffield Academic Press,
1992); Benjamin R. Foster, "The Epic of Creation," in *Canonical Compositions from
the Biblical World* (vol. 1 of *The Context of Scripture;* ed. William W. Hallo and
K. Lawson Younger Jr.; Leiden: Brill, 1997), 390–91.
[21] Other parallels may be found in Pritchard, *Ancient Near East,* 66–71.

each, male and female, came to Noah into the ark." Gilg XI:84–85: "All my
family and kin I made go aboard the ship. The beasts of the field, the wild
creatures of the field."
(4) Coming of the rains. Gen 7:12: "The rain fell on the earth forty days
and forty nights." Gilg XI:125–126: "Six days and [six] nights blows the
flood wind ... when the seventh day arrived." Both accounts use typological numbers, forty in the Bible and seven in Gilgamesh.
(5) Receding of the waters. Gen 8:1: "The waters subsided." Gilg XI:131:
"The sea grew quiet."
(6) Landing of the ark. Gen 8:4: "The ark came to rest on the mountains
of Ararat." Gilg XI:140: "On Mount Nisir the ship came to a halt."
(7) Opening of a window. Gen 8:6: "Noah opened the window of the
ark." Gilg XI:135: "I opened a hatch."
(8) Sending out birds. Gen 8:7–8: "[Noah] sent out the raven ... then he
sent out the dove." Gilg XI:146–154: "I set free a dove ... and set free a
swallow ... and set free a raven."
(9) Offering of sacrifices. Gen 8:20: "Then [Noah] offered burnt offerings
on the altar." Gilg XI:155: "I offered a sacrifice. I poured out a libation."
(10) Acceptance of the offering. Gen 8:21: "The LORD smelled the pleas-
ing odor." Gilg XI:160: "The gods smelled the sweet savor."

Though these parallels are impressive, the major differences should
also be noted. The story of Noah is monotheistic: the storm occurs because
of extreme but natural manifestations. The Akk flood story is polytheistic:
the storm is caused by the actions of various gods. The Noah story is
embedded in a wider story of the wickedness of humankind, whereas the
Akk flood story consists of a recounting by one person, Utnapishtim,
whose name means "he has found (eternal) life," of how he became
immortal. Both accounts differ as to the cause of the flood and what occurs
at its conclusion. Since it is his story, Utnapishtim does not know the reason for the flood, but he does know that he was made immortal at the end;
that is, he had to withdraw from the world. In the Bible humanity is the
cause of the flood, but the climax of the story is the covenant made by
God never again to send a deluge against humanity. As for Noah, unlike
Utnapishtim, he is told not to withdraw from the world but, on the contrary, to help build it up again.[22]

2.3. HISTORY

One reason why the public was so intrigued by the early Assyriologi-
cal finds was that these excavations were discovering documents that

---

[22] Tikva Frymer-Kensky, "What the Babylonian Flood Stories Can and Cannot
Teach Us about the Genesis Flood," *BAR* 4/4 (1978): 32–41.

contained names of people similar to names found in the Bible. Of course, it is to be expected in a kindred Semitic language, especially one with such a lengthy textual history, that many names corresponding to names found in the Bible would also occur in the Akk onomasticon. Thus, names such as Adamu, Abramu, Yaqub, Sumuilu, and even Dudiya (= David?), who was the first king of Assyria, have indeed been found in Akk documents, but not one of the people bearing these names is remotely related in time or place to any biblical figure.

The situation is very different with material coming from the Neo-Assyrian and later periods. In these texts many biblical kings, starting with Ahab, king of Israel in the ninth century B.C.E., are mentioned by name, so a study of them is of the utmost importance for biblical history. Ahab is prominently mentioned by the Neo-Assyrian king Shalmaneser III (859–824) in a stela found at his capital Calah (Nimrud). The occasion was the Battle of Qarqar (853), where Shalmaneser, in one of his campaigns to the west, had to face a coalition of Aramean and western kings. Shalmaneser lists the kings of the coalition, which included Hadad-ezer, king of Damascus (= biblical Ben-hadad), and Ahab, king of Israel (*a-ḫa-ab-bu māt sir-ʾi-la-a-a*), who is said to have had two thousand chariots and ten thousand foot soldiers and, therefore, must have been one of the coalition leaders. Shalmaneser claimed an overwhelming victory at Qarqar, but the Bible does not record this battle.

The only contemporary representation of an Israelite figure known from the Bible is that of Jehu, king of Israel (841–814). He is depicted on one of the registers of the Black Obelisk of Shalmaneser as bowing down and offering tribute to Shalmaneser.[23] The inscription on the register reads "tribute of Jehu, son of Omri" (*ia-ú-a mār ḫu-um-ri-i*). Since Jehu was not the real son of Omri (2 Kgs 9:2, 14), the name Omri is probably being used as designating the country Israel.

Three other celebrated comparisons between Mesopotamian annals and the biblical record are the accounts of the fall of Samaria, the siege of Jerusalem, and the fall of Jerusalem. The fall of Samaria is described by Sargon II (721-705): "I besieged and conquered Samaria [*sa-me-ri-na*], led away as booty 27,290 inhabitants of it. I formed from among them a contingent of 50 chariots and made remaining (inhabitants) assume their (social) positions. I installed over them an officer of mine and imposed upon them the tribute of the former king." The siege of Jerusalem in 701 is described by Sennnacherib (704–681) in his annals in the following way: "As to Hezekiah, the Judean [*ḫa-za-qi-a-ú amēl ia-ú-da-ai*], he did not

---

[23] E. Strommenger, *Five Thousand Years of the Art of Mesopotamia* (New York: Abrams, 1956), no. 208.

submit to my yoke. I laid siege to 46 of his strong cities.... I drove out (of them) 200,150 people, young and old, male and female, horses, mules, donkeys, camels, big and small cattle beyond counting, and considered (them) booty. Himself I made a prisoner in Jerusalem, his royal residence, like a bird in a cage."[24] A relief from the same campaign depicts the conquest of Lachish and contains an inscription describing Sennacherib sitting on his throne while the booty taken from the city of Lachish (*la-ki-su*) passes in review (cf. 2 Kgs 18:14; 19:8).

The fall of Jersualem in 598 is reported by Nebuchadnezzar II (604–562) in the following manner: "Year 7, month Kislimu: The king of Akkad moved his army into Hatti land [Syria], laid siege to the city of Judah [*ia-a-ḫu-du*], and the king took the city on the second day of the month of Addaru. He appointed in it a (new) king of his liking, took heavy booty from it and brought it into Babylon"[25] (cf. 2 Kgs 24:14–16; Jer 52:31–34).

2.4. LAW

Law played a major role in ancient Near Eastern society, and, as a result, thousands of legal contracts (adoptions, invoices, marriages, etc.) written in Akk have come to light. There are not too many parallels between these documents and the Bible because the Bible contains only a few examples of contracts or remnants of contracts. But of greatest significance for the Bible are those Mesopotamian legal texts involving covenantal agreements between a king and his subject or between a suzerain and his vassal kings. There were two types of covenants. One was a promissory-type covenant in which a king granted land to a servant or his descendants unconditionally and in perpetuity in recognition of a servant's loyal service. These covenants have typological and functional comparisons with covenants to the patriarchs and to David.[26] The second type were obligatory covenants or vassal treaties in which a king or superpower stipulated the terms of his relationship with a smaller power or vassal, demanding future loyalty. When applied to Israel, God metaphorically becomes Israel's suzerain and Israel his vassal. It is now generally held that much of the book of Deuteronomy is patterned after such a vassal treaty.[27]

---

[24] The quotations in this paragraph are based on *ANET,* 284–85, 288.

[25] Ibid., 564.

[26] Moshe Weinfeld, "The Covenant of Grant in the Old Testament and in the Ancient Near East," *JAOS* 90 (1970): 184–203; repr., *Essential Papers on Israel and the Ancient Near East,* 69–102.

[27] On vassal treaties, see Moshe Weinfeld, *Deuteronomy and the Deuteronomic School* (Oxford: Clarendon, 1972); idem, "The Loyalty Oath in the Ancient Near East," *UF* 8 (1976): 379–414.

One of the main sources of comparison in the area of law between the Bible and Mesopotamia is the codes or legal collections. The largest collections written in Akk are those of Eshnunna (1770 B.C.E.), Hammurabi (1750 B.C.E.), and the Middle Assyrian period (twelfth century B.C.E.). These collections, based on Sumerian models, reveal a basic consistency of thought that continued throughout the two thousand years of Mesopotamian civilization. That there should be correspondences between biblical law and ancient Near Eastern law is not surprising because of the centrality of law in both cultures. Parallels may be seen both in form and content. In form, these law codes ideally contain a prologue often recounting the historical and military accomplishments of the king (cf. the prologue to the Ten Commandments in Exod 20; Deut 5) and are followed by an epilogue containing blessings and curses (cf. Lev 26; Deut 28). Secondly, these codes and the biblical laws contain a mixture of casuistic ("If a person ...") and apodictic law ("you shall/you shall not ..."). Of the scores of parallel laws between these codes and biblical law we present for illustrative purposes just a few examples in the area of personal injury from the Covenant Code in Exodus (NRSV) and the Code of Hammurabi (= CH).

> (1) Striking a parent. Exod 21:15: "Whoever strikes father or mother shall be put to death." CH §195: "If a child should strike his father, they shall cut off his hand."
> (2) Unintentional injury. Exod 21:18–19: "When individuals quarrel and one strikes the other with a stone or fist so that the injured party, though not dead, is confined to bed, but recovers..., the assailant shall be free of liability, except to pay for the loss of time, and to arrange for full recovery" (compensation and medical expenses). CH §206: "If a man strikes another man in a brawl and has inflicted upon him a wound, that man shall swear, 'I did not strike him deliberately' and he shall satisfy the physician" (pay his fees).
> (3) Goring ox. Exod 21:28: "When an ox gores a man or a woman to death, the ox shall be stoned ... but the owner of the ox shall not be liable." CH §250: "If an ox gores to death a man while it is passing through the streets, that case has no basis for a claim."
> (4) Injury to a third party. Exod 21:22: "When people who are fighting injure a pregnant woman so that there is a miscarriage..." CH §209: "If a man strikes another man's daughter and thereby causes her to miscarry..."

It must be stressed that despite these apparent similarities there are fundamental differences of outlook between Israelite and Mesopotamian law codes because both systems reflect their disparate cultural values. For example, the two societies have different ideas about the origin of law (in Mesopotamia it is the king; in Israel it is God). Hence, violation of criminal law in Israel is a sin against God and an absolute wrong, and mitigation of punishment in cases of murder or adultery is not permitted, whereas cuneiform law allows it. The severity of biblical law in cases of homicide is also due to divergent underlying principles, as is the prohibition in Israel of vicarious punishment, which is permitted in cuneiform law.[28]

2.5. PROPHECY

Akkadian texts have revealed a considerable amount of material dealing with divination and methods of divination, including omens and dreams. Most of the divination methods condemned in the Bible as being improper for Israelites can be found in Akk texts.[29] The only legitimate form of divination in the Bible, the use of Urim and Thummim, has striking parallels with a recently published Akk divination text. Parallels with Mesopotamian divination can be found in biblical stories such as those of Balaam (Num 22) and Daniel and in the few biblical accounts of dream interpretation.[30] The closest parallels to biblical prophecy, particularly examples of intuitive prophecy, can be seen in texts from Mari. The word *nābû,* now attested at Emar as referring to an office holder, is evidently related to the Hebrew word for "prophet" (*nābî*).[31]

2.6. WISDOM

Akkadian has contributed many texts elucidating Israelite wisdom literature both of the didactic (Psalms, Proverbs) and reflective or meditative

---

[28] For more on biblical law, see Moshe Greenberg, "Some Postulates of Biblical Criminal Law," in *Studies in Bible and Jewish Religion: Yehezkel Kaufmann Jubilee Volume* (ed. M. Haran; Jerusalem: Magnes, 1950), 5–28; repr., *Essential Papers on Israel and the Ancient Near East,* 333–52.

[29] Ann K. Guinan, "Divination," in *Canonical Compositions,* 421–22.

[30] On the use of Urim and Thummim, see Wayne Horowitz and Victor Hurowitz, "Urim and Thummim in Light of a Psephomancy Ritual from Assur (LKA 137)," *JANESCU* 21 (1992): 95–115. Parallels to the stories of Balaam and Daniel can be found in Guinan, "Divination," 422. Connections between the biblical and Mesopotamian materials in the area of dream interpretation are discussed in A. Leo Oppenheim, *The Interpretation of Dreams in the Ancient Near East* (Philadelphia: American Philosophical Society, 1956); Frederick H. Cryer, *Divination in Ancient Israel and Its Near Eastern Environment: A Socio-Historical Investigation* (JSOTSup 142; Sheffield: Sheffield Academic Press, 1994).

[31] On Mari, see Abraham Malamat, "A Forerunner of Biblical Prophecy: The Mari Documents," in *Ancient Israelite Religion: Essays in Honor of Frank Moore Cross* (ed. P. D. Miller Jr., P. D. Hanson, and S. D. McBride; Philadelphia: Fortress, 1987), 33–52; repr., *Essential Papers on Israel and the Ancient Near East,* 153–75; Maria de Jong Ellis, "Observations on Mesopotamian Oracles and Prophetic Texts: Literary and Historiographic Considerations," *JCS* 41 (1989): 127–86. The Emar material is treated in Daniel Fleming, "Two *Kissu* Festivals," in *Canonical Compositions,* 442–43.

(Job, Qohelet) types. There are proverbs and truth statements in Akk wisdom literature akin to those in the book of Proverbs. An example of this is seen in the proverb, "When an ant is swatted, does it not fight back and bite the hand of the man who swats it?" This adage illustrates how ants respond to a particular stimulus (cf. Prov 6:6–8; 30:25, where the ant is praised for its industry and resourcefulness). There are a number of apprentice-type texts that offer advice to princes, such as The Instruction of Shuruppak and The Counsels of Wisdom, that can be compared to similar biblical material (e.g., Words of Lemuel [Prov 31:1–9]). The reflective works are more extensive, and a number of them have parallels with biblical wisdom books. Both the Babylonian Theodicy and *Ludlul bēl nēmeqi* ("Let me praise the lord of wisdom") deal, like Job and parts of Qohelet, with the problem of innocent suffering. The Babylonian Theodicy is in the form of an acrostic and consists of a dialogue between a sufferer and a friend. In the seventh stanza the sufferer opines: "Most particular friend, your advice is e[xcellent]. Let me [put] but one matter before you: those who seek not after a god can go the road of favor, those who pray to a goddess have grown poor and destitute" (cf. Qoh 8:14 and Job). To this sentiment the friend responds: "O just, knowledgeable one, your logic is perverse. You have cast off justice, you have scorned divine design … the strategy of a god is [as remote as] innermost heaven, the command of a goddess cannot be dr[awn out]" (cf. the response of Eliphaz in Job 5:1-7).[32]

3. ANCIENT SOURCES, MODERN RESOURCES

Sign lists for all dialects of Akk may be found in W. von Soden and W. Röllig, *Das Akkadische Syllabar;* and R. Labat, *Manuel d'épigraphie Akkadienne.* Aids in learning the cuneiform signs and the language may be found in workbooks such as D. C. Snell, *A Workbook of Cuneiform Signs;* and D. B. Miller and R. M. Shipp, *An Akkadian Handbook: Paradigms, Helps, Glossary, Logograms, and Sign List.* The two standard dictionaries are the *Akkadisches Handwörterbuch (Ahw)* and the *Assyrian Dictionary of the Oriental Institute of the University of Chicago (CAD).* A useful one-volume English dictionary is now available in J. Black et al., *A Concise Dictionary of Akkadian.* The universally recognized reference grammar is W. von Soden, *Grundriß der akkadischen Grammatik,* with its essential features included in the smaller A. Ungnad, *Akkadian Grammar.* Other descriptive grammars include R. Caplice, *Introduction to Akkadian;* and J. Huehnergard, *A Grammar of Akkadian.* An inductive learning approach

---

[32] These translations are taken from Foster, "The Babylonian Theodicy," in *Canonical Compositions,* 493.

to the essentials of Akk grammar may be found in D. Marcus, *A Manual of Akkadian*. A fine selection of basic texts such as the Code of Hammurabi and the Annals of Sennacherib in cuneiform and transliteration with a full glossary may be found in R. Borger, *Babylonisch-assyrische Lesestücke*. Nearly every major Akk text has been published with a transliteration and translation. References to text editions may be found in the introductory material to translations of collected texts such as J. B. Pritchard, ed., *Ancient Near Eastern Texts Relating to the Old Testament;* idem, *The Ancient Near East: An Anthology of Texts and Pictures;* B. R. Foster, *Before the Muses: An Anthology of Akkadian Literature;* and W. H. Hallo and K. L. Younger Jr., eds., *The Context of Scripture.* The most up-to-date work on Akk and biblical parallels may be found in F. Greenspahn, ed., *Essential Papers on Israel and the Ancient Near East;* W. H. Hallo, *The Book of the People;* and J. Sasson, ed., *Civilizations of the Ancient Near East.* A recent work of particular interest to Hebrew Bible scholars is P. V. Mankowski, *Akkadian Loanwords in Biblical Hebrew.*

4. BIBLIOGRAPHY

Black, Jeremy, Andrew George, and Nicholas Postgate. *A Concise Dictionary of Akkadian.* Wiesbaden: Harrasowitz, 1999.

Borger, Rykle. *Babylonisch-assyrische Lesestücke.* Rome: Pontifical Biblical Institute, 1963.

Budge, E. A. Wallis. *The Rise and Progress of Assyriology.* London: Martin Hopkinson, 1925.

Caplice, Richard I. "Akkadian." *ABD* 4:170–73.

———. *Introduction to Akkadian.* 3d rev. ed. Studia Pohl: Series Maior 9. Rome: Biblical Institute Press, 1988.

Cohen, Harold R. *Biblical Hapax Legomena in the Light of Akkadian and Ugaritic.* SBLDS 37. Missoula, Mont.: Scholars Press, 1978.

Cooper, Jerrold S. "Sumerian and Akkadian." Pages 37–57 in *The World's Writing Systems.* Edited by Peter T. Daniels and William Bright. Oxford: Oxford University Press, 1996.

Cryer, Frederick H. *Divination in Ancient Israel and Its Near Eastern Environment: A Socio-Historical Investigation.* JSOTSup 142. Sheffield: Sheffield Academic Press, 1994.

Daniels, Peter T. "Semitic Scripts." Pages 236–60 in *Introduction to the Semitic Languages: Text Specimens and Grammatical Sketches.* Edited by G. Bergsträsser. Translated with notes and bibliography and an appendix on the scripts by Peter T. Daniels. Winona Lake, Ind.: Eisenbrauns, 1983.

Ellis, Maria de Jong. "Observations on Mesopotamian Oracles and Prophetic Texts: Literary and Historiographic Considerations." *JCS* 41 (1989): 127–86.

Finkelstein, Jacob J. "Bible and Babel: A Comparative Study of the Hebrew and Babylonian Religious Spirit." *Commentary* 26 (1958): 431–44. Repr., pages 355–80 in *Essential Papers on Israel and the Ancient Near East*. Edited by Frederick E. Greenspahn. New York: New York University Press, 1991.

Fleming, Daniel. "Two *Kissu* Festivals." Pages 442-43 in *Canonical Compositions from the Biblical World*. Vol. 1 of *The Context of Scripture*. Edited by William W. Hallo and K. Lawson Younger Jr. Leiden: Brill, 1997.

Foster, Benjamin R. "The Babylonian Theodicy." Pages 492–95 in *Canonical Compositions from the Biblical World*. Vol. 1 of *The Context of Scripture*. Edited by William W. Hallo and K. Lawson Younger Jr. Leiden: Brill, 1997.

———. *Before the Muses: An Anthology of Akkadian Literature*. 2 vols. Bethesda: CDL, 1993.

———. "The Epic of Creation." Pages 390–402 in *Canonical Compositions from the Biblical World*. Vol. 1 of *The Context of Scripture*. Edited by William W. Hallo and K. Lawson Younger Jr. Leiden: Brill, 1997.

Friedrich, Johannes. *Extinct Languages*. New York: Philosophical Library, 1957.

Frymer-Kensky, Tikva. "What the Babylonian Flood Stories Can and Cannot Teach Us about the Genesis Flood." BAR 4/4 (1978): 32–41.

Greenberg. Moshe. "Some Postulates of Biblical Criminal Law." Pages 5–28 in *Studies in Bible and Jewish Religion: Yehezkel Kafuman Jubilee Volume*. Edited by M. Haran. Jerusalem: Magnes, 1950. Repr., pages 333–52 in *Essential Papers on Israel and the Ancient Near East*. Edited by Frederick E. Greenspahn. New York: New York University Press, 1991.

Greenspahn, Frederick E., ed. *Essential Papers on Israel and the Ancient Near East*. New York: New York University Press, 1991.

Guinan, Ann K. "Divination." Pages 421–26 in *Canonical Compositions from the Biblical World*. Vol. 1 of *The Context of Scripture*. Edited by William W. Hallo and K. Lawson Younger Jr. Leiden: Brill, 1997.

Hallo, William W. *The Book of the People*. BJS 225. Atlanta: Scholars Press, 1991.

Hallo, William W., and K. Lawson Younger Jr., eds. *The Context of Scripture*. Vol. 1: *Canonical Compositions from the Biblical World*. Vol. 2: *Monumental Inscriptions from the Biblical World*. Leiden: Brill, 1997, 2000.

Horowitz, Wayne, and Victor Hurowitz. "Urim and Thummim in Light of a Psephomancy Ritual from Assur (LKA 137)." *JANESCU* 21 (1992): 95–115.

Huehnergard, John. *The Akkadian of Ugarit*. HSS 34. Atlanta: Scholars Press, 1989.

———. *A Grammar of Akkadian*. HSS 45. Atlanta: Scholars Press, 1997.

Hurowitz, Victor (Avigdor). *I Have Built You an Exalted House: Temple Building in the Bible in Light of Mesopotamian and Northwest Semitic Writings*. JSOTSup 115. Sheffield: Sheffield Academic Press, 1992.

Joüon, Paul. *A Grammar of Biblical Hebrew*. Translated and revised by T. Muraoka. 2 vols. SubBi 14/1–2. Rome: Biblical Institute Press, 1991.

Kramer, Samuel Noah. *The Sumerians: Their History, Culture, and Character*. Chicago: University of Chicago Press, 1963.

Labat, René. *Manuel d'épigraphie Akkadienne (Signes, Syllabaire, Idéogrammes)*. Rev. and corr. by Florence Malbran-Labat. Paris: Librairie Orientaliste Paul Geuthner, 1976.

Machinist, Peter. "The Question of Distinctiveness in Ancient Israel: An Essay." Pages 196–212 in *Ah Assyria ... Studies in Assyrian History and Ancient Near Eastern Historiography Presented to Hayim Tadmor*. Edited by Mordechai Cogan and Israel Eph'al. Jerusalem: Magnes, 1991. Repr., pages 420–42 in *Essential Papers on Israel and the Ancient Near East*. Edited by Frederick E. Greenspahn. New York: New York University Press, 1991.

Malamat, Abraham. "A Forerunner of Biblical Prophecy: The Mari Documents." Pages 33–52 in *Ancient Israelite Religion: Essays in Honor of Frank Moore Cross*. Edited by P. D. Miller Jr., P. D. Hanson, and S. D. McBride. Philadelphia: Fortress, 1987. Repr., pages 153–75 in *Essential Papers on Israel and the Ancient Near East*. Edited by Frederick E. Greenspahn. New York: New York University Press, 1991.

Mankowski, Paul V. *Akkadian Loanwords in Biblical Hebrew*. HSS 47. Winona Lake, Ind.: Eisenbrauns, 2000.

Mann, Thomas W. *Divine Presence and Guidance in Israelite Traditions: The Typology of Exaltation*. JHNES 9. Baltimore: Johns Hopkins University Press, 1977.

Marcus, David. *A Manual of Akkadian*. Washington, D.C: University Press of America, 1978.

Miller, Douglas B., and R. Mark Shipp. *An Akkadian Handbook: Paradigms, Helps, Logograms, and Sign Lists*. Winona Lake, Ind.: Eisenbrauns, 1996.

Oppenheim, A. Leo. *The Interpretation of Dreams in the Ancient Near East*. Philadelphia: American Philosophical Society, 1956.

Oppenheim, A. Leo, et al., eds. *Assyrian Dictionary of the Oriental Institute of the University of Chicago*. Chicago: University of Chicago Press, 1956–.

Pritchard, James B., ed. *The Ancient Near East: An Anthology of Texts and Pictures*. 3d ed. Princeton, N.J.: Princeton University Press, 1971.

———, ed. *Ancient Near Eastern Texts Relating to the Old Testament*. 3d ed. Princeton, N.J.: Princeton University Press, 1969.

Rainey, Anson F. *Canaanite in the Amarna Tablets: A Linguistic Analysis of the Mixed Dialect Used by the Scribes from Canaan.* Leiden: Brill, 1996.

Reiner, Erica. "Akkadian." Pages 274–303 in *Linguistics in South West Asia and North Africa.* Edited by T. A. Sebeok. Current Trends in Linguistics 6. The Hague: Mouton, 1970.

Saggs, H. W. F. *Assyriology and the Study of the Old Testament.* Cardiff: University of Wales Press, 1969.

Sasson, Jack M., ed. *Civilizations of the Ancient Near East.* 4 vols. New York: Charles Scribner's Sons, 1995.

Snell, Daniel C. *A Workbook of Cuneiform Signs.* Aids and Research Tools in Ancient Near Eastern Studies 3. Malibu: Undena, 1979.

Soden, Wolfram von. *Akkadisches Handwörterbuch.* 3d ed. Wiesbaden: Harrassowitz, 1995.

———. *Grundriß der akkadischen Grammatik.* AnOr 47. Rome: Pontifical Biblical Institute, 1969.

Soden, Wolfram von, and Wolfgang Röllig. *Das Akkadische Syllabar.* 3d rev. and enl. ed. AnOr 42. Rome: Pontifical Biblical Institute, 1976.

Strommenger, E. *Five Thousand Years of the Art of Mesopotamia.* New York: Abrams, 1956.

Ungnad, Arthur. *Akkadian Grammar.* Translated by Harry A. Hoffner Jr. Atlanta: Scholars Press, 1993.

Waltke, Bruce K., and M. O'Connor. *An Introduction to Biblical Hebrew Syntax.* Winona Lake, Ind.: Eisenbrauns, 1990.

Weinfeld, Moshe. "The Covenant of Grant in the Old Testament and in the Ancient Near East." *JAOS* 90 (1970): 184–203. Repr., pages 69–102 in *Essential Papers on Israel and the Ancient Near East.* Edited by Frederick E. Greenspahn. New York: New York University Press, 1991.

———. *Deuteronomy and the Deuteronomic School.* Oxford: Clarendon, 1972.

———. "The Loyalty Oath in the Ancient Near East." *UF* 8 (1976): 379–414.

AMMONITE, EDOMITE, AND MOABITE

Simon B. Parker

1. PRELIMINARY OBSERVATIONS

Although the largest Northwest Semitic inscription from Palestine, the Moabite Stone (or Mesha Stela), was discovered in Moab over a century and a quarter ago, other inscriptions from Transjordan have begun to appear in any numbers only within the last few decades. Those now known, however, are still both few and short. Thus knowledge of the peculiarities of the language of Transjordan is still very limited.

But there are other difficulties in defining the varieties of Northwest Semitic in Transjordan. Despite the eventual establishment of national monarchies in the course of the Iron Age, the people of Transjordan shared a broadly common culture. Ammon may have been more subject to Aramean and even Phoenician influence than Moab or Edom, but their commonalities remain more striking than their differences.

It is not clear precisely when the peoples of Transjordan—from the area around the Zerqa (Jabbok) in the north to the head of the Gulf of Aqaba in the south—can be defined as three distinct entities, nor when they became monarchies (if the two were not simultaneous). It seems likely that Ammon was the first to become a centralized monarchy, then Moab, and finally Edom and that Ammon would have been the most developed form of early state and Edom the most elementary.[1] But these distinctions are made at a very simple level of state development. In any case, the borders of the ancient monarchies were not precisely defined, as are modern state borders, by treaties and maps or by customs and immigration barriers, but rather were roughly marked by major geographical barriers and occasional strategically placed, fortified towns representing the power of the monarch. Most political borders were not stable over time but moved with the imbalance of resources and power.

---

[1] Øystein S. LaBianca and Randall W. Younker, "The Kingdoms of Ammon, Moab, and Edom: The Archaeology of Society in Late Bronze/Iron Age Transjordan," in *The Archaeology of Society in the Holy Land* (ed. Thomas E. Levy; New York: Facts on File, 1995), 399–415.

In times of significant imbalance in the power of neighboring monarchies, particular border settlements and towns may themselves have judged it advantageous to shift allegiance from one monarchy to another. In times of generally weak central powers, such populations would simply assert their independence. Particularly strong monarchs, on the other hand, might have judged it advantageous to conquer and incorporate settlements previously independent or claimed by another. In any case, there may have been a significant difference between royal control at the center and more nominal claims of control at the periphery of such monarchies. Through much of the Iron Age, frontiers were in many areas zones rather than boundaries. All this means that dialectal distinctions were unlikely to be significantly affected by monarchic territorial claims.

Given the simplicity of these early states, it is inappropriate to think of them as having each a discrete national language. There is no a priori reason why the populations of the territories (with their ill-defined and shifting borders) claimed by the three monarchs at any one time should have had three distinct languages. Granting that all the textual witnesses attest the use of a Northwest Semitic language throughout the region, it is most likely that there would have been dialectal variations also throughout the region and that dialectal boundaries would reflect settlement patterns and the degree of isolation of particular settlements or groups of settlements. Major geographical barriers such as the River Jordan, the Dead Sea, and, to a lesser extent, the Arabah to the west; the desert to the east; and in varying degrees the rivers cutting from east to west were probably more significant and stable boundaries of dialects than the shifting political boundaries. It is an oversimplification to conclude that the variations in the evidence for the Canaanite language of Transjordan reflect three distinct languages spoken in three regions coterminous with the three monarchies that we know from historical and literary documents.[2]

We do not have a fraction of the number of linguistic samples needed to produce a precise "dialect geography." In any case, since we are of necessity confined to written documentation, only a "written dialect geography" would be possible, and that would of course be shaped by centers in which writing was important, the relations among those centers, and the relations between them and peripheral sites where writing is found. When our documentation comes from the royal city, it may reasonably be assumed that the language inscribed reflects the dialect of that community.

---

[2] On dialects and dialectology, see J. K. Chambers and P. Trudgill, *Dialectology* (Cambridge: Cambridge University Press, 1980); W. N. Francis, "Dialectology," *International Encyclopaedia of Linguistics* 1:349–55; and S. Romaine, "Dialect and Dialectology," *The Encyclopaedia of Language and Linguistics* 2:900–907.

Inscriptions found elsewhere, if they were the work of the royal administration, might also reflect the dialect of the court, which might be classified
as a prestige dialect. If the court, or at least the royal city, was the source
of all literacy, all written remains may be expected to conform more or less
to the dialect of instruction in that center. The written form of the language
would not then reflect dialectal variations in pronunciation. Otherwise,
however, the writing in other towns may reflect local variations in speech,
and this appears to be the case. It is also possible that the language of an
inscription reflects that of a trader or other traveler from a different region.
It is worth remembering that a major north-south route, the King's High-
way, ran through the length of the region. Literate people may move—for
reasons of trade or diplomacy or safety—from one linguistic area to
another and, assuming mutually comprehensible dialects, continue to write
in their own dialect, not that of their current environment. Larger groups
of people may also be moved by deportation or forced resettlement.[3]
Thus, assumptions about the language of the place where an inscription is
found are not an infallible guide to the precise dialect of the inscription,
and generalizations about a "language" based on where a few inscriptions
are found may be misleading.

The distinguishing features of the Transjordanian dialects that have
been identified suggest that we should be speaking of dialectal variation
rather than discrete languages.[4] Although Garr explicitly accepts the "traditional classification" of texts as Ammonite, Edomite, or Moabite,[5] he uses
the term "dialectal continuum" when summarizing relations among the
three. Aufrecht, in his "corpus" of Ammonite inscriptions, considers it
"impossible at this time" to resolve the question of whether Ammonite is a
language or a dialect.[6] Given the uncertainties mentioned in the preceding
paragraphs and the lack of a systematic study of all the data for the language of Transjordan without the prior imposition of a tripartite
geographical/political grid, references to three discrete linguistic entities
should be regarded as hypothetical and provisional. These reservations
should be kept in mind when reference is made in the following discussion to the Ammonite, Edomite, or Moabite dialects as representing the
varieties of the Canaanite language spoken in Transjordan.

---

[3] See, for example, the Moabite Stone, lines 13–14.

[4] W. Randall Garr, *Dialect Geography of Syria-Palestine, 1000–586 B.C.E.*
(Philadelphia: University of Pennsylvania Press, 1985).

[5] Ibid., 13.

[6] Walter E. Aufrecht, *A Corpus of Ammonite Inscriptions* (Lewiston, N.Y.: Mellen,
1990), xv.

2. THE LANGUAGE

The dialects of Transjordan as defined above generally belong to the Canaanite group of Syro-Palestinian (traditionally Northwest Semitic) languages, which also includes Phoenician and Hebrew. However, some dialects, especially those found north of the Zerqa (Jabbok), have significant isoglosses with Aramaic. Unlike Phoenician, Hebrew, and Aramaic, however, there are very few continuous texts from Transjordan, and it is sometimes debatable which of the three supposed dialects—Ammonite, Moabite, or Edomite—a given text represents. The debate over the language of the Tell Deir ʿAllā plaster texts, from which several lines of continuous narrative prose have been recovered, is the best known example of this kind of problem, with claims for other languages beyond these three making significant appearances in the scholarly literature about those texts. The linguistic attribution of other texts from Tell Deir ʿAllā and of texts from Tell el-Mazar is also disputed. Hübner and Knauf rightly observe that in view of the complexity of the population in the mid-Jordan valley— as suggested by and reflected in the archaeology, epigraphy, and history of the region—we should expect a range of dialects to be represented, even in the same time and place.[7] It is not a priori necessary that the Deir ʿAllā plaster texts should have been written in any other than the local dialect. While noting the varying relations of their language with other Northwest Semitic languages, we should be content simply to classify them as written in a Deir ʿAllā dialect.

Official texts from the royal cities of the three states provide the firmest foundation for speaking of the dialect of each monarchy. But without abundant documentation and precise criteria it is impossible to be certain where precisely the boundaries lay between groups speaking different dialects. The Heshbon ostraca, from a traditionally Moabite site, are classified as Ammonite by Aufrecht, while their Moabite character is defended by Hübner. The best course in the study of any inscription from outside the capital city or of unknown provenance is to describe the language and other features of the text and note its relations with contiguous dialects, remembering that it is not necessary to claim that it is identical with any one of them.

A good model is provided by the discussion of the language of the unprovenanced *marzeaḥ* papyrus by Bordreuil and Pardee.[8] After their introduction and commentary, they summarize the orthography, phonology, morphology, syntax, and vocabulary of the text. They then discuss the

---

[7] Ulrich Hübner and Ernst Axel Knauf, review of W. Aufrecht, *A Corpus of Ammonite Inscriptions, ZDPV* 110 (1994): 82–87.

[8] Pierre Bordreuil and Dennis Pardee, "Le papyrus du marzeaḥ," *Sem* 38 (1990): 49–68.

paleography and, rather than rushing to attribute it to one of the standard "national" scripts, judiciously observe that it "does not correspond entirely to any of the known systems."[9] Next they carefully eliminate dialects to which it does not precisely conform and conclude that it is written in "a Moabite dialect somewhat different from that of Mesha's stela."[10] Not least important, they conclude with a careful discussion of the authenticity of the papyrus.

The linguistic situation in Iron Age Transjordan is thus probably best envisaged, for the present, as a range of Canaanite dialects shifting toward Aramaic north of the Jabbok and including the three prevailing in the courts of the three monarchies, which we may call official Ammonite, Moabite, and Edomite. The Moabite texts now known date from roughly the ninth century B.C.E., Ammonite from the eighth, and Edomite from the seventh. Aramaic increasingly displaced the local dialects in texts from the fifth century on. Not only is the period covered by the documentation limited, but also the number of texts preserved is minuscule compared with that of most of the other languages covered in this volume. Moreover, most of the inscriptions are very short (e.g., seal inscriptions) and relatively unrevealing of linguistic peculiarities. Thus one is ill-advised to propose any general development of the language on the basis of present knowledge.

It has been argued, however, that there are scraps of evidence that suggest that Transjordanian dialects preserved older phonemes not represented in the standard Phoenican script. Thus t, represented by $š$ in the PN $b^{\epsilon}lyš^{\epsilon}$ on two Ammonite seals, may be reflected in the s of Hebrew $b^{\epsilon}lys$ (Jer 40:14 MT); z in the name of the Edomite tribe $zrḥ$ (Gen 36:13, 17) may reflect Edomite d, still preserved in the modern place name Udruḥ; and Assyrian lt, in the Assyrian writing of the name of the Moabite king Kamâšḫaltâ (presumably *$kamoš$-$^{\epsilon}aśâ$) reflects $ś$.[11]

Moabite was first recognized when the so-called Moabite Stone or Mesha Stela, a thirty-four-line memorial inscription of King Mesha, was brought to the attention of Western scholars in 1868. It remains by far the

---

[9] Ibid., 61. "System" is surely the wrong word with reference to the Transjordanian scripts, as presently known.

[10] Ibid., 63.

[11] Ernst Axel Knauf and S. Maáni, "On the Phonemes of Fringe Canaanite: The Cases of Zerah-Udruḥ and 'Kamâšḫaltâ,'" *UF* 19 (1987): 91–94. On the first of these, however, see Ronald S. Hendel, "Sibilants and *šibbolet* (Judges 12:6)," *BASOR* 301 (1996): 69–75. For the recently published second Ammonite seal, see Robert Deutsch, "Seal of Ba$^{\epsilon}$alis Surfaces," *BAR* 25/2 (1999):46–49, 66. Further evidence for the preservation of old phonemes in the Canaanite dialects is available in the representation of Canaanite loanwords in Egyptian texts of the period. See James E. Hoch, *Semitic Words in Egyptian Texts of the New Kingdom and Third Intermediate Period* (Princeton, N.J.: Princeton University Press, 1994).

most extensive Moabite text—and indeed the most extensive text in any of these dialects. Ammonite began to come to light in the second half of the nineteenth century. Although Edomite ostraca and seals had been identified in previous decades, the first more or less continuous prose text appeared only with the discovery in 1983 of the Ḥorvat ʿUza ostracon (published in 1985). The dialect(s) of the area south of the Dead Sea (Edomite) remain(s) the least known of the three.

Apart from the general difficulty of reading ancient, damaged or worn, and usually incomplete inscriptions, none of the Transjordanian scripts and dialects posed problems of decipherment when they were discovered. Their close resemblance to the already known Syro-Palestinian scripts and languages rendered them immediately accessible to those who first studied them. All Transjordanian dialects are attested in Iron Age inscriptions written in the standard Syro-Palestinian alphabet of twenty-two consonants, with some use of some of these to represent vowels. Hence, as in the case of other Syro-Palestinian languages of this period, we have a partial and inadequate basis for determining the pronunciation of the language. While comparative and historical linguistics generally permit the assignation of vowel phonemes, no conclusions can be drawn as to whether the speakers of the different areas were mutually comprehensible. Many phonetic features of regional dialects in Transjordan, as in Cisjordan, would not be reflected in the script.

A few summary remarks concerning the paleography of the inscriptions are in order. The Ammonite script is the closest to Aramaic. It is disputed whether Ammon used the Aramaic script found contemporaneously further north or whether it developed more slowly than its Aramaic source, becoming somewhat distinct until overtaken by the Aramaic script of the Persian Empire.[12] This obviously has implications for dating inscriptions: the former hypothesis leads to higher dates, the latter to lower. In any case, the Aramaic character of the script allows it to be distinguished from the scripts used further south and in Cisjordan. In relation to other Transjordanian scripts, it is characterized by the vertical stance of the stems of those letters that have stems. The Moabites initially used the same form of the script as that used by the Israelites and Judahites. Unlike the Ammonite script, the Moabite generally has very curved stems, even more so than the Hebrew script. The Edomite script is very similar to the Moabite. Distinctive is an inverted *d*. Despite greater claims made by some for the distinctive character of each script, difficulties remain, since among

---

[12] The first hypothesis is that of Joseph Naveh, *Early History of the Alphabet* (Jerusalem: Magnes; Leiden: Brill, 1982), 109–10; the latter is that of Frank Moore Cross, "Notes on the Ammonite Inscription from Tell Sīrān," *BASOR* 212 (1973): 13–14.

the few inscriptions we have, some are cursive and some formal, some clearly carefully shaped, others rather more casually. The limitations of attempts to specify the distinct scripts of the three areas are illustrated by the fact that in some inscriptions letters allegedly characteristic of what have been identified as different "national" scripts are used side by side. Thus while there are clearly different letter forms favored by different scribes, primarily on a regional basis, their identification with politically defined areas or languages is suspect. It is also noteworthy that on seals the shapes of letters are sometimes influenced by the space available.

Turning to the language itself, we can make a few observations about the distinctive character of each dialect and the cultural relations of its speakers to the Judahites and Israelites. The Ammonite dialect is closely related to Hebrew. But if the seal of Abinadab is Ammonite, the relative pronoun appears once as š as against epigraphic Hebrew ᵓšr, though š is attested in various places in biblical literature. Ammonite has the definite article h- but uses it infrequently. In the area of vocabulary, it appears that *tmk* is the equivalent of Hebrew ᵓḥz in personal names: "DN grasped/held fast."[13] But it should be noted that *tmk* also appears in Hebrew and Phoenician PNs.[14] The most common divine name in personal names on Ammonite seals is El; in blessing formulae it is Milcom. The Ammonites were neighbors of the Israelites and presumably shared much the same culture, though we still have relatively little evidence of Ammonite culture.

Moabite, the best known of the three dialects, thanks to the Mesha inscription, preserves a number of older features of the language: final *n* on the absolute plural of masculine nouns and adjectives, final *t* as the marker of feminine singular absolute nouns, and an infixed *t* stem of the simple conjugation. On the other hand, it shares with Hebrew the relative pronoun ᵓšr, the accusative marker ᵓt, and apocopation of the third weak verb in the *wayyqtl* form. Like Ammonite, it has the definite article h- but makes less use of it than Hebrew. The diphthongs *aw* and *ay* have been monophthongized, as in Northern (Israelite) Hebrew and Phoenician. Moabite shares with both Old Aramaic and Phoenician the form of the feminine ending on the word for "year" *št*.

The Moabites were also sometime neighbors of the Israelites, though partly separated by the Dead Sea. It is clear from Mesha's inscription, as

---

[13] Michael Heltzer, "The Root *tmk* in Ammonite, Phoenician and Hebrew," *ZAH* 8 (1995): 140–43.

[14] André Lemaire, "Les critères non-iconographiques de la classificiation des sceaux nord-ouest sémitiques inscrits," in *Studies in the Iconography of Northwest Semitic Inscribed Seals* (ed. Benjamin Sass and Christoph Uehlinger; Freiburg: Universitätsverlag, 1993), 12.

well as from biblical narratives, that Israel and Moab fought over disputed territory in Transjordan (cf. 2 Kgs 3). The border between Moab and Ammon was similarly unstable. Hence, without the discovery of numerous inscriptions in this area, we cannot be sure whether the dialect used by the population of a particular site at a particular time was closer to Moabite, Hebrew, or Ammonite. (It is noteworthy that the dialect represented in Heshbon ostracon IV apparently had [ʾ]lš as its relative pronoun; cf. the Ammonite and Hebrew forms noted above.)

Edomite, little known as it is, is perhaps least distinguishable from contemporary Judahite. If there were differences between the dialects of the two areas, they are minimally reflected in the limited Edomite documentation. Possibly distinctive features either occur only once, such as the use of the *hipʿil* of *brk* instead of the *piʿel* in a performative blessing, or are based on disputed interpretation of the texts. This, of course, says nothing about differences in pronunciation. This linguistic closeness may correspond to a much broader social and cultural closeness (expressed in the Bible in terms of brotherhood). Edom was the southeastern neighbor of Judah. Here, too, the political boundary apparently shifted widely during the period between the origin of the two states and the Persian occupation, so that many settlements were under the control of Judah at one time and Edom at another. In particular, in the later Iron Age the Edomites moved into the Negev, presumably mingling with some of the former Judahite population. Again, only abundant documentation would make clear what dialect the population of any one area spoke at any one time.

The commonalities among the various dialects may be illustrated by the opening formulae used in letters. The Ḥorvat ʿUza ostracon (Edomite) opens with the formulaic *ʾmr* PN1 *ʾmr* *l*PN2 "PN1 says: 'Say to PN2'"—as in the Tell el-Mazar ostracon 3 (central Jordan valley) and Kuntillet ʿAjrūd pithos 1 (ninth-century Hebrew). The Ḥorvat ʿUza ostracon continues: *hšlm* *ʾt* "Are you well?" The same expression follows in the Tell el-Mazar ostracon, though apparently without the interrogative *h,* and in Kuntillet ʿAjrūd pithos 2. Biblical literature typically uses the interrogative *h* and the preposition *l* + suffixed pronoun (or third-person reference)—"Are you (Is X) well?"—but may omit the interrogative (as in 2 Sam 18:29) or the preposition (as in Gen 43:27). All the above sources begin the body of the letter with *wʿt,* "Now, ..." Thus the written form of these several linguistic expressions is indistinguishable in these dialects.

3. SIGNIFICANCE FOR THE BIBLE

Because of the close political and cultural relations between the Transjordanian states and the states of Judah and Israel and the probable general similarity of the institutions of the various states, every discovery of a new text from Transjordan is potentially of great significance for illuminating not only the language, history, and institutions of Ammon, Moab, and Edom but also those of the two states that figure so largely in the Bible. The Mesha inscription, still the one lengthy prose text we have from Transjordan and the most important in relation to the Bible, is, aside from the grammatical distinctions mentioned above, strikingly similar in language and even style to classical Hebrew prose. The beliefs and institutions it reveals are also strikingly similar. Thus its view of the relations among the land of Moab, its king, and the monarchy's deity (Chemosh) were more or less the same as the relations among land, king, and national deity in Judah (and presumably Israel), and the two monarchies seem to have shared such institutions as the *ḥrm,* the vow, the dedication of booty to the deity in his temple, the provision of an adequate water supply in fortified cities, and the building of cities, temples, and a royal palace with associated defenses. Ammonite inscriptions that have some importance for biblical studies—especially the Tell Siran bottle inscription—(see below) are beginning to appear. Edomite is too sparsely attested to be of any importance as yet.

The major methodological problem we face in dealing with inscriptions (allegedly) from Transjordan is the definition of their dialect and, in the case of unprovenanced texts, their place of origin, since these dialects are known to us through such a limited number of inscriptions, composed of at most a few lines (except for the Moabite Stone). In *A Corpus of Ammonite Inscriptions,* Aufrecht includes virtually all those inscriptions that some scholars have claimed are Ammonite. But in an appendix to his book ("Appendix I—Classification") he classifies the inscriptions he has included as (genuinely) Ammonite, probably Ammonite, possibly Ammonite, and other—the last category including inscriptions that are actually in other languages and those that are probably forgeries.[15] The book thus consists of a corpus of inscriptions that, according to the author, are, may be, or are not Ammonite. Further, in their review of this book, Hübner and Knauf argue for the inclusion of texts Aufrecht omitted and the exclusion of texts he considered definitely Ammonite.[16]

In the case of short or damaged inscriptions, it is often not possible to identify features characteristic of the language of the few recovered official texts from central sites. Moreover, since Edomite is so sparsely attested and so far is virtually indistinguishable from Hebrew, there are no reliable linguistic criteria for classifying inscriptions as Edomite. The following criteria have been used to identify the language of inscriptions: provenance, onomastics (specifically divine names), paleography, and, in the case of seals,

[15] Aufrecht, *Corpus of Ammonite Inscriptions,* 349–50.
[16] Hübner and Knauf, review of Aufrecht.

iconography. But given the limited amount of source material and the present state of our knowledge, none of these is a completely reliable indicator of language or dialect, although we may speak of their relative reliability. A few comments on each of the above criteria are appropriate.

3.1. PROVENANCE

As noted above, political boundaries varied over time, and their precise lines in any one era are not precisely known to us. In any case, through written correspondence (assuming the neighboring dialects were mutually comprehensible) or trade, short texts in one dialect might appear beyond the boundaries of the community speaking that dialect. Seals, especially, are very easily transported and usually travel with their owner. Bullae may also travel with the letters or contracts on which they are stamped.[17]

3.2. ONOMASTICS

Where there was a distinctive national or regional deity, as in Moab (Chemosh) and Edom (Qaus), it may reasonably be concluded that personal names containing those divine names belong to people from the corresponding region. While biblical literature suggests that Milcom plays a comparable role in Ammon, the relative frequency of Il and rarity of Milcom in personal names on apparently Ammonite inscriptions means that Milcom is not as valuable for identification purposes as the other two divine names. In any case, while personal names containing the names of Chemosh, Qaus, or Milcom probably belonged, respectively, to Moabites, Edomites, or Ammonites, it does not follow that the text in which the personal name occurs is written in the corresponding dialect. Personal names containing such divine names may belong to natives of one region resident in other linguistic communities. It is even possible that the author of a text may have a name invoking the deity of the country of his origin or of his parents' origin, but write in the dialect of the community in which he is resident. Beyond the divine name, personal names are of even more limited value for identifying the language of an inscription. Most elements, and even whole names, are used in more than one region.

3.3. PALEOGRAPHY

Given the very limited number of features that can be claimed to be consistently characteristic of one of the three regions, paleography alone

---

[17] For an example of a seal found in a controlled investigation in Amman, which, on the basis of paleography and iconography was judged to be Moabite, see Lemaire, "Les critères non-iconographiques," 2–3.

is rarely a reliable criterion for identification of the language of an inscription. Some inscriptions have letters that have distinctive features associated with different dialects. While scribes in the royal city may have conformed to a common standard, scribes in peripheral areas would not have been subject to such professional reinforcement. Thus, without other compelling indications, paleography is usually of limited value.

3.4. ICONOGRAPHY

Iconography is also of little help in identifying the language of an inscription, since iconographic motifs found in Transjordanian seals are also common elsewhere. What is more, certain motifs common elsewhere in Palestine are absent from Transjordan to date. This may be due to the limited size of the corpus, but it is not surprising, given the relatively isolated cultures east of the Jordan. Even if it were possible to identify local variations of common iconographic motifs on an inscription, we could not be certain that both the inscription and the iconography come from the same region; one may have been engraved after the other and in a different location.

Thus provenance and divine names provide the strongest evidence for the language of an inscription, especially if they both point in the same direction. Obviously an inscription that is found in the heartland of one of the three regions, that includes the name of the national deity of that region, and that has letter forms or linguistic features characteristic of that region would provide the greatest cumulative argument for identification. It is a combination of the more distinctive features in each category that makes identification of the language most certain. The fewer such characteristic features there are, the more reservations must accompany any identification. But conclusions based on provenance, onomastics, paleography, and iconography do not always point in the same direction. When such characteristics point in different directions, identification must remain uncertain at present—or the language simply be classified as the local dialect, as suggested above.

Special considerations attach to the largest category of inscriptions, namely, those on seals. Most seals are found, not in a controlled excavation, but on the antiquities market, where provenance is unknown or questionable and forgeries are numerous. Few have been authenticated by scientific tests. Inscribed seals, unlike other inscriptions, may offer evidence of their place of origin in their manufacture, design, and iconography. On the other hand, even when they are found in a controlled excavation, so that their precise find site is known, their manufacture, iconographic decoration, and inscription may all have taken place in different locations. In any case, seals go where their owners go. Thus the language of a seal inscription may not necessarily reflect that of the place where a seal is found, of the place where it was made, or of the place where its iconography was carved (if these were different).

4. ANCIENT SOURCES, MODERN RESOURCES

As mentioned, the largest inscription from the whole region is the so-called Moabite Stone from Dibon, a ninth-century B.C.E. memorial inscription of King Mesha, thirty-four lines long. A fragmentary, second royal inscription (reportedly from Kerak), possibly in the name of Mesha's father, adds little to our knowledge of Moabite.[18] A recently studied, unprovenanced inscription may also be Moabite: the so-called *marzeaḥ* papyrus (see below).

Inscriptions identified as Ammonite include a handful of short formal texts, only one complete, and a number of ostraca with lists of names, patronymics, or commodities. Other ostraca contain no more than a few letters.

In Edomite, we have only a few fragmentary inscriptions consisting of parts of a few lines. Most notable are a brief letter on an ostracon from Ḥorvat ʿUza and a list of names from Tell el-Kheleifeh (no. 6043), that is, from the northern and southern extremities, respectively, of Edomite occupation. Both inscriptions include the name of the Edomite deity Qaus.

There are also a number of inscribed seals and bullae (seal impressions) from or attributed to all three areas: about seventy fairly certainly from Ammon, of those only nine with a known find spot;[19] about four dozen from Moab, of which only about ten mention the characteristic Moabite deity, Chemosh; and a handful from Edom (i.e., containing the divine name Qaus and/or from an excavation in Edom). However, the precise number is disputed in each case, since opinions on the provenance or the authenticity of many diverge. The seals contain personal names and a number of terms referring to the owner's status. One allegedly Ammonite seal is noteworthy, as it takes the form of a votive inscription (see below).

The following inscriptions are the most important for students of the Hebrew Bible.

4.1. MOABITE STONE

The Moabite Stone is preserved almost completely for twenty-seven lines, which are followed by another seven lines of decreasing length. A squeeze of the whole monument as it appeared in 1868 has been preserved,

---

[18] But cf. P. Swiggers, "The Moabite Inscription of el-Kerak," *AION* 42 (1982): 521–25.

[19] Ulrich Hübner, *Die Ammoniter: Untersuchungen zur Geschichte, Kultur und Religion eines transjordanien Volkes im 1. Jahrtausend v. Chr.* (ADPV 1; Wiesbaden: Harrassowitz, 1992), 133.

along with approximately two-thirds of the stone itself. Both are now in the Louvre, where the exhibit displays the stone supplemented by the squeeze. Surprisingly, there has never been an authoritative edition of this text, although in 1994 André Lemaire announced that he was preparing one. Numerous translations, however, have been published based on photographs and hand copies.[20] After more than a century, new explanations and interpretations of particular words and expressions continue to appear. The inscription is valuable as a source of information on the geography of Moab, the history of Mesha's reign, and Moabite religious, political, and military practices and beliefs. It has close connections with the briefer accounts of warfare and references to royal construction projects in the Deuteronomistic History, using similar expressions, style, historiography, and ideology. The present author has undertaken an extensive analysis of the inscription and comparison with biblical materials, focusing especially on individual campaign narratives and sequences of campaign narratives.[21]

4.2. *MARZEAḤ* PAPYRUS

The *marzeaḥ* papyrus, known only from photographs, contains a complete inscription and a damaged seal impression. The language is not identical with palatine Moabite of the ninth century, since it preserves the diphthong *ay*. But it has other features that distinguish it clearly from the other Canaanite and Aramaic dialects, so it is probably best classified as representing a dialect of a marginal district of greater Moab, perhaps in the northwest. It records a divine judgment concerning ownership of a *marzeaḥ* (a voluntary association with its own building), its millstones, and its house.[22] It is thus a legal record of a divine decision on a case. It may be compared with biblical references to cases in which such divine judgment is sought (e.g., Exod 22:6–8; 1 Kgs 8:31–32).

4.3. TELL SIRAN INSCRIPTION

The Tell Siran inscription is written on a bronze bottle, found during excavations at the site of that name (ca. 10 km. northwest of Amman) and

---

[20] See the photo, hand copy, and translation in André Lemaire, "'House of David' Restored in Moabite Inscription," *BAR* 20/3 (1994): 30–37; and the recent translations in Simon B. Parker, *Stories in Scripture and Inscriptions* (New York: Oxford University Press, 1997), 44–46; and Klaas A. D. Smelik, "The Inscription of King Mesha," in *Monumental Inscriptions from the Biblical World* (vol. 2 of *The Context of Scripture*, ed. W. W. Hallo; Leiden: Brill, 2000), 137–38.

[21] Parker, *Stories in Scripture*, 43–75.

[22] Bordreuil and Pardee, "Le papyrus du marzeaḥ."

now in the Archaeological Museum in Amman. The inscription is clearly preserved in its entirety. The most valuable and compelling study of this inscription and its relation to biblical material was published by Müller in 1996.[23] It includes a philological commentary, discussion of style and genre, and careful comparison with various biblical texts, most notably Qoh 2:1–11 and several passages in the Song of Songs.

4.4. AMMAN CITADEL INSCRIPTION

The Amman Citadel inscription was discovered in 1961 on a limestone slab during excavations of the Iron Age citadel at Amman and is now in the Archaeological Museum there. There is a good photograph of the inscription on the West Semitic Research website.[24] The remains of eight lines are preserved, but unfortunately neither the beginnings nor the ends of them. The text seems to consist of directions and promises given by a deity concerning a building. It thus invites comparison with ancient Near Eastern texts answering to the same description and with the divine instructions concerning the tabernacle and the temple in the Bible.

4.5. TELL EL-MAZAR OSTRACA

Of the nine ostraca found at Tell el-Mazar (3 km. east of the Jordan above the Jabbok and 3 km. northwest of Tell Deir ʿAllā) and now in the University of Jordan Museum, most are poorly preserved, and two are practically illegible. Several are from the Hellenistic period. Ostracon 3, found on the floor of a sixth-century building, preserves parts of the first few lines of a letter (see above, p. 50).

4.6. SEALS

Even the smallest inscriptions, such as those on seals, may be of significance for biblical studies. One of uncertain origin, though considered Ammonite by many, and now in the Bibliotheque Nationale in Paris, reads: "[PN, son of ?] Abinadab, who vowed to ʿšt in Sidon. May she bless him," or perhaps better: "[Seal which?] Abinadab vowed to ..." The reference is to a vow made away from home—as allegedly by Absalom in Geshur (2 Sam 15:8)—and then fulfilled in some other place—Hebron, in Absalom's case. Here the seal itself is the fulfillment, as indicated by the final wish for a blessing. Thus the owner's testimony to the goddess's response

---

[23] Hans-Peter Müller, "Kohelet und Amminadab," in *"Jedes Ding hat seine Zeit...":* *Studien zur israelitischen und altorientalischen Weisheit Diethelm Michel zum 65. Geburtstag* (ed. A. A. Diesel et al; BZAW 241; Berlin: de Gruyter, 1996).

[24] The address is: http://www.usc.edu/dept/LAS/wsrp/educational_site.

to his vow is stamped on every document he seals. Two other seals refer to a servant of *bʿlyšʿ*, perhaps the king of Ammon called Baalis in Jer 40:14.

4.7. DEIR ʿALLĀ TEXTS

Finally, although it might be questioned whether the Tell Deir ʿAllā plaster texts belong in this chapter, they should not be ignored since they represent a distinct dialect in the north of the linguistic area covered and are of particular importance for students of the Bible. They were originally inscribed in the early eighth century in black and red ink on the plaster of a wall but survived only in plaster fragments in the debris near where the wall had been. They are now in the Archaeological Museum in Amman. Many fragments have been rejoined in two "combinations." Unfortunately, parts of the reconstruction remain uncertain, and much of the text is fragmentary. However, the first nine or ten lines of Combination I are almost complete and reliably restored. From these it is clear that this, unlike most Northwest Semitic Iron Age inscriptions, was a literary text. It begins with a superscription identifying it as "the story of Balaam, son of Beor, who was a seer of (the) gods." It recounts that the gods came to Balaam at night and that he saw a vision like a divine oracle. The next day his people found him weeping profusely. In answer to their inquiries, he told them the acts of the gods, beginning with a divine assembly in which there was a call for the heavens to be obscured, at which point the text becomes obscured. It seems to describe dire events in nature, but the order of the fragments and their restoration are subjects of scholarly speculation and debate.

The main character is clearly the same as that of Num 22–24. The two texts together suggest the prominence of stories about the seer Balaam in and around the Jordan Valley in the Iron Age and later. But the Deir ʿAllā texts also clearly have relations with various passages in biblical prophetic literature.[25]

5. BIBLIOGRAPHY

5.1. PRIOR CONSIDERATIONS

5.1.1. ON POLITICAL DEVELOPMENT

LaBianca, Øystein S., and Randall W. Younker. "The Kingdoms of Ammon, Moab, and Edom: The Archaeology of Society in Late Bronze/Iron Age Transjordan." Pages 399–415 in *The Archaeology of Society in the Holy Land*. Edited by Thomas E. Levy. New York: Facts on File, 1995.

---

[25] See the numerous references in Hallo, ed., *Monumental Inscriptions from the Biblical World*, 142–45.

5.1.2. On Dialects

Chambers, J. K., and P. Trudgill. *Dialectology.* Cambridge: Cambridge University Press, 1980.

Francis, W. N. "Dialectology." Pages 349–55 in vol. 1 of *International Encyclopaedia of Linguistics.* Edited by W. Bright. 4 vols. Oxford: Oxford University Press, 1992.

Romaine, S. "Dialect and Dialectology." Pages 900–907 in vol. 2 of *The Encyclopaedia of Language and Linguistics.* Edited by R. E. Asher. 10 vols. Oxford: Pergamon, 1994.

5.2. GENERAL

Garr, W. Randall. *Dialect Geography of Syria-Palestine, 1000–586 B.C.E.* Philadelphia: University of Pennsylvania Press, 1985.

Hallo, William W., ed. *Monumental Inscriptions from the Biblical World.* Vol. 2 of *The Context of Scripture.* Leiden: Brill, 2000.

Hoch, James E. *Semitic Words in Egyptian Texts of the New Kingdom and Third Intermediate Period.* Princeton, N.J.: Princeton University Press, 1994.

Hoftijzer, Jacob, and K. Jongeling. *Dictionary of the North-West Semitic Inscriptions.* Leiden: Brill, 1995.

Israel, F. "Rassegna critico-bibliografica ed epigrafica su alcune onomastiche palestinesi: la Transgiordania." *SEL* 9 (1992): 95–114.

Knauf, Ernst Axel, and S. Maáni. "On the Phonemes of Fringe Canaanite: The Cases of Zerah-Uḏruḫ and ʿKamâšḫaltâ.ʾ" *UF* 19 (1987): 91–94.

Lemaire, André. "Epigraphy, Transjordanian." *ABD* 2:561–68.

Young, Ian. *Diversity in Pre-Exilic Hebrew.* FAT 5. Tübingen: Mohr Siebeck, 1993.

The following four items are concerned specifically with seals:

Avigad, Naʿaman. *Corpus of West Semitic Stamp Seals.* Revised and completed by Benjamin Sass. Jerusalem: Israel Exploration Society, 1997.

Bordreuil, Pierre. "Sceaux inscrits des pays du Levant." *DBSup* 12.86–212.

Lemaire, André. "Les critères non-iconographiques de la classification des sceaux nord-ouest sémitiques inscrits." Pages 1–26 in *Studies in the Iconogaphy of Northwest Semitic Inscribed Seals.* Edited by Benjamin Sass and Christoph Uehlinger. Freiburg: Universitätsverlag, 1993.

Uehlinger, Christoph. "Westsemitisch beschriftete Stempsiegel: Ein Corpus und neue Fragen." *Bib* 79 (1998): 103–19.

The following four items treat paleography:

Herr, Larry G. "The Formal Scripts of Iron Age Transjordan." *BASOR* 238 (1988): 21–34.

————. "The Palaeography of West Semitic Stamp Seals." *BASOR* 312 (1998): 45–77.

————. *The Scripts of Ancient Northwest Semitic Seals.* HSM 18. Missoula, Mont.: Scholars Press, 1978.

Naveh, Joseph. *Early History of the Alphabet: An Introduction to West Semitic Epigraphy and Palaeography.* Jerusalem: Magnes, 1982.

5.3. AMMONITE

Aufrecht, Walter E. "The Ammonite Language of the Iron Age." *BASOR* 266 (1987): 85–95.

————. "Ammonite Texts and Language." Pages 163–88 in *Ancient Ammon.* Edited by B. Macdonald and R. W. Younker. Studies in the History and Culture of the Ancient Near East 17. Leiden: Brill, 1999.

————. *A Corpus of Ammonite Inscriptions.* Lewiston, N.Y.: Mellen, 1990.

Deutsch, Robert. "Seal of Ba'alis Surfaces." *BAR* 25/2 (1999): 46–49, 66.

Heltzer, Michael. "The Root *tmk* in Ammonite, Phoenician and Hebrew." *ZAH* 8 (1995): 140–43.

Hendel, Ronald S. "Sibilants and *šibbolet* (Judges 12:6)." *BASOR* 301 (1996): 69–75.

Hübner, Ulrich. *Die Ammoniter: Untersuchungen zur Geshichte, Kultur und Religion eines transjordanien Volkes im 1. Jahrtausend v. Chr.* ADPV 16. Wiesbaden: Harrassowitz, 1992.

Hübner, Ulrich, and Ernst Axel Knauf. Review of W. Aufrecht, *A Corpus of Ammonite Inscriptions. ZDPV* 110 (1994): 82–87.

Israel, F. "The Language of the Ammonites." *OLP* 10 (1979): 143–59.

Jackson, Kent. P. *The Ammonite Language of the Iron Age.* HSM 27. Chico, Calif.: Scholars Press, 1983.

Müller, Hans-Peter. "Kohelet und Amminadab." Pages 149–65 in *"Jedes Ding hat seine Zeit...": Studien zur israelitischen und altorientalischen Weisheit Diethelm Michel zum 65. Geburtstag.* Edited by A. A. Diesel et al. BZAW 241. Berlin: de Gruyter, 1996.

O'Connor, Michael Patrick. "The Ammonite Onomasticon: Semantic Problems." *AUSS* 25 (1987): 51–64.

Sivan, Daniel. "On the Grammar and Orthography of the Ammonite Findings." *UF* 14 (1982): 219–34.

5.4. MOABITE

Andersen, Francis I. "Moabite Syntax." *Or* 35 (1966): 81–120.

Blau, Joshua. "Short Philological Notes on the Inscription of Meša'." *Maarav* 2 (1979–1980): 143–57.

Bordreuil Pierre, and Dennis Pardee. "Le papyrus du marzeaḥ." *Sem* 38 (1990): 49–68.

Dearman, Andrew, ed. *Studies in the Mesha Inscription and Moab.* SBLABS 2. Atlanta: Scholars Press, 1989.

Lemaire, André. "'House of David' Restored in Moabite Inscription." *BAR* 20/3 (1994): 30–37.

————. "Notes d'épigraphie nord-ouest sémitique." *Syria* 64 (1987): 205–16.

Niccacci, A. "The Stele of Mesha and the Bible: Verbal System and Narrativity." *Or* 63 (1994): 226–48.

Parker, Simon B. *Stories in Scripture and Inscriptions.* New York: Oxford University Press, 1997.

Segert, Stanislav. "Die Sprache der Moabitischen Königsinschrift." *ArOr* 29 (1961): 197–267.

Sekine, M. "Subdivisions of the North-West Semitic Languages." *JSS* 18 (1973): 205–21.

Swiggers, P. "The Moabite Inscription of el-Kerak." *AION* 42 (1982): 521–25.

Timm, Stefan. *Moab zwischen den Mächten: Studien zu historischen Denkmälern und Texten.* Ägypten und Altes Testament 17. Wiesbaden: Harrassowitz, 1989.

van Wyk, Koot. *Squatters in Moab: A Study of Iconography, History, Epigraphy, Orthography, Ethnography, Religion and Linguistics of the Ancient Near East.* Berrien Springs, Mich.: Louis Hester, 1993.

5.5. EDOMITE

Beit-Arieh, Itzhaq, and Bruce Cresson. "An Edomite Ostracon from Ḥorvat ʿUza." *TA* 12 (1985): 96–101.

Bartlett, John R. *Edom and the Edomites.* JSOTSup 77. Sheffield: Sheffield Academic Press, 1989.

Naveh, Joseph. "The Scripts of Two Ostraca from Elath." *BASOR* 183 (1966): 27–30.

Vanderhooft, David S. "The Edomite Dialect and Script: A Review of the Evidence." Pages 135–57 in *You Shall Not Abhor an Edomite For He Is Your Brother: Edom and Seir in History and Tradition.* Edited by D. V. Edelman. SBLABS 3. Atlanta: Scholars Press, 1995.

5.6. DEIR ʿALLĀ

Hackett, Jo Ann. *The Balaam Text from Deir ʿAlla.* HSM 31. Chico, Calif.: Scholars Press, 1984.

Hoftijzer, Jacob, and G. van der Kooij. *Aramaic Texts from Deir ʿAlla.* Documenta et Monumenta Orientis Antiqui 19. Leiden: Brill, 1976.

————, eds. *The Baalam Text from Deir ʿAlla Reevaluated: Proceedings of the International Symposium Held at Leiden, 21–24 August 1989.* Leiden: Brill, 1991.

ARABIC

John Kaltner

1. THE LANGUAGE

Arabic is universally classified as a Semitic language, but its precise place within the Semitic family has been the subject of debate. Traditionally, it has been common to identify it as a South Semitic language along with Old South Arabian, Modern South Arabian, and Ethiopic. But recently it has been suggested that it should more properly be classified as a Central Semitic language, a category also containing the Northwest Semitic languages Aramaic and Canaanite.

The primary reason for the ambiguous position of Arabic is the fact that it shares certain features with languages found in both the southern and northern branches of the Semitic family. Phonetically, it appears to have more in common with the southern languages, while from the morphological point of view it shares more with the northern languages. Some of these features will be discussed below.[1]

Until the present day, Arabic has continued to function as a spoken and written means of communication. This is not to say that it has remained unchanged and has not evolved or developed over the centuries. Just the opposite is true. But, unlike many of the languages in this volume, it did not experience a period of abandonment followed by its rediscovery and decipherment centuries later. Certain pre-Islamic inscriptions and texts written in scripts different from the later Classical Arabic script have been identified as a type of "proto-Arabic" (see below), but this is quite different from the decipherment of a previously unknown language.

---

[1] For a discussion of the alternative models and the debate over the placement of Arabic within them, see Alice Faber, "Genetic Subgrouping of the Semitic Languages," in *The Semitic Languages* (ed. Robert Hetzron; London: Routledge, 1997), 3–15. Other studies that treat these issues include Robert Hetzron, "Two Principles of Genetic Classification," *Lingua* 38 (1976): 89–108; Rainer M. Voigt, "The Classification of Central Semitic," *JSS* 32 (1987): 1–21; Andrzej Zaborski, "The Position of Arabic within the Semitic Language Continuum," *Budapest Studies in Arabic* 3–4 (1991): 365–75.

1.1. HISTORY

The development and spread of the Arabic language was a lengthy and complex process, and this has a significant bearing on how the Hebrew Bible scholar should make use of the resources it offers. As the Muslim community extended beyond the Arabian peninsula beginning in the mid-seventh century C.E., it brought the language of the Qurʾān with it. Arabic eventually became the lingua franca of a vast area covering large portions of western Asia, northern Africa, and western Europe. In the present day, Arabic has a worldwide presence, since speakers of the language can be found in every part of the globe.[2]

As the oldest and most respected literary work written in Arabic, the Qurʾān enjoys a privileged position in the history of the language. The form of Arabic found in Islam's sacred text became the standard expression of the language, and it, along with the poetry of the pre-Islamic period, formed the basis of what is known as Classical Arabic (hereafter CA). The earliest Arabic grammarians consulted these two resources in order to determine proper usage and to establish the rules of the language. The elevation of the Qurʾānic form of the language was also instrumental in the development of one of the defining features of Arabic: diglossia, a situation in which high and low varieties of a language coexist and mark a division between written and spoken forms of communication. For biblical scholars CA is the most important and useful form of Arabic, but other aspects of the historical development of the language are also worth noting and will now be briefly discussed.[3]

There is a lack of sufficient evidence to trace the emergence and development of Arabic in its earliest stages. The Arabian peninsula was settled in the second millennium B.C.E., but the language of its earliest inhabitants is unknown. Between the thirteenth and tenth centuries B.C.E. fairly advanced civilizations were established in the area. The earliest inscriptions exhibiting features related to later CA are written in a language termed Early North Arabic, sometimes called Proto-Arabic or Early Arabic. The scripts of these inscriptions appear to be derived from those found in earlier inscriptions from the southern part of the peninsula, which are

---

[2] Information on the spread and influence of Arabic can be found in Anwar G. Chejne, *The Arabic Language: Its Role in History* (Minneapolis: University of Minnesota Press, 1969); and Bertold Spuler, "Die Ausbreitung der arabischen Sprache," in *Semitistik* (ed. B. Spuler; HO 1/3; Leiden: Brill, 1964), 245–52.

[3] An excellent overview of the historical development of Arabic is presented in Kees Versteegh, *The Arabic Language* (New York: Columbia University Press, 1997).

unrelated to later Arabic and are written in a language designated Old (or Epigraphic) South Arabian.

Discovered in the nineteenth century and numbering in the tens of thousands, these inscriptions are mostly fragmentary and are often comprised of nothing but personal names. They date from the middle part of the first millennium B.C.E. to the first half of the first millennium C.E. (ca. 600 B.C.E.–400 C.E.) and are divided into four groups named after places with which they are associated: Thamūdic, Liḥyānitic, Ṣafāʾitic, and Ḥasāʾitic. These Early North Arabic inscriptions contain some interesting similarities with Northwest Semitic languages, as seen, for example, in their use of the preposed definite article *h(n)* (c.f. Heb. *ha-*) rather than the article *al* found in later Arabic. There is also some limited evidence of shared vocabulary with Northwest Semitic, as, for example, in the word *mdbr* "desert" (c.f. Heb. *midbār*).[4]

The earliest recorded evidence for the definite article *al* is seen in inscriptions written in Nabatean and Palmyrene. These inscriptions are in the Aramaic script, but they come from places where Arabic was commonly spoken, and it appears that the form of the language spoken in these areas was related to CA. Approximately four thousand inscriptions, most of which date from between the first century B.C.E. and the first century C.E., have been discovered from the Arab kingdom of Nabatea, which had its capital at Petra in modern Jordan. The Palmyrene texts number around two thousand and come from the oasis of Tadmur, an important trade outpost in the Syrian desert between the first and third centuries C.E. The usefulness of these two sets of inscriptions in understanding the development of Arabic is limited by the fact that they are written in Aramaic, which was the language of written communication then current. Evidence of the Arabic spoken by the local populations is found primarily in the many personal names present in the inscriptions and in the few places where the spoken language has infiltrated the written language. The most important contribution the Nabatean and Palmyrene inscriptions have made to the study of Arabic is in the area of orthography. In particular, they highlight the key role the Aramaic script played in the order and

---

[4] For detailed data on these inscriptions and the linguistic situation in Arabia prior to the rise of Islam, see Alfred F. L. Beeston, "Languages of Pre-Islamic Arabia," *Arabica* 28 (1981): 178–86; Walter M. Müller, "Das Altarabische der Inschriften aus vorislamischer Zeit," in *Grundriß der arabischen Philologie I. Sprachwissenschaft* (ed. Wolfdietrich Fischer; Wiesbaden: Reichert, 1983), 30–36; Christian Robin, *L'Arabie antique de Karibʾîl à Mahomet: nouvelles données sur l'histoire des Arabes grâce aux inscriptions* (Aix-en-Provence: Editions Edisud, 1992); M. C. A. Macdonald, "Reflections on the Linguistic Map of Pre-Islamic Arabia," *Arabian Archaeology and Epigraphy* 11 (2000): 28–79.

arrangement of the CA alphabet, and they provide important data on the spelling of long vowels.[5]

The oldest Arabic text is probably one discovered in 1979 at ʿEn ʿAvdat that is part of an inscription to the god Obodas. The inscription, from perhaps as early as the first century c.e., is written in Nabatean Aramaic script, and a two-line portion of it is generally held to be the earliest example of Arabic. Although there is disagreement over how to read and interpret the text, the presence of the definite article *al* leaves no doubt that the inscription is Arabic.[6]

Although it contains elements that are clearly Arabic, the ʿEn ʿAvdat inscription is not written in an Arabic script. The evidence for written Arabic in the period prior to Islam is quite limited, but five brief inscriptions written in the language have been found and published. The primary value of these five inscriptions is in what they tell us about the early development of the Arabic script. It is now generally agreed that the Arabic alphabet came from a form of cursive Nabatean. Comparative evidence from Nabatean suggests that perhaps as early as the second century c.e. an Arabic script was already emerging that contained some of the characteristic features of the later language, including ligatures between letters and different forms for individual letters depending on their position within a word.[7]

The early Arab grammarians indicate that there were differences among the spoken languages of the various tribes in pre-Islamic Arabia, but it is impossible to pinpoint the precise distribution of these differences. The basic distinctions are drawn in broad geographic terms with a primary division between the Northern and Southern Arabs. The language of the Southern Arabs was characterized by the use of the definite article *ʾam,* and this feature continues to be found in the dialects of modern Yemen. The languages of the Northern Arabs are divided into two groups, one comprising the western portion of the peninsula and the other the eastern

---

[5] A comprehensive treatment of this aspect of Arabic is provided in Beatrice Gruendler, *The Development of the Arabic Scripts: From the Nabataean Era to the First Islamic Century according to Dated Texts* (Atlanta: Scholars Press, 1993).

[6] James A. Bellamy, "Arabic Verses from the First/Second Century: The Inscription of ʿEn ʿAvdat," *JSS* 25 (1990): 73–79, translates the lines "For (Obodas) works without reward or favor and he, when death tried to claim us, did not let it claim (us) for when a wound (of ours) festered, he did not let us perish." See also A. Negev, "Obodas the God," *IEJ* 36 (1986): 56–60; David Testen, "On the Arabic of the ʿEn ʿAvdat Inscription," *JNES* 55 (1996): 281–92.

[7] Versteegh, *Arabic Language,* 33–34.

section. These are referred to as the language of the Hijāz and language of the Tamīm, respectively. In a general way, this division also delineates the boundaries between the sedentary lifestyle of the pre-Islamic cities of the Hijāz region in the western part of Arabia and the nomadic existence of the desert areas.[8]

The Hijāz was the birthplace of Islam, and two of its major cities, Mecca and Medina, were important centers for the early Muslim community. Interestingly, the language of the Qur'ān is different from the language spoken in that area and is in fact closer to the dialects of the eastern part of Arabia. For example, the orthography of the Qur'ān includes the letter *hamza* ('), the character designating the glottal stop, and this is a feature that is found in the eastern dialects but is completely missing from the western ones. It therefore appears that the forms of Arabic in the eastern part of the peninsula were closer to CA than those in the western part, where Islam began. This is often attributed to the important role of pre-Islamic poetry as it emerged in the east and eventually spread to settled areas such as Mecca and Medina. Because poetry was considered to be the purest form of Arabic and transcended tribal divisions, it was the ideal vehicle by which to convey the message of Islam's sacred text, even if it was not the vernacular of the area in which the religion first appeared.

This situation in which a poetic or literary language coexists with a colloquial language is an example of diglossia, a phenomenon mentioned above that appears to predate Islam and continues to be a characteristic feature of Arabic to the present day. Throughout the Arabic-speaking world, two varieties of the language separate the domains of writing and speaking, with a standard form being used for written expression or formal speaking and a colloquial form used for informal speech. Presently, CA is a form of the language that is only encountered when reading the Qur'ān or other ancient texts. Modern Standard Arabic, which began to develop in the nineteenth century, is used for writing or formal speaking and serves to unite all Arabic speakers. Local dialects are used for informal speech, and the differences among them can be so profound that two native speakers of Arabic are unable to understand each other and must resort to communicating in Modern Standard Arabic or another language.[9]

---

[8] An excellent overview of the pre-Islamic dialects of Arabia is provided in Chaim Rabin, *Ancient West-Arabian* (London: Taylor's Foreign Press, 1951).

[9] For more literature on diglossia, see Mauro Fernandez, *Diglossia: A Comprehensive Bibliography 1960–90 and Supplements* (Amsterdam and Philadelphia: Benjamins, 1993).

A type of written Arabic that has been of interest to Hebrew Bible scholars is Middle Arabic (MA), a designation for texts exhibiting deviations from the norms of CA. MA is not a chronological category that refers to texts from a particular period but is used to speak of any text that does not strictly follow the rules of CA. An example of this is texts that use the pattern *yaf'alū* for the third-person plural masculine of the indicative of a verb, a form that is a subjunctive in CA but is commonly found in colloquial speech to express the indicative. While such usage can be due to the unintentional influence of spoken Arabic on written texts, it is also sometimes the result of an intentional desire to use the vernacular. It is common to categorize MA texts as Muslim, Jewish, or Christian depending on their provenance.

The MA of Jewish texts is often called "Judaeo-Arabic." The colloquial language of Jews conquered by Muslim armies became Arabic quite early, and the first Jewish literary works written in Arabic come from the ninth century C.E. The MA of these texts tends to have more colloquialisms than the MA of Islamic works. A primary reason for this is that CA was less of a constraint on the Jewish community than it was on Muslims, for whom it functioned as the sacred language of their revealed book the Qur'ān. Judaeo-Arabic is written in a Hebrew script that employs a system of dots to transliterate Arabic letters not found in the Hebrew alphabet. Jewish texts written in MA contain many loanwords from Hebrew and also exhibit an interesting tendency to arabicize Hebrew words. For example, Hebrew verbs in the *hip'il* conjugation are occasionally written in the pattern of the fourth Arabic verbal conjugation (*'af'ala*), which, like the *hip'il,* expresses the causative. Similarly, Hebrew nouns in these works are sometimes pluralized using the broken plural forms that are found in Arabic.[10]

The biblical scholar who wishes to consult Arabic needs to keep in mind the long and complex development of the language. This is particularly the case when one is engaging in the work of comparative lexicography, the primary way that Arabic has been used in Hebrew Bible studies. The lengthy history and wide geographic distribution of Arabic, as well as the presence of diglossia leading to different forms of the language, can complicate the attempt to arrive at an accurate understanding of how a particular word or meaning functions in Arabic and

---

[10] The standard work on Middle Arabic is Joshua Blau, *The Emergence and Linguistic Background of Judeo-Arabic: A Study of the Origins of Middle Arabic* (London: Oxford University Press, 1965). Some of Blau's most important articles have been collected in his *Studies in Middle Arabic and Its Judaeo-Arabic Variety* (Jerusalem: Magnes, 1988).

its possible relevance for biblical Hebrew. For reasons that will be explained below (see §2), biblical scholarship is best served when the data and resources associated with CA are the ones primarily used and given the most weight. While evidence from dialects and colloquial forms of the language can be of some assistance to the Bible scholar, it would be a mistake to base one's conclusions on it alone without any reference to CA.

1.2. WRITING SYSTEM

As noted earlier, the epigraphic evidence suggests that the CA script derived from Nabatean Aramaic. Because Arabic has more consonants than Aramaic, some letters had to represent more than one consonant. By the seventh century C.E. a series of dots placed above and below letters helped to differentiate the various consonants. Other signs were also introduced to indicate short vowels, the lack of vocalization, and the doubling of consonants. A major impetus in these developments was the status of the Qur'ān as a revealed text. These diacritical dots and marks helped to ensure an unambiguous reading of Islam's sacred book, and this system has survived intact until the present day. In other words, the phonological and morphological features of Modern Standard Arabic are virtually identical to those found in CA.[11]

There are twenty-eight letters in the Arabic script, with each letter representing one consonant. It is a cursive script written from right to left in which letters must be joined where possible, but six letters (ʾ, d, ḏ, r, z, w) cannot be connected to what follows them. There are four possible positions for each letter within a word: isolated, initial, medial, and final. As this list of the Arabic letters shows, a letter will often be written somewhat differently depending on its position in a word.[12]

---

[11] An important work on the development of Classical Arabic is Johann Fück, *Arabiya: Untersuchungen zur arabischen Sprach- und Stilgeschichte* (Berlin: Akademie-Verlag, 1950). On orthography, see Nabia Abbott, *Studies in Arabic Literary Papyri III: Language and Literature* (Chicago: University of Chicago Press, 1972); Gerhard Endreß, "Die arabische Schrift," in *Grundriß der arabischen Philologie I. Sprachwissenschaft* (ed. Wolfdietrich Fischer; Wiesbaden: Reichert, 1983), 165–97. On the diacritical marks, see E. J. Revell, "The Diacritical Dots and the Development of the Arabic Alphabet," *JSS* 20 (1975): 178–90.

[12] There are a number of different transliteration systems for Arabic. The one adopted here is used in Hans Wehr, *A Dictionary of Modern Written Arabic* (Ithaca, N.Y.: Spoken Language Services, 1976), except for ġ in place of Wehr's ḡ.

Name	Isolated	Initial	Medial	Final	Transliteration
alif	ا			ا	ʾ
bāʾ	ـب	ـبـ	ـبـ	ـب	b
tāʾ	ـت	ـتـ	ـتـ	ـت	t
ṯāʾ	ـث	ـثـ	ـثـ	ـث	ṯ
jīm	ج	ـجـ	ـجـ	ـج	j
ḥāʾ	ح	ـحـ	ـحـ	ـح	ḥ
ḵāʾ	خ	ـخـ	ـخـ	ـخ	ḵ
dāl	د			ـد	d
ḏāl	ذ			ـذ	ḏ
rāʾ	ر			ـر	r
zāʾ	ز			ـز	z
sīn	س	ـسـ	ـسـ	ـس	s
šīn	ش	ـشـ	ـشـ	ـش	š
ṣād	ص	ـصـ	ـصـ	ـص	ṣ
ḍād	ض	ـضـ	ـضـ	ـض	ḍ
ṭāʾ	ط	ط	ـطـ	ـط	ṭ
ẓāʾ	ظ	ظ	ـظـ	ـظ	ẓ
ʿain	ع	ـعـ	ـمـ	ـع	ʿ
ġain	غ	ـغـ	ـغـ	ـغ	ġ
fāʾ	ف	ـفـ	ـفـ	ـف	f
qāf	ق	ـقـ	ـقـ	ـق	q
kāf	ك	كـ	كـ	ـك	k
lām	ل	لـ	ـلـ	ـل	l
mīm	م	مـ	ـمـ	ـم	m
nūn	ن	نـ	ـنـ	ـن	n
hāʾ	ه	هـ	ـهـ	ـه	h
wāw	و			ـو	w
yāʾ	ي	يـ	ـيـ	ـي	y

The vowel system of Arabic is similar to those of other Semitic languages. The three short vowels *a, i,* and *u* are indicated by the marks (´ `) written above or below a consonant and known in Arabic as *fatḥa, kasra,* and *ḍamma,* respectively. As in biblical Hebrew, the Arabic consonants *alif, yāʾ,* and *wāw* do double duty and can function as markers of the long vowels *ā, ī,* and *ū.* When a consonant is unvocalized, this is indicated by the presence of the sign (°), known as *sukūn,* above the letter. Another marker placed above consonants is the *shadda,* written (´), which denotes the gemination, or doubling, of the letter. It is important to note that Arabic texts are hardly ever fully vocalized. While the Qurʾān is always written with all vowels and signs present to prevent the possibility of variant readings, this is not the case with other texts. Familiarity with the rules and principles of morphology usually prevents serious errors in reading, but in those cases where radically different readings of a word are possible, vowel signs or other marks are often found.

A morphological feature unique to Arabic among the Semitic languages is the use of the ending *-n* as a marker to designate an indefinite noun. The term used to describe this is *nunation* (in Arabic, *tanwīn*), coming from the name of the letter *nūn*. Nunation is indicated by the doubling of the short vowel signs in the following manner: ˊ (pronounced *-an*), ˏ (*-in*), and ˊ (*-un*). There are two other signs commonly used in Arabic that deserve mention. The first is the *hamza*, written (ء), which represents the glottal stop and is usually carried by either the *alif, yā'*, or *wāw*, although it can stand alone.[13] The other is the *tā' marbūṭa*, which is the letter *h* with two dots above it (ة) and designates the consonant *t* when it functions as the feminine ending as, for example, in the word مَدِينَةٌ (*madīnatun*, "city").

1.3. GRAMMATICAL FEATURES

As is the case with all Semitic languages, most words in Arabic are derived from a root comprised of three letters, although roots with four letters are not rare. A basic lexical meaning is found in these three radicals, and the meaning of a given form is communicated morphologically through its vowel pattern and, often, the addition of auxiliary consonants. For example, the root letters *k-r-j* convey the general sense of going out or departing. Some of the words and meanings derived from this root include: *karaja* "he went out," *yakruju* "he goes out," *istakraja* "he extracted," *karj* "expenditures," *kurāj* "swelling," *kārij* "exterior, outside," and *makraj* "exit."

Early on, Arab grammarians made the decision to use the letters *f-ʿ-l*, a root associated with the idea of making or doing (cf. Hebrew *pāʿal*), as a paradigm to describe morphological patterns.[14] They would simply insert the vowels and additional consonants into this root in order to describe the pattern of a given word. For example, the patterns of the Arabic words listed in the previous paragraph would be identified in grammars as *faʿala, yafʿulu, istafʿala, faʿl, fuʿāl, fāʿil*, and *mafʿal*. This same approach will be used at times in the following discussion.[15]

---

[13] The five possible ways the *hamza* can be written are found in Thomas Bauer, "Arabic Writing," in *The World's Writing Systems* (ed. Peter T. Daniels and William Bright; Oxford: Oxford University Press, 1996), 561.

[14] The Arab grammarians use of *faʿala* is what led their Jewish counterparts to make the unfortunate decision to use the Hebrew cognate *pāʿal* as their own paradigm root.

[15] There are many Arabic grammars available. Among the best are William Wright, *A Grammar of the Arabic Language* (ed. W. Robertson Smith and M. J. de

1.3.1. Nouns

The three categories of words in Arabic are noun, verb, and particle. All nouns possess case, gender, and number. CA has the three cases nominative, accusative, and genitive, but there is no clear evidence for or against declensions in the inscriptions of the pre-Islamic period. Case is indicated by the vowel endings -*u* (nominative), -*a* (accusative), and -*i* (genitive) on the noun. When a noun is indefinite, nunation is used, and the case endings are -*un, -an,* and -*in.* Note, however, that the standard citation form in Western languages of indefinite Arabic nouns does not include the nunation. For example, "a king" is typically rendered as *malik* rather than *malikun.*

A separate class of nouns, referred to as diptotes, has only two endings, one for the nominative, and one for the accusative and genitive. The latter ending is identical to the accusative of other nouns (i.e., -*a*). When they are indefinite, diptotes lack nunation and lose the usual genitive ending, but when they are definite all three endings are found.

All Arabic nouns are either masculine or feminine, although a small number may be either gender. Morphologically, the clearest indicator that a noun is feminine is the presence of the *tā' marbūṭa* at the end of the word (*madīnatun* "city"). Here, as in the case of nunation, it is standard practice in Western languages not to transliterate the final *tā' marbūṭa*. Consequently, "a city" is usually written *madīna.* Some words are feminine because they fit certain categories such as: denoting females (*umm* "mother"), names of cities or countries (*miṣr* "Egypt"), or designation of body parts that come in pairs (*yad* "hand"). Still other nouns are feminine simply due to usage (*dār* "house," *šams* "sun"). An interesting feature of CA is the fact that the plural forms of nouns that refer to inanimate objects or irrational animate objects are grammatically feminine singular. For example, if the phrase "famous books" were translated into Arabic (*kutubun mašhūratun*) the word "famous" would be written with a *tā' marbūṭa* (مَشْهُورَةٌ *mašhūratun*), making it feminine singular. An adjective must agree with the noun it modifies in case, gender, and number. In this instance, because the word "books" is grammatically feminine singular its adjective must follow suit.

Arabic nominal forms can be singular, dual, or plural. There are two dual endings, one for nominative and the other for accusative/genitive.

Goeje; 2 vols.; 3d rev. ed. Cambridge: Cambridge University Press, 1896–1898); Carl Brockelmann, *Arabische Grammatik: Paradigmen, Literatur, Übungsstücke und Glossar* (ed. Manfred Fleischhammer; 16th ed.; Leipzig: VEB Verlag Enzyklopädie, 1965); Alfred F. L. Beeston, *Written Arabic: An Approach to Basic Structures* (London: Cambridge University Press, 1968); Wolfdietrich Fischer, *Grammatik des klassischen Arabisch* (2d ed.; Wiesbaden: Harrassowitz, 1987).

The masculine endings are -$\bar{a}ni$ (nom.) and -$ayni$ (acc./gen.), while the feminine ones are -$at\bar{a}ni$ (nom.) and -$atayni$ (acc./gen.). Thus, "two books" would either be $kit\bar{a}b\bar{a}ni$ or $kit\bar{a}bayni,$ depending on its case. However, the final -ni of the dual ending is dropped when the word is followed by a noun in the genitive case. For example, "the man's two books" would either be $kit\bar{a}b\bar{a}$ al-$rajuli$ or $kit\bar{a}bay$ al-$rajuli,$ depending on the case of "books."

In Arabic a distinction is made between sound and broken plurals. Sound plurals are so called because all of the vowels and consonants of the singular form are found in the plural, which is designated by endings attached to the noun. These endings are -$\bar{u}na$ (nom.) or -$\bar{i}na$ (acc./gen.) for the masculine and -$\bar{a}tun$ (nom.) or -$\bar{a}tin$ (acc./gen.) for the feminine. These forms are used almost solely for the plurals of animate beings and certain adjectives as well as for the participles. For example, to pluralize "teacher" ($mudarris$) one would write $mudarris\bar{u}na,$ $mudarris\bar{i}na,$ $mudarris\bar{a}tun,$ or $mudarris\bar{a}tin$ depending on the gender and case required.

One of the most distinctive, and perplexing, aspects of the Arabic language is the presence of broken plurals. These are forms that are often markedly different from their singular counterparts due to a change in vocalization and/or the addition or elision of consonants. No other Semitic language exhibits this phenomenon to the degree that Arabic does with its more than thirty-five distinct patterns of broken plurals. Since there are no rules for determining under which pattern a particular noun will fall, the only surefire way to know the broken plural of a given noun is through memorization. The following is a sampling of some of the broken plural patterns.[16]

Singular	Plural
$walad$ (boy)	$^{\textquoteright}awl\bar{a}d$
$bayt$ (house)	$buy\bar{u}t$
$kit\bar{a}b$ (book)	$kutub$
$faq\bar{i}r$ (poor)	$fuqar\bar{a}^{\textquoteright}u$
$\d{s}ad\bar{i}q$ (friend)	$^{\textquoteright}a\d{s}diq\bar{a}^{\textquoteright}u$
$bil\bar{a}d$ (country)	$buld\bar{a}n$

---

[16] For a more complete listing of the Arabic broken plural forms, see Wright, *Grammar of the Arabic Language,* 1:199–234. On the issue of broken plurals in Semitic languages more generally, see Federico Corriente, *Problemática de la pluralidad en semítico: el plural fracto* (Madrid: Consejo Superior de Investigaciones Científicas, 1971).

The presence of broken plurals is one of the main reasons why Arabic has often been categorized as a South Semitic language. It is a feature that is missing in most other Semitic languages but is found in Old South Arabian, Modern South Arabian, and Ethiopic, and this has led many scholars to conclude that it is part of the same linguistic family with them.

1.3.2. VERBS

The Arabic verbal system is comprised of two conjugations, perfect and imperfect, and Western grammarians have disagreed over whether the distinction between the two is primarily one of tense or aspect. Similar to biblical Hebrew, Arabic has a first, or ground, form (*qal* in Hebrew) and a number of derived forms that each exhibit unique morphological traits. There are sixteen derived forms in Arabic, but only the first ten are commonly used and therefore of primary importance. The discussion in the next few paragraphs relates to the first verbal form. The derived forms will be discussed below.[17]

The lexical form by which roots are found in dictionaries is the third-person singular masculine perfect. For example, the root *ḵ-r-j* is typically listed in lexicons as *ḵaraja* "he went out." In both conjugations, the vowel of the second root letter can be *a, i,* or *u,* which leads to three possible vocalizations of the perfect (*faʿala, faʿila,* or *faʿula*) and imperfect (*yafʿalu, yafʿilu,* and *yafʿulu*). The vowel of the second radical in the perfect does not always indicate what it will be in the imperfect, although some rules do apply. A root of the pattern *faʿila* in the perfect almost always has *yafʿalu* for the imperfect, and *faʿula* can only have a *yafʿulu* imperfect. But verbs of the pattern *faʿala* in the perfect will have an imperfect of either *yafʿilu* or *yafʿulu,* and there is no way of predicting which of the two will be correct. Another rule that helps determine vocalization states that a root having a guttural letter for the second or third radical will usually be of the *yafʿalu* pattern in the imperfect.

The main difference between perfect and imperfect in terms of their inflection is that the markers indicating person, number, and gender are suffixed to the root in the perfect, while for the imperfect they are both suffixed and prefixed. This is the very same situation we find in biblical Hebrew, and, in fact, the prefixes and suffixes used in the two languages are quite similar in many cases. The following table showing both conjugations for the first form of the Arabic verb will make this clear.

---

[17] A good discussion of the Arabic verbal system is found in Kjell Aartun, *Zur Frage altarabischer Tempora* (Oslo: Universitetsforlaget, 1963).

	Perfect		**Imperfect**	
3d masc. sg.	faʿala	فَعَلَ	yafʿulu	يَفْعُلُ
3d fem. sg.	faʿalat	فَعَلَت	tafʿulu	تَفْعُلُ
2d masc. sg.	faʿalta	فَعَلْتَ	tafʿulu	تَفْعُلُ
2d fem. sg.	faʿalti	فَعَلْت	tafʿulīna	تَفْعُلِينَ
1st com. sg.	faʿaltu	فَعَلْتُ	ʾafʿulu	أَفْعُلُ
3d masc. dual	faʿalā	فَعَلَا	yafʿulāni	يَفْعُلَانِ
3d fem. dual	faʿalatā	فَعَلَتَا	tafʿulāni	تَفْعُلَانِ
2d com. dual	faʿaltumā	فَعَلْتُمَا	tafʿulāni	تَفْعُلَانِ
3d masc. pl.	faʿalū	فَعَلُوا	yafʿulūna	يَفْعُلُونَ
3d fem. pl.	faʿalna	فَعَلْنَ	yafʿulna	يَفْعُلْنَ
2d masc. pl.	faʿaltum	فَعَلْتُم	tafʿulūna	تَفْعُلُونَ
2d fem. pl.	faʿaltunna	فَعَلْتُنَّ	tafʿulna	تَفْعُلْنَ
1st com. pl.	faʿalnā	فَعَلْنَا	nafʿulu	نَفْعُلُ

The imperfect column of this table shows the forms for the indicative mood. The subjunctive and jussive moods are identical to the indicative as far as the prefixes are concerned, but the differences among them appear in the suffixes. For those forms ending with a *u* in the indicative, the subjunctive ending is an *a* (*yafʿula, tafʿula,* etc.), while the jussive has no vowel at all (*yafʿul, tafʿul,* etc.). Elsewhere, both the subjunctive and jussive forms are identical and exhibit a tendency to abbreviate through the loss of the final *-na* or *-ni*. For instance, the second-person feminine singular is *tafʿulī,* the third-person masculine dual is *yafʿulā,* and the second-person masculine plural is *tafʿulū.* The only places where there are no changes and the subjunctive and jussive forms are the same as the indicative are in the second- and third-person feminine plurals, where all three are *yafʿulna* and *tafʿulna* respectively. The future is formed by adding the prefix *sa-* to the imperfect (*sayafʿulu, satafʿulu,* etc.). This prefix is an abbreviation of the particle *sawfa,* and the future tense can also be conveyed by having it precede the imperfect (*sawfa yafʿulu*).

As observed, the existence of the broken plurals in Arabic is an argument in favor of grouping it among the South Semitic languages, where the same phenomenon is found. From the point of view of the verbal system, however, there is evidence that suggests Arabic is closer to the Northwest Semitic family. We see this, for example, in the conjugation of the perfect, where the suffixes of the first- and second-person singular forms contain the letter *t*. This is similar to what is found in biblical Hebrew (*kātabtî, kātabt,* etc.) and other Northwest Semitic languages and is different from the South Semitic family, where *k* is used in the suffix for these forms. There are several other features outside the verbal system that Arabic has in common with the Northwest Semitic languages but are not found in South Semitic. These include the use of a definite article (*al* in Arabic and *ha* in biblical Hebrew) and third-person pronoun forms beginning with the letter *h* (*hūwa/hīya* in Arabic and *hû'/hî'* in biblical Hebrew).[18] It has already been noted that it is the presence of features from both the Northwest and South Semitic language groups that has led to a scholarly debate over the classification of Arabic.[19]

The Arabic imperative is formed by replacing the prefixes of the second-person jussive forms with a short vowel. When the vowel of the second root letter is *a* or *i,* the initial vowel is *i* (*iḍrib* "strike"), and when it is *u* the initial vowel is *u* (*uktub* "write"). Another mood in Arabic that is formed from the jussive is the energic, used to give emphasis. It is created by adding the suffix *-anna* or *-an* to the jussive, resulting in the forms *yafʿulanna* and *yafʿulan*. Biblical Hebrew contains a number of words that end in the *nun energicum,* and scholars typically understand these words to be remnants from earlier periods of the Hebrew language when the energic mood functioned in a way analogous to what is found in Arabic.[20]

The passive voice in Arabic is formed by a revocalization of the active forms in which the most distinctive feature is the presence of the vowel *u* in the first syllable. In the perfect, the vowel of the second radical is an *i* (*fuʿila, fuʿilat,* etc.), while in the imperfect it is an *a* (*yufʿalu, tufʿalu,* etc.). There are a number of words in biblical Hebrew that suggest that at one time it, too, possessed a passive form in its basic, or *qal,* stem. It appears that a distinguishing element of it, as in Arabic, is the presence of the vowel *u* in the first syllable in both the perfect and imperfect, as seen, for example, in the forms *luqqaḥ* (Gen 3:23) and *yuqqaḥ* (Gen 18:4).[21]

---

[18] Third-person pronouns with *h* are found in the Old South Arabian dialect Sabaean. OSA is most often classified as a South Semitic language, although there have been attempts to attach it to Central Semitic. Ethiopic also has *h* pronouns that are lost in the independent forms but preserved in the suffix forms.

[19] An overview of the debate over the divisions within the Semitic language family is presented in Angel Sáenz-Badillos, *A History of the Hebrew Language* (trans. John Elwold; Cambridge: Cambridge University Press, 1993), 6–15.

[20] Bruce K. Waltke and M. O'Connor, *An Introduction to Biblical Hebrew Syntax* (Winona Lake, Ind.: Eisenbrauns, 1990), §§20.2f; 31.7.

[21] Ibid., §22.6.

As stated earlier, there are ten commonly used derived verbal forms, or measures, in CA that are structured and function in a way similar to what is found in biblical Hebrew (*nipʿal, piʿel, hipʿil,* etc.). Each exhibits one or more unique features, such as a lengthened vowel, a doubled consonant, or an infixed letter, that are found throughout the entire conjugation system of a given measure. Since the Middle Ages, it has been the convention among Western grammarians and linguists to number these ten derived forms. The most common way of designating them has been to assign each a Roman numeral, and this is the way they are typically identified in dictionaries written in European languages. The list below shows the pattern of each verbal measure for the active voice of the third-person masculine singular in the perfect and imperfect and the masculine singular imperative form. The prefixes and suffixes for the rest of each measure are the same as those described earlier for the first form of the Arabic verb.

	Perfect		**Imperfect**		**Imperative**	
II	*faʿʿala*	فَعَّلَ	*yufaʿʿilu*	يُفَعِّلُ	*faʿʿil*	فَعِّل
III	*fāʿala*	فَاعَلَ	*yufāʿilu*	يُفَاعِلُ	*fāʿil*	فَاعِل
IV	*ʾafʿala*	أَفْعَلَ	*yufʿilu*	يُفْعِلُ	*aʾfʿil*	أَفْعِل
V	*tafaʿʿala*	تَفَعَّلَ	*yatafaʿʿalu*	يَتَفَعَّلُ	*tafaʿʿal*	تَفَعَّل
VI	*tafāʿala*	تَفَاعَلَ	*yatafāʿalu*	يَتَفَاعَلُ	*tafāʿal*	تَفَاعَل
VII	*infaʿala*	انْفَعَلَ	*yanfaʿilu*	يَنْفَعِلُ	*infaʿil*	انْفَعِل
VIII	*iftaʿala*	افْتَعَلَ	*yaftaʿilu*	يَفْتَعِلُ	*iftaʿil*	افْتَعِل
IX	*ifʿalla*	افْعَلَّ	*yafʿallu*	يَفْعَلُّ	*ifʿalil*	افْعَلِل
X	*istafʿala*	اسْتَفْعَلَ	*yastafʿilu*	يَسْتَفْعِلُ	*istafʿil*	اسْتَفْعِل

The morphological changes to the stem found in these derived forms exert semantic influence, and, in each measure, several types of effects on meaning can be found. Here, the most common are identified for each. The second form normally conveys an intensive or iterative sense (*kasara* "to break," *kassara* "to break in pieces"). The third form communicates the idea of reciprocity (*kataba* "to write," *kātaba* "to correspond with another"). The primary meaning of the fourth verbal form is causative (*ʿalima* "to know," *ʾaʿlama* "to cause someone to know, to inform"). The fifth form gives a reflexive sense to the second form and is therefore often translated passively (*kassara* "to break in pieces," *takassara* "to be broken in pieces"). The sixth form is generally the reflexive of the third form and often carries a sense of reciprocity (*qātala* "to fight another," *taqātala* "to fight each other"). The passive sense of the first form is found in the seventh form (*kasara* "to break," *inkasara* "to be broken"). The eighth form conveys the reflexive sense of the first form (*faraqa* "to divide," *iftaraqa* "to become divided"). The ninth form, which is quite rare, is primarily used to identify colors and physical defects (*ibyaḍḍa* "to be white"). The tenth form is the reflexive of the fourth form (*ʾaʿadda* "to make ready," *istaʿadda* "to make oneself ready").

Each of the measures contains distinct verbal adjectives in both the active and passive that often become substantives (*kātib* "writing, a writer," *maktūb* "written, a letter"). The most common patterns in the first form are *fāʿil* in the active voice (cf. Heb. *qōṭēl*) and *mafʿūl* in the passive. There are many other patterns for the first form, and a complex set of rules can often help determine when a pattern will be found in a particular root.[22] The adjectives of the derived forms are more predictable and exhibit many of the same morphological changes to the root letters that are found in their perfect and imperfect conjugations. They are listed in the following chart.

	Active		**Passive**	
II	*mufaʿʿil*	مُفَعِّل	*mufaʿʿal*	مُفَعَّل
III	*mufāʿil*	مُفَاعِل	*mufāʿal*	مُفَاعَل
IV	*mufʿil*	مُفْعِل	*mufʿal*	مُفْعَل
V	*mutafaʿʿil*	مُتَفَعِّل	*mutafaʿʿal*	مُتَفَعَّل
VI	*mutafāʿil*	مُتَفَاعِل	*mutafāʿal*	مُتَفَاعَل
VII	*munfaʿil*	مُنْفَعِل	*munfaʿal*	مُنْفَعَل
VIII	*muftaʿil*	مُفْتَعِل	*muftaʿal*	مُفْتَعَل
IX	*mufʿall*	مُفْعَلّ		
X	*mustafʿil*	مُسْتَفْعِل	*mustafʿal*	مُسْتَفْعَل

Another important form in Arabic is the verbal noun or *maṣdar*. These substantives can also be used as adjectives and express the action or state of the verb without any reference to object, subject, or time (*fahm* "understanding," *faraḥ* "joy"). This is the equivalent of the infinitive construct in biblical Hebrew. As with the participles, there are many patterns of the verbal noun in the first form, with more than forty attested.[23] Most roots have only one, and rarely are there more than three for a given root. The most common patterns are *faʿl, faʿal, fuʿūl, faʿālatun, fuʿūlatun,* and *fiʿālatun.* Here, too, the derived forms have fewer patterns, with the most

---

22 These rules are in Wright, *Grammar of the Arabic Language,* 1:133–41.

23 Ibid., 1:110–12

common being the following: II *tafʿīl*, III *mufāʿalatun*, IV *ʾifʿāl*, V *tafaʿʿul*, VI *tafāʿul*, VII *infiʿāl*, VIII *iftiʿāl*, IX *ifʿilāl*, X *istifʿāl*.

As in biblical Hebrew, the presence of certain letters can render roots in CA "defective." In such cases, these letters introduce changes in vocalization and/or spelling that do not adhere to the patterns that have been identified above. In Arabic, these are roots that contain the letters *wāw* (Heb. *wāw*) or *yāʾ* (Heb. *yôd*). A small number of roots contain both these letters and are therefore doubly defective. When these letters are found in the initial position (*waṣala* "to arrive"), the changes are relatively minor and straightforward. When they occur in the second or third positions, however, the situation is more complicated. Roots with a *wāw* or *yāʾ* for the middle radical are referred to as "hollow," and they are divided into three groups that differ from one another only in the first verbal form (*qāla/yaqūlu* "to speak," *bāʿa/yabīʿu* "to sell," *ḵāfa/yaḵāfu* "to fear"). Roots with a *wāw* or *yāʾ* in the third position are referred to as "weak." They are divided into four groups that also differ from one another only in the first verbal form (*ramā/yarmī* "to throw," *daʿā/yadʿū* "to call," *baqiya/yabqā* "to remain," *saʿā/yasʿā* "to run"). A detailed discussion of this aspect of CA is not possible here. Suffice it to say that Arabic roots in the last two categories are classified within a particular group based on the vowel of their middle root letter and whether their weak letter is a *wāw* or a *yāʾ*.[24]

1.3.3. PARTICLES

There are four categories of particles in CA. The first is the prepositions, some of which are attached to the following noun, such as *bi-* "in, at" and *li-* "to, for" (cf. Heb. *b* and *l*), while others stand on their own, such as *fī* "in" and *ʿalā* "over, upon" (cf. Heb. *ʿal*). Prepositions are always followed by a noun in the genitive case (*fī kitābin* "in a book"). The second category of particles is the adverbs, of which there are many different types, including interrogatives, affirmatives, negatives, and demonstratives. The third category of particles is comprised of conjunctions that connect two sentences or parts of a sentence. The most common are *wa* "and" (cf. Heb. *wa*), which joins words or clauses, and *fa*, which is attached to the following word and typically conveys the idea that what comes before and after it are temporally linked. The final category are the interjections such as *yā* "oh," *ḥayyā* "come," *ṣah* "hush," and so on.[25]

---

[24] Roots with an *alif* or *hamza* in the middle position are also problematic. For a full treatment of the hollow verbs, see ibid., 1:71–96.

[25] The Arabic particles are discussed in ibid., 1:278–96.

The system of negation in Arabic is different from that found in biblical Hebrew. The hollow verb *laysa* is used at the beginning of a nominal sentence to deny the attribution of the predicate to the subject. It is found only in the perfect conjugation, but it is imperfect in meaning. With the addition of *laysa* the subject of the nominative sentence remains in the nominative case, but the predicate becomes accusative. For example, the sentence *al-waladu marīḍun* ("the boy is sick") is negated as *laysa al-waladu marīḍan* ("the boy is not sick"). The negation of verbal sentences is more complex. With an imperfect verb, the particle *lā* is used and can be translated either in the present or the future tense: *lā yaktubu* can mean either "he does not write" or "he will not write." Another way to express negation in the future is to use the particle *lan* and the subjunctive mood (*lan yaktuba* "he will not write"). The negation of a past act can be expressed through the use of the particle *lam* followed by the jussive (*lam yaktub* "he did not write"). Yet another way of negating a verbal sentence in Arabic is through the use of the particle *mā*. When followed by a verb in the perfect, it has a past meaning (*mā kataba* "he did not write"), and when followed by a verb in the imperfect its meaning is present (*mā yaktubu* "he is not writing").

2. SIGNIFICANCE FOR THE BIBLE

The primary way that Arabic has contributed to study of the Hebrew Bible is through comparative lexicography, the branch of linguistics that is concerned with the meanings of words. Owing to its long period of use and the important role lexicography has played throughout its history, the Arabic language has a richer and more extensive corpus upon which to draw than any other Semitic language. The fact that Arabic has preserved many ancient Semitic features such as the case system and verbal conjugations has also made it a valuable resource for biblical scholars. Until relatively recent times, Arabic was the principal language of comparison in Hebrew Bible scholarship, and those engaged in serious study of the text needed a basic familiarity with it. But the discovery and decipherment of Akkadian, Ugaritic, and other languages in the nineteenth and twentieth centuries caused Arabic to lose the privileged place it once enjoyed in comparative Semitic study. Nonetheless, it remains an extremely important and valuable resource for Hebrew Bible scholars to the present day.

The earliest Arabic literary texts were written centuries after the latest biblical texts in places far removed from the biblical lands. Consequently, they do not hold the same importance for biblical scholars as texts written in languages such as Ugaritic or Aramaic that predate or are contemporaneous with the biblical material. Since such texts are often from the same general area as the Bible, many scholars study them to determine what light they might shed on its content or background. While Arabic literary texts do not function in the same way for Bible scholars, there are other texts that have had an impact on the course of Hebrew Bible scholarship. These texts come in the form of the Arabic lexicons and dictionaries that have been a significant part of the language throughout its history and are among the oldest examples of such lexicographic resources in the world. In this section, the use of Arabic in biblical Hebrew lexicography will be considered with particular emphasis on its tools and method.

Medieval Jewish scholars engaged in comparative study of Arabic and Hebrew as early as the tenth and eleventh centuries, first in Babylon and later in Spain. During this period, many Jews lived in the Arabic-speaking world where lexicography and grammar were among the first sciences developed. Their study of Hebrew was therefore greatly influenced by Arab scholars, and many of them acknowledge this in their work. Jewish scholars like Saadyah Gaon, Ibn Qoreish, Judah Hayyūj, and Ibn Barūn were highly indebted to their Arab predecessors, and their scholarship set the standard for comparative lexicography for centuries.[26]

Prior to the eighteenth century, the tendency was to see Hebrew as the parent language in the Semitic family, with Arabic and others as its descendants. This was largely due to the sacred status Hebrew had as a biblical language, but there was no factual basis for this view. With the work of A. Shultens in the first half of the eighteenth century, things changed dramatically. He argued for an approach that did not privilege one language over the others, but he believed that Arabic could be particularly useful due to the immense amount of material available in the Arabic dictionaries. In particular, Shultens thought the Arabic vocabulary could be of assistance in understanding the many obscure and problematic Hebrew words in the Bible. This led to a period of "hyperarabism" in which a flood of scholarly material began to appear that attempted to analyze biblical Hebrew in light of the Arabic data. Until the present day, commentaries and articles written by Bible scholars regularly cite evidence from Arabic in support of a particular meaning for a Hebrew word or passage. Most of these attempts to use Arabic in biblical Hebrew lexicography have been carefully done, but enough problems exist to warrant caution in how one goes about the task. The two crucial areas are the tools and the method. One needs to be aware of both the value and the limitations of each Arabic dictionary and to be attentive to how the material contained in the dictionaries is interpreted and applied to Hebrew.

---

[26] Information on the role of Arabic in the work of the medieval Jewish Bible scholars can be found in H. Hirschfeld, *Literary History of Hebrew Grammarians and Lexicographers* (Oxford: Oxford University Press, 1926); Edward L.Greenstein, "Medieval Bible Commentaries," in *Back to the Sources: Reading the Classic Jewish Texts* (ed. Barry W. Holtz; New York: Summit Books, 1984), 213–59.

2.1. TOOLS

The Bible scholar wishing to study a particular Arabic word is immediately confronted with a problem: there is a dizzying array of resources
from which to choose. As noted above, lexicography has played a central
role throughout the history of the Arabic language, resulting in the availability of a very large number of dictionaries and types of dictionaries.
Hebrew Bible scholars need to have a basic familiarity with these various
tools in order to make proper use of them and to evaluate the use that others make of them.[27]

One of the most obvious and basic ways of distinguishing among these
dictionaries is to categorize them according to the languages in which they
are written. The most thorough and reliable are written entirely in Arabic,
and, ideally, these are the works Bible scholars should consult. Three in
particular merit some brief comment. The *Lisān al-ʿArab* (*The Tongue of the
Arabs*) was compiled by Ibn Manẓūr (1232–1311) and continues to be the
major lexicon for many educated Arabs. It contains a comprehensive treatment of virtually the entire Arabic vocabulary and is a massive work. A
recent edition comprises fifteen volumes, each containing approximately
five hundred pages with double columns. The *al-Qamūs al-Muḥīṭ* (*The
Surrounding Ocean*) was put together by al-Fīrūzābādī (1326–1414), who
attempted to present a more streamlined version of what is found in the
Lisān. Through the use of sigla and abbreviations he was able to compile
a dictionary that, at two volumes, is much shorter than the *Lisān* but almost
as comprehensive. Another valuable resource is the *Tāj al-ʿArūs* (*The
Crown of the Bride*) of al-Zabīdī (1732–1791), which doubled the size of the
Qamūs and is the largest Arabic dictionary ever compiled.

An interesting aspect of all three of these works is that they are
arranged in a rhyming format, with each root listed by its final letter. The
arrangement by initial root letter in alphabetical order is one that had been
introduced as early as the eleventh century but did not become very popular until more recent times. There are many other dictionaries written in
Arabic that Hebrew Bible scholars might consult, but these three are the
most reliable and best known. Another very useful tool that is not, strictly
speaking, a lexicon is the *Maqāyīs al-Luġa* (*The Standards of the Language*) of Ibn Fāris (d. 1005), which is dedicated to the meanings of
consonantal roots and lists the meanings of each one in a clear and concise manner.

---

[27] Discussions of Arabic lexicography are in Helmut Gätje, "Arabische Lexiko-
graphie," *Bustan* 5 (1964): 3–11; John Haywood, *Arabic Lexicography* (Leiden:
Brill, 1965); Stefan Wild, "Arabische Lexikographie," in *Grundriß der arabischen
Philologie 2* (ed. Helmut Gätje; Wiesbaden: Harrassowitz, 1987), 37–47.

Each of these tools requires knowledge of Arabic that is beyond that of the majority of Hebrew Bible scholars, so their use in biblical scholarship is limited. But there are other resources written in European languages that are readily available and more accessible. The choice one makes on this matter is critical. The quality of these works and their relevance for biblical Hebrew scholarship varies considerably, so that caution and discretion must be exercised in determining which sources to consult. It is particularly important that scholars use works that are as thorough as possible regarding the semantic range of roots and forms, how the various meanings relate to each other, and how words are used in context. As will be seen in the section below on method, these are among the factors most important in determining whether or not a given Arabic word or meaning is relevant for biblical Hebrew.

There are many one-volume Arabic dictionaries in European languages available, but such works by themselves do not meet the demands of serious comparative Semitic lexicography. These tools simply translate the meanings of words into the target language without any discussion or explanation of such issues as how the meanings relate or how the words are used in sentences. Two dictionaries of this type that are often used by Bible scholars are J. G. Hava's *Arabic-English Dictionary* and Hans Wehr's *A Dictionary of Modern Written Arabic*. Both of these works do in fact contain much information that is quite ancient and could be applicable to biblical Hebrew, but because they lack a full discussion of roots and individual words it would be a mistake for Hebrew Bible scholars to base their conclusions or suggestions solely on them. A further problem with Wehr's dictionary is implied in its title. It is primarily interested in Modern Standard Arabic, the most recent form of literary Arabic, and therefore often leaves out older meanings that are no longer current. It is precisely this material that is most relevant and important when studying biblical Hebrew in light of the Arabic evidence.

More useful for the purposes of Hebrew Bible scholars are a number of multivolume lexicons in European languages that present a more complete picture of what is found in works written in Arabic, such as the *Lisān al-ʿArab* and the *Tāj al-ʿArūs*. In fact, these lexicographers all tend to translate the prior lexicons and use them as the basis of their own works. They all adopt the modern arrangement of listing roots in alphabetical order according to the first letter. Roots and words are typically written in Arabic script, and so use of these tools requires some general familiarity with the Arabic alphabet and basic rules of morphology.

The first European to compile an Arabic dictionary was Jacobus Golius, whose *Lexicon Arabico-Latinum* appeared in 1653. This one-volume work remained the standard resource in European Arabic studies for close to two centuries. While important in its day, it was eventually replaced by Georg

Wilhelm Freytag's *Lexicon Arabico-Latinum,* which was published in four volumes between 1830 and 1837. A major drawback of both these dictionaries is that they simply list words and meanings and do not give examples of usage in literary contexts. This is a particularly serious problem for the user who is trying to understand the precise sense of rare words and meanings.

This issue was addressed by William Edward Lane, whose eight-volume *Arabic-English Lexicon* (1863–1893) remains the most important resource for Bible scholars who do not have access to works written solely in Arabic. Lane's lexicon is distinguished by a precision not seen in its predecessors, as he draws upon the work of dozens of Arab grammarians and lexicographers and gives abundant examples of words used in context from literary and poetic sources. The primary source of Lane's dictionary was al-Zabīdī's *Tāj al-ʿArūs.* An important aspect of Lane's lexicon that must be kept in mind is that its last two volumes are not as reliable as the rest of the work. Lane died before finishing the dictionary, and his nephew tried to complete the project by publishing his uncle's notes in progress. As a result, many entries are incomplete or not fully developed. Bible scholars who make use of the material in volumes 7 and 8 of Lane should keep this limitation in mind and not rely solely on it to reach their conclusions.

A work that is often cited by Hebrew Bible scholars discussing Arabic cognates to Hebrew roots is the *Supplément aux Dictionnaires Arabes* by R. P. A. Dozy. This two-volume work, published in 1881, was meant to augment Lane's lexicon and contains many words and meanings not found in it. But Dozy's lexicon should be used with care by Bible scholars because much of the additional material it contains comes from Arab Spain and may therefore not be directly relevant to biblical Hebrew. Another more recent attempt to complete Lane's lexicon is the *Wörterbuch der klassischen arabischen Sprache,* a project that first began to appear in fascicles in 1957 under the direction of A. Fischer and continued by A. Kraemer, A. Spitaler, and H. Gätje. In keeping with its intention to supplement Lane, the dictionary begins with the letter *kāf,* the point at which Lane's lexicon becomes less dependable. This work will be of immense value to Hebrew Bible scholars and others once it is finished. But progress on it has been slow, as the material on the letter *lām* is just now nearing completion.

2.2. METHOD

In studying the relationship between a Hebrew word and a possible Arabic cognate, the work of comparative lexicography entails two steps. One must first consult the Arabic resources to identify the precise meaning(s) of the word, and then one should determine the relevance of this information for biblical Hebrew. The primary aim of the first step is to understand the historical background and semantic range of the word. Is the word well attested in Arabic? Is it commonly used, or is it unique to particular times and/or places? What are its possible meanings? Which meanings are primary? What are the relationships among its various meanings? These and similar questions must be carefully considered, and it is often the case that Hebrew Bible scholars who make untenable suggestions regarding Arabic have not paid sufficient attention to these matters.

Only sources that allow one fully to understand the historical and semantic contexts should be used. The lexicons that are most useful in this regard are the ones written in Arabic mentioned above. Among them, either the *Lisān al-ʿArab* or the *Tāj al-ʿArūs* is sufficient to meet the needs of Bible scholars. If one is unable to consult these resources, Lane's dictionary is the next best alternative. An issue that must be kept in mind when using Lane is the relatively inferior quality of its final two volumes. Some of the entries in these volumes are more complete and reliable than others, but it is advisable not to base one's conclusions solely on Lane for words that begin with *qāf* and letters subsequent to it. If the word one is studying is found in the as yet unfinished *Wörterbuch der klassischen arabischen Sprache,* this is an excellent supplement to the material in the latter part of Lane. If not, it would be best to ask someone who is able to read Arabic to consult the *Lisān al-ʿArab* or the *Tāj al-ʿArūs* and summarize its content in order to ensure a proper understanding of the Arabic data. It is also the case that, on occasion, Lane's lexicon does not contain material found in the *Lisān* and the *Tāj,* at times even excluding entire roots. For this reason, these latter sources are to be used as much as possible.

Because so many of the meanings in Dozy's dictionary come from Arab Spain, it is not recommended that it be used by itself. Material in Dozy that is not found in Lane or another dependable dictionary should not be used as the basis for proposals regarding biblical Hebrew. Such words and meanings probably come from a later point in the development of Arabic and are therefore not relevant. Unfortunately, it is not uncommon to see Dozy cited as the only authority for a meaning in proposals put forward by Bible scholars. Exclusive use of modern dictionaries such as Hava and Wehr should be avoided at all costs, since their presentation of the material does not allow one to evaluate it properly. Such tools do indeed contain much information that can be of value for comparative lexicography, but they should only be used in tandem with Lane and other more reliable resources.

Discretion must also be exercised regarding proposals that have been put forward by Hebrew Bible scholars on matters of Hebrew/Arabic comparative lexicography. Commentaries and scholarly articles regularly refer to the Arabic evidence when trying to make sense of difficult Hebrew words or to suggest new meanings for those that are well known. Such published proposals, particularly when they come from someone who is considered to be an expert in comparative lexicography, are sometimes uncritically accepted as correct even though careful study of the Arabic resources indicates that there is no support for them.[28] The same holds true for Arabic cognate forms that are listed in *The Hebrew and Aramaic Lexicon of the Old Testament* and similar works. The Arabic data in the entries should not be blindly accepted but need to be checked and verified through careful use of the Arabic dictionaries. As will be illustrated below, even the most reliable of biblical Hebrew lexicons can contain errors in the use and citation of Arabic.

Evaluating the evidence in the Arabic sources and determining its relevance for biblical Hebrew is the second step of the method. It must first be established that a given Arabic root or word is, in fact, a true cognate of the Hebrew root or word under consideration. This must be the case both etymologically and semantically. Each Arabic letter has its etymological equivalent in Hebrew, and for words in the two languages to be true cognates each root letter must correspond to its equivalent in the other language. For example, it would be improper to claim that the Hebrew verb *kābēd* ("to be heavy") is a cognate of Arabic *kabara* ("to be large") because only their first two root letters are the same. The situation can become muddled at times, since metathesis and the interchange of consonants (called *badal* in Arabic) are well-attested phenomena in Arabic and other languages. *Badal* is a particularly complex aspect of Arabic lexicography, and some scholars of the language have identified dozens of examples of possible interchange of consonants. For instance, the letters ʿ and *ḫ* can, on occasion, be interchanged, as in the verbs *baḫtara* and *baʿtara*, which both mean "to scatter." Some scholars, most notably Alfred Guillaume, have attempted to explore the implications of this phenomenon for biblical Hebrew lexicography, and this has led to the identification of presumed cognates in Hebrew and Arabic that appear to be etymologically unrelated according to the strict rules of equivalence.[29] Since there are often few external controls in such an approach, proposals of this sort should be put forth judiciously and evaluated cautiously.

---

[28] Numerous examples of these proposals can be found in the works in the bibliography that are written by G. R. Driver, Alfred Guillaume, and Lothar Kopf. A work that discusses specific examples of problematic proposals is John Kaltner, *The Use of Arabic in Biblical Hebrew Lexicography* (CBQMS 28; Washington, D.C.: Catholic Biblical Association of America, 1996).

[29] See Alfred Guillaume, *Hebrew and Arabic Lexicography* (Leiden: Brill, 1965). This work is a collection of four articles Guillaume published in the journal *Abr-Nahrain* between 1959 and 1965. In the introduction to each article he discusses his method and the phenomenon of *badal*.

Determining if the Hebrew and Arabic forms are true semantic cognates entails careful study and analysis of their various meanings. Some of the most common mistakes made by biblical scholars working with the Arabic data are the result of insufficient attention to semantic matters. At times, the semantic range of a word is not fully understood, or a well-attested meaning is extended beyond what the evidence can allow. Other times, meanings that are identified as extremely rare in the Arabic dictionaries are focused on to the exclusion of more basic meanings in a way that presents a distorted picture of the evidence. A similar type of mistake occurs when one bases a proposal on an Arabic word or meaning that is temporally or geographically limited. If the word or meaning enters the Arabic lexicon at a late point or if it is unique to a particular locale, its relevance for biblical Hebrew lexicography diminishes considerably.[30] Some of these possible pitfalls will now be illustrated by the following examples taken from the first volume of *The Hebrew and Aramaic Lexicon of the Old Testament* (*HALOT*).

2.2.1. HEBREW *dālap*//ARABIC *dalafa*

These roots are proper etymological cognates, but there is a problem concerning their relationship on the semantic level. According to *HALOT*, the Hebrew verb can mean "to be leaky" or "to weep," and the Arabic verb carries the sense "to drip through."[31] But study of the Arabic sources indicates that the latter meaning is a modern one. Neither Lane nor the *Lisān al-ʿArab* lists meanings connected to dripping or leaking in their entries on the root. The primary meanings of the verb in both of those lexicons have to do with walking leisurely or with short steps. However, meanings associated with water are found in both the dictionaries of Wehr and Hava. In Wehr, which is primarily interested in modern written Arabic, the verb means "to leak, drip, trickle." In two places in Hava's dictionary meanings having to do with the oozing of water are mentioned. In both cases the siglum for the modern Syrian dialect is found, indicating the meaning is not present in the older lexicons Hava consulted.[32] The evidence therefore

---

[30] For a detailed discussion of etymological and semantic equivalence, see Chaim Cohen, "The 'Held Method' for Comparative Semitic Philology," *JANESCU* 19 (1989): 9–23.

[31] *HALOT* 1:223.

[32] Edward W. Lane, *Arabic-English Lexicon* (8 vols.; London: Williams & Norgate, 1863–1893; repr., Beirut: Librairie du Liban, 1980), 3:904–5; Ibn Manẓūr, *Lisān al-ʿArab* (15 vols.; Beirut: Dār Bayrūt lil-Ṭibāʿa wal-Našr, 1968), 9:106–7; Wehr, *Dictionary of Modern Written Arabic*, 290; J. G. Hava, *Arabic-English Dictionary* (Beirut: Catholic Press, 1951), 214.

points in the direction of seeing "to drip through" as a relatively recent meaning in Arabic that should have no bearing on matters of biblical Hebrew lexicography.

2.2.2. HEBREW ḥāgar//ARABIC ḥajara

In this case, too, roots that are etymological cognates are lacking semantic equivalence. *HALOT* lists the meaning of the Arabic as "to fence in, close off," and this is well documented in the *Lisān* and Lane as the basic sense of the eighth verbal form.[33] But, according to *HALOT,* the primary meaning of the Hebrew verb is to gird oneself or another, and this is quite different from the act of fencing in or closing off. If the entry is implicitly arguing for an extension of meaning from fencing in to girding for the Arabic, such a claim has no basis, since there is no evidence anywhere in the Arabic dictionaries that words under this root ever convey the idea of girding or binding oneself. The lack of overlap in meaning between the two roots means they are not true semantic cognates. *HALOT* seems to recognize this problem, since it includes a question mark in its reference to this Arabic root and meaning.

2.2.3. HEBREW ḥādâ//ARABIC kadā^y AND ḥadā^{u}/^{y}

HALOT proposes two Arabic cognates for this Hebrew root, which is found only in the *qal* and *pi'el* verbal forms with the meanings "to rejoice" and "to make joyful," respectively. There are semantic problems with this identification. The meaning of the first Arabic verb (*kadā^y*) is listed as "to walk briskly" in *HALOT.* This verb is not found in Lane's lexicon at all, but it is in the *Lisān,* where it has this meaning. However, the Arabic word simply refers to the act of walking quickly and does not convey the idea of rejoicing that is central to the Hebrew root.[34] The same thing is true for the second Arabic verb, which is found in both the *Lisān* and Lane with the meaning "to drive (camels) with song" as listed in *HALOT.*[35] It describes the activity of chiding an animal along with song, but the entries make no reference to meanings associated with joy or rejoicing. These Arabic roots are therefore not really semantic cognates of the Hebrew one.

---

[33] *HALOT* 1:291; Lane, *Arabic-English Lexicon,* 2:516–18; Ibn Manẓūr, *Lisān al-ʿArab,* 4:165–72.

[34] *HALOT* 1:292; Ibn Manẓūr, *Lisān al-ʿArab,* 14:224–25.

[35] *HALOT* 1:292; Lane, *Arabic-English Lexicon,* 2:532–33; Ibn Manẓūr, *Lisān al-ʿArab,* 14:168–69.

2.2.4. HEBREW *zēr*//ARABIC *zirr*

The meaning "button" that is given in *HALOT* for the Arabic word is well attested in the sources, but it is not a proper semantic equivalent to the Hebrew word, which refers to the edge or border of something. The entry in Lane's dictionary indicates that it is the act of joining together the two parts of a garment that is central to the meaning "button." This is evident in another possible sense of the word that refers to a section of wood into which a tent peg is driven. These meanings do not have a clear semantic association with the Hebrew word. However, there is another meaning of the Arabic term that comes closer to the apparent sense of the Hebrew. The word can also refer to the edge of a sword, and it would have been better if *HALOT* had included this meaning in its entry. In this instance, the Arabic sources have been misused by not identifying the meaning that is the closest semantic equivalent to the Hebrew one.[36]

While such examples of misuse of the Arabic data in biblical Hebrew lexicography in *HALOT* and elsewhere could be multiplied, they do not reflect the general state of affairs. Most of the time, Bible scholars have adopted a methodologically sound approach in their use of the Arabic resources and their application to the Hebrew Bible. But the possibility of errors and faulty conclusions remains ever present, and even a work as highly regarded as *HALOT* is not immune to them. For this reason, it is imperative that careful attention be paid to the tools at one's disposal and how they are used. Only then can the benefits Arabic offers to the study of the Hebrew Bible be fully realized.

3. ANCIENT SOURCES, MODERN RESOURCES

3.1. HISTORICAL DEVELOPMENT

A fine overview of Arabic that discusses the chronological development of the language is K. Versteegh, *The Arabic Language*. For a treatment of the languages of the Arabian peninsula prior to the rise of Islam, see A. F. L. Beeston's article, "Languages of Pre-Islamic Arabia," and C. Robin, *L'Arabie antique de Karib'îl à Mahomet: nouvelles données sur l'histoire des Arabes grâce aux inscriptions.* The inscriptions of the pre-Islamic period and other matters related to paleography are discussed in A. Grohmann's handbook, *Arabische Paläographie. II. Das Schriftwesen: Die Lapidarschrift.*

B. Gruendler's book *The Development of the Arabic Scripts: From the Nabataean Era to the First Islamic Century according to Dated Texts* presents

---

[36] *HALOT* 1:279; Lane, *Arabic-English Lexicon,* 3:1223.

a thorough analysis of the evolution of the scripts and also includes tracings of some of the most important inscriptions. On the relevance of Nabatean orthography for the development of the Arabic writing system, see W. Diem's article, "Die nabatäischen Inschriften und die Frage der Kasusflexion im Altarabischen." Later developments in the Arabic script are studied in N. Abbott, *The Rise of the North Arabic Script and Its Kurʾanic Development.*

The best presentation of the origin of CA is found in C. Rabin, "The Beginnings of Classical Arabic." The development of CA is treated in J. Fück, *Arabiya: Untersuchungen zur arabischen Sprach- und Stilgeschichte.* For a discussion of the language of poetry and the lexicon of the poets, see M. Ullman, *Untersuchungen zur Raǧazpoesie: ein Beitrag zur arabischen Sprach- und Literaturwissenschaft.* A careful analysis of the textual history of the Qurʾān is available in T. Nöldeke and F. Schwally, *Geschichte des Qorans.*

3.2. GRAMMAR/LEXICON

The standard English language work on CA grammar is W. Wright's *A Grammar of the Arabic Language,* which is based on C. P. Caspari, *Arabische Grammatik,* and M. S. Howell, *A Grammar of the Classical Arabic Language Translated and Compiled from the Most Approved Native or Naturalized Authors.* Among the shorter grammars, the best are R. Blachère, *Eléments de l'arabe classique,* and C. Brockelmann, *Arabische Grammatik: Paradigmen, Literatur, Übungsstücke und Glossar.* A good study of the Arabic theory of grammar is G. Bohas and J.-P. Guillaume, *Etude des théories des grammairiens arabes. I. Morphologie et phonologie.*

General treatments of Arabic lexicography are available in H. Gätje, "Arabische Lexikographie"; J. Haywood, *Arabic Lexicography;* and F. Sezgin, *Lexicographie bis ca. 430 H.* The issue of loanwords into Arabic is discussed in A. Schall, "Geschichte des Arabischen Wortschatzes: Lend– und Fremdwörter im klassischen Arabisch." The most important and useful Arabic dictionaries for Hebrew Bible scholars are identified and described in the section above titled "Tools" (§2.1).

Works that directly treat Hebrew/Arabic comparative lexicography with references to specific examples and methodological issues include A. Guillaume, *Hebrew and Arabic Lexicography;* J. Kaltner, *The Use of Arabic in Biblical Hebrew Lexicography;* and L. Kopf's two articles titled "Arabische Etymologien und Parallelen zum Bibelwörterbuch."

4. BIBLIOGRAPHY

Aartun, Kjell. *Zur Frage altarabischer Tempora.* Oslo: Universitetsforlaget, 1963.

Abbott, Nabia. *The Rise of the North Arabic Script and Its Kurʾanic Development.* Chicago: University of Chicago Press, 1939.

———. *Studies in Arabic Literary Papyri III: Language and Literature.* Chicago: University of Chicago Press, 1972.

Bauer, Thomas. "Arabic Scripts." Pages 559–64 in *The World's Writing Systems.* Edited by Peter T. Daniels and William Bright. Oxford: Oxford University Press, 1996.

Beeston, Alfred F. L. "Languages of Pre-Islamic Arabia." *Arabica* 28 (1981): 178–86.

———. *Written Arabic: An Approach to Basic Structures.* London: Cambridge University Press, 1968.

Bellamy, James A. "Arabic Verses from the First/Second Century: The Inscription of ʿEn ʿAvdat." *JSS* 25 (1990): 73–79.

Blachère, Régis. *Eléments de l'arabe classique.* 4th ed. Paris: Maisonneuve & Larose, 1985.

Blau, Joshua. *The Emergence and Linguistic Background of Judeo-Arabic: A Study of the Origins of Middle Arabic.* London: Oxford University Press, 1965.

———. *Studies in Middle Arabic and Its Judaeo-Arabic Variety.* Jerusalem: Magnes, 1988.

Bohas, Georges, and Jean-Patrick Guillaume. *Etude des théories des grammairiens arabes. I. Morphologie et phonologie.* Damascus: Institut Français de Damas, 1984.

Brockelmann, Carl. *Arabische Grammatik: Paradigmen, Literatur, Übungsstücke und Glossar.* Edited by Manfred Fleischhammer. 16th ed. Leipzig: VEB Verlag Enzyklopädie, 1965.

Caspari, C. P. *Arabische Grammatik.* Edited by August Müller. Halle, 1887.

Chejne, Anwar G. *The Arabic Language: Its Role in History.* Minneapolis: University of Minnesota Press, 1969.

Cohen, Chaim. "The 'Held Method' for Comparative Semitic Philology." *JANESCU* 19 (1989): 9–23.

Corriente, Federico. *Problemática de la pluralidad en semítico: el plural fracto.* Madrid: Consejo Superior de Investigaciones Científicas, 1971.

Diem, Werner. "Die nabatäischen Inschriften und die Frage der Kasusflexion im Altarabischen." *ZDMG* 123 (1973): 227–37.

Dozy, R. P. A. *Supplément aux Dictionnaires Arabes.* 2 vols. Leiden: Brill, 1881.

Driver, G. R. Isaiah I–XXXIX: Textual and Linguistic Problems." *JSS* 13 (1968): 36–57.

———. "Linguistic and Textual Problems: Jeremiah." *JQR* 28 (1937–1938): 97–129.

———. "Notes on the Psalms." *JTS* 36 (1935): 147–56.

———. "Problems and Solutions." *VT* 4 (1954): 225–45.

———. "Problems in Job." *AJSL* 52 (1935–1936): 160–70.

————. "Studies in the Vocabulary of the Old Testament IV." *JTS* 33 (1932): 38–47.

————. "Supposed Arabisms in the Old Testament." *JBL* 55 (1936): 101–20.

Endreß, Gerhard. "Die arabische Schrift." Pages 165–97 in *Grundriß der arabischen Philologie I. Sprachwissenschaft.* Edited by Wolfdietrich Fischer. Wiesbaden: Reichert, 1983.

Faber, Alice."Genetic Subgrouping of the Semitic Languages." Pages 3–15 in *The Semitic Languages.* Edited by Robert Hetzron. London: Routledge, 1997.

Fernandez, Mauro. *Diglossia: A Comprehensive Bibliography 1960–90 and Supplements.* Amsterdam and Philadelphia: Benjamins, 1993.

Fīrūzābādī, al-. *Al-Qāmūs al-Muḥīṭ.* 4 vols. Beirut: al-Muʾassasa al-ʿArabīya lil-Ṭibāʿa wal-Našr, 1970.

Fischer, August, et al., eds. *Wörterbuch der klassischen arabischen Sprache.* Wiesbaden: Harrassowitz, 1957–.

Fischer, Wolfdietrich. *Grammatik des klassischen Arabisch.* 2d ed. Wiesbaden: Harrassowitz, 1987.

Fück, Johann. *Arabiya: Untersuchungen zur arabischen Sprach- und Stilgeschichte.* Berlin: Akademie-Verlag, 1950.

Gätje, Helmut. "Arabische Lexikographie." *Bustan* 5 (1964): 3–11.

Greenstein, Edward L. "Medieval Bible Commentaries." Pages 213–59 in *Back to the Sources.* Edited by Barry W. Holtz. New York: Summit Books, 1984.

Grohmann, Adolph. *Arabische Paläographie. II. Das Schriftwesen: Die Lapidarschrift.* Vienna: Österreichische Akademie der Wissenschaften, 1971.

Gruendler, Beatrice. *The Development of the Arabic Scripts: From the Nabataean Era to the First Islamic Century according to Dated Texts.* Atlanta: Scholars Press, 1993.

Guillaume, Alfred. "The Arabic Background of the Book of Job." Pages 106–27 in *Promise and Fulfillment: Essays Presented to S. H. Hooke in Celebration of His Ninetieth Birthday.* Edited by F. F. Bruce. Edinbourgh: T&T Clark, 1963.

————. *Hebrew and Arabic Lexicography.* Leiden: Brill, 1965.

Hava, J. G. *Arabic-English Dictionary.* Beirut: Catholic Press, 1951.

Haywood, John. *Arabic Lexicography.* Leiden: Brill, 1965.

Hetzron, Robert. "Two Principles of Genetic Classification." *Lingua* 38 (1976): 89–108.

Hirschfeld, H. *Literary History of Hebrew Grammarians and Lexicographers.* Oxford: Oxford University Press, 1926.

Howell, Mortimer Slope. *A Grammar of the Classical Arabic Language Translated and Compiled from the Most Approved Native or Naturalized Authors.* 1883–1911. Repr., Delhi: Gian, 1986.

Ibn Fāris. *Maqāyīs al-Luġa.* 6 vols. Cairo: al-Dār al-Islāmīya, 1990.

Ibn Manẓūr. *Lisān al-ʿArab*. 15 vols. Beirut: Dār Bayrūt lil-Ṭibāʿa wal-Našr, 1968.

Kaltner, John. *The Use of Arabic in Biblical Hebrew Lexicography*. CBQMS 28. Washington, D.C.: Catholic Biblical Association of America, 1996.

Koehler, Ludwig, Walter Baumgartner, and J. J. Stamm. *The Hebrew and Aramaic Lexicon of the Old Testament*. Translated and edited under the supervision of M. E. J. Richardson. 5 vols. Leiden: Brill, 1994–2000.

Kopf, Lothar. "Arabische Etymologien und Parallelen zum Bibelwörterbuch." *VT* 8 (1958): 161–215; 9 (1959): 247–87.

Lane, Edward W. *Arabic-English Lexicon*. 8 vols. London: Williams & Norgate, 1863–1893. Repr., Beirut: Librairie du Liban, 1980.

Macdonald, M. C. A. "Reflections on the Linguistic Map of Pre-Islamic Arabia." *Arabian Archaeology and Epigraphy* 11 (2000): 28–79.

Müller, Walter M. "Das Altarabische der Inschriften aus vorislamischer Zeit." Pages 30–36 in *Grundriß der arabischen Philologie I. Sprachwissenschaft*. Edited by Wolfdietrich Fischer. Wiesbaden: Reichert, 1983.

Negev, A. "Obodas the God." *IEJ* 36 (1986): 56–60.

Nöldeke, Theodor, and Friedrich Schwally. *Geschichte des Qorans*. Edited by Gotthelf Bergsträßer and Otto Pretzl. 3d ed. Hildesheim: G. Olms, 1961.

Rabin, Chaim. *Ancient West-Arabian*. London: Taylor's Foreign Press, 1951.

———. "The Beginnings of Classical Arabic." *Studia Islamica* 4 (1955): 19–37.

Revell, E. J. "The Diacritical Dots and the Development of the Arabic Alphabet." *JSS* 20 (1975): 178–90.

Robin, Christian. *L'Arabie antique de Karibʾîl à Mahomet: Nouvelles données sur l'histoire des Arabes grâce aux inscriptions*. Aix-en-Province: Editions Edisud, 1992.

Sáenz-Badillos, Angel. *A History of the Hebrew Language*. Translated by John Elwolde. Cambridge: Cambridge University Press, 1993.

Schall, Anton. "Geschichte des Arabischen Wortschatzes: Lend- und Fremdwörter im klassischen Arabisch." Pages 142–53 in *Grundriß der arabischen Philologie I. Sprachwissenschaft*. Edited by Wolfdietrich Fischer. Wiesbaden: Reichert, 1983.

Sezgin, Fuat. *Lexicographie bis ca. 430 H*. Leiden: Brill, 1982.

Spuler, Bertold. "Die Ausbreitung der arabischen Sprache." Pages 245–52 in *Semitistik*. Edited by B. Spuler. HO 1/3. Leiden: Brill, 1964.

Testen, David. "On the Arabic of the ʿEn ʿAvdat Inscription." *JNES* 55 (1996): 281–92.

Ullman, Manfred. *Untersuchungen zur Raǧazpoesie: ein Beitrag zur arabischen Sprach- und Literaturwissenschaft*. Wiesbaden: Harrassowitz, 1966.

Versteegh, Kees. *The Arabic Language*. New York: Columbia University Press, 1997.

Voigt, Rainer M. "The Classification of Central Semitic." *JSS* 32 (1987): 1–21.

Waltke Bruce K., and M. O'Connor. *An Introduction to Biblical Hebrew Syntax*. Winona Lake, Ind.: Eisenbrauns, 1990.

Wehr, Hans. *A Dictionary of Modern Written Arabic*. Ithaca, N.Y.: Spoken Language Services, 1976.

Wild, Stefan. "Arabische Lexikographie." Pages 37–47 in *Grundriß der arabischen Philologie 2*. Edited by Helmut Gätje. Wiesbaden: Harrassowitz, 1987.

Wright, William. *A Grammar of the Arabic Language*. Edited by W. Robertson Smith and M. J. de Goeje. 2 vols. 3d. rev. ed. Cambridge: Cambridge University Press, 1896–1898.

Zabīdī, al-. *Tāj al-ʿArūs*. 10 vols. Libya, n.d.

Zaborski, Andrzej. "The Position of Arabic within the Semitic Language Continuum." *Budapest Studies in Arabic* 3–4 (1991): 365–75.

ARAMAIC

Frederick E. Greenspahn

Aramaic is unique among the languages relevant to biblical studies in that, like Hebrew, it is found both within and beyond the canon. Not only are several sections of the "Hebrew" Bible (most notably Daniel and Ezra) written in Aramaic, but so are several important bodies of texts outside of the Bible that are relevant to understanding it.

The name "Aramaic" comes from the Bible itself. It reports that the leaders of Judah asked an Assyrian general who was besieging the city of Jerusalem toward the end of the eighth century to speak to them in *'ărāmît* rather than Judean (i.e., Hebrew) so that the general population would not understand what was being said (2 Kgs 18:26 = Isa 36:11). The term is also found in Dan 2:4 and Ezra 4:7, where it indicates the shift from Hebrew to Aramaic that takes place in those verses, and in one of the papyri from Elephantine.[1] Early Greek sources identify the language as "Syrian,"[2] except at Dan 2:26, where the Old Greek uses the term "Chaldean."[3]

The name is taken from that of the Aramean people, who are first mentioned by that name in the eleventh century B.C.E., when the Assyrian emperor Tiglath-pileser I reports having encountered them during a military campaign in Syria.[4] There they created several small kingdoms that reached as far east as the Persian Gulf; several of these are mentioned in the Bible, including Beth-rehob, Damascus, Geshur, Hamath, Maacah, Tob, and Zobah.

---

[1] A. Cowley, *Aramaic Papyri of the Fifth Century B.C.* (Oxford: Clarendon, 1923), no. 28, lines 4 and 6.

[2] LXX Dan 2:4; Job 42:17; and *Aristeas* 11; this is the basis for the rabbinic pejorative pun *lăšôn sûrsî* ("clipped tongue," *b. Soṭ.* 49b; *b. B. Qam.* 82b–83a; and *y. Soṭ.* 7:2 21c; cf. *Gen. Rab.* 71:14).

[3] Cf. also Jerome's introduction to Daniel (PL 28:1357). Occasionally, one finds the term "Hebrew" where the reference appears to be to Aramaic (e.g., John 19:13, 17 and, perhaps, Eusebius's references to the sources used by Matthew, *Ecclesiastical History* 3:39 §16, LCL 1:296–97).

[4] Albert Kirk Grayson, *Assyrian Royal Inscriptions* (Wiesbaden: Harrassowitz, 1976) part 2, "From Tiglath-Pileser I to Ashur-nasir-apli II," pp. 13 (§34), 27 (§97), and 23 (§83).

By the time that Israel's monarchy fell in the early part of the sixth century, Aramaic had become the lingua franca of the ancient Near East. That,
after all, is why the leaders of Judah could expect the Assyrian Rabshakeh
to use it to communicate with them. Further evidence of that role can be
seen in an Aramaic letter that was found at the Egyptian site of Saqqara,
which records the request of a Philistine city (probably Ekron) for Egyptian
assistance against the army of Babylon late in the seventh century B.C.E.[5]

The Judeans who were taken captive by Nebuchadnezzar after the
Jerusalem temple was destroyed in 586 B.C.E. adopted the Aramaic language along with the Aramean script. (Hebrew was previously written in
Phoenician characters, which are sometimes called Paleo-Hebrew.) As a
result, biblical literature written after the exile is heavily influenced by Aramaic, and substantial sections of the books of Daniel and Ezra are actually
written in it. Later on, Aramaic was extensively used within the Jewish
community as well as among various Christian groups, most notably the
Syrian Orthodox and also the Samaritans, Mandeans, and Nabateans. It
continues in use within a handful of isolated communities to this day;
among these are some in Syria, Turkey, and Iraq, as well as Jews and
Christians from Kurdistan, virtually all of whom have now migrated to
Israel and the United States.

1. THE LANGUAGE

Aramaic is one of two major branches of Northwest Semitic. (The other
branch, which is called Canaanite, includes Hebrew as its most prominent
member.) Because of its long history and widespread usage, it is divided
into several dialects on the basis of chronological and geographical factors.

The oldest surviving Aramaic texts, which were written between the
tenth and seventh centuries B.C.E., are said to be in Old or Ancient Aramaic.
Sources from the sixth through the third century B.C.E. are said to be in
Official, Imperial, or Standard Literary Aramaic (the German term is *Reichs-
aramäisch*) because it manifests a degree of standardization as a result of
having been used for administrative purposes in the Persian Empire, which
eventually reached from Egypt to India. This is the dialect found in the
Bible, although Daniel is sometimes considered to reflect a later form of
the language.[6]

The fall of Persia led to variation in the dialects of different regions.
This may account for the reference to Peter's distinctive accent in Matt

---

[5] *KAI* §266; cf. Bezalel Porten, "The Identity of King Adon," *BA* 44 (1981): 36–52.

[6] Among the book's idiosyncrasies are its use of *himmôn* for the third masculine
plural pronoun where Ezra has *himmô* and the second- and third-person plural
pronominal suffixes *-kôn* and *-hôn* where Ezra has *-kōm* and *-hōm* as well.

26:73. Although Greek became increasingly important in Judea at this time, Aramaic continued to play a prominent role in Jewish life and culture until it was displaced by Arabic many centuries later. The language of this period, which extends from the second century B.C.E. to the second century CE, is designated Middle Aramaic. This is the form of Aramaic found in the Dead Sea Scrolls and the New Testament. Some scholars also trace the earliest layers of the targumim to the Pentateuch (*Onqelos*) and the Prophets (*Jonathan*) to this time. Other dialects from this period are those of the Nabatean Arab tribes and the cities of Palmyra (biblical Tadmor) and Edessa in Syria, as well as Hatra, which is in Mesopotamia.

Texts from the second through the ninth centuries C.E. (or sometimes later) are said to be in Late Aramaic. These include writings from the Jewish communities of both Palestine (the Palestinian Talmud, various midrashim, and several targumim) and Babylonia (the Babylonian Talmud) as well as among the Christians and Samaritans in the West and the Mandean and Syrian communities in the East.

As mentioned above, Aramaic is still used to this day. The dialects of these communities are called Modern Aramaic.

Among the distinguishing features of Aramaic are certain characteristic words, such as *bar* rather than *bēn* for "son," *qōdem* rather than *lipnê* for "before," and the verbs *ʾth* instead of *bwʾ* for "come" and *slq* rather than *ʿlh* for "ascend." It also retains long *a,* which became long *o* in the Canaanite languages. (This is, therefore, conventionally called the Canaanite shift.) Thus the word for "good" appears as *ṭāb* in Aramaic rather than *ṭôb,* as in Hebrew.

Plural nouns are marked with the suffix *-n* in Aramaic where Hebrew uses *-m.* The masculine ending was apparently *-īn* and the feminine *-ān,* although some feminine plurals end with *-āt.* In light of the Canaanite shift, this latter suffix can be recognized as equivalent to the Hebrew *-ôt.* Aramaic also uses a suffix *-āʾ* where Hebrew places the definite article *ha-* at the beginning of words. Although some scholars regard the Aramaic ending as a definite article, others think of it as creating a separate state ("determined" or "emphatic"), much like the absolute and the construct. Over time, this suffix lost its force and came to be used on almost all nouns. In a similar way, the masculine plural suffix *-ē,* which was used for the construct in earlier dialects of Aramaic (alongside the determined plural *-ayyā*), came to be the standard determined ending in some later dialects.

Like biblical Hebrew, Aramaic verbs appear in two major tenses (or aspects), one characterized by suffixes ("perfect") and the other by prefixes ("imperfect"), albeit with suffixes to mark the plural. These prefixes and suffixes are very similar to those in Hebrew, though the vowels (at least as attested in biblical Aramaic) are not the same.

	perfect		**imperfect**	
	singular	plural	singular	plural
1	-*ēt*	-*nā*ʾ	ʾ*e-*	*nī-*
2m	-*t(â)*	-*tûn* (or *tûm*)	*t-*	*t-ûn*
2f	-*tî*	-*tēn*	*t-în*	*t-ān*
3m	—	-*û*	*y-*	*y-ûn*
3f	-*at*	-*â*	*t-*	*y-ān*

The Aramaic conjugations ("stems") are similar to those of Hebrew. There is even a *qal* (*pəʿal*) passive participle, called *pəʿîl* because it is formed with the vowel *î*. However, unlike Hebrew, in biblical Aramaic there is also a perfect passive, as in *siprîn pətîḥû* (Dan 7:10), which means "the books were opened."

Aramaic does not have a prefixed *n* stem (*nipʿal*), although there are a variety of conjugations beginning with *n* in rabbinic texts (e.g., *nitpaʿel* and *nupʿal*). Instead, the passive is expressed by shifting the vowels to the pattern *u-a* in the derived stems. (Because of the ways in which these are realized, active and passive forms are sometimes identical.)

Like Hebrew, Aramaic uses the prefix *hit-* to express the reflexive, adding it both to the stem in which the middle root letter is lengthened (*paʿʿēl*), as in the Hebrew *hitpaʿʿel,* and to the basic (*qal*) stem (*hitpəʿēl*). In Middle Aramaic, this prefix was also added to the prefixed *h* stem (*hapʿēl*), creating ʾ*ethapʿal* forms, which became ʾ*ettapʿal*. Over time, all these stems came to function as passives, replacing the internal passive forms described above. The *h* prefix on various derived forms also weakened to an ʾ*ālep,* a process that was already underway during the biblical period, resulting in stems such as ʾ*apʿēl* and ʾ*itpaʿʿēl*.[7] On the other hand, *h* does not always elide in Aramaic as it does in imperfect and participial forms of the Hebrew *hipʿil* or when serving as a definite article on a word that has a prefixed preposition.

Aside from these generally prevailing features, each dialect has distinctive traits (isoglosses) of its own. These are useful both for classifying texts and for tracing the language's history. For example, Old Aramaic texts share several features with Hebrew that are not found in later strata of the language. Particularly revealing is the use of *zayin, ṣādê,* and *šîn* to represent the consonants *ð, θ̣,* and *θ* respectively; this is the same way that they appear in Hebrew, though not how they are shown in most of the language's later forms. It is likely that the pronunciation of these phonemes had not yet developed into the sounds that would eventually

---

[7] Stephen Kaufman suggests that these were the original forms and that the *hit-* prefix is a Hebraism ("Languages [Aramaic]," *ABD* 4:177).

become characteristic of Aramaic. On the other hand, the original Semitic consonant ś, which appears as ṣādê in Hebrew, is written with qôp in this period, so that the word for "land" (ʾereṣ in Heb.) is spelled ʾrq in early Aramaic texts. Also, when there are two emphatic letters in a single word, the first tends to dissimilate; thus, the word for "summer" (i.e., qayiṣ) occurs as kyṣ' and the verb "to kill" (qṭl) as kṭl.

Also found in this period is the particle ʾiyāt, which marks the direct object. This is apparently the origin of the Hebrew ʾet. The later form yāt can already be seen in Dan 3:12. Finally, inscriptions from this period demonstrate the use of the letters hê, wāw, and yôd to mark long vowels (matres lectionis), especially at the end of words, as they often do in biblical Hebrew, although it is not clear that Hebrew scribes borrowed this idea from the Arameans.[8]

Aramaic began to function as a lingua franca during the Neo-Assyrian and Babylonian periods. It was at this time that several phonological features that would become characteristic of Aramaic emerged. Among these is the use of a prefix m for the qal (pəʿal) infinitive.[9] It is also in this period that the changes in the representation of the letters mentioned above first occurs. For example, the consonant ś was now written with an ʿayin instead of a qôp, as it had been earlier, so that the word for "land" (Heb. ʾereṣ), which was written ʾrq in Old Aramaic, now appears as ʾrʿ. (Remarkably, both forms appear in Jer 10:11.) Several other consonants that had been represented in early Aramaic inscriptions the same way that they occur in Hebrew also took on a distinctive spelling at this time. These include ð, which appears as dālet in Aramaic rather than zayin as in Hebrew, so that the word for "sacrifice" is dbḥ in Aramaic rather than zbḥ; θ is now represented with ṭêt in Aramaic rather than ṣādê as in Hebrew, yielding the Aramaic word qyṭ ("summer") in contrast to Hebrew qyṣ; and Aramaic represents θ with tāw instead of šîn as in Hebrew, so that the Hebrew word yšb corresponds to the Aramaic ytb.

Biblical Aramaic also tends to nasalize double consonants, presumably as a result of dissimilation. Examples include forms of the root ydʿ, such as the second-person singular imperfect *tiddaʿ, which became tindaʿ, and the noun maddaʿ, which became mandaʿ. (This last word, which means "knowledge," is the basis for the name Mandean, which is used for a gnostic sect that claimed special, secret knowledge.) In similar fashion, the infinitive of the root slq, in which lāmed often assimilates

---

[8] Cf. Ziony Zevit, *Matres Lectionis in Ancient Hebrew Epigraphs* (Cambridge, Mass.: American Schools of Oriental Research, 1980), 4.

[9] This is anticipated in the ninth-century inscription from Tell Fekheriye, the significance of which is discussed below.

to the following *qôp* much as it does in forms of the Hebrew root *lqḥ,* is (*lə*)*ḥansāqâ,* which is derived from the form **ḥassāqâ.* Of special interest is the way this process worked out for the second-person independent pronoun. Originally *'antâ,* it appears as *'t* in Old Aramaic as a result of the *nûn,* which did not have a vowel of its own, assimilating into the *tāw* (cf. Heb. *'attâ*); however, this doubled *tāw* then dissimilated in biblical Aramaic, yielding the form *'antâ*—exactly what the word had originally been!

Also characteristic of Official Aramaic is the reduction of short, pretonic vowels, which generally lengthen in Hebrew. Thus, the word for "prophet" (*nabî'*), which is familiar in the Hebrew form *nābî',* appears as *nəbî'* in Aramaic. This affects many perfect forms of verbs in the *qal* stem. For example, the Hebrew third-person masculine singular *kātab* developed from *katab,* which became *kətab* in Aramaic.

Biblical Aramaic also has several characteristic syntactic features. For example, direct objects are marked with the preposition *l*- rather than the Old Aramaic particle *'iyāt.* There are also several distinctive verbal forms, such as the use of the verb *hwh* with the participle to create a kind of compound tense, much like our present perfect; examples include *hăwāt bāṭəlā'* for "and [the work] ceased" (Ezra 4:24) and *hāzēh hăwêt* for "I saw" (Dan 4:10 [Eng. 4:13]). A similar effect is achieved with the existential particle *'îtay* (cf. the Hebrew *yēš*), as in *lā' 'îtaynā' pāləḥîn* (Dan 3:18, cf. v. 14), which means "we do not worship." Third-person personal pronouns can also be used as a copula, even when the accompanying verb is not in the third person, as in *'ănaḥnā' himmô 'abdôhî dî 'ĕlāh šəmayyā',* literally, "we are they (who are) his servants of the God of heaven," that is, "we are servants of the God of heaven" (Ezra 5:11).

The Bible's Aramaic passages contain numerous terms that were borrowed from other languages, testifying to the rich mixture of cultures experienced by postexilic Jews. Among these are Persian words, such as *'osparnā'* ("completely"), *gizbār* ("treasurer"), *dāt* ("order"), *zan* ("sort"), *ništəwān* ("decree"), *paršegen* ("copy"), and *pitgām* ("report"). There are also Greek terms (most notably the musical instruments listed several times in Dan 3) and several Akkadian words, including *'iggərâ* ("letter"), *bîrtā'* ("citadel"), *zəman* ("time"), and *kārsē'* ("seat"). In addition, there are several verbal forms that appear to belong to the *šap'ēl* (i.e., prefixed *šîn*) conjugation (e.g., *šêzīb* in Dan 3:28; *šêṣî'* in Ezra 6:15; and *šaklēl* in Ezra 4:12). Since there is no evidence that this conjugation was actively used to create verbs in biblical Aramaic, these, too, may have been borrowed from Akkadian, which does have a causative conjugation based on prefixed *šîn.*

There is also reason to believe that the spirantization of the six stops *b, g, d, k, p,* and *t* when they follow a vowel emerged in this period. This phenomenon came to be normative in classical Hebrew.

During the Middle Aramaic period, participles assumed an even broader role than they had in Official Aramaic, when they were joined with *ʾîtay* and forms of *hwh*. In Eastern dialects, pronouns were attached to the end of active participles, enabling them to function as a full tense, as in the use of *ʾāmar-nāʾ* for "I am saying." At the same time, passive participles followed by the preposition *l-* came to serve as a past tense, as in the Syriac *šmîʿ-lan* (lit. "it was heard to us") for "we heard." It was also during this period that Eastern dialects used the prefixes *l-* and *n-* as a third-person prefix. The use of *l-* actually goes back to Old Aramaic, where it functioned as the jussive ("let him. . ."); it is also found in Official Aramaic for the third-person imperfect of the root *hwh*, as in the biblical form *lehĕwēʾ*.

2. SIGNIFICANCE FOR THE BIBLE

Because Aramaic's relationship to the Bible is multifaceted—it is itself both a biblical language as well as the language of one of Israel's neighbors and an important vehicle in postbiblical Jewish and Christian history—its significance for biblical studies is multifaceted as well.

The greatest importance of Aramaic for biblical studies is obviously the fact that sections of the Bible are in Aramaic. Several of these occur within biblical books, most notably Daniel (2:4–7:28) and Ezra (4:8–6:18; 7:12–26), in both of which the Aramaic passages are preceded and followed by sections in Hebrew. How this might have come to be is clearest in the case of Ezra 7:12–26, where the Aramaic section comprises an official Persian document that is, presumably, being cited in its original language.

The mixture of languages in the other cases is peculiar. Some have speculated that the books of Ezra and Daniel were written entirely in Hebrew and that the Aramaic sections are a translation that was substituted for the original. Others have proposed that these books were first written in Aramaic, in which case the Hebrew sections are a replacement. Alternatively, the shift may have been intentional, whether as a result of combining passages that were originally written in different languages or for some particular stylistic effect.[10]

The same problem applies to Jer 10:11, which is also in Aramaic, although this case is less difficult, since most scholars agree that the verse is a late insertion. There is no question about the appropriateness of the changing language in Gen 31:47, where the Aramaic phrase *yəgār śāhădûtāʾ* ("pile of witness") is attributed to Laban, whom Gen 31:20 identifies as an Aramean; the Israelite Jacob gives the same place the equivalent Hebrew name *galʿēd* (i.e., Gilead).

---

[10] See the standard introductions and commentaries, such as Otto Eissfeldt, *The Old Testament: An Introduction* (New York: Harper & Row, 1965), 516–17, 543–44.

Interestingly, the New Testament contains a similar phenomenon, with occasional phrases and even sentences in Aramaic, though obviously written out in Greek script.[11] Examples include the reference to God as *abba* ("father") in Mark 14:36; Rom 8:15; and Gal 4:6; the slogan *maranatha* ("our lord, come") in 1 Cor 16:22; and Jesus' instruction to the dead girl: *talitha koum* ("arise, little girl") in Mark 5:41. There is even an entire biblical verse in Aramaic when Jesus quotes Ps 22:2 (Eng. 22:1) while hanging on the cross, according to Matt 27:46 and Mark 15:34.

It is hardly surprising to find Aramaic elements in the New Testament, given that language's status as the lingua franca of Judea in the time of Jesus.[12] This surely accounts for the numerous proper names that are of plainly Aramaic origin, including Golgotha (Matt 27:33; Mark 15:22; John 19:17), Martha (Luke 10:38–41), Tabitha (Acts 9:36), and Kephas (John 1:42; NRSV Cephas). The recurring use of the phrase "son of man" (especially in Rev 1:13 and 14:14) may also reflect Aramaic influence, since that language typically refers to "a person" with the phrase *bar naš*.[13]

Hebrew texts that were written after the exile also show Aramaic influence. Among the numerous words of demonstrably Aramaic origin that are found in such passages are *'ns* (Esth 1:8), *btl* (Qoh 12:3), *gənāzîm* (Esth 3:9; 4:7), and *ršm* (Dan 10:21). Aramaic grammatical features, such as the plural *-în* rather than the normal Hebrew *-îm*, are also common in these books (e.g., *ḥiṭṭîn* in Ezek 4:9, *tannîn* in Lam 4:3, and *ḥayyāmîn* in Dan 12:13). Some scholars have even suspected that individual biblical books were translated from Aramaic originals, an assertion that conforms to the statement at the end of the Septuagint version of Job, which refers to that book as written in Aramaic (lit. "Syrian").[14]

---

[11] These are listed in E. Kautzsch, *Grammatik des Biblisch-Aramäisch* (Leipzig: Vogel, 1884).

[12] Cf. Joseph A. Fitzmyer, "The Study of the Aramaic Background of the New Testament," in *A Wandering Aramean: Collected Aramaic Essays* (Chico, Calif.: Scholars Press, 1979), 1–27.

[13] Cf. Joseph A. Fitzmyer, "The New Testament Title, 'Son of Man' Philologically Considered," in *A Wandering Aramean,* 143–60; and John Bowker, "The Son of Man," *JTS* NS 28 (1977): 19–48.

[14] Cf. the comment of the twelfth-century Spanish exegete Abraham ibn Ezra at Job 2:11; more recently, N. H. Tur-Sinai, *The Book of Job, A New Commentary* (rev. ed., Jerusalem: Kiryath Sepher, 1967), xxx–xl. A more extensive argument is laid out by Frank Zimmermann, *Biblical Books Translated from the Aramaic* (New York: Ktav, 1973). Charles C. Torrey took a similar position regarding the Synoptic Gospels in "The Translations Made from the Original Aramaic Gospels," in *Studies in the History of Religions Presented to Crawford Howell Toy by Pupils, Colleagues and Friends* (ed. D. G. Lyon and G. F. Moore; New York: Macmillan, 1912), 269–317.

Because Hebrew absorbed elements from Aramaic during and after the Babylonian exile, the presence of such features can be used as a criterion for determining when individual passages were written. Unfortunately, this technique is not without problems, since some Aramaic-like features are found in what are usually considered the oldest texts in the Bible.[15] For example, the Song of Deborah (Judg 5), which is almost universally dated to the twelfth or eleventh centuries, includes the plural form *middîn* (v. 10) and the verb *tnḥ* (5:11), which is cognate to the Hebrew *šnḥ*.[16] The Aramaic verb *mḥq* is also found there alongside its Hebrew equivalent *mḥṣ* (v. 26), although in that case the latter may be a gloss.[17]

Aramaic is also helpful for understanding the nature and history of Hebrew itself. To be sure, almost any other Semitic language is valuable for that purpose; however, the close linguistic and historical relationship between Hebrew and Aramaic makes it a particularly rich resource for comparisons and contrasts.

In addition to providing evidence that can be used to date individual passages, the relationship between the two languages can also serve as a valuable tool for identifying cognate relationships between words and forms[18] and for understanding how Hebrew developed. For example, Aramaic retention of the H stem's (*hapʿēl*) characteristic prefixed-*h* in forms where it elides in the equivalent Hebrew *hipʿil* (thus Hebrew *yašpîl*, but Aramaic *yəhašpîl*) suggests that the former was an internal Hebrew development. The absence of an Aramaic cognate for the relative pronoun *še-* (Aramaic uses *dî*) suggests that it, too, developed within Hebrew, whereas the cognate relationship between later Hebrew's relative pronoun *ʾăšer* and the Aramaic noun *ʾătar* ("place") demonstrates the origin of that Hebrew usage. The presence of *hit-* prefixes in several Aramaic conjugations suggests the possibility that it may also have been more widespread in Hebrew than is usually thought; in fact, the Bible contains examples of it on verbs that do not belong to the *piʿel* stem (e.g., *pqd* in

---

[15] For qualifications about this method, see Avi Hurvitz, "The Chronological Significance of 'Aramaisms in Biblical Hebrew,'" *IEJ* 18 (1968): 238–40; for a recent study that revolves around these issues, see Gary R. Rendsburg, "Some False Leads in the Identification of Late Biblical Hebrew Texts: The Cases of Genesis 24 and 1 Samuel 2:27–36," *JBL* 121 (2002): 23–46.

[16] Cf. Judg 11:40 and perhaps Ps 8:2 and Prov 31:31.

[17] These features have alternatively been explained as belonging to northern Hebrew; cf. Gary A. Rendsburg, *Linguistic Evidence for the Northern Origin of Selected Psalms* (Atlanta: Scholars Press, 1990), 6.

[18] This has been recognized since early in the tenth century, as in *The Risāla of Judah ben Quraysh* (ed. Dan Becker; Tel Aviv: Tel Aviv University, 1984), 116–17.

Judg 20:15, 17; 21:9; cf. Num 1:47; 2:33; 26:62; and 1 Kgs 20:27; also *lḥm* in the Moabite Stone).[19]

Similar insight can be applied to phonological and orthographic phenomena. We have already suggested that Hebrew's two different pronunciations of *b, g, d, k, p, t* and the use of *matres lectionis* were adopted from Aramaic. The merging of the consonants *sāmek* and *śîn* in Aramaic may also account for later examples of that phenomenon in Hebrew.

Beyond their linguistic value, Aramaic texts are a valuable resource for understanding the historical background of the Bible. That this should be so is clear from its ample references to Israelite interaction with Arameans. According to Deut 26:5, Israel's ancestors were related to the Arameans, a point supported by the genealogies of Genesis, which describe Aram as the grandson of Abraham's brother (22:20–21).[20] It is, therefore, hardly surprising to find that the patriarchs interacted with their relatives from that region on several occasions, most notably going there in order to find suitable (i.e. related) wives (Gen 24:1–10; 28:1-5). Both Bethuel and Laban, the fathers of Rebekah and of Leah and Rachel, are called Arameans (Gen 25:20; 31:20).

During the monarchy period, Israel had numerous and complex relations with the Arameans. Saul is said to have fought them along with several other neighboring peoples (1 Sam 14:47), including the Ammonites, who hired Aramean mercenaries for their conflict with David (2 Sam 10:6–19). He also defeated Hadadezer, the ruler of Zobah (2 Sam 8:3–10). King Solomon fought with Rezon, who fled from Zobah and then ruled over Damascus (1 Kgs 11:23–25). After the Israelite kingdom split near the end of the tenth century, the Israelites were at various times subordinate to (1 Kgs 15:8–20; 20:34; 2 Kgs 10:32; 12:17; 13:7, 22) or dominant over (1 Kgs 20:34; 2 Kgs 13:25) the Arameans. According to Assyrian sources, northern Israel was part of an alliance that included Damascus, Hamath, and nine other countries, who appear to have withstood the powerful ruler Shalmaneser III (853 B.C.E.); however, just a decade later (841 B.C.E.) the Assyrian emperor defeated these same nations.[21]

In the eighth century, the Arameans joined with northern Israel and the Phoenicians of Tyre in an apparent effort to create another coalition that could take on Assyria. When Judah's king Ahaz refused to participate, the alliance attempted to replace him with a ruler of their own choosing. In response, he turned to Assyria for assistance, as a result of

---

[19] See the discussion in Simon B. Parker's chapter on "Ammonite, Edomite, and Moabite," pp. 54–55.

[20] Contrast Gen 10:22–23, where he is said to have been descended from Shem.

[21] Cf. *ANET,* 278–81.

which Tiglath-pileser III conquered Damascus, bringing an end to Aramean power and autonomy.[22] According to 2 Kgs 16:10–13, Ahaz was so impressed by an altar he saw in Damascus that he had an imitation built within Jerusalem itself.[23]

These accounts clearly show that there was abundant political and cultural interaction between Israel and the nearby Aramean kingdoms. This has now been reinforced by an Aramaic inscription that was discovered in 1993–1994 at Tel Dan in northern Israel. It appears to have been written on behalf of a ninth-century Aramean ruler, who reports having killed a king from the house of David.[24] This suggests that the southern kingdom of Judah, which was ruled by David's descendants, had been involved in a battle against Aramean peoples in this region.

The only other Aramaic inscription to mention a biblical personality was discovered in 1930 at the Russian convent on Jerusalem's Mount of Olives.[25] Probably written toward the end of the Second Temple period, it states that the bones of Judah's king Uzziah had been brought "there," presumably from the site outside the city where they had been buried according to 2 Chr 26:23. (By contrast, 2 Kgs 15:7 states that he was buried in the city of David.)[26]

An entire archive of documents written by Jewish mercenaries who were serving in a Persian military colony at the southern border of Egypt during the fifth pre-Christian century was found on the island of Yeb (Elephantine), which is located across from the settlement of Syene, just north of the first cataract of the Nile. These provide valuable information about Jewish history and practices at about the time that Judean exiles were returning to their homeland after the exile.[27]

Several other Aramaic documents have been found in nearby regions. These include papyri from Wadi ed-Daliyeh, which were apparently written

---

[22] Cf. Isa 7:1–9 and 2 Kgs 16:5–9.

[23] 2 Chr 28:23 reports that Ahaz actively worshiped the gods of Damascus.

[24] Published by Avraham Biran and Joseph Naveh in *IEJ* 43 (1993): 81–98 and 45 (1995): 1–18; a different understanding of the inscriptions can be found in Philip R. Davies, "'House of David' Built on Sand, The Sins of the Biblical Maximizers," *BAR* 20/4 (1994): 54–55.

[25] Joseph A. Fitzmyer and Daniel J. Harrington, *A Manual of Palestinian Aramaic Texts* (Rome: Biblical Institute Press, 1978), §70.

[26] See also *t. B. Bat.* 1:11.

[27] Cf. Bezalel Porten, *Archives from Elephantine: The Life of an Ancient Jewish Military Colony* (Berkeley and Los Angeles: University of California Press, 1968); and idem, *The Elephantine Papyri in English: Three Millennia of Cross-Cultural Continuity and Change* (Leiden: Brill, 1996).

in Samaria near the middle of the fourth century. Although their contents are primarily legal, they mention several individuals with plainly Yahwistic names as well as an official named Sanballat, the same name as that of an official who is mentioned in the book of Ezra (although these texts were written nearly a century later than the period with which Ezra is concerned). Other correspondence found in the region was written by a Persian official and families living at Luxor and Syene.

In addition to these texts, which relate explicitly to ancient Israelites and Judeans, there are several inscriptions from the ancient Aramean kingdoms.[28] One of these, which was found near Aleppo, speaks of a ruler named "Bar Haddad ... king of Aram" (*KAI* §201). Although that name was shared by several rulers of Damascus about whom we have other information, a careful examination of the stela has suggested that it refers to an entirely different individual.[29] Other inscriptions are from Zakkur, an eighth-century ruler of Hamath and Luʿash and Panammuwa and Barrakib of Samʾal.[30] Some scholars also consider the inscription about the Moabite prophet Balaam from Tell Deir ʿAllā to be in Aramaic. Whatever its language, that inscription is treated elsewhere in this book.[31]

In addition to direct linguistic and historical connections, it is possible to glean useful insights into biblical culture and theology from Aramaic texts that do not bear directly on people or events mentioned in the Bible. For example, an inscription from Tell Fekheriye (ancient Sikan), which is located near the upper Habur River, refers to the statue on which it is inscribed as both a *ṣlm* and a *dmwt* in a way that suggests these words were synonyms. (The accompanying Assyrian version uses the Sumerian term NU, which corresponds to the Akkadian *ṣalmu*.) This inscription is, therefore, frequently cited to help clarify the significance of the Bible's statement that human beings are in God's image (*ṣelem*) and likeness (*dəmût*).[32]

---

[28] Cf. Scott C. Layton's survey in "Old Aramaic Inscriptions," *BA* 51 (1988): 172–89.

[29] Wayne T. Pitard has identified the king's father as ʿAttar-hamek ("The Identity of the Bir-Hadad of the Melqart Stela," *BASOR* 272 [1988]: 3–21). A Bar-Hadad who was the son of Tabrimmon is mentioned in 1 Kgs 15:18; 1 Kgs 20:1, 20 and 2 Kgs 6:24 seem to refer to a different ruler with the same name, and the Zakkur inscription (*KAI* §202) mentions yet another, who was the son of Hazel.

[30] Cf. *KAI* §§201, 214–18.

[31] Cf. Jo Ann Hackett, *The Balaam Text from Deir ʿAllā* (Chico, Calif.: Scholars Press, 1984), 109–24; and Simon B. Parker's chapter on "Ammonite, Edomite, and Moabite," p. 57.

[32] Gen 1:26 and 5:3; the text was published by Ali Abou-Assaf, Pierre Bordreuil, and Alan R. Millard, *La statue de Tell Fekherye et son inscription bilingue assyro-araméene* (Paris: Editions Recherche sur les civilisations, 1982).

Another important document that is often used for biblical studies is an eighth-century treaty that was found in the Syrian village of Sefire. It prescribes the relationship between the king of Arpad and his Mesopotamian master, who was from KTK. This document has yielded valuable insights into the nature of ancient Semitic treaties and, thus, the Bible's concept of covenant. It is especially useful for understanding the blessings and curses that are contained in such agreements.[33]

Among the Elephantine papyri was found a collection of proverbs attributed to a wise man named Ahiqar, who is said to have served as an advisor to the Assyrian king Sennacherib. The story of Ahiqar was already well known in a variety of versions, which parallel several biblical narratives. The proverbs in the middle of this text belong to the same tradition as much of the Bible's wisdom literature.[34]

In addition to documents from the biblical period, there are also important Aramaic texts from the post-Israelite period. These include several of the Dead Sea Scrolls, which were composed during the last two pre-Christian and the first Christian century. For example, the Genesis Apocryphon (1QapGen) retells several events from the book of Genesis, and the Prayer of Nabonidus (4QprNab) is based on an incident that is similar to that recounted in Dan 4, but with Nabonidus rather than Nebuchadnezzar as the Babylonian ruler. Several books from the apocryphal and pseudepigraphical writings also seem to have been composed in Aramaic, although they have typically survived in other languages. However, Aramaic copies of Tobit, Enoch, and a form of the *Testament of Levi* have now been found among the Dead Sea Scrolls. From the same region also come Aramaic letters written by the second-century Jewish leader Simon Bar-Kosiba (Bar Kokhba).

Later Aramaic Jewish texts that relate to the Bible include substantial sections of both the Palestinian and the Babylonian Talmudim as well as several midrashim. *Megillat Ta'anit,* an early rabbinic text listing dates on which it is forbidden to fast, is in Aramaic, as are some isolated sentences in the Mishnah, which was put into its current form near the end of the second century C.E.; among these are two sayings attributed to the first-century sage Hillel.[35] To these, one should add the Targumim, which are Aramaic paraphrases and translations of the Bible that were written beginning during the Second Temple period and continuing into

---

[33] Joseph A. Fitzmyer, *The Aramaic Inscriptions of Sefire* (rev. ed., Rome: Pontifical Biblical Institute, 1995).

[34] Cf. James M. Lindenberger, *The Wisdom Proverbs of Ahiqar* (JHNES; Baltimore: Johns Hopkins University Press, 1983).

[35] At *m. 'Abot* 1:13; 2:6; 5:22–23.

the Middle Ages. Targumim to Leviticus and Job were also found at Qumran.[36]

Finally, the Masorah—marginal notes to the biblical text, which were compiled by the same schools that developed the familiar vowels and accents in the sixth and seventh centuries C.E.—are generally written in a heavily abbreviated form of Aramaic, presumably because that was the language of those who composed them.

There are also several corpora of Aramaic texts that are important for the history of Christianity and include material relevant to understanding the Bible and how it has been interpreted. Most conspicuous among these are the writings of the Syrian (Orthodox) Christian community, which are in a dialect called Syriac. Besides its rich interpretive tradition, this is the language of the Peshitta, an ancient translation of the Bible that is important in its own right as well as for the light it can shed onto the original text of the Bible.[37] And, of course, many later Jewish texts, most notably having to do with mystical and legal matters, are in Aramaic.

3. ANCIENT SOURCES, MODERN RESOURCES

The same text-editions, lexica, and concordances that are used for the Bible's Hebrew sections are appropriate for studying its Aramaic passages. In addition, Ernestus Vogt's *Lexicon linguae aramaicae veteris testamenti documentis antiquis illustratum* (Rome: Pontifical Biblical Institute, 1971) is devoted solely to biblical Aramaic.

The best English grammar of biblical Aramaic is Franz Rosenthal, *A Grammar of Biblical Aramaic* (Wiesbaden: Harrasowitz, 1963); more technical material can be found in Hans Bauer and Pontus Leander, *Grammatik des Biblisch-Aramäische* (Halle: Niemeyer, 1927). Introductory textbooks to the language include Frederick E. Greenspahn, *An Introduction to Aramaic* (SBLRBS 38; Atlanta: Society of Biblical Literature, 1999); and Alger F. Johns, *A Short Grammar of Biblical Aramaic* (Berrien Springs, Mich.: Andrews University Press, 1972). Isaac Jerusalmi's *The Aramaic Sections of Ezra and Daniel* (Cincinnati: Hebrew Union College-Jewish Institute of Religion, 1972) is also a helpful tool.

A good overview of the history of the Arameans and their relationship to ancient Israel is in Wayne T. Pitard, "Arameans" in *People of the Old Testament World* (ed. Alfred J. Hoerth, Gerald L. Mattingly, and Edwin M.

---

[36] They are published in volumes 6 and 23 of the series Discoveries in the Judaean Desert (Oxford: Clarendon, 1977 and 1998); see also Michael Sokoloff, *The Targum to Job from Qumran Cave XI* (Ramat-Gan: Bar Ilan University Press, 1974).

[37] Cf. Michael P. Weitzman, *The Syriac Version of the Old Testament: An Introduction* (Cambridge: Cambridge University Press, 1999).

Yamauchi; Grand Rapids, Mich.: Baker, 1994), 207–30. There are several general surveys of the Aramaic language; these include Eduard Yechezkel Kutscher, "Aramaic," *EncJud* 3:259–87; Joseph A. Fitzmyer, "The Phases of the Aramaic Language," in *A Wandering Aramaean: Collected Aramaic Essays* (Chico, Calif.: Scholars Press, 1979), 57–84; Klaus Beyer, *The Aramaic Language* (Göttingen: Vandenhoeck & Ruprecht, 1986); and Stephen A. Kaufman, "Languages (Aramaic)," *ABD* 4:173–78. Joseph A. Fitzmyer and Stephen A. Kaufman have also published the first part of *An Aramaic Bibliography* (Baltimore: Johns Hopkins University Press, 1993–) as part of a project to produce a comprehensive Aramaic lexicon.

Additional information can be found in the standard overviews of comparative Semitics. Among these are I. M. Diakonof, *Semito-Hamitic Languages: An Essay in Classification* (Moscow: Nauka, 1965); Sabbatino Moscati et al., *An Introduction to the Comparative Grammar of the Semitic Languages* (Wiesbaden: Harrassowitz, 1969); Gotthelf Bergsträsser, *Introduction to the Semitic Languages* (Winona Lake, Ind.: Eisenbrauns, 1983); and W. Randall Garr, *Dialect Geography of Syria-Palestine, 1000–586 B.C.E.* (Philadelphia: University of Pennsylvania Press, 1985).

The most recently discovered inscriptions are likely to be available only in professional journals. Collections of West-Semitic inscriptions, such as those of Herbert Donner and Wolfgang Röllig (*Kananäische und Aramäische Inschriften* [3 vols.; Wiesbaden: Harrassowitz, 1971–1976]) and John C. L. Gibson (*Aramaic Inscriptions* [vol. 2 of *Textbook of Syrian Semitic Inscriptions;* Oxford: Clarendon, 1975]), include sections devoted to Aramaic. Many of these texts are translated in James Pritchard's now dated volume, *Ancient Near Eastern Texts Relating to the Old Testament* (3d ed.; Princeton, N.J.: Princeton University Press, 1969). More specialized collections can be found in Joseph A. Fitzmyer and Daniel J. Harrington, *A Manual of Palestinian Aramaic Texts* (Rome: Biblical Institute Press, 1978); Arthur E. Cowley, *Aramaic Papyri of the Fifth Century B.C.* (Oxford: Clarendon, 1923); Emil G. Kraeling, *The Brooklyn Museum Aramaic Papyri* (New Haven, Conn.: Yale University Press, 1953); G. R. Driver, *Aramaic Documents of the Fifth Century B.C.* (rev. ed.; Oxford: Clarendon, 1965); Bezalel Porten and Ada Yardeni, *Textbook of Aramaic Documents from Ancient Egypt* (4 vols.; Jerusalem: Hebrew University Press, 1986–1999); and Bezalel Porten, *The Elephantine Papyri in English: Three Millennia of Cross-Cultural Continuity and Change* (Leiden: Brill, 1996).

Postbiblical inscriptions are published in widely scattered sources. The Aramaic texts found among the Dead Sea Scrolls can be found in B. Jongeling, C. J. Labuschagne, and A. S. van der Woude, *Aramaic Texts from Qumran* (Leiden: Brill, 1976–); Klaus Beyer, *Die aramäischen Texte vom Toten Meer* (Göttingen: Vandenhoeck & Ruprecht, 1987); and Florentino

García Martínez and Eibert J. C. Tigchelaar, *The Dead Sea Scrolls Study Edition* (2 vols.; Leiden: Brill, 1997–1998).

Alexander Sperber's *The Bible in Aramaic* (5 vols.; Leiden: Brill, 1959–1973) includes several of the most important Targumim. Others have been published by E. G. Clarke (*Targum Pseudo-Jonathan of the Pentateuch* [Hoboken, N.J.: Ktav, 1984]); Alejandro Diez Macho (*Neophyti I* [Madrid: Consejo Superio de Investigaciones Cientificas, 1968]); and Michael L. Klein (*The Fragment-Targums of the Pentateuch according to the Extant Sources* [Rome: Biblical Institute Press, 1980]). Many of these are translated in The Aramaic Bible series, which was initiated by Michael Glazier and is now published by Liturgical Press.

Important resources for studying nonbiblical texts include Jacob Hoftijzer and Karel Jongeling, *Dictionary of the North-West Semitic Inscriptions* (2 vols.; Leiden: Brill, 1995); Marcus Jastrow, *A Dictionary of the Targumim, the Talmud Babli and Jerusalmi, and the Midrashic Literature* (New York: G. P. Putnam's Sons, 1903; reprinted often); and Michael Sokoloff, *A Dictionary of Jewish Palestinian Aramaic of the Byzantine Period* (Ramat Gan: Bar-Ilan University Press, 1990). The Peshitta Institute is publishing a critical edition of the Peshitta under the title, *The Old Testament in Syriac according to the Peshitta Version* (Leiden: Brill, 1977–).

EGYPTIAN

Donald B. Redford

1. THE LANGUAGE

Unlike Hebrew, Arabic and Greek, Egyptian has not enjoyed an uninterrupted continuum in the collective consciousness of the world. This has proven a mixed blessing. On the one hand, the scholar cannot refer to a "received" textual tradition, expurgated and authorized by a surviving community (either spiritual or ethnic). On the other hand, the absence of an archival hegemony has permitted the recovery ad hoc of pieces, preserved by chance, which a surviving tradition would not have countenanced.

1.1. DECIPHERMENT

With Egypt's political subjugation to Persia in 525 B.C.E. and to Macedon in 332 B.C.E., the Egyptians found themselves in subjection to regimes that replaced the language of the autochthonous inhabitants first with Aramaic and later with Greek as the language of government. The Egyptian language and script, in the "Demotic" stage at the time, remained the vehicles for the expression of native religious custom and business transactions among the native population. But when foreigners became involved with Egyptians in any kind of interaction, the language favored by the conquerors had to be used. This situation created a great incentive for Egyptians increasingly to abandon their native script (if not their language), which thus retreated to a purely cultic register. In consequence, the temples of Egypt increasingly adopted the (self-imposed) role of guardians of the classical cultic, prescriptive, and belletristic literature, which was lodged now solely within temple archives.[1] After the disaster of 343 B.C.E., when the conquering Persians confiscated the contents of temple libraries throughout Egypt, the priesthood became wary of outside authorities and committed a good deal of this written material to inscribed form on temple walls. A "siege mentality" developed among the priesthood that was

---

[1] Donald B. Redford, *Pharaonic King-Lists, Annals and Daybooks* (Mississauga, Ont.: Benben, 1986).

only exacerbated when Rome added Egypt to its empire in 30 B.C.E. The new rulers introduced fiscal and legal disincentives to weaken and reduce the native clergy by curtailing recruitment. The overall result was a vastly diminished body of those who could read the native script, numbering in the third century C.E. only a few hundred.[2] By 200 C.E. the use of Demotic, even in business transactions, was beginning to die out, and beyond the middle of the third century, the practice of rendering the emperor's name in hieroglyphs was discontinued. During the late third and early fourth centuries C.E. native temples began to close down under the impact of the expansion of Christianity. Encouraged by the anathema they pronounced on all "pagan" culture, the Christians ransacked temple archives, committing the papyri to the flames.[3]

The end followed swiftly. The last known hieroglyphic inscription dates to 394 C.E., within half a decade of the edict of Theodosius closing the pagan places of worship, and the last Demotic text fifty-eight years later. Within a single generation accurate knowledge of the script was lost. The diletantish work of one Horapollo, toward the end of the fifth century, purporting to "explain" the hieroglyphic script, is in fact a mishmash of a few dimly remembered facts, distorted by a fixation with symbolic interpretation. For fourteen centuries the hieroglyphs were to remain a closed book.

This tragic loss derives as much from a classical "attitude" as from Christian animosity. In spite of the proverbial fascination shown by Greeks for the physical remains of ancient Egypt, no writer in Greek save Manetho, the *Egyptian* priest, cared enough to master the hieroglyphic script. They knew of the latter solely through its appearance on temple walls (hence ἱερογλυφικός, "sacred script"), a use that seemed to be consonant with the insistence of Middle- and Neoplatonic thinkers on the value of symbols to convey profound, philosophical truths.[4] This mistaken semiotic preconception was abetted by the hidden agenda of such marginal, though influential, movements as Gnosticism and Hermeticism, which, while containing a solid core of material of Egyptian origin, strangely promoted the allegorical reading of all things Egyptian, including the script. Hence, throughout the Middle Ages and well into the

---

[2] Roger S. Bagnall, *Egypt in Late Antiquity* (Princeton, N.J.: Princeton University Press, 1993), 237.

[3] This was especially true for the magical papyri. See Hans Dieter Betz, *The Greek Magical Papyri in Translation* (Chicago: University of Chicago Press, 1986), xli–xlii.

[4] Erik Iversen, *The Myth of Egypt and Its Hieroglyphs in European Tradition* (2d ed.; Princeton, N.J.: Princeton University Press, 1993).

Renaissance the conviction that the hieroglyphic script conveyed a language of symbols continued to cloud the minds of the European intelligentsia.

It was not until Napoleon's Egyptian expedition (1798–1801) that sufficient textual comparanda had become available to aid in a successful decipherment. The recovery by the French, excavating the foundations of a fort at Rashid in the Delta, of the trilingual decree of 195 B.C.E. (the "Rosetta" Stone) and the 1815 discovery at Philae of an obelisk with a bilingual text provided European savants with Greek texts done into Egyptian. Through a close comparison of the hieroglyphic renderings of the personal names "Ptolemy" and "Kleopatra," J. F. Champollion was able to determine that the signs of which the cartouche ovals were composed stood for consonantal sounds. His list of phonetic equivalents expanded markedly as an increasing number of cartouches yielded the names of Ptolemaic kings and Roman emperors. The unexpected, though welcome, consistency with which Thutmoside and Ramesside royal names submitted to decipherment along the same lines, proved that the essentially phonetic nature of the core of the sign-list had informed the script from the start.

1.2. ADVANCES IN THE STUDY OF THE LANGUAGE

The nineteenth century witnessed a whirlwind of activity in text collection and grammatical and syntactic studies.[5] Champollion himself toured Egypt in 1828 in search of new inscriptional material, and his labors issued (posthumously) in *Notices Descriptive, Monuments d'Egypte et de la Nubie* and in a grammar (1838). Thanks to the enlightened patronage of a monarch, Frederick William IV, R. Lepsius undertook the first scientific epigraphic mission to Egypt in the 1840s and from 1849 to 1858 produced the monumental *Denkmäler aus Ägypten und Äthiopen,* which is still used today.[6] European consuls in Egypt, such as B. Drovetti (France), G. Anastasi (Sweden), and H. Salt (Great Britain) and his agent G. B. Belzoni, indulged in collecting antiquities in vast quantities, and the papyri and inscriptions they amassed today form the heart of several museum collections. At the same time, formal, if not scientific, excavations in Egypt began to produce inscriptions. A. Mariette at the behest of the Khedive founded the *Service des antiquités de l'Égypte,* and from 1850 to 1881 he controlled extensive clearing operations at such sites as Karnak, Abydos, Saqqara, and Tanis. For advances in the study of Egyptian grammar, syntax, and lexicon, we are most indebted to German scholars, especially those of Berlin. Among these A. Erman

---

[5] Jean Vercoutter, *The Search for Ancient Egypt* (New York: Abrams, 1992).

[6] R. Lepsius, *Denkmäler aus Ägypten und Äthiopen* (6 vols.; Berlin: Nicolaische Buchhandlung, 1849–1858).

occupies a prominent place for his groundbreaking work on Middle and Late Egyptian grammar. He is closely followed by K. Sethe for his monumental work on the Egyptian verb and W. Spiegelberg for his studies in Demotic grammar and syntax.[7]

The advances in language studies during the twentieth century owe most to the application of modern linguistic theory and lexicography. B. Gunn inaugurated the modern era with his *Studies in Egyptian Syntax* (Paris, 1924), to be followed three years later by (Sir) A. H. Gardiner's *Egyptian Grammar,* which underwent two further editions into the 1950s.[8] One of Sethe's students, H. J. Polotsky, made a signal breakthrough in the study of the Egyptian verbal system with his publication in 1944 of *Études de syntaxe copte* and his introduction of "Standard Theory," which applied observations based on Coptic grammar to Middle Egyptian.[9] Subsequent decades witnessed contributions to the discussion (many based on Polotsky) of Middle and Late Egyptian grammar[10] and of Coptic.[11] It remained

---

[7] Adolf Erman, *Ägyptisch Grammatik* (4th ed.; 3 vols.; Porta linguarum orientalium; Berlin: Reuther & Reichard, 1928–1929); Kurt Sethe, *Das ägyptische Verbum in altägyptischen, neuägyptischen und koptischen* (3 vols.; Leipzig: Hinrichs, 1899–1902); Wilhelm Spiegelberg, *Demotische Grammatik* (Heidelberg: Winter, 1975).

[8] B. Gunn, *Studies in Egyptian Syntax* (Paris: Geuthner, 1924); Alan H. Gardiner, *Egyptian Grammar* (3d ed.; Oxford: Griffith Institute Ashmolean Museum, 1957).

[9] H. J. Polotsky, *Études de syntaxe copte* (Cairo: Société d'archéologie copte, 1944); idem, "The Coptic Conjugation System," *Or* 29 (1960): 392–422; and idem, *Egyptian Tenses* (Jerusalem: Central, 1965). For more on standard theory, see Leo Depuydt, "The Standard Theory of the 'Emphatic' Forms in Classical (Middle) Egyptian: A Historical Survey," *OLP* 14 (1983): 13–53; and James P. Allen, *Middle Egyptian: An Introduction to the Language and Culture of Hieroglyphs* (Cambridge: Cambridge University Press, 2000), 389–410.

[10] Elmar Edel, *Altägyptische Grammatik* (AnOr 34, 39; Rome: Biblical Institute Press, 1955–1964); Gertie Englund and Paul John Frandsen, *Crossroad: Chaos or the Beginning of a New Paradigm: Papers from the Conference on Egyptian Grammar, Helsingor 28–30 May 1986* (Copenhagen: Carsten Niebuhr Institute of Ancient Near East Studies, 1986); Paul John Frandsen, *An Outline of the Late Egyptian Verbal System* (Copenhagen: Akademisk, 1974); Jaroslav Černý and Sarah Israelit-Groll, assisted by Christopher Eyre, *A Late Egyptian Grammar* (Studia Pohl, series maior 4; Rome: Biblical Institute Press, 1975); D. Mueller, *A Concise Introduction to Middle Egyptian Grammar* (Lethbridge: unpublished, 1975).

[11] Thomas O. Lambdin, *Introduction to Sahidic Coptic* (Macon, Ga: Mercer University Press, 1983); Jozef Vergote, *Grammaire Copte* (2 vols.; Leuven: Peeters, 1973–1983; repr., 1992); W. C. Till, *Koptisches Grammatik (Saïdischer Dialekt)* (Leipzig: Harrassowitz, 1955).

at the end of the century for scholars such as A. Loprieno and F. Junge to bring language study in Egyptology to the peak of modernity.[12]

Lexical studies owe a similar debt to the Berlin school. A dictionary project, conceived by A. Erman at the close of the nineteenth century, came to fruition with the publication of the *Wörterbuch der ägyptischer Sprache*.[13] Without the vast effort at text collection entailed by this enterprise, subsequent lexica could not have been compiled.[14]

1.3. HISTORY

Egyptian belongs to the Afro-Asiatic family of languages and occupies a middle ground, both in terms of geography and structure, between the two "wings," African and Asiatic.[15] Its area of origin has plausibly been located on the lower Nile between the first cataract and the apex of the Delta, within a time-frame of roughly 12,000 to 8000 B.P.[16] While other languages of the family may boast a comparable antiquity, Egyptian enjoys the distinction of being the earliest to appear in writing. The origins of the script are to be sought in the advent of complex society in the Nile Valley at the close of the fourth millennium B.C.E. and in the demands of an incipient bureaucracy for graphic means of enumerating, commemorating, and identifying personnel and commodities.[17] The early attempts

---

[12] Antonio Loprieno, *Ancient Egyptian: A Linguistic Introduction* (Cambridge: Cambridge University Press, 1995); Friedrich Junge, *Einführung in die Grammatik des Neuägyptischen* (Wiesbaden: Harrassowitz, 1996).

[13] Adolf Erman and H. Grapow, *Wörterbuch der ägyptischer Sprache* (5 vols.; Leipzig: Hinrichs, 1926–1931).

[14] E.g., Walter E. Crum, *Coptic Dictionary* (Oxford: Clarendon, 1939; repr., Oxford: Oxford University Press, 1990); Wolja Erichsen, *Demotisches Glossar* (Copenhagen: Munksgaard, 1954); Raymond O. Faulkner, *A Concise Dictionary of Middle Egyptian* (Oxford: Griffith Institute, 1962).

[15] Marcel S. R. Cohen, *Essai comparatif sur le vocabulaire et la phonétique du chamito-sémitique* (Paris: Champion, 1947); J. H. Greenberg, *Studies in African Linguistic Classification* (Branford, Conn.: Compass, 1955); C. T. Hodge, ed., *Afro-Asiatic: A Survey* (The Hague: Mouton, 1971); K. Petrácek, *Altägyptisch, Hamito-semitisch und ihre Beziehungen zu einigen Sprachfamilie in Afrika und Asien: Vergleichende Studien* (Prague: Universita Karlova, 1988); H. J. Polotsky, "Egyptian," in *Collected Papers* (Jerusalem: Magnes, 1971), 320–28; J. Vergote, "Egyptian," in *Current Trends in Linguistics* (ed. T. A. Seboek; The Hague: Mouton, 1970).

[16] I. M. Diakonoff, "The Earliest Semitic Society: Linguistic Data," *JSS* 43 (1998): 209–20.

[17] W. Helck, "Gedanken zum Ursprung der ägyptischen Schrift," *Mélanges Mokhtar* 1 (1985): 395–408; J. D. Ray, "The Emergence of Writing in Egypt," *World Archaeology* 17/3 (1986): 307–16.

at simple representation of referents were followed fairly quickly by the development of indexical, symbolic, and phonetic sign-types, so that by the middle of the First Dynasty, the script had graduated to the status of a vehicle capable of recording any level of speech.

Old Egyptian (floruit ca. 2700–2200 B.C.E.) represents the language of the Memphite region. Here the earliest paramount chiefs had laid claim to a united country and had founded their residence. Their speech and that of their entourage reflects a "courtly" register cultivated by the royal family and the aristocracy.[18] As the Old Kingdom draws to a close, a vernacular can be detected in the speech attributed to the lower classes in the relief art of the time. With the demise of the aristocratic lifestyle and the Memphite monarchy around 2200 B.C.E., this vernacular, *Middle Egyptian,* remains as the only acceptable dialect.[19] The kings of the Twelfth Dynasty (ca. 1991–1786 B.C.E.) promoted Middle Egyptian as a literary vehicle. It is during this period and shortly thereafter that many of the novellas, hymns, and didactic pieces that Egyptians ever after considered "classics" were written. The shape of the language at this stage of its development exerted an irresistible attraction on "literati" and rhetoricians centuries later, and even in Ptolemaic times scribes reproduced Middle Egyptian or attempted to compose in it.[20] As early as the Thirteenth Dynasty signs of diglossia herald the presence of a patois, or perhaps better a proletarian argot, inexorably diverging from the static literary register. The differences encompassed phonemic modification as well as new or remodelled forms in grammar and lexicon. Between approximately 1550 and 1450 B.C.E. the creation of an empire in Africa and Asia brought new linguistic influences from such language groups as Nubian, Canaanite, Akkadian, and Hittite.

In post-Amarna times *Late Egyptian,* possibly derived immediately from the dialect of the eastern Delta, was sanctioned by the outgoing

---

[18] This is somewhat different from the language of the Pyramid Texts, which may have striven for an archaic or sacerdotal cast. See James P. Allen, *The Inflection of the Verb in the Pyramid Texts* (Bibliotheca Aegyptia 2/1–2; Malibu, Calif.: Undena, 1974); and the articles in Serge Sauneron, ed., *Textes et langages de l'Égypte pharaonique: Cent cinquante années derecherches, 1822–1972: Hommage Jean-Francois Champollion* (3 vols.; Cairo: Institut français d'archéologie orientale, 1973).

[19] Elke Blumenthal, "Die literarische Verarbeitung der Übergangszeit zwischen Altem und Mittlerem Reich," in *Ancient Egyptian Literature: History and Forms* (ed. Antonio Loprieno; Leiden: Brill, 1996), 105–36.

[20] See the articles by Antonio Loprieno, "Defining Egyptian Literature," and Pascal Vernus, "Langue littéraire et diglossie," in Loprieno, *Ancient Egyptian Literature,* 39–58 and 555–66.

Eighteenth Dynasty as a language of business, commerce, epistolography, and government.[21] So drastic had been the phonological changes Egyptian had undergone in the preceding six centuries, and so numerous the loanwords entering the language from Asia, that Late Egyptian developed a redundant "syllabic orthography," itself derived from Old and Middle Egyptian scribal attempts to transcribe foreign words. By the end of the New Kingdom even monumental inscriptions, written in the "bastard" Middle Egyptian of the period, were couched wholly in the new syllabic system. Cursive scripts had, from the dawn of history, always existed side by side with the formal hieroglyphs, but the New Kingdom "hieratic" was an especially florid version, and one ideally suited to syllabic orthography. Much Late Egyptian material has come down in this cursive form, which continued to be used for literary creations well into Ptolemaic times.[22]

The evolution of the language between approximately 1050 and 700 B.C.E. is barely reflected in the meager texts that have survived. But increasingly numerous papyri and inscriptions from the Kushite-Saite period (ca. 711–525 B.C.E.) help in reconstruction. During this so-called "dark age," Late Egyptian entered a sort of intermediate stage, characterized by a refinement of the verbal system and the introduction of an abbreviated cursive called "abnormal hieratic." With the establishment of the Twenty-Sixth Dynasty in the Delta, abnormal hieratic was superceded by an even more abbreviated script, a veritable shorthand called *Demotic,* which served the interests of a revived bureaucracy and priesthood.[23] The term *Demotic* also is applied to that stage of the language that the script was used to convey, and this double usage extends down to the obsolescence of the script in the fourth century C.E. As pointed out above, the imposition of Aramaic by the Persians and Greek by the Ptolemies on the Egyptian administration proved fatal to the survival of the script, if not the language. By Roman times Demotic had become a "purified and filtered vernacular."[24]

Although attempts to transcribe Egyptian into Greek characters, especially in the onomasticon, date back to Ptolemaic times, success came in

---

[21] H. J. Polotsky, "Notre connaissance du neo-égyptien," in Sauneron, *Textes et langages de l'Égypte pharaonique,* 2:133–41.

[22] Ursula Verhoeven, "Von hieratischen Literaturwerken in der Spätzeit," in *Literatur und Politik im pharaonischen Ägypten* (ed. Jan Assmann and E. Blumenthal; Cairo: Institut français d'archéologie orientale, 1999): 255–66.

[23] W. J. Tait, "Demotic Literature and Egyptian Society," in *Life in a Multi-cultural Society: Egypt from Cambyses to Constantine and Beyond* (SAOC 51; ed. Janet H. Johnson; Chicago: Oriental Institute Press, 1990), 303–10.

[24] J. D. Ray, "How Demotic Is Demotic?" in *Acta Demotica* (ed. E. Besciani; Pisa: Giardini, 1994) = *EVO* 17 (1994): 251–64.

the third century C.E. with the adaptation of the alphabet to the phonemic needs of the Egyptian language. The nascent Christian church capitalized on the invention of this Coptic script, and a considerable effort was expended in translating scriptural and liturgical texts into the Coptic language.[25] The latter marks the third to fourth–centuries C.E. stage in the written language, at several removes from the now obsolete Demotic. The lack of any central scribal authority or tradition to promote a single grammar and lexicon means that, for the first time in the history of the Egyptian language, scholars are able to study local dialect.

1.4. STRUCTURE

Egyptian is beset by a number of problems most other languages do not have. The lack, for the most part, of any indication of vocalization (in Old and Middle Egyptian, to a lesser extent in Late Egyptian) has successfully concealed the presence of distinct verb forms. The absence of textual corpora from certain periods prevents us from appreciating linguistic change and thus being able to establish cladograms and transformation series. The failure to take into account shared semantic space has sometimes led scholars to postulate forms and patterns that in reality do not exist.[26]

The Egyptian *root system* shows radicals ranging from bi-literals to quinquiliterals, many represented by West Semitic. Gemination and reduplication are common. Causative preformative *s* and reflexive preformative *n* occur as in Semitic.

Nouns are formed from roots in several ways. Although the absence of vocalization markers deprives us of certainty, it is likely that such forms as *quṭl, quṭul,* and *qaṭil* occurred in Egyptian as elsewhere in the family. Nouns formed with preformative *m-* of place, manner, or instrument are common, as are those with an *r-* augment in similar position. The noun distinguishes two genders—masculine and feminine (in *-at*), the latter doubling as a neuter—and three numbers: singular, dual, and plural. There are no case endings. Bound constructions are regular, but Egyptian also possesses an "indirect genitive" construction, mediated by a *nisbe* possessive adjective.[27] When attributive, adjectives follow their nouns and agree in

---

[25] M. Krause, "Koptische Sprache," *LÄ* 3:731–37.

[26] On what follows, see in general the works of Polotsky listed in the bibliography; also Antonio Loprieno, *Ancient Egyptian;* Pascal Vernus, *Future at Issue: Tense, Mood, and Aspect in Middle Egyptian: Studies in Syntax and Semantics* (Yale Egyptological Studies 4; New Haven, Conn.: Yale University Press, 1990); and idem, "Procèssus de grammaticalisation dans la langue égyptienne," *CRAI* (1998): 191–209.

[27] Leo Depuydt, "Egyptian 'Split' Genitives and Related Phenomena: Exotic Debris from Conflicting Forces," *Mus* 112 (1999): 273–300.

number and gender; when predicative, they occupy initial position and show a constant masculine singular. When in subjunct position, a special adjective verb replaces the predicate adjective. Egyptian is fond of the *nisbe*-adjective, as is Arabic, especially those formed from prepositions, and these enter commonly into titles.

Verbal nouns fall under the categories of infinitive, negatival complement, participle, *sḏm.ty.fy* form, and relative form. With the exception of the negatival complement, all can occupy N-position in most patterns. Infinitives show either masculine or feminine forms, the negatival complement only masculine. Participles and relative forms are adjectival, denoting actor and object of verbal functions. The *sḏm.ty.fy* is regularly the equivalent of a future participle in translation languages.[28]

Pronouns show interrogative, deictic, and personal forms. The last may be divided into independent (normally occupying initial position), dependent (in postpositive position), or suffixal. In Late Egyptian one of the deictics has graduated to the status of definite article.

The *narrative verbal system,* especially during the Old and Middle Egyptian phases, continues to be debated in scholarly circles. In general it has been assumed that Old and Middle Egyptian show an aspectual system—from action standpoint—with incipient tenses in the process of developing, while Late Egyptian is characterized by a consistent shift to a tense system.[29] The narrative verb in Old and Middle Egyptian is essentially object-prominent and synthetic, building the paradigm on the basis of suffixes and infixes. Late Egyptian generates tenses by recourse to a periphrasis employing the pattern conjugation base-subject-adverbial comment and could be said to be subject-prominent. Old and Middle Egyptian forms include an aorist, a perfect, a "prospective" (used in subjunct position), and an "emphatic" form.[30] The passive is expressed by two suffixal forms by recourse to an infix or (in later times) by the indefinite use of the third plural.

Negation is expressed in several ways. Negative particles preceding the verbal statement negate either the verb or the nexus between subject and predicate. In Old Egyptian a word signifying "completion" backgrounds and negates the following proposition. Nominal forms of the verb are negated by a special "negative" verb.

---

[28] Leo Depuydt, "Twixt Relative Verb Form and Passive Participle in Egyptian," *ZDMG* 146 (1996): 1–24.

[29] In addition to Vernus, *Future at Issue,* see John B. Callender, "Problems of Tense and Aspect in Egyptian," *ZÄS* 113 (1986): 8–18.

[30] Friedrich Junge, *"Emphasis" and Sentential Meaning in Middle Egyptian* (Göttinger Orientforschungen 4/20; Wiesbaden: Harrassowitz, 1989).

Numerous *modal indicators* serve to nuance meaning. These include enclitic and initial particles (used to emphasize, foreground, modify clause status, and provide adverbial comment), infixes in verbal forms of consequence or sequence, and tense converters. These last, in Late Egyptian especially, are employed to provide the language (often in agglutinative sequences) with gnomic, circumstantial, preterite, and relative patterns.

The study of syntax and morphosyntax is by no means complete, and here only a few broad remarks must suffice.[31] Lacking case endings, word order and prosody assume an overriding importance in Egyptian. While prosody remains largely beyond the competence of modern researchers, word order can be closely analyzed. In terms of the use of finite narrative verbs, position (initial or medial) assumes considerable importance. Verbal sentences are usually constructed on the sequence particle/converter-verb-subject-object-adverbial comment. Nonverbal patterns show both subject and object prominence. In all patterns fronting is common. While subordination can be clearly indicated by the use of prepositions, conjunctions, and particles, parataxis is much more usual than is commonly admitted, and the *inta mabsut ana mabsut* construction is regular.

2. SIGNIFICANCE FOR THE BIBLE

In the realm of language and literature, as in other spheres of cultural expression, the Israelites found themselves both geographically and spiritually within the *Kulturgebiet* of Mesopotamia. There is no clear, fundamental debt to northeast Africa in intellectual heritage or material culture. Those cultural elements from Egypt that have been demonstrated were borrowed only sporadically and made but superficial impact on the Israelites. This has meant that, in terms of cognate languages and cultures to be selected by the student of the Hebrew Bible to "round out" his or her approach, those from the Tigris-Euphrates and Syria have been preferred to their counterparts in Egypt. Akkadian, Ugaritic, and Aramaic have long since proven of far greater help than Egyptian in elucidating the minutiae of the Hebrew text.

That having been said, in the realm of *form* there are some Egyptian genres that furnish exemplars of equal value to Akkadian pieces as comparanda. Of particular importance is the *Märchen* or *Novella*. The Joseph story especially is greatly illumined through comparison with a plot motif common from the second quarter of the first millennium B.C.E. This involves the "rags-to-riches" theme in which a wise, divinely inspired young man

---

[31] In general, see Junge, *"Emphasis" and Sentential Meaning;* and Leo Depuydt, "Sentence Pattern and Verb Form: Egyptian Grammar Since Polotsky," *Mus* 108 (1995): 39–48.

saves Pharaoh and the entire nation when catastrophe looms. A related theme in the Joseph story—the Potiphar's wife incident—enjoys numerous parallels from Egypt to Greece. In the sphere of lyric, Egypt offers numerous points of contact with Hebrew belletristics. New Kingdom love poetry has a bearing on the Song of Songs in both form and content. The well-known type of lament dubbed the "penitential psalm" finds a striking parallel in Egypt of the Ramesside age; appeals to god for forgiveness and healing and thankgiving for salvation come from the workers' community at Deir el-Medina. Perhaps it is to Egypt also that biblical scholars should look for the closest parallels to Hebrew proverbial literature. The study of the "wisdom" of such legendary Egyptian worthies as Ptahhotpe and Anii will be found especially rewarding. Amenemope, of course, is paraphrased in Proverbs and Ipuwer in part of the "Song of Hannah" in 1 Sam 2.

Other Egyptian genres have relevance only remotely, if at all. Declamations to or on behalf of the deity and predictions of what is to come will be found in Egyptian literature, but the cultural differences between Egypt and the Levant render connection to or influence upon Hebrew prophecy highly suspect. The *Königsnovelle* (a *Tendenz* in Egyptian royal propaganda rather than a form) has been compared to certain biblical accounts, especially the "Succession Narrative" in 2 Samuel, but the comparisons fail to convince. Again, the fable is known from ancient Egypt, but examples have little relevance for material in the Hebrew Bible. No parallels exist in the Bible to Egyptian prosody and satire or to the voluminous corpora of religious, mythological, and magical texts. Parallels to Egyptian cosmogony in Gen 1 and to solar hymns in Ps 104 are exceptional.

The best-known connection between Egypt and the Bible concerns the origin traditions for Israel in Genesis and Exodus, specifically the stories of Joseph and the exodus. I have treated this matter in detail previously and cannot repeat that treatment here.[32] It is not a matter of comparative historiography, since there is simply no mention in Egyptian historical records of any of the events described in these biblical stories. As suggested above, the Joseph story is a *composition* rather than a *record,* a novella, probably created sometime during the late Judean monarchy or the exile (seventh to sixth century B.C.E.). The story of the exodus contains dim memories from the Canaanite perspective of the occupation and expulsion of the Hyksos, including the name of the illustrious Hyksos ruler Yaʿaqob(har). But these have been elaborated and fictionalized by the biblical writers again in the seventh to sixth centuries (the Saite period in Egypt and into the Persian period).

---

[32] Donald B. Redford, *Egypt, Canaan, and Israel in Ancient Times* (Princeton, N.J.: Princeton University Press, 1992).

3. ANCIENT SOURCES, MODERN RESOURCES

The surviving corpus of ancient Egyptian texts tends to be somewhat spotty and imbalanced, at least in terms of the wealth of writings that once existed. "Checklists" of books, mainly from temples, but also from administrative locations, apprise us of the sometime presence of extensive temple libraries, government archives, and private collections, the growth of which over the centuries remained largely uninterrupted, in contrast to the checkered fate of similar *bibliotheca* in Western Asia. But almost all of these suffered dispersal or destruction in the trauma of successive invasions (especially that of the Persians in 343 B.C.E.), government restrictions under Rome, and the Christian persecution of the native religion.

3.1. ADMINISTRATIVE TEXTS

Since the hieroglyphic script was in origin devised as a tool of the new phenomenon of the civil service of a complex society, it is appropriate to begin our survey with government documents. First and foremost are the royal decrees and rescripts that issued as transcriptions of royal statements, copied on papyrus and sealed in the king's presence. None of this extensive corpus of legal documents survives, but a significant number of hieroglyphic copies exist on stone set up for display and public reference. Annals were kept on perishable media (wood, ivory) during the Old Kingdom and are represented by derivative labels (First Dynasty) used to date the contents of containers and store chambers. Toward the close of the Old Kingdom, complete sets of annals were published on stone and set up in Memphis, the capital. The Middle Kingdom witnessed the evolution of a new form of recording, namely, the "day-book" or journal, a combination of an account book and diary, which was kept by such institutions as the king's house, the temples, and the army.[33] Many royal stelae (especially "Triumph-"stelae and building inscriptions) derive ultimately from day-book entries.

Public display for purposes of information, dissemination, and societal admonition involved the transfer to a stone or wood medium of administrative texts originally on papyrus and the creation of new genres on the basis of oral tradition.[34] Thus, beginning in the late First

---

[33] Redford, *Pharaonic King-Lists, Annals and Daybooks.* One good example is Papyrus Boulaq XVIII.

[34] See W. Helck, *Altägyptische Aktenkunde des 3. und 2. Jahrtausends v. Chr.* (Munich: Deutscher Kunstverlag, 1974); and Donald B. Redford, "Scribe and Speaker: The Interface between Written and Oral Tradition in Ancient Egypt," in *Writings and Speech in Israelite and Ancient Near Eastern Prophecy* (ed. Ehud Ben Zvi and Michael H. Floyd; Atlanta: Society of Biblical Literature, 2000), 145–218.

Intermediate Period and continuing through the end of the New Kingdom, the practice was followed of copying *verbatim* on a stela the
speech of the king delivered at a royal seance. A similar oral tradition,
probably within a court setting and designed to adulate the king, led in
the Eighteenth Dynasty to the creation of a type of stela called the "Compilation of the Mighty Deeds" of Pharaoh. By the Nineteenth Dynasty a
veritable genre of encomium had come into being, to be sung to harp
accompaniment, in which each stanza of grandiose epithets terminated
in the double cartouche of the king. There was also a more elaborate
and discursive hymnody, clearly produced at court, which eulogized
royal accoutrements and lauded the monarch on his accession or the
anniversary thereof.[35]

Loosely related to the above are the aforementioned "Triumph"-stelae,
often derived remotely from a day-book entry, in which the mighty deeds
of Pharaoh are recounted in high-flown style. The "triumphs" frequently
assume the form of records of construction. Public display—often with
pious intent—coupled with the desire for permanent reference, explains
the Egyptian penchant for inscribing records of mining or quarrying expe-
ditions or private commissions.[36]

Such stelae as we have just passed in review were often placed at the
approach to temple pylons, and the latter, along with adjacent wall surfaces, provided ideal space for complementary texts and scenes. Thus,
depictions of head-smiting and formal presentation of enemy captives to
the gods frequently adorn pylons. These are often accompanied by
toponym lists, purporting to represent the far-flung conquests of the king.
During the New Kingdom there developed a "battle art" consisting of a
sequence of relief scenes with accompanying text, depicting a military
campaign from start to finish.[37]

Administrative texts on papyrus or ostraca have an uneven history of
preservation. From the Old Kingdom come the Abusir Papyri, account texts

---

[35] A. Erman, *Hymnen an das Diadem der Pharaonen* (Berlin, 1911); Alan H.
Gardiner, "A Pharaonic Encomium," *JEA* 41 (1955): 30.

[36] J. Couyat and P. Montet, *Les inscriptions hiéroglyphiques et hiératiques du
Ouaïdi Hammamat* (Cairo: Institut français d'archéologie orientale, 1912); Alan H.
Gardiner and T. Eric Peet, *The Inscriptions of Sinai* (ed. Jaroslav Černý; 2 vols.; Memoir of the Egypt Exploration Society 36, 45; London: Egypt Exploration Society,
1952–1955); Georges Goyon, *Nouvelles inscriptions rupestres du Wadi Hammamat*
(Paris: Adrien Maisonneuve, 1957); Karl-Joachim Seyfried, *Beiträge zu den Expeditionen des Mittleren Reiches in die Ost-Wüste* (Hildesheimer ägyptologische Beiträge
15; Hildesheim: Gerstenberg, 1981); Zbigniew Zába, *The Rock Inscriptions of Lower
Nubia: Czechoslovak Concession* (Prague: Charles University, 1974).

[37] S. Curto, "Krieg," *LÄ* 3:785–86.

from the pyramid temple of Neferirkare I (twenty-fifth century B.C.E.);[38] and from the Middle Kingdom the Kahun papyri, a tax-assessor's journal, dispatches from a Nubian fort, and accounts from a building site.[39] The New Kingdom has yielded considerably more, especially from the late Nineteenth and Twentieth Dynasties (ca. 1250–1070 B.C.E.). We now dispose of tax-assessors' journals, tax receipts, transcripts of treason trials, transcripts of tomb robbery trials, and commission reports and inventories.[40] From Deir el-Medina, the village of the workers responsible for carving the royal tombs in the Kings' Valley, comes a wealth of ostraca and papyri that overlap the official administration and the private sector.[41] Of interest to economic historians are the legions of bills of sale, promissory notes, receipts, salary sheets, and food dockets that come largely from the west bank at Thebes and Amarna.[42]

3.2. BELLETRISTICS

What we might classify as "belles lettres" has a solid basis of origin in oral composition.[43] But a number of pieces have survived in written form, either as *aides memoires* or school texts.[44] The category of *Märchen,* or

---

[38] Paula Posener-Kriéger, *Les archives du temple funéraire de Néferirkareï-Kakaï (Le papyrus d'Abousir)* (Cairo: Institut français d'archéologie orientale, 1976).

[39] On these documents, see, respectively, Stephen Quirke, ed., *Middle Egyptian Studies* (New Malden, Surrey: SIA Publications, 1991); P. C. Smither, "A Tax-Assessor's Journal of the Middle Kingdom," *JEA* 27 (1941): 74–77; idem, "The Semna Despatches," *JEA* 31 (1945): 3–19; and William Kelly Simpson, *Papyrus Reisner I–IV* (4 vols.; Boston: Museum of Fine Arts, 1963–1986).

[40] For the first two of these, see Alan H. Gardiner, *Ramesside Administrative Documents* (Leiden: P. Lund, Humphries, 1940). On the others, see Susan Redford, *The Harem Conspiracy: A Study of the Murder of Ramesses III* (Dekalb: Northern Illinois University Press, 2002); T. E. Peet, *The Great Tomb-Robbery Papyri of the Egyptian XXth Dynasty* (Oxford: Oxford University Press, 1930); Pierre Grandet, *Le Papyrus Harris I, BM 9999* (2 vols.; Cairo: Institut français d'archéologie orientale, 1994).

[41] Leonard H. Lesko, *Pharaoh's Workers: The Villagers of Deir el-Medina* (Ithaca, N.Y.: Cornell University Press, 1994); Raphael Ventura, *Living in a City of the Dead* (OBO 69; Freiburg: Universitätsverlag, 1986).

[42] Jac J. Janssen, *Commodity Prices from the Ramessid Period* (Leiden: Brill, 1975); David A. Warburton, *State and Economy in Ancient Egypt: Fiscal Vocabulary of the New Kingdom* (OBO 151; Freiburg: Universitätsverlag, 1997).

[43] Egyptian *sdd n rmt* translates almost literally as "popular oral transmission" or even folklore. Cf. Redford, "Scribe and Speaker."

[44] Translations of the following pieces may be found in A. K. Grayson and Donald B. Redford, *Papyrus and Tablet* (Englewood Cliffs, N.J.: Prentice-Hall, 1973);

novella, a short story usually with timeless setting and anonymous characters, is represented by the Shipwrecked Sailor, the Doomed Prince, and the
initial pericope of the Tale of Two Brothers. Wonder tales from history,
associated with magicians or especially clever individuals, focus on a single
novel ploy or trick, such as bringing slaughtered animals to life, rolling back
the waters, animating images of noisome beasts, or deceiving the enemy by
the Ali-Baba trick. Adventure tales, of verisimilitude if not historicity, are
represented by the Story of Sinuhe, the Tale of Wenamun, the Moscow Letter, and sundry fragments. Both tales of magicians and adventure stories are
known to continue as popular genres into the Late Period and the Greco-
Roman era. But by then they take on a somber cast, centered upon the
theme of "the hero who saves the nation" or a fate that cannot be averted.
Some examples from the Ptolemaic period, such as the Amazon Romance
and the Armor of Inaros, show strong Greek influence

A large portion of ancient Egyptian narrative belongs within a category that we might call "mythological tales." Myth, as it appears in an
Egyptian context, remains yet to be defined and delineated adequately,
but it is fair to say that the category arises out of the twofold need to
probe the essence of the supernatural ("... in his name of ...") and etio-
logically to explain cultic norms.[45] However, while myth in other parts of
the Near East (e.g., Mesopotamia) has achieved graduation to an aesthetic
plane and masquerades in the guise of full-blown epic, Egyptian myths
are most frequently found as "asides," more or less extended in written
form, but by no means claiming the status of *editio princeps*. Most frequently they are found, baldly told, as magical incantations within larger
corpora, such as hemerologies, the Coffin Texts, or the Book of Going
Forth by Day (see below). But a few take on an extended almost "literary"
form with picaresque or even pornographic overtones.[46] In spite of the

---

Miriam Lichtheim, *Ancient Egyptian Literature: A Book of Readings* (3 vols.; Berke-
ley and Los Angeles: University of California Press, 1973–1980); and William Kelly
Simpson, *The Literature of Ancient Egypt: An Anthology of Stories, Instructions, and
Poetry* (new ed.; New Haven, Conn.: Yale University Press, 1973). For Middle Kingdom pieces, see especially Richard B. Parkinson, "Teachings, Discourses and Tales
from the Middle Kingdom" in Quirke, *Middle Egyptian Studies,* 123–40; idem,
Voices from Ancient Egypt: An Anthology of Middle Kingdom Writings (Norman:
University of Oklahoma Press, 1991). Other specific treatments are listed in the bib-
liography.

[45] Eberhard Otto, *Das Verhältnis vom Rite und Mythen im ägyptischen* (Heidelberg: Winter, 1958); Siegfried Schott, *Mythe und Mythenbildung im alten Ägypten*
(Leipzig: Hinrichs, 1945).

[46] For examples, see Michel Broze, *Les aventures d'Horus et Seth dans le papyrus
Chester Beatty I: mythe et roman en Egypte ancienne* (Leuven: Peeters, 1996); Erik

apparently cavalier treatment of these themes, many of these narratives attained a quasi-"official," canonical status.

One genre that achieved some degree of popularity during the Middle and New Kingdoms was the "lament" (*nhwt*), such as those of Ipuwer and Khakheperresonbu. This was couched in a monologue, in which a lector-priest or some other wise man bemoaned the lamentable condition of anarchy the land was experiencing. Occasionally the piece was coupled (in promotion of dynastic acceptance) with a prophecy of better times to come.[47] Formal "prophecies" (*sr*) enjoyed a currency during the First Intermediate Period and experienced a revival in the latest period of Egypt's history, when deliverance from foreign oppression loomed large.[48]

Other genres, though once popular, are now poorly represented in the surviving corpus. Fables occur, but not in the same profusion as in other cultures; allegory is rare. Dialogues, popular didactic forms in the Middle and New Kingdoms, survive in such pieces as the debate between a man and his *ba* over the efficacy of mortuary arrangements.[49] The existence of "dramatic texts" as a legitimate category is still debated, the myth of Horus of Edfu being the most famous.[50]

Hornung, *Der ägyptische Mythos von der Himmelskuh: Eine Ätiologie des Unvollkommenen* (2d ed.; OBO 46; Freiburg: Universitätsverlag, 1982); A. Massart, "The Egyptian Geneva Papyrus MAH 15274," *MDAI* 15 (1957): 172–85; Alessandro Roccati, "Une légende égyptienne d'Anat," *REg* 24 (1972): 152–59; John Wilson, trans., "Isis and the Hidden Name of Re," *ANET*, 12–14.

[47] Cf. the Prophecy of Neferty: E. Blumenthal, "Die Prophezeihung des Neferti," *ZÄS* 109 (1982): 1–27; W. Helck, *Die Prophezeihung des Nfr.tj* (Kleine ägyptische Texte; 2d ed.; Wiesbaden: Harrassowitz, 1970).

[48] E.g., the prophecy of the Potter: L. Koenen, "Die Prophezeihung des 'Topfers,'" *ZPE* 2 (1968), 178–209; and the prophecy of the Ram: László Kákosy, "Prophecies of Ram-Gods," *AcOr* 19 (1966): 341–58.

[49] Winfried Barta, *Das Gespräch eines Mannes mit seinem Ba (Papyrus Berlin 3024)* (Berlin: Hessling, 1969); Odette Renaud, *Le dialogue du déséspéré avec son aïme: Une interprétation littéraire* (Geneva: Société d'égyptologie, 1991); V. A. Tobin, "A Re-assessment of the Lebensmüde," *BO* 48 (1991): 341–63.

[50] Hartwig Altenmüller, "Zur Lesung und Deutung des dramatischen Ramesseumspapyrus," *JEOL* 19 (1964–1965): 421–42; Etienne Drioton, *Le Texte dramatique d'Edfou* (Cairo: Institut français d'archéologie orientale, 1948; repr., Cairo: Organisation égyptienne générale du livre, 1984); H. W. Fairman, *The Triumph of Horus: The Oldest Play in the World* (Berkeley and Los Angeles: University of California Press, 1974); J. Gwyn Griffiths, "Horusmythe," *LÄ* 3:54–59; L. Mikhail, "The Egyptological Approach to Drama in Ancient Egypt: Is It Time for a Revision?" *GM* 77 (1984): 25–34; Kurt Sethe, *Dramatische Texte zu altägyptischen Mysterienspielen* (Leipzig: Hinrichs, 1928).

While most of the texts reviewed above display metrical arrangement, there exists a substantial corpus of true lyrical creations.[51] Many fall under the category of *hymnody* and belong within a cultic context (see below), but two types might be classed by us moderns as "secular." One finds its origin in songs at parties, surviving examples often enjoying a mortuary context within tombs. These "harpers' songs" show a scene in which an accomplished bard, often old and blind, serenades the tomb owner to the accompaniment of the harp. The extemporized lyric sometimes contains a *carpe diem* tone that calls into question the certainty of the conventional belief system.[52] The other, love poetry, comparable in form and content to that of Mesopotamia and the Levant, is found in three New Kingdom corpora but clearly enjoyed popularity over an extended span of time.[53]

3.3. WISDOM AND DIDACTIC TEXTS

One term used widely (and somewhat loosely) by the ancient Egyptians was *seboyet,* "teaching," a term roughly comparable semantically to what elsewhere in the Near East would be called "wisdom" (Heb. *ḥokmâ*). One of the principal forms *seboyet* took was the "father-to-son" chat, in which an old man gives his offspring good, practical, and worldly wisdom on how to get ahead in life. Seven such exemplars of "Teaching" became very popular and range in age of composition from the end of the third millennium B.C.E. to Roman times: Ptahhotpe, Gemnikai, Merikare, Amenemhet I, Anii, Loyalist literature, Amenemope, and Onkhshesonqy.[54] But in the minds of the Egyptians, *seboyet* also encompassed such disparate genres as "discourses" or monologues, panegyrics, policy statements, teaching aids, word lists, and even satyrical pieces.

Didactic literature, whether within the professions or for private use, is represented by a number of papyri, but many more examples are known by name only. Medical papyri fall within this category. Six major books dealing with such branches of medicine as surgery, gynecology and child birth, mechanical injuries, gastronomical problems, ophthalmology, and

---

[51] John L. Foster, *Echoes of Egyptian Voices: An Anthology of Ancient Egyptian Poetry* (Norman: University of Oklahoma Press, 1992).

[52] Jan Assmann, "Fest des Augenblicks—Verheissung der Dauer: Die Kontroverse der ägyptischen Harfnerlieder," in *Fragen an die altägyptischen Literatur* (ed. Jan Assmann, Erika Feucht, and Reinhard Grieshammer; Wiesbaden: Reichert, 1977), 55–84; Michael V. Fox, "A Study of Antef," *Or* 46 (1977): 393–423; Miriam Lichtheim, "The Songs of the Harpers," *JNES* 4 (1945): 178–212.

[53] Michael V. Fox, *The Song of Songs and the Ancient Egyptian Love Songs* (Madison: University of Wisconsin Press, 1985).

[54] Detailed treatments of each of these works are listed in the bibliography.

pharmacology are preserved.[55] Problems in engineering are touched on in the Rhind Mathematical Papyrus and Papyrus Anastasi I.[56] Prognostication by dreams is the burden of the Chester Beatty "Dream-Book," and prediction by astronomical omina, though a late arrival in Egypt, is addressed by sundry Demotic fragments.[57] Eliciting the divine will through oracles was endemic in Egyptian religion, and some fine accounts of oracles have been preserved.[58] Equally popular were the "self-help" books for daily use and guidance, the hemerologies, which advised the individual on day-to-day comportment on the basis of the cultic associations of a particular calendar date.[59]

3.4. PRIVATE TEXTS

In the realm of purely private texts the "autobiography," conventionally so-called, looms large. This piece of self-laudation is inevitably found either in a mortuary context, where it is couched within the "Address to the Living" (i.e., visitors to the tomb) or in a statue inscription to be set up in the ambulatory of a temple. When in a tomb setting the text is often amplified by the addition of scenes (painted or in relief) illustrating the speaker's life and appointments. Exemplars range in relative abundance throughout all periods of Egypt's history. Some, especially in the Late Period, approach the length and character of an *apologia pro vita sua*.[60]

---

[55] John F. Nunn, *Ancient Egyptian Medicine* (Norman: University of Oklahoma Press, 1996).

[56] On the former, see Gay Robins and Charles Shute, *The Rhind Mathematical Papyrus: An Ancient Egyptian Text* (New York: Dover, 1987); on the latter, Hans-Werner Fischer-Elfert, *Die satirische Streitschrift des Papyrus Anastasi I: Übersetzung und Kommentar* (Wiesbaden: Harrassowitz, 1986).

[57] Alan H. Gardiner, *Hieratic Papyri in the British Museum:* 3d series: *Chester Beatty Gift* (London: British Museum Publications, 1935); George R. Hughes, "A Demotic Astrological Text," *JNES* 10 (1951): 256–64; Richard A. Parker, *A Vienna Demotic Papyrus on Eclipse- and Lunar-Omina* (Providence, R.I.: Brown University Press, 1959).

[58] E.g., Richard A. Parker, *A Saite Oracle Papyrus from Thebes in the Brooklyn Museum* (Providence, R.I.: Brown University Press, 1962).

[59] Abd el-Mohsen Bakir, *The Cairo Calendar no. 86637* (Cairo: General Organization for Government Printing Offices, 1966).

[60] Ricardo A. Caminos, *The Chronicle of Prince Osorkon* (AnOr 37; Rome: Biblical Institute Press, 1958); A. Gnirs, "Die ägyptische Autobiographie," in Loprieno, *Ancient Egyptian Literature,* 191–242; Karl Jansen-Winkeln, *Ägyptische Biographien der 22. und 23. Dynastie* (ÄAT 8; Wiesbaden: Harrassowitz, 1985); Jean Leclant, *Montouemhat, quatrième prophète d'Amon, prince de la ville* (Bibliothèque d'étude 35; Cairo: Institut français d'archéologie orientale, 1961); Miriam Lichtheim, *Ancient Egyptian Autobiographies Chiefly of the Middle Kingdom: A Study and an*

Private letters, mainly on papyri and ostraca, abound, especially in the New Kingdom and Late Period, and show a wide range of use. Deeds, wills, bills of sale, contracts, and receipts are all mentioned from the dawn of Egyptian history, but they begin to appear in numbers only in Ramesside times, becoming legion in the Late Period and Hellenistic times.[61]

3.5. RELIGIOUS TEXTS

Texts of religious import are of frequent occurrence and cover a wide range of forms and functions.[62] Those of mortuary application, broadly speaking, are perhaps most numerous. Chief in terms of importance to the ancients are the "beatification" texts (*s3ḫw*), designed to transfigure the dead and assist them in their passage to the afterlife. These fall into three great corpora: the Pyramid Texts, the Coffin Texts, and the "Book of Going Forth by Day" (popularly known as the "Book of the Dead").[63] None of this material conformed to a canonical, static form; rather, it continued to evolve over time, adding new spells and excising or modifying others. The Pyramid Texts are found in their original form inscribed for royal use in pyramid tombs of the outgoing Old Kingdom and First Intermediate Period, while the Coffin Texts occur in more than fifty exemplars, written in ink on the insides of the standard wooden coffins of the later First Intermediate Period and Middle Kingdom. The Book of Going Forth by Day, first found in the early New Kingdom, comprises hundreds of spells (many descended from the Coffin Texts) written on papyrus and secreted in the coffin. Both before and after the final redaction of this great corpus in the Twentieth Dynasty, hundreds of exemplars were written up, and many

---

Anthology (OBO 84; Freiburg: Universitätsverlag, 1988); Georges Posener, *La première domination perse en Égypte: Receuil d'inscriptions hiéroglyphiques* (Cairo: Institut français d'archéologie orientale, 1936); Redford, "Scribe and Speaker."

[61] On letters, see E. F. Wente, *Letters from Ancient Egypt* (SBLWAW 1; Atlanta: Scholars Press, 1990). On the other genres mentioned, see Schafik Allam, *Hieratische Ostraka und Papyri aus der Ramessidenzeit* (2 vols.; Tübingen: self-published, 1973); Janssen, *Commodity Prices;* Sally L. D. Katary, *Land Tenure in the Ramesside Period* (London: Kegan Paul, 1989); Michel Malinine, *Choix de textes juridiques en hiératique anormal et en démotique* (2 vols.; Paris: Institut français d'archéologie orientale du Caire, 1953, 1983); Warburton, *State and Economy.*

[62] Donald B. Redford, "Egyptian Religion: Literature," *ER* 5:54–65.

[63] See, respectively, Raymond O. Faulkner, *The Ancient Egyptian Pyramid Texts* (2 vols.; Oxford: Clarendon, 1969; repr., Warminster: Aris & Phillips, 1985); idem, *The Ancient Egyptian Coffin Texts* (3 vols.; Warminster: Aris & Phillips, 1973); and idem, *The Ancient Egyptian Book of the Dead* (ed. Carol Andrews; rev. ed.; London: British Museum Publications, 1985; repr., Austin: University of Texas Press, 1990).

may now be found in the museums of the world. Before the demise of ancient Egyptian civilization, the Book of Going Forth by Day was joined by additional works with the same purpose, such as the Book of Breathings and the Book of Traversing Eternity.

Of a markedly different nature, principally because they constitute esoteric descriptions of the "secrets of heaven and the hidden things of earth," are the "books" copied on the walls of the royal burial hypogea of New Kingdom date at Thebes and later excerpted for royal burials at Tanis, Mendes, and (presumably) Sais. The contents derive from papyrus originals kept in the sacred "House of Life"[64] and subsumed under the heading "The Souls of Re" (i.e., highly potent, mystical literature of a classified nature). But, as none of these originals has survived, the royal copies alone are known to us. The titles clearly convey the thrust of the works: for example, the Book of That Which Is in the Underworld, the Book of Gates, and the Book of Caverns. The Litany of Re reveals the names and essence of the sun-god, while the Book of the Cow of Heaven tells of the destruction of humankind and the aetiological origins of various cultic acts and paraphernalia.[65]

Egyptian religious literature is rich in hymns. These fall broadly into two types: "invocations" (*ind-ḥr.k*) and "adorations" (*dwꜣ*, originally "morning hymn"). The two overlap considerably. Hymns were used in the service of temples where they were intoned (perhaps sometimes with didactic intent) by choirs of female choristers. They appear also with very great frequency in private devotions, wherein any god or goddess might be the object of the adoration. Sun-hymns, to be sung by an individual at sunrise and sunset, are especially common, while adorations of and lamentations over Osiris and his cycle were almost equally popular. One genre of note, with parallels elsewhere in the Near East, is the category of "penitential psalm" (our term) in which the devotee either confesses sin and appeals to the deity or praises god for having forgiven and healed him or her from sickness.[66]

---

[64] Alan H. Gardiner, "The House of Life," *JEA* 24 (1938): 157–79.

[65] See, respectively, Erik Hornung, *The Ancient Egyptian Books of the Afterlife* (Ithaca, N.Y.: Cornell University Press, 1999); idem, *Das Buch der Anbetung des Re im Westen (Sonnenlitanie): Nach den Versionen des Neuen Reiches* (Geneva: Éditions de Belles-Lettres, 1975); and idem, *Der ägyptische Mythos von der Himmelskuh*.

[66] For treatments of Egyptian hymns, see Jan Assmann, *Ägyptische Hymnen und Gebete* (Zürich: Artemis, 1975); idem, *Egyptian Solar Religion in the New Kingdom: Re, Amun and the Crisis of Polytheism* (trans. Anthony Alcock; London: Kegan Paul, 1995); idem, "Grundformen hymnischer Rede im Alten Ägypten," in Loprieno, *Ancient Egyptian Literature,* 313–34; idem, *Sonnenhymnen im thebanischen Gräbern* (Mainz: Zabern, 1983); Pierre Auffret, *Hymnes d'Égypte et d'Israël* (Freiburg: Éditions universitaires, 1981); Raymond O. Faulkner, *The Papyrus Bremner-Rhind*

Prescriptive texts governing the cult abounded in temple libraries. These included ritual texts, inventories, instruction manuals, receipts, and the like. While most are known to us only by their *incipits,* contained in temple checklists, a few have survived intact on papyrus or temple walls.[67]

3.6. MAGICAL TEXTS

It should come as no surprise that, in a culture that valued magic to an extreme, spells and incantations should constitute one of the largest groups of surviving texts. The magic spell (*r3*) belonged within the purview of "that art of the lector-priest," the temple reader who read from the ritual papyri and whose title and persona in later times approximated those of our "magician." A large proportion of the beatifications in the Pyramid Texts, the Coffin Texts, and the Book of Going Forth by Day have magical force and are provided with rubrics giving purpose and mode of use. Checklists from temple libraries show that an overwhelming percentage of their contents were magical and were designed to ensure that the ritual and the celebrants were magically protected from malevolent forces. But magical texts could also form part of private collections and are found in medical compendia and pharmacopeia as well. The social situations in which magic could be invoked were deemed to be legion and could involve active enforcement of will as well as the prophylactic. Since gods in their very essence partook of magic, identification with them and their actions could elevate the magician to a higher plane of power. Consequently, many spells identify the speaker with a god and might contain a snippet of a myth.[68]

(Brussels: Éditions de la fondation égyptologique Reine Élisabeth, 1933); Louis V. Zabkar, *Hymns to Isis at Her Temple at Philae* (Hanover, N.H.: University Press of New England, 1988).

[67] Cf. Émile Chassinat, *Le mystère d'Osiris au mois de Khoiak* (Cairo: Institut français d'archéologie orientale, 1968); A. Rosalie David, *A Guide to Religious Ritual at Abydos* (rev. ed.; Warminster: Aris & Phillips, 1981); Henre Gauthier, *Les fêtes du dieu Min* (Cairo: Institut français d'archéologie orientale, 1931); Alexandre Moret, *Le rituel du culte divin journalier en Égypte, d'apres les papyrus de Berlin et les texts du temple de Séti 1er* (Paris: E. Leroux, 1902); Otto, *Das Verhältnis vom Rite und Mythen;* Redford, *Pharaonic King-Lists, Annals and Daybooks;* J. C. Goyon, *Confirmation du pouvoir royal au nouvel an, Brooklyn museum papyrus 47.218.50* (Bibliothèque d'étude 52; Cairo: Institut français d'archéologie orientale, 1971).

[68] Betz, *Greek Magical Papyri;* J. F. Borghouts, trans., *Ancient Egyptian Magical Texts* (Nisaba 9; Leiden: Brill, 1978); Robert K. Ritner, *The Mechanics of Ancient Egyptian Magical Practice* (SAOC 54; Chicago: Oriental Institute, 1993).

4. BIBLIOGRAPHY

Allam, Schafik, *Hieratische Ostraka und Papyri aus der Ramessidenzeit.* 2 vols. Tübingen: self-published, 1973.

Allen, James P. *The Inflection of the Verb in the Pyramid Texts.* Bibliotheca Aegyptia 2/1–2. Malibu, Calif.: Undena, 1974.

———. *Middle Egyptian: An Introduction to the Language and Culture of Hieroglyphs.* Cambridge: Cambridge University Press, 2000.

Altenmüller, Hartwig. "Zur Lesung und Deutung des dramatischen Ramesseumspapyrus." *JEOL* 19 (1964–1965): 421–42.

Assmann, Jan. *Ägyptische Hymnen und Gebete.* Zürich: Artemis, 1975.

———. *Egyptian Solar Religion in the New Kingdom: Re, Amun and the Crisis of Polytheism.* Translated by Anthony Alcock. London: Kegan Paul, 1995.

———. "Fest des Augenblicks—Verheissung der Dauer: Die Kontroverse der ägyptischen Harfnerlieder." Pages 55–84 in *Fragen an die altägyptischen Literatur.* Edited by Jan Assmann, Erika Feucht, and Reinhard Grieshammer. Wiesbaden: Reichert, 1977.

———. "Grundformen hymnischer Rede im Alten Ägypten." Pages 313–34 in *Ancient Egyptian Literature: History and Forms.* Edited by Antonio Loprieno. Leiden: Brill, 1996.

———. *Sonnenhymnen im thebanischen Gräbern.* Mainz: Zabern, 1983.

Auffret, Pierre. *Hymnes d'Égypte et d'Israeïl.* Freiburg: Éditions universitaires, 1981.

Bakir, Abd el-Mohsen. *The Cairo Calendar no. 86637.* Cairo: General Organization for Government Printing Offices, 1966.

Barta, Winfried. *Das Gespräch eines Mannes mit seinem Ba (Papyrus Berlin 3024).* Berlin: Hessling, 1969.

Betz, Hans Dieter. *The Greek Magical Papyri in Translation.* Chicago: University of Chicago Press, 1986.

Blumenthal, Elke. "Die literarische Verarbeitung der Übergangszeit zwischen Altem und Mittlerem Reich." Pages 105–36 in *Ancient Egyptian Literature: History and Forms.* Edited by Antonio Loprieno. Leiden: Brill, 1996.

———. "Die Prophezeihung des Neferti." *ZÄS* 109 (1982): 1–27.

Broze, Michel. *Les aventures d'Horus et Seth dans le papyrus Chester Beatty I: mythe et roman en Egypte ancienne.* Leuven: Peeters, 1996.

Callender, John B. "Problems of Tense and Aspect in Egyptian." *ZÄS* 113 (1986): 8–18.

Caminos, Ricardo A. *The Chronicle of Prince Osorkon.* AnOr 37. Rome: Biblical Institute Press, 1958.

Černý, Jaroslav, and Sarah Israelit-Groll, assisted by Christopher Eyre. *A Late Egyptian Grammar.* Studia Pohl, series maior 4. Rome: Biblical Institute Press, 1975.

Chassinat, Émile. *Le mystère d'Osiris au mois de Khoiak.* Cairo: Institut français d'archéologie orientale, 1968.

Cohen, Marcel S. R. *Essai comparatif sur le vocabulaire et la phonétique du chamito-sémitique.* Paris: Champion, 1947.

Couyat, J., and P. Montet. *Les inscriptions hiéroglyphiques et hiératiques du Ouaïdi Hammamat.* Cairo: Institut français d'archéologie orientale, 1912.

Crum, Walter E. *Coptic Dictionary.* Oxford: Clarendon, 1939. Repr., Oxford: Oxford University Press, 1990.

Curto, S. "Krieg." *LÄ* 3:785–86.

David, A. Rosalie. *A Guide to Religious Ritual at Abydos.* Rev. ed. Warminster: Aris & Phillips, 1981.

Depuydt, Leo. "Egyptian 'Split' Genitives and Related Phenomena: Exotic Debris from Conflicting Forces." *Mus* 112 (1999): 273–300.

———. "Sentence Pattern and Verb Form: Egyptian Grammar since Polotsky." *Mus* 108 (1995): 39–48.

———. "The Standard Theory of the 'Emphatic' Forms in Classical (Middle) Egyptian: A Historical Survey." *OLP* 14 (1983): 13–53.

———. "Twixt Relative Verb Form and Passive Participle in Egyptian." *ZDMG* 146 (1996): 1–24.

Diakonoff, I. M. "The Earliest Semitic Society: Linguistic Data." *JSS* 43 (1998): 209–20.

Drioton, Etienne. *Le Texte dramatique d'Edfou.* Cairo: Institut français d'archéologie orientale, 1948. Repr., Cairo: Organisation égyptienne générale du livre, 1984.

Edel, Elmar. *Altägyptische Grammatik.* AnOr 34, 39. Rome: Biblical Institute Press, 1955–1964.

Englund, Gertie, and Frandsen Paul John. *Crossroad: Chaos or the Beginning of a New Paradigm: Papers from the Conference on Egyptian Grammar, Helsingor 28–30 May 1986.* Copenhagen: Carsten Niebuhr Institute of Ancient Near East Studies, 1986.

Erichsen, Wolja. *Demotisches Glossar.* Copenhagen: Munksgaard, 1954.

Erman, Adolf. *Ägyptische Grammatik.* 4th ed. Porta linguarum orientalium. Berlin: Reuther & Reichard, 1928–1929.

———. *Hymnen an das Diadem der Pharaonen.* Berlin, 1911.

Erman, Adolf, and H. Grapow. *Wörterbuch der ägyptischer Sprache.* 5 vols. Leipzig: Hinrichs, 1926–1931.

Eyre, Christopher J. "Irony in the Story of Wenamun: The Politics of Religion in the Twenty-First Dynasty." Pages 235–54 in *Literatur und Politik in pharaonischen und ptolemäischen Ägypten.* Edited by Jan Assmann. Cairo: Institut français d'archéologie orientale, 1999.

Fairman, H. W. *The Triumph of Horus: The Oldest Play in the World.* Berkeley and Los Angeles: University of California Press, 1974.

Faulkner, Raymond O. *The Ancient Egyptian Book of the Dead*. Rev. ed. Edited by Carol Andrews. London: British Museum Publications, 1985. Repr., Austin: University of Texas Press, 1990.

———. *The Ancient Egyptian Coffin Texts*. 3 vols. Warminster: Aris & Phillips, 1973–1978.

———. *The Ancient Egyptian Pyramid Texts*. 2 vols. Oxford: Clarendon, 1969. Repr., Warminster: Aris & Phillips, 1985.

———. *A Concise Dictionary of Middle Egyptian*. Oxford: Griffith Institute, 1962.

———. *The Papyrus Bremner-Rhind*. Brussels: Éditions de la fondation égyptologique Reine Élisabeth, 1933.

Fischer-Elfert, Hans-Werner. *Die satirische Streitschrift des Papyrus Anastasi I: Übersetzung und Kommentar*. Wiesbaden: Harrassowitz, 1986.

Foster, John L. *Echoes of Egyptian Voices. An Anthology of Ancient Egyptian Poetry*. Norman: University of Oklahoma Press, 1992.

Fox, Michael V. *The Song of Songs and the Ancient Egyptian Love Songs*. Madison: University of Wisconsin Press, 1985.

———. "A Study of Antef." *Or* 46 (1977): 393–423.

Frandsen, Paul John. *An Outline of the Late Egyptian Verbal System*. Copenhagen: Akademisk, 1974.

Gardiner Alan H. *The Admonitions of an Egyptian Sage from a Hieratic Papyrus in Leiden, Pap. Leiden 344 recto*. Leipzig, 1909. Repr., Hildesheim: Olms, 1969.

———. *Egyptian Grammar*. 3d ed. Oxford: Griffith Institute Ashmolean Museum, 1957.

———. *Hieratic Papyri in the British Museum*. 3d series: *Chester Beatty Gift*. London: British Museum Publications, 1935.

———. "The House of Life." *JEA* 24 (1938): 157–79.

———. "A Pharaonic Encomium." *JEA* 41 (1955): 30.

———. *Ramesside Administrative Documents*. Leiden: P. Lund, Humphries, 1940.

Gardiner, Alan H., and T. Eric Peet. *The Inscriptions of Sinai*. Edited by Jaroslav Černý. 2 vols. Memoir of the Egypt Exploration Society 36, 45. London: Egypt Exploration Society, 1952–55.

Gauthier, Henri. *Les fêtes du dieu Min*. Cairo: Institut français d'archéologie orientale, 1931.

Gnirs, A. "Die ägyptische Autobiographie." Pages 191–242 in *Ancient Egyptian Literature: History and Forms*. Edited by Antonio Loprieno. Leiden: Brill, 1996.

Goedicke, Hans. *Königliche Dokumente aus dem Alten Reich*. Ägyptische Abhandlungen 14. Wiesbaden: Harrassowitz, 1967.

Goldwasser, Orly. *From Icon to Metaphor: Studies in the Semiotics of Hieroglyphs*. OBO 142. Freiburg: Universitätsverlag, 1995.

Goyon, Georges. *Confirmation du pouvoir au nouvel an.* Bibliothèque d'étude 52. Cairo: Institut français d'archéologie orientale, 1971.

———. *Nouvelles inscriptions rupestres du Wadi Hammamat.* Paris: Adrien Maisonneuve, 1957.

Grandet, Pierre. *Le Papyrus Harris I, BM 9999.* 2 vols. Cairo: Institut français d'archéologie orientale, 1994.

Grayson, A. K., and Donald B. Redford. *Papyrus and Tablet.* Englewood Cliffs, N.J.: Prentice-Hall, 1973.

Greenberg, Joseph H. *Studies in African Linguistic Classification.* Branford, Conn.: Compass, 1955.

Griffiths, J. Gwyn. "Horusmythe." *LÄ* 3:54–59.

Helck, W. *Altägyptische Aktenkunde des 3. und 2. Jahrtausends v. Chr.* Munich: Deutscher Kunstverlag, 1974.

———. "Gedanken zum Ursprung der ägyptischen Schrift." *Mélanges Mokhtar* 1 (1985): 395–408.

———. *Die Prophezeihung des Nfr.tj. Kleine ägyptische Texte.* 2d ed. Wiesbaden: Harrassowitz, 1970.

Hoch, James. *Semitic Words in Egyptian Texts of the New Kingdom and Third Intermediate Period.* Princeton, N.J.; Princeton University Press, 1994.

Hodge, C. T., ed., *Afro-Asiatic: A Survey.* The Hague: Mouton, 1971.

Hornung, Erik. *Der ägyptische Mythos von der Himmelskuh: Eine Ätiologie des Unvollkommenen.* 2d ed. OBO 46; Freiburg: Universitätsverlag, 1982.

———. *The Ancient Egyptian Books of the Afterlife.* Ithaca, N.Y.: Cornell University Press, 1999.

———. *Das Buch der Anbetung des Re im Westen (Sonnenlitanie): Nach den Versionen des Neuen Reiches.* Geneva: Éditions de Belles-Lettres, 1975.

Hughes, George R. "A Demotic Astrological Text." *JNES* 10 (1951): 256–64.

Iversen, Erik. *The Myth of Egypt and Its Hieroglyphs in European Tradition.* 2d ed. Princeton, N.J.: Princeton University Press, 1993.

Jansen-Winkeln, Karl. *Ägyptische Biographien der 22. und 23. Dynastie.* ÄAT 8. Wiesbaden: Harrassowitz, 1985.

Janssen, Jac J. *Commodity Prices from the Ramesside Period.* Leiden: Brill, 1975.

Junge, Friedrich. *Einführung in die Grammatik des Neuägyptischen.* Wiesbaden: Harrassowitz, 1996.

———. *"Emphasis" and Sentential Meaning in Middle Egyptian.* Göttinger Orientforschungen 4/20. Wiesbaden: Harrassowitz, 1989.

Kákosy, László. "Prophecies of Ram-Gods." *AcOr* 19 (1966): 341–58.

Katary, Sally L. D. *Land Tenure in the Ramesside Period.* London: Kegan Paul, 1989.

Kitchen, Kenneth A. *Ramesside Inscriptions, Historical and Biographical.* 3 vols. Oxford: Blackwell, 1969.

Koch, Roland. *Die Erzählung des Sinuhe.* Bibliotheca Aegyptiaca 17. Brussels: Éditions de la fondation égyptologique Reine Élisabeth, 1990.

Koenen L. "Die Prophezeihungen des 'Töpfers.'" *ZPE* 2 (1968): 178–209.

Krause, M. "Koptische Sprache." *LÄ* 3:731–37.

Lambdin, Thomas O. *Introduction to Sahidic Coptic.* Macon, Ga: Mercer University Press, 1983.

Leclant, Jean. *Montouemhat, quatrième prophète d'Amon, prince de la ville.* Bibliothèque d'étude 35. Cairo: Institut français d'archéologie orientale, 1961.

Lepsius, R. *Denkmäler aus Ägypten und Äthiopen.* 6 vols. Berlin: Nicolaische Buchhandlung, 1849–1858.

Lesko, Leonard H. *Pharaoh's Workers: The Villagers of Deir el-Medina.* Ithaca, N.Y.: Cornell University Press, 1994.

Lichtheim, Miriam. *Ancient Egyptian Autobiographies Chiefly of the Middle Kingdom: A Study and an Anthology.* OBO 84. Freiburg: Universitätsverlag, 1988.

―――. *Ancient Egyptian Literature: A Book of Readings.* 3 vols. Berkeley and Los Angeles: University of California Press, 1973–1980.

―――. "The Songs of the Harpers." *JNES* 4 (1945): 178–212.

Loprieno, Antonio. *Ancient Egyptian: A Linguistic Introduction.* Cambridge: Cambridge University Press, 1995.

―――. "Defining Egyptian Literature." Pages 39–58 in *Ancient Egyptian Literature: History and Forms.* Edited by Antonio Loprieno. Leiden: Brill, 1996.

―――, ed. *Ancient Egyptian Literature: History and Forms.* Leiden: Brill, 1996.

Malinine, Michel. *Choix de textes juridiques en hiératique "anormal" et en démotique.* 2 vols. Paris: Institut français d'archéologie orientale, 1953, 1983.

Massart, A. "The Egyptian Geneva Papyrus MAH 15274." *MDAI* 15 (1957): 172–85.

Mikhail, L. B. "The Egyptological Approach to Drama in Ancient Egypt II: Is It Time for a Revision?" *GM* 77 (1984): 25–33.

Moret, Alexandre. *Le Rituel du culte divin journalier en Égypte, d'apres les papyrus de Berlin et les texts du temple de Séti 1er.* Paris: Leroux, 1902.

Mueller, D. *A Concise Introduction to Middle Egyptian Grammar.* Lethbridge: unpublished, 1975.

Nunn, John F. *Ancient Egyptian Medicine.* Norman: University of Oklahoma Press, 1996.

Otto, Eberhard. *Das Verhältnis vom Rite und Mythen im ägyptischen.* Heidelberg: Winter, 1958.

Parker, Richard A. *A Saite Oracle Papyrus from Thebes in the Brooklyn Museum.* Providence, R.I.: Brown University Press, 1962.

————. *A Vienna Demotic Papyrus on Eclipse- and Lunar-Omina.* Providence, R.I.: Brown University Press, 1959.

Parkinson, Richard B. "Teachings, Discourses and Tales from the Middle Kingdom." Pages 123–40 in *Middle Kingdom Studies.* Edited by Stephen Quirke. New Malden, Surrey: SIA Publications, 1991.

————. *Voices from Ancient Egypt: An Anthology of Middle Kingdom Writings.* Norman: University of Oklahoma Press, 1991.

Peet, T. E. *The Great Tomb-Robbery Papyri of the Egyptian XXth Dynasty.* Oxford: Oxford University Press, 1930.

Polotsky, Hans Jakob "The Coptic Conjugation System." *Or* 29 (1960): 392–422.

————. "Egyptian." Pages 320–28 in *Collected Papers.* Jerusalem: Magnes, 1971.

————. *Egyptian Tenses.* Jerusalem: Central, 1965.

————. *Études de syntaxe copte.* Cairo: Société d'archéologie copte, 1944.

————. "Notre connaissance du neo-égyptien." Pages 133–41 in vol. 2 of *Textes et langages de l'Égypte pharaonique: Cent cinquante années de recherches, 1822–1972: Hommage Jean-Francois Champollion.* Edited by Serge Sauneron. 3 vols. Cairo: Institut français d'archéologie orientale, 1973.

Posener, Georges. *La première domination perse en Égypte: Receuil d'inscriptions hiéroglyphiques.* Cairo: Institut français d'archéologie orientale, 1936.

Posener-Kriéger, Paula. *Les archives du temple funéraire de Néferirkareï-Kakaï (Le papyrus d'Abousir).* Cairo: Institut français d'archéologie orientale, 1976.

Quirke, Stephen., ed. *Middle Egyptian Studies.* New Malden, Surrey: SIA Publications, 1991.

Ray, J. D. "The Emergence of Writing in Egypt." *World Archaeology* 17/3 (1986): 307–16.

————. "How Demotic Is Demotic?" Pages 251–64 in *Acta Demotica.* Edited by E. Besciani. Pisa: Giardini, 1994 = *EVO* 17 (1994).

Redford, Donald B. *Egypt, Canaan, and Israel in Ancient Times.* Princeton, N.J.: Princeton University Press, 1992.

————. "Egyptian Religion: Literature." *ER* 5:54–65.

————. *Pharaonic King-Lists, Annals and Daybooks.* Mississauga: Benben, 1986.

————. "Scribe and Speaker: The Interface between Written and Oral Tradition in Ancient Egypt." Pages 145–218 in *Writings and Speech in Israelite and Ancient Near Eastern Prophecy.* Edited by Ehud Ben Zvi and Michael H. Floyd. Atlanta: Society of Biblical Literature, 2000.

Redford, Susan. *The Harem Conspiracy: A Study of the Murder of Ramesses III.* Dekalb: Northern Illinois University Press, 2001.

Renaud, Odette. *Le dialogue du désésperé avec son aïme: Une interprétation littéraire.* Geneva: Société d'égyptologie, 1991.

Ritner, Robert K. *The Mechanics of Ancient Egyptian Magical Practice.* SAOC 54. Chicago: Oriental Institute Press, 1993.

Robins, Gay, and Charles Shute. *The Rhind Mathematical Papyrus: An Ancient Egyptian Text.* New York: Dover, 1987.

Robinson, Andrew. *The Story of Writing.* New York: Thames & Hudson, 1995.

Roccati, Alessandro. "Une légende égyptienne d'Anat." *RdÉ* 24 (1972): 152–59.

Sauneron, Serge, ed. *Textes et langages de l'Égypte pharaonique: Cent cinquante années derecherches, 1822–1972: Hommage Jean-Francois Champollion.* 3 vols. Cairo: Institute français d'archéologie orientale, 1973.

Schott, Siegfried. *Mythe und Mythenbildung im alten Ägypten.* Leipzig: Hinrichs, 1945.

Sethe, Kurt. *Das ägyptische Verbum in altägyptischen, neuägyptischen und koptischen.* 3 vols. Leipzig: Hinrichs, 1899–1902.

———. *Dramatische Texte zu altägyptischen Mysterienspielen.* Leipzig: Hinrichs, 1928.

Seyfried, Karl-Joachim. *Beiträge zu den Expeditionen des Mittleren Reiches in die Ost-Wüste.* Hildesheimer ägyptologische Beiträge 15. Hildesheim: Gerstenberg, 1981.

Simpson, William Kelly. *The Literature of Ancient Egypt: An Anthology of Stories, Instructions, and Poetry.* New ed. New Haven, Conn.: Yale University Press, 1973.

———. *Papyrus Reisner I–IV.* 4 vols. Boston: Museum of Fine Arts, 1963–1986.

Smith, H. S., and W. J. Tait. *Saqqâra Demotic Papyri I.* London: Egypt Exploration Society, 1983.

Smither, P. C. "The Semna Despatches." *JEA* 31 (1945): 3–19.

———. "A Tax-Assessor's Journal of the Middle Kingdom." *JEA* 27 (1941): 74–77.

Spiegelberg, Wilhelm. *Demotische Grammatik.* Heidelberg: Winter, 1975.

Tait, W. J. "Demotic Literature and Egyptian Society." Pages 303–10 in *Life in a Multi-cultural Society: Egypt from Cambyses to Constantine and Beyond.* Edited by Janet H. Johnson. SAOC 51. Chicago: Oriental Institute Press, 1990.

Till, W. *Koptisches Grammatik (Saïdischer Dialekt).* Leipzig: Harrassowitz, 1955.

Tobin, V. A. "A Re-assessment of the Lebensmüde," *BO* 48 (1991): 341–63.

Ventura, Raphael. *Living in a City of the Dead.* OBO 69. Freiburg: Universitätsverlag, 1986.

Vercoutter, Jean. *The Search for Ancient Egypt*. New York: Abrams, 1992.

Vergote, Jozef. "Egyptian." Pages 531–37 in *Current Trends in Linguistics*. Edited by Thomas A. Seboek. The Hague: Mouton, 1970.

———. *Grammaire Copte*. 2 vols. Leuven: Peeters, 1973–1983. Repr., 1992.

Verhoeven, Ursula. "Von hieratischen Literaturwerken in der Spätzeit." Pages 255–66 in *Literatur und Politik im pharaonischen Ägypten*. Edited by Jan Assmann and E. Blumenthal. Cairo: Institut français d'archéologie orientale, 1999.

Vernus, Pascal. *Future at Issue: Tense, Mood, and Aspect in Middle Egyptian: Studies in Syntax and Semantics*. Yale Egyptological Studies 4. New Haven, Conn.: Yale University Press, 1990.

———. "Langue littéraire et diglossie." Pages 555–66 in *Ancient Egyptian Literature: History and Forms*. Edited by Antonio Loprieno. Leiden: Brill, 1996.

———. "Procèssus de grammaticalisation dans la langue égyptienne." *CRAI* (1998): 191–209.

Warburton David A. *State and Economy in Ancient Egypt: Fiscal Vocabulary of the New Kingdom*. OBO 151. Freiburg: Universitätsverlag, 1997.

Wente, E. F. *Letters from Ancient Egypt*. SBLWAW 1. Atlanta: Scholars Press, 1990.

Zabkar, Louis V. *Hymns to Isis at Her Temple at Philae*. Hanover, N.H.: University Press of New England, 1988.

HEBREW (BIBLICAL AND EPIGRAPHIC)

Jo Ann Hackett

1. THE LANGUAGE

Biblical Hebrew (BH) and epigraphic Hebrew are umbrella terms used to describe a number of dialects and periods of the language from the Iron Age until the Hellenistic era. Hebrew is a member of the Canaanite family of languages, which descend from Northwest Semitic languages, which in turn are part of the larger Central Semitic languages and finally West Semitic.[1]

In the Bible itself, the word "Hebrew" (*'ibrît*) is not used by Israelites or Judahites to describe their own language. We find *śapat kəna'an*, "the language of Canaan," in Isa 19:18, and *yəhûdît*, "Judahite," is used in the famous reply to the Assyrian Rabshakeh in 2 Kings: Elyakim and Shebnah say to the Rabshakeh, "Speak to your servants in Aramaic [*'ărāmît*], because we understand it, but don't speak to us in Judahite within the hearing of the people who are on the wall" (2 Kgs 18:26 = Isa 36:11). The Rabshakeh, however, refuses and continues to speak Judahite (2 Kgs 18:28 = Isa 36:13; 2 Chr 32:18 is also similar). When Nehemiah complains that Jewish men had married women from Ashdod, Ammon, and Moab, part of his complaint is that half their children spoke *'ašdôdît* or the language of each nation, and did not know *yəhûdît* (13:23–24). The first attestation we have of "Hebrew" being used of the language occurs in Greek, in the prologue to Ben Sira, in which Ben Sira's grandson claims to have translated his grandfather's words from the original Hebrew.

The earliest evidence we have of a language like BH comes in Canaanite glosses and verb forms within the mixed language of the Amarna letters, written in a form of West Peripheral Akkadian and dating to the fourteenth century B.C.E. The Canaanite of these letters exhibits a verbal system with a suffix conjugation **qatala* (Heb. *qāṭal*) for most past-tense and nondurative constructions and three prefix conjugations: **yaqtul* (Heb. *yiqṭōl*) for jussive and past tense; **yaqtulu* (Heb. *yiqṭōl*) for future tense and durative uses; **yaqtula* for volitive (cf. the Heb. cohortative with -*â*

---

[1] See John Huehnergard's introduction to this volume.

ending).[2] In the strong verb in BH, both *yaqṭul* and *yaqṭulu* develop into *yiqṭōl,* but the earlier difference can be seen in some weak verbs: compare BH *yīben* "let him build," with *yibneh* "he will build"; *yīben* is the realization of earlier *yaqṭul,* while *yibneh* is the realization of earlier *yaqṭulu.*

The earliest examples of what is clearly Hebrew, however, come to us from the Hebrew Bible itself. Biblical Hebrew is usually divided into three large chronological periods: early poetry, Standard Biblical Hebrew (SBH), and Late Biblical Hebrew (LBH). The phrase "early poetry" refers to a body of biblical literature that is defined differently by different scholars but is usually said to consist of at least the poems in Exod 15; Judg 5; Deut 33; and Gen 49.[3] Some would add to this list the oracles of Balaam in Num 23–24 and the poems in Deut 32; 1 Sam 2; 2 Sam 22 = Ps 18; Pss 29; 68; 72; 78; 2 Sam 1; 23; and Hab 3,[4] but others consider this list too inclusive for the very earliest poetry.[5] These poems are thought to date to the twelfth or eleventh centuries because of linguistic and stylistic features that remind scholars of slightly earlier literature: the structure of and figures in Israel's archaic poetry (including vocabulary) and certain grammatical and syntactical features have been compared to those of the fourteenth-century Ugaritic epics from Ras Shamra and to the Canaanite known from the fourteenth-century Amarna letters found in Egypt (see above). Examples of such features include the appearance of enclitic *mêm*[6] and the use of a prefix-conjugation verb—usually a present-future in SBH—to denote simple past-tense actions.[7]

---

[2] The asterisk (*) designates reconstructed proto-Hebrew forms.

[3] See, for instance, Frank Moore Cross Jr. and David Noel Freedman, *Studies in Ancient Yahwistic Poetry* (SBLDS 21; Missoula, Mont.: Scholars Press, 1975; repr. Grand Rapids, Mich.: Eerdmans, 1997).

[4] For instance, W. F. Albright, *Yahweh and the Gods of Canaan* (Garden City, N.Y.: Doubleday, 1968), 1–46; David Noel Freedman, "Divine Names and Titles in Early Hebrew Poetry," "Early Israelite History in the Light of Early Israelite Poetry," and "Early Israelite Poetry and Historical Reconstructions," conveniently gathered in *Pottery, Poetry, and Prophecy* (Winona Lake, Ind.: Eisenbrauns, 1980).

[5] For example, David A. Robertson, *Linguistic Evidence in Dating Early Hebrew Poetry* (SBLDS 3; Missoula, Mont.: Scholars Press, 1972), 153–56, lists only Exod 15 (the earliest, according to Robertson) and Judg 5 (next), with Deut 32, 2 Sam 22 = Ps 18, Hab 3, Job, and Ps 78 probably in the eleventh to tenth centuries.

[6] Enclitic *mêm* is an unnecessary addition of *m* at the end of a word. In 2 Sam 22:49, the word *ḥămāsîm* occurs, whereas the same verse in the parallel poem in Ps 18 has only *ḥāmās.* The "extra" *mêm* in the 2 Samuel version is often said to be an example in BH of enclitic *mêm.*

[7] See, for instance, the several prefix conjugation verbs in Exod 15:5, 12, 14, and 15 that clearly refer to past time.

By SBH is generally meant the narrative prose of the Deuteronomistic History and the Pentateuch. LBH differs from SBH in quite a few respects, including: reduced use of the infinitive absolute; increased use of the infinitive construct with *lə;* the appearance of *-hm* for both the third-person masculine and feminine plural suffixes; increased Aramaisms; and, less significantly, vocabulary, to a certain extent.[8] Most would agree that the following books exhibit, in part or completely, LBH features: Chronicles (in those portions not parallel to Samuel-Kings); Ezra; Nehemiah; Esther; Ecclesiastes; Daniel; Ben Sira.

The Hebrew of the Dead Sea Scrolls (DSS) is the latest LBH. The Hebrew of the rabbinic writings (the Mishnah and the Talmuds), called Mishnaic Hebrew (MH), is not a continuation of any strand of BH but rather a different dialect of Hebrew. It is commonly assumed that MH is the written version of the vernacular spoken in Yehud/Judea from the sixth century on, which theory also assumes that LBH is strictly a literary language, patterned after SBH. (Whether SBH represents spoken Hebrew or is itself a strictly literary language is debated. It is important to note, however, that even informal epigraphic Hebrew of the monarchic period is very much like SBH [see below].) MH was still spoken in the second century C.E., but after the failure of the Bar Kokhba revolt, Hebrew became a literary language and lingua franca for Jews all over the world, until its revival in modern times.

Epigraphic Hebrew spans almost the entire biblical period, beginning with the Gezer Calendar (if the language of that inscription is indeed Hebrew) through the Second Temple period. The few reasonably long compositions in preexilic epigraphic Hebrew are remarkably like the Hebrew prose in the Bible. We find the typical uses of the consecutive imperfect and consecutive perfect; the infinitive absolute substituting for a finite verb, both imperative and perfect; the typical use of the definite article and occasionally the definite direct object marker *'t;* the use of the imperfect as an indirect imperative; the use of a consecutive perfect after an imperative to continue the imperative sense; the use of locative *-h,* even in the middle of a construct chain; the use of *'yš* in a distributive sense; the divine name YHWH and even *byt* YHWH; the use of *hnh* to mean something has "just now" happened; and an "inferior" referring to himself or herself as "your servant" when addressing a "superior."

---

[8] LBH is described at length in Robert Polzin, *Late Biblical Hebrew: Toward an Historical Typology of Biblical Hebrew Prose* (HSM 12; Missoula, Mont.: Scholars Press, 1976); and Avi Hurvitz, *A Linguistic Study of the Relationship between the Priestly Source and the Book of Ezekiel: A New Approach to an Old Problem* (Paris: Gabalda, 1982).

In epigraphic Hebrew we can identify at least two dialects: a northern dialect, known from the Samaria ostraca and seals, and a southern dialect, known from several inscriptions as well as seals. The northern dialect is very similar to Phoenician. One obvious similarity is that diphthongs have collapsed in northern Hebrew, as in Phoenician. The word for wine, biblical *yayin,* is written *yn* /yēn/ in the eighth-century Samaria ostraca, like the biblical construct singular form. In BH, original **yayn* has become triphthongized to *yayin* in the absolute state, but the *ay* diphthong collapses in the construct state: *yên.* In northern Hebrew and Phoenician the word for wine is always *yn* (i.e., not only in the construct state), suggesting that the diphthong had collapsed in all environments, and the word was consistently pronounced /yēn/.

Another similarity between northern Hebrew and Phoenician is their spelling and pronunciation of the word for "year." In southern Hebrew and in BH, the original *-at* ending (**šanat-*)[9] became /ā/, written *-â* (*šānâ*), like so many feminine singular nouns. The **-at* ending is only one possibility for the feminine singular, however; a simple **-t* is also possible, and northern Hebrew and Phoenician apparently used this alternative feminine ending for this particular word, giving an original **šant-*, which became **šatt-*, and finally **šat-*, written *št* instead of *šnt.*[10]

In theophoric names in demonstrably northern texts, the ending that represents Yahweh is consistently *yw* /yaw/, whereas in demonstrably southern texts it is *yhw* /yahū/. Compare *šmryw* /šamaryaw/ from the Samaria ostraca (*KAI* 183.1/2) with *smkyhw* /samakyahū/ from Lachish (*KAI* 194.6).

The southern or Judahite dialect is the one in which most of the SBH texts are written. Scholars have proposed, however, that a northern dialect occasionally shows through in the Bible, especially in texts that might come from northern writers or circles, like the stories of northern kings in the books of Kings.

2. SIGNIFICANCE FOR THE BIBLE

The Masoretic Text (MT) is the received text of the Hebrew Bible. It is so called because the vocalization and accentuation of the text we use

---

[9] The dash following **šanat* represents any of the three original case endings (*-u* for nominative, *-i* for genitive, and *-a* for accusative), which have disappeared from Hebrew by the biblical period.

[10] See, e.g., *KAI* 183.1. *KAI* (H. Donner and W. Röllig, *Kanaanäische und aramäische Inschriften* [Wiesbaden: Harrassowitz, 1966–1969], now unfortunately out of print) is a collection of Phoenician, Moabite, Hebrew, and Aramaic inscriptions, and the *KAI* number is one standard way of citing inscriptions: "183.1" means the word *št* can be found in *KAI* inscription no. 183 (one of the Samaria ostraca), line 1.

was added to the consonantal text by medieval scholars known as Masoretes. These scholars were called Masoretes because they passed on the tradition, the Masorah, of their pronunciation of the Hebrew text. They also contributed thousands of marginal notes on the text, for the most part concerned with the correct transmission of the text from one copyist to the next. These marginal notes are also called Masorah. A selection of the vast Masorah to the MT is included in many modern Bibles, and the *Biblia Hebraica Stuttgartensia* (*BHS*) includes notes in the margins and in an apparatus at the bottom of each page. The notes in the margins are called Masorah Parva (Mp), and there are footnotes in the Mp to the apparatus at the bottom of the page that point the reader to the relevant sections of the Masorah Magna (Mm), available in several collections.

The Tiberian Masoretic tradition is the one most commonly available today, and it is itself only one of three (or more) in antiquity: Tiberian, Babylonian, and Palestinian. Within the Tiberian system there were at least two schools, named after the family names of their most famous adherents: the Ben Asher school and the Ben Naphtali school. The Ben Asher version of the Tiberian MT is generally held to be the better of the two, and it is that version that is represented by the Leningrad Codex (ca. 1000 C.E., the basis for *BHS*) and by the Aleppo Codex, an earlier (tenth century C.E.) and better but incomplete exemplar (the basis for the Hebrew University Bible). It is possible to narrow the dates for the addition of vowel signs and accents to around 600–750 C.E., on the basis of citations in external sources. The Ben Asher family of Masoretes was active in the eighth through the tenth centuries C.E. So the "biblical Hebrew" discussed in this essay is actually the vocalized Hebrew of the MT of the Ben Asher Tiberian tradition, as represented by the Leningrad Codex.[11]

We know from early translations of the Hebrew Bible and from some of the biblical texts found among the Dead Sea Scrolls at Qumran that the Masoretic tradition of the biblical text is only one of several extant earlier. The Hebrew text from which the Greek version (called Septuagint or LXX) was translated, for instance, must have differed from the Masoretic tradition, because in places the LXX is not a translation of a proto-Masoretic text, and there is evidence, especially from the scrolls from Qumran, of still other ancient text types. So the Masoretic tradition is not only a system of vowel and accent signs, but it is also one tradition among others of the consonants themselves. By the end of the first century C.E. the Masoretic-

---

[11] There is a lengthy discussion of the variety of early Hebrew texts in Emanuel Tov, *Textual Criticism of the Hebrew Bible* (2d ed.; Minneapolis: Fortress, 2001).

type text had become dominant, as shown by second-century biblical texts found at Masada and at Wadi Murabbaʿat.

There is some evidence that the Hebrew of the scribes who wrote the consonantal text was slightly different from that preserved by the Masoretes. One piece of evidence is the second-person masculine singular possessive pronominal suffix, almost always written ךְ. That the suffix is only rarely written with the *h mater lectionis* suggests that the scribes who wrote the consonantal text were not, in fact, pronouncing a long *ā* vowel after the *k*: the suffix was more likely something like *-ak* for them. The Hebrew of the Masoretes, however, has *-kā* for this suffix, and so the Masoretes did what they could with the consonantal text handed down to them and nestled the *qameṣ* within the final *k*. (The Masoretes did not alter the consonantal text; the many Ketib/Qere combinations attest to this same fact.)

The earliest inscription generally recognized as Hebrew is the Gezer Calendar from the late tenth century B.C.E., although this brief and cryptic text is difficult to classify. The earliest Hebrew script is an offshoot of the Phoenician script, itself a continuation of an earlier Old Canaanite tradition that goes as far back as the eighteenth century B.C.E. (the earliest exemplars of which have only been known since their discovery in 1998). In early Hebrew inscriptions, like Phoenician inscriptions throughout their history, only the consonants were written. In the ninth century, Aramaic inscriptions show the beginnings of the use of *matres lectionis* ("mothers of reading"), that is, consonants used to indicate a (long) vowel sound. Hebrew inscriptions, probably under Aramaic influence, have final *matres lectionis* beginning in the eighth century and internal *matres lectionis* at the end of the eighth. The earliest Hebrew system of final *matres lectionis* used *w* to mark a final *ū*, *y* for final *ī*, and *h* for all other final long vowels (plus the vowel that in BH is represented by final *sǝgôl*). The earliest Hebrew system of internal *matres lectionis* copied the system of final *matres lectionis* and used *w* to mark *ū* and *y* to mark *ī*. Eventually, the system was expanded so that both final and internal *w* could represent *ō* as well as *ū*, and final and internal *y* could mark *ē* as well as *ī*; *h* was used for all other final long vowels (and for eventual *sǝgôl*) and was never used as an internal *mater lectionis*.

The earliest biblical texts antedate the monarchy and the latest, Daniel, dates from the second century B.C.E. Within this span of about a thousand years, the Hebrew language must have changed considerably. Yet the Masoretic tradition imposed the same vocalization and accentuation system on the entire text, and the standardization that this process accomplished surely conceals any number of differences in pronunciation, including possible changes in accentuation (i.e., changes in which syllable was accented in a given word). Occasionally dialect differences are a part of the text, as in the *shibboleth* story in Judg 12:6 and the use of *mḥṣ* to gloss *mḥq* in Judg 5:26. The biblical Hebrew that we are investigating in this chapter, then, is somewhat artificial and presents texts from vastly different time periods and perhaps even different dialects as a single, unchanging entity.

The Tiberian Masoretic vowel system is usually interpreted according to Joseph Kimchi's (twelfth century) system of corresponding short and long vowels: *ḥîreq* (*i*) and *ḥîreq gādôl* (*ī*); *səgôl* (*e*) and *ṣērê* (*ē*); *pataḥ* (*a*) and *qāmeṣ* (*ā*); *q̇ameṣ ḥātûṗ/qāṭōn* (*o*) and *ḥōlem* (*ō*); *qibbûṣ* (*u*) and *šûreq* (*ū*). (Vocal and silent *šəwa*, the *ḥaṭēṗ* vowels, and diphthongs [such as *ṣērê-yôd*] are all secondary to this basic short/long system.) The pointing itself, however, suggests seven basic vowels plus *šəwa*, differentiated by vowel quality rather than quantity: *ḥîreq* [i][12] (pronounced like the *ee* in *beet*), *səgôl* [ɛ] (like the *e* in *bet*), *ṣērê* [e] (like the *ai* in *bait*), *pataḥ* [a] (like the *o* in *bottle*), *qameṣ* [ɔ] (like the *ou* in *bought* or the *au* in *caught* in those English dialects that distinguish *cot* and *caught*), *ḥōlem* [o] (like the *oa* in *boat*), and *šûreq* [u] (like the *oo* in *boot*).[13]

Medieval grammatical manuscripts, further, specify that each of the seven vowels could be either long or short.[14] Moreover, *šəwa* in this system is simply pronounced as the shortest possible vowel sound in any given environment, including the possibility of no vowel sound at all. Modern grammarians who criticize the Kimchi interpretation and prefer this second system argue that the Masoretes, who took such care to vocalize the text precisely in order that the exact "correct" pronunciation could be reproduced, would not have used the same symbol (i.e., *qāmeṣ* or *šəwa*) for two different sounds.

On the following page is a chart of the consonants of the Tiberian pronunciation system and following that a review of some of the changes linguists believe took place during the long history of Hebrew pronunciation.

---

[12] Brackets indicate phonetic realization, i.e., proposed actual pronunciation. The symbols within brackets are those of the International Phonetic Alphabet (IPA), a standard set used by linguists.

[13] For a discussion of the two systems, see W. Randall Garr, "Interpreting Orthography," in *The Hebrew Bible and Its Interpreters* (ed. William H. Propp, Baruch Halpern, and David Noel Freedman; Winona Lake, Ind.: Eisenbrauns, 1990), 53–80.

[14] See Geoffrey Khan, "The Orthography of Karaite Hebrew Bible Manuscripts in Arabic Transcription," *JSS* 38 (1993): 49–70.

manner of articulation[15]	place of articulation[16]							
	bilabial	interdental	dental	lateral	palatal	velar	pharyngeal	glottal
voiced stop	b (ב)		d (ד)			g (ג)		
voiceless stop	p (פ)		t (ת)			k (כ)		ʾ (א)
emphatic stop			ṭ (ט)			q (ק)		
voiced fricative	ḇ (ב)	ḏ (ד)	z (ז)			ḡ (ג)	ʿ (ע)	
voiceless fricative	p̄ (פ)	ṯ (ת)	s (ס)	ś (שׂ)	š (שׁ)	ḵ (כ)	ḥ (ח)	h (ה)
emphatic fricative			ṣ (צ)					
voiced approximant	w (ו)		r? (ר)	l (ל)	y (י)			
voiced nasal	m (מ)		n (נ)					

1. ח in Biblical Hebrew represents a merger of two originally separate phonemes, *ḥ and *ḫ, and ע in BH also masks two originally distinct phonemes, *ʿ and *ġ. We know that these consonants in fact remained separate in pronunciation, at least until the third century B.C.E. when the Septuagint of the Pentateuch was translated, because personal names and place names that are simply transliterated in the Septuagint show an almost entirely consistent distinction in their transliteration into Greek.[17]

When a BH word is spelled with ח that we know from cognate evidence was originally Semitic *ḥ, the Greek either does not transliterate the ח at all or shows evidence of vowel mutation. For instance, the name קֹרַח is transliterated κορε, and the familiar יִצְחָק is transliterated ισαακ. But when a BH word is spelled with ח that we know was originally Semitic *ḫ, the Greek transliterates the ח as χ. For instance, the BH place name חָרָן

---

[15] With regard to *manner of articulation,* a *stop* is a consonant produced by shutting off the passage of air somewhere in the oral cavity. A "voiced" consonant is one that is pronounced with vibration of the vocal cords. An *emphatic* is pronounced with a secondary velarization or glottalization (see *velar* and *glottal* in n. 16 below). A *fricative* is a consonant pronounced so that there is a narrowing in some area of the oral cavity that causes friction in the movement of air through that area. An *approximant* is pronounced with a movement of air, but without friction (cf. *fricative*).

[16] With regard to *place of articulation,* a *lateral* is pronounced with the air flowing along the sides of the tongue rather than down the center. A *palatal* is pronounced with the tongue raised toward the hard palate. A *velar* is pronounced with the tongue raised toward the soft palate. A *pharyngeal* is pronounced with the pharynx constricted. A *glottal* is pronounced with the vocal cords constricted.

[17] See especially Joshua Blau, *On Polyphony in Biblical Hebrew* (Proceedings: The Israel Academy of Sciences and Humanities 6/2; Jerusalem: Israel Academy of Sciences and Humanities, 1982); and John W. Wevers, "Ḥeth in Classical Hebrew," in *Essays on the Ancient Semitic World* (ed. John W. Wevers and Donald B. Redford; Toronto: University of Toronto Press, 1970), 101–12.

(cf. Akkadian *ḫarrānu*) is transliterated χαρραν, and gentilic חֹרִי (cf. Ugaritic *ḫry*) is χορραι. There are scores of such examples. So the people who translated the Bible into Greek heard a difference in the pronunciation of ח in these place names, and it is a difference that corresponds almost exactly to the distinction between the original phonemes *ḥ and *ḫ, a distinction we determine from the study of languages cognate to Hebrew. Outside the Pentateuch, this distinction between *ḥ and *ḫ is kept with a bit less consistency, and in Ezra-Nehemiah the distinctions made in the Greek often do not correspond correctly with the etymological evidence.

A similar argument can be made for the retention of the distinction between *ʿ and *ġ. Those עs that we know to have been originally Semitic *ġ either are not transliterated or show evidence of vowel mutation: אֱלִיעֶזֶר becomes ελιεζερ, and גִּלְעָד is γαλααδ. But those עs that were originally Semitic *ġ are transliterated with Greek γ, most famously Gaza, BH עַזָּה and Greek γαζα, and Gomorrah, BH עֲמֹרָה and Greek γομορρα.

2. Spirantization, or *lenition*, a "weakening" of a consonant, is a common sound change in languages all over the world. Spirantization of the six BH consonants—*b, g, d, k, p,* and *t*—is usually understood to enter Hebrew through Aramaic, where it took place probably at least by the fifth century B.C.E. In theory, during the Second Temple period when many Jews were speaking Aramaic as their first language, such an Aramaic feature as spirantization would have made its way into their pronunciation of Hebrew as well.

3. Recently, many Semitic linguists have come to the conclusion that the consonant שׂ, pronounced [š] in BH, was originally probably pronounced [s]. Alice Faber, in particular, has argued for this earlier pronunciation, based on comparisons with cognate languages (the same phoneme is pronounced [s] in Arabic and in some dialects of Akkadian, for instance), and on the behavior of languages in general: it is much more common for [s] to develop into [š] over time than for [š] to develop into [s]. Faber has used this theory to give a convincing explanation of the *shibboleth* episode in Judg 12:6, suggesting, to shorten a complicated argument, that the Ephraimites were still pronouncing [s] after the rest of Hebrew had shifted to [š].[18]

4. Geoffrey Khan, who has made an exhaustive study of the sounds of Tiberian Hebrew utilizing medieval documents that describe in detail the pronunciation of the letters,[19] has suggested three possible pronunciations

---

[18] Alice Faber, "Second Harvest: *šibbōleθ* Revisited (Yet Again)," *JSS* 37 (1992): 1–10.

[19] Especially, "The Tiberian Pronunciation Tradition of Biblical Hebrew," *ZAH* 9 (1996): 1–23; see also "The Pronunciation of the *reš* in the Tiberian Tradition of Biblical Hebrew," *HUCA* 66 (1995): 67–80.

for *reš* in that Hebrew: a uvular[20] trill, a uvular approximant,[21] and an alveolar emphatic[22] trill. One reason the suggestion of a uvular pronunciation is attractive is that one feature of BH *r* aligns it with the "gutturals" ʾ, *ḥ*, *ḥ*, and ʿ, that is, that it cannot be doubled. A uvular pronunciation, like the French *r*, is much closer to the guttural pronunciation of the other four than is an alveolar trill, like Spanish or Italian *r*.

5. There has been much discussion of the original pronunciation of the "emphatic" consonants *ṭ*, *ṣ*, and *q*. It is generally agreed that they incorporate some kind of secondary feature of pronunciation, but whether velarized (i.e., a consonant pronounced in the usual way, along with the back of the tongue arched up toward the soft palate) or glottalized (pronounced with a constriction of the vocal cords) is unclear.

6. Khan notes that the usual Tiberian pronunciation of ו was [v], but it was pronounced [w] when preceded by a *u* vowel; [w] was the original pronunciation of the letter, and it is, for instance, the Classical Arabic pronunciation as well.

3. RESOURCES[23]

After students complete a first-year grammar, there are a number of resources available for further study of BH. The Hebrew Bible most often used in scholarly research is *Biblia Hebraica Stuttgartensia* (*BHS*) (published by the Deutsche Bibelgesellschaft; available in many bookstores or from the American Bible Society), which includes the text from the Leningrad Codex plus text-critical notes and Masoretic notes (Masora parva in the margins, Masora magna citations beneath the biblical text). It is also now possible to buy a facsimile edition of the Leningrad Codex for under $200 in a beautiful volume, though it is much too large to carry around as a research Bible.[24] Jewish bookstores sell a paper version of a Torah scroll for under $50, so that students can see what the unpointed liturgical text looks like.

William Scott's *A Simplified Guide to BHS* is an excellent short compilation of useful information to help readers make their way through

---

[20] Produced by vibration of the uvula, the small teardrop-shaped tissue that hangs down from the roof of the mouth, toward the beginning of the throat.

[21] See n. 15 above.

[22] An alveolar consonant is pronounced by placing the tip of the tongue on the bony ridge directly behind the upper teeth; for "emphatic," see directly below.

[23] I would like to express my gratitude to my fellow members of the Wabash Center Consultation on Teaching Biblical Hebrew, who generously gave of their time and knowledge to make this section much more useful.

[24] David Noel Freedman, ed., *The Leningrad Codex: A Facsimile Edition* (Grand Rapids, Mich.: Eerdmans, 1998).

BHS, including short explanations of the accent marks, translations of Latin terms used in the text-critical apparatus, and translations and explanations of the most common Masora parva notes.[25] A larger discussion of *BHS,* but still on an introductory level, is Page Kelley, Daniel S. Mynatt, and Timothy G. Crawford, *The Masorah of Biblical Hebraica Stuttgartensia.*[26] This book contains a wealth of information, easily and attractively explained for the beginner. Reinhard Wonneberger's *Understanding BHS: A Manual for the Users of Biblical Hebraica Stuttgartensia* is a more detailed and complicated discussion for the advanced student.[27] The Masora article in the *Encyclopedia Judaica* is also useful; the 1994 version (also on CD-ROM) has been updated.[28] Finally, for the more advanced student, Israel Yeivin's *Introduction to the Tiberian Masorah* explains in some detail the history and contents of the Tiberian Masorah, including the meaning of the patterns of accentuation in the Hebrew text.[29]

Emanuel Tov's *Textual Criticism of the Hebrew Bible* (see n. 11) is a treasure trove of information about the formation of the text, as well as about the mechanics of textual criticism. The *Text of the Old Testament: An Introduction to the Biblia Hebraica* by Ernst Würthwein is an older and shorter treatment of much of the same material, but as the subtitle indicates is focused specifically on information of use to readers of *BHS.*[30]

The most commonly used scholarly dictionary in the United States is BDB, shorthand for its editors, Brown, Driver, and Briggs.[31] The other familiar scholarly dictionary is the English translation now available of the German *HAL* (Koehler and Baumgartner's *Hebräisches und aramäisches Lexikon zum Alten Testament*) entitled *The Hebrew and Aramaic Lexicon*

---

[25] William Scott, *A Simplified Guide to BHS* (3d ed.; N. Richland Hills, Tex.: BIBAL, 1995).

[26] Page H. Kelley, Daniel S. Mynatt, and Timothy G. Crawford, *The Masorah of Biblical Hebraica Stuttgartensia* (Grand Rapids, Mich.: Eerdmans, 1998).

[27] Reinhard Wonneberger, *Understanding BHS: A Manual for the Users of Biblia Hebraica Stuttgartensia* (2d ed.; trans. Dwight R. Daniels; Rome: Biblical Institute Press, 1990).

[28] Aron Dotan, "Masorah," *Encyclopedia Judaica Supplementary Volume* (*EncJud* 16; Jerusalem: Keter, 1972), cols. 1401–82.

[29] Israel Yeivin, *Introduction to the Tiberian Masorah* (trans. E. J. Revell; SBLMasS 5; Missoula, Mont.; Scholars Press, 1980).

[30] Ernst Würthwein, *The Text of the Old Testament: An Introduction to the Biblia Hebraica* (2d ed.; trans. Erroll F. Rhodes; Grand Rapids, Mich.: Eerdmans, 1995).

[31] Francis Brown, S. R. Driver, and Charles A. Briggs, *A Hebrew and English Lexicon of the Old Testament* (repr. Oxford: Clarendon, 1962), with a less expensive version available from Hendrickson Publishers (Peabody, Mass., 1979).

of the Old Testament (*HALOT*).[32] BDB is organized according to root, so students must be able to identify the root of a word in order to use the dictionary at all. Even, for instance, a *mem*-preformative noun like *midbār* must be analyzed as such and looked up under the root *dbr*. *HALOT* is organized alphabetically, so that the example above, *midbār,* would be listed under *mem.* Both BDB and *HALOT* give information from cognate languages about each root, as well as a complete listing of extant forms for each verb and a complete (or nearly complete, in the case of very common words) roster of passages catalogued under specific meanings of the word. The cognate information in *HALOT* is more up to date than that in BDB, which was written even before Ugaritic was known to exist; on the other hand, many American linguists are more comfortable with the analysis of root phonology that is found in BDB.[33] William Holladay's *A Concise Hebrew and Aramaic Lexicon of the Old Testament,* also organized alphabetically, is an abridgment of older versions of *HAL*.[34] It is a handy first dictionary, since it also includes complete listings of forms and passages (except, as before, when the word in question occurs very frequently). The small Langenscheidt's *Pocket Dictionary* is the easiest to carry of all the BH dictionaries.[35] It is organized alphabetically, as well, although the size precludes complete listings of forms or meanings.

Sheffield Academic Press is publishing a dictionary that takes a different approach to lexicography from the ones above: *The Dictionary of Classical Hebrew.*[36] The "Classical Hebrew" of the title includes Ben Sira, Qumran Hebrew, and other epigraphic Hebrew, as well as biblical Hebrew. The dictionary lists each form of a given word and its several meanings, as do the scholarly dictionaries above. But it differs from others in providing a tally of the various uses of each word as well, for instance, when a noun appears as the subject of a clause and when it is the object of a verb. Also, unlike the dictionaries described above, this one does not

---

[32] Ludwig Koehler, Walter Baumgartner, and J. J. Stamm, *The Hebrew and Aramaic Lexicon of the Old Testament* (trans. and ed. M. E. J. Richardson; 5 vols.; Leiden: Brill, 1994–1999).

[33] Ernest Klein's *A Comprehensive Etymological Dictionary of the Hebrew Language for Readers of English* (New York: Macmillan, 1987) provides cognates for Hebrew words of all periods.

[34] William Holladay, *A Concise Hebrew and Aramaic Lexicon of the Old Testament* (Grand Rapids, Mich.: Eerdmans, 1971).

[35] Karl Feyerabend, *Langenscheidt's Pocket Dictionary to the Old Testament: Hebrew-English* (12th ed.; New York: Barnes & Noble, 1961).

[36] David J. A. Clines, ed., *The Dictionary of Classical Hebrew* (5 vols. to date; Sheffield: Sheffield Academic Press, 1993–2001).

provide cognates from other Semitic languages. As of this writing, five volumes covering ʾ-n have been published, out of an expected eight.

The most common reference grammar in the United States is *Gesenius' Hebrew Grammar* (GKC = Gesenius-Kautzsch-Cowley, after the author, editor, and translator).[37] This is one of a long line of grammars published in Gesenius's name because he wrote the first thirteen editions. A newer reference grammar, very similar to Gesenius but with up-to-date bibliography, is "Joüon/Muraoka" (= T. Muraoka's update of P. Joüon's *A Grammar of Biblical Hebrew*).[38] Both books cover the phonology, orthography, and morphology of BH, as well as elementary syntax; both are arranged in numbered sections (and cited by section number, i.e., §15e). For a longer discussion of syntax, the major work in English is B. Waltke and M. O'Connor's *An Introduction to Biblical Hebrew Syntax*.[39] This book is meant as an intermediate Hebrew textbook, among other things, and is best used by reading entire sections through, rather than as a reference grammar. Waltke and O'Connor provide many, many examples of the topics they pursue. Also intended for students with one year of BH is *A Biblical Hebrew Reference Grammar*, by C. H. J. van der Merwe, Jackie A. Naudeg, and Jan H. Kroeze.[40] The authors remind the student of the basic information a first-year course would most likely cover, adding many details and a more systematic presentation than a lesson grammar can adopt. There is a new reprint of Davidson's *Introductory Hebrew Grammar—Syntax*.[41] This is a companion volume to Davidson's *Introductory Hebrew Grammar* (also recently issued in a revised edition)[42] and is also seen as a textbook for the second level of Hebrew study. It is shorter than the four previously mentioned grammars, but, like Waltke-O'Connor, concentrates on syntax alone. Ronald Williams's *Hebrew Syntax: An Outline* is, as the title implies, a shorter presentation of the syntax in an easy-to-use format.[43] F. C. Putnam's

[37] F. W. Gesenius, *Gesenius' Hebrew Grammar* (ed. E. Kautzsch; trans. A. E. Cowley; 2d ed.; Oxford: Clarendon, 1910).

[38] Paul Joüon, *A Grammar of Biblical Hebrew* (trans. and rev. T. Muraoka; 2 vols.; SubBi 14/1–2; Rome: Biblical Institute Press, 1991).

[39] Bruce K. Waltke and Michael Patrick O'Connor, *An Introduction to Biblical Hebrew Syntax* (Winona Lake, Ind.: Eisenbrauns, 1990).

[40] Christo H. J. van der Merwe, Jackie A. Naudeg, and Jan H. Kroeze, *A Biblical Hebrew Reference Grammar* (Sheffield: Sheffield Academic Press, 1999).

[41] A. B. Davidson, *Introductory Hebrew Grammar; Hebrew Syntax* (ed. and rev. J. C. L. Gibson; 4th ed.; Edinburgh: T&T Clark, 1994).

[42] A. B. Davidson, *Introductory Hebrew Grammar* (rev. James D. Martin; Edinburgh: T&T Clark, 1993).

[43] Ronald Williams, *Hebrew Syntax: An Outline* (2d ed.; Toronto: University of Toronto Press, 1978). Unfortunately, this work was completed in 1976, without a

A Cumulative Index to the Grammar and Syntax of Biblical Hebrew is a verse-by-verse listing of the locations in each of the grammars mentioned above (plus others) where a given verse is treated.[44]

For building vocabulary, both Larry Mitchel's *A Student's Vocabulary for Biblical Hebrew and Aramaic*[45] and George Landes's new, revised edition of his vocabulary book, *Building Your Biblical Hebrew Vocabulary,*[46] give lists of vocabulary organized according to frequency of appearance in the Bible. Mitchel lists words strictly by frequency, while Landes groups all the words he treats according to root. Landes's book also includes a useful short chapter on the formation of Hebrew words.

Several books include aids to make using the dictionaries and grammars easier. Armstrong, Busby, and Carr's *Reader's Hebrew-English Lexicon of the Old Testament* lists every word, verse by verse, that occurs fewer than fifty times in the Bible.[47] It is keyed to BDB as well. Students can keep this book open while reading new material and have unfamiliar words defined for them, and with the BDB citation they can turn to the dictionary if they want further information. Bruce Einspahr's *Index to Brown, Driver and Briggs Hebrew Lexicon* proceeds verse by verse through the Bible, listing the words in each verse that are used as examples in BDB and giving the page and section of BDB where the verse is mentioned, as well as an English gloss for the word.[48] Einspahr is not meant to be used as a lexicon but rather as an aid for students who want to know whether BDB has discussed a particular word in a specific verse. The much larger *Analytical Key to the Old Testament* analyzes every word in the Hebrew text, verse by verse, with additional reference to BDB and Gesenius's grammar, plus an English translation.[49] Davidson's *Analytical Hebrew and Chaldee Lexicon* also analyzes

---

computer, so that the Hebrew vowels are drawn in by hand, making the Hebrew a bit difficult to read.

[44] Frederic C. Putnam, *A Cumulative Index to the Grammar and Syntax of Biblical Hebrew* (Winona Lake, Ind.: Eisenbrauns, 1996).

[45] Larry Mitchel, *A Student's Vocabulary for Biblical Hebrew and Aramaic* (Grand Rapids, Mich.: Zondervan, 1984).

[46] George Landes, *A Student's Vocabulary of Biblical Hebrew: Listed According to Frequency and Cognate* (2d ed.; SBLRBS 41; Atlanta: Society of Biblical Literature, 2001).

[47] Terry A. Armstrong, Douglas L. Busby, and Cyril F. Carr, *A Reader's Hebrew-English Lexicon of the Old Testament* (Grand Rapids, Mich.: Zondervan, 1989).

[48] Bruce Einspahr, *Index to Brown, Driver and Briggs Hebrew Lexicon* (Chicago: Moody Press, 1976).

[49] John Joseph Owens, *Analytical Key to the Old Testament* (4 vols.; Grand Rapids, Mich.: Baker, 1989–1992).

every word in the Bible, but not verse by verse; rather, it proceeds alphabetically, but completely so (with the exception of prefixed *wāw*), so that *hā'āb* is listed under *he,* as is *hipqadtî*.[50] Students with very little Hebrew can use the Hebrew index to *Strong's Exhaustive Concordance of the Bible* (the English Bible, that is) to determine which Hebrew words are being used in a particular verse and to compare passages where the same Hebrew words are used, for word studies, for instance.[51]

Concordance work has been made enormously easier with the advent of computers. There are several good Hebrew Bible concordance programs available that also include information such as verb parsing. For Macintosh users, Gramcord's Accordance program is a powerful tool; the Windows version is called Gramcord for Windows. Bible Windows (Silver Mountain Software) is a popular concordance version for PCs with Windows, and Logos also makes a number of programs that include concordance capability. One can still buy concordances in book form, of course: Even-Shoshan's *A New Concordance of the Bible* is probably the most widely used.[52]

For students interested in pursuing epigraphic Hebrew, or just in finding the inscriptions, there are two fairly recent listings of known Hebrew inscriptions: G. I. Davies, *Ancient Hebrew Inscriptions: Corpus and Concordance;* and the appendices to *A Grammar of Epigraphic Hebrew,* by Sandra Landis Gogel, in the same series as this volume.[53] Gogel's book includes a lexicon, but the best proper dictionary for epigraphic Hebrew is the two-volume *Dictionary of the North-West Semitic Inscriptions,* edited by J. Hoftijzer and K. Jongeling.[54] All of Northwest Semitic is included, but it is complete (as of the time of the book's publication) for Hebrew inscriptions dating from before 300 c.e. The official publications of the Dead Sea Scrolls are in the Discoveries in the Judaean Desert series; the best collection is the one edited by Florentino García Martínez and Eibert J. C.

---

[50] Benjamin Davidson, *Analytical Hebrew and Chaldee Lexicon* (repr., Grand Rapids, Mich.: Zondervan, 1972).

[51] James Strong, *The Strongest Strong's Exhaustive Concordance of the Bible* (rev. John R. Kohlenberger III and James A. Swanson; Grand Rapids, Mich.: Zondervan, 2001). The Bible to which this concordance is keyed is the King James Version.

[52] Avraham Even-Shoshan, ed., *A New Concordance of the Old Testament Using the Hebrew and Aramaic Text* (2d ed.; Grand Rapids, Mich.: Baker, 1989).

[53] G. I. Davies, *Ancient Hebrew Inscriptions: Corpus and Concordance* (Cambridge: Cambridge University Press, 1991); Sandra Landis Gogel, *A Grammar of Epigraphic Hebrew* (SBLRBS 23; Atlanta: Scholars Press, 1998).

[54] J. Hoftijzer and K. Jongeling, eds., *Dictionary of the North-West Semitic Inscriptions* (Leiden: Brill, 1995).

Tigchelaar, and it is complete enough for most purposes.[55] E. Qimron's *Hebrew of the Dead Sea Scrolls,* currently being revised, is the only grammar of the scrolls in general.[56]

There are several websites that serve as clearinghouses for information about the Bible or the ancient Near East. James West's site is a very good place to start for information about Hebrew and Hebrew Bible on the web (http://web.infoave.net/~jwest), and for the ancient Near East, Charles Jones's Abzu site at the University of Chicago is the place to go (http://www-oi.uchicago.edu/OI/DEPT/RA/ABZU/ABZU.HTML).

4. BIBLIOGRAPHY

Albright, William F. *Yahweh and the Gods of Canaan.* Garden City, N.Y.: Doubleday, 1968.

Armstrong, Terry A., Douglas L. Busby, and Cyril F. Carr. *A Reader's Hebrew-English Lexicon of the Old Testament.* Grand Rapids, Mich.: Zondervan, 1989.

Blau, Joshua. *On Polyphony in Biblical Hebrew.* Proceedings: The Israel Academy of Sciences and Humanities 6/2. Jerusalem: Israel Academy of Sciences and Humanities, 1982.

Brown, Francis, S. R. Driver, and Charles A. Briggs. *A Hebrew and English Lexicon of the Old Testament.* Oxford: Clarendon, 1962.

Clines, David J. A. *The Dictionary of Classical Hebrew.* 5 vols. to date. Sheffield: Sheffield Academic Press, 1993–2001.

Cross, Frank Moore, Jr., and David Noel Freedman. *Studies in Ancient Yahwistic Poetry.* SBLDS 21. Missoula, Mont.: Scholars Press, 1975. Repr., Grand Rapids, Mich.: Eerdmans, 1997.

Davidson, A. B. *Introductory Hebrew Grammar.* Edited by James D. Martin. Edinburgh: T&T Clark, 1993.

———. *Introductory Hebrew Grammar; Hebrew Syntax.* Edited and revised by J. C. L. Gibson. 4th ed. Edinburgh: T&T Clark, 1994.

Davidson, Benjamin. *Analytical Hebrew and Chaldee Lexicon.* Repr., Grand Rapids, Mich.: Zondervan, 1972.

Davies, G. I. *Ancient Hebrew Inscriptions: Corpus and Concordance.* Cambridge: Cambridge University Press, 1991.

Donner, H., and W. Röllig. *Kanaanäische und aramäische Inschriften.* 3 vols. Wiesbaden: Harrassowitz, 1966–1969.

---

[55] Florentino García Martínez and Eibert J. C. Tigchelaar, *The Dead Sea Scrolls Study Edition* (2 vols.; Leiden: Brill, 2000).

[56] E. Qimron, *The Hebrew of the Dead Sea Scrolls* (Atlanta: Scholars Press, 1986). My thanks to Sidnie White Crawford for the most up-to-date information on Qumran Hebrew.

Dotan, Aron. "Masorah." Cols. 1401–82 in *Encyclopedia Judaica Supplementary Volume. EncJud* 16. Jerusalem: Keter, 1972.

Einspahr, Bruce. *Index to Brown, Driver and Briggs Hebrew Lexicon.* Chicago: Moody Press, 1976.

Even-Shoshan, A., *A New Concordance of the Old Testament Using the Hebrew and Aramaic Text.* 2d ed. Grand Rapids, Mich.: Baker, 1990.

Faber, Alice. "Second Harvest: *šibbōleθ* Revisited (Yet Again)." *JSS* 37 (1992): 1–10.

Feyerabend, Karl. *Langenscheidt's Pocket Dictionary to the Old Testament: Hebrew-English.* 12th ed. New York: Barnes & Noble, 1961.

Freedman, David Noel. *Pottery, Poetry, and Prophecy.* Winona Lake, Ind.: Eisenbrauns, 1980.

———, ed. *The Leningrad Codex: A Facsimile Edition.* Grand Rapids, Mich.: Eerdmans, 1998.

Garr, W. Randall. "Interpreting Orthography." Pp. 53–80 in *The Hebrew Bible and Its Interpreters.* Edited by William H. Propp, Baruch Halpern, and David Noel Freedman. Winona Lake, Ind.: Eisenbrauns, 1990.

García Martínez, Florentino, and Eibert J. C. Tigchelaar. *The Dead Sea Scrolls Study Edition.* 2 vols. Leiden: Brill, 2000.

Gesenius, F. W. *Gesenius' Hebrew Grammar.* Edited by E. Kautzsch. Translated by A. E. Cowley. 2d ed. Oxford: Clarendon, 1910.

Gogel, Sandra L. *A Grammar of Epigraphic Hebrew.* SBLRBS 23. Atlanta: Scholars Press, 1998.

Hoftijzer, J., and K. Jongeling, *Dictionary of the North-West Semitic Inscriptions.* Leiden: Brill, 1995.

Holladay, William. *A Concise Hebrew and Aramaic Lexicon of the Old Testament.* Grand Rapids, Mich.: Eerdmans, 1971.

Hurvitz, Avi. *A Linguistic Study of the Relationship between the Priestly Source and the Book of Ezekiel: A New Approach to an Old Problem.* Paris: Gabalda, 1982.

Joüon, Paul. *A Grammar of Biblical Hebrew.* Translated and revised by T. Muraoka. 2 vols. SubBi 14/1–2. Rome: Biblical Institute Press, 1991.

Kelley, Page H., Daniel S. Mynatt, and Timothy G. Crawford. *The Masorah of Biblia Hebraica Stuttgartensia: Introduction and Annotated Glossary.* Grand Rapids, Mich.: Eerdmans, 1998.

Khan, Geoffrey. "The Orthography of Karaite Hebrew Bible Manuscripts in Arabic Transcription." *JSS* 38 (1993): 49–70.

———. "The Pronunciation of the *reš* in the Tiberian Tradition of Biblical Hebrew." *HUCA* 66 (1995): 67–80.

———. "The Tiberian Pronunciation Tradition of Biblical Hebrew." *ZAH* 9 (1996): 1–23.

Klein, Ernest. *A Comprehensive Etymological Dictionary of the Hebrew Language for Readers of English.* New York: Macmillan, 1987.

Koehler, Ludwig, Walter Baumgartner, and J. J. Stamm. *The Hebrew and Aramaic Lexicon of the Old Testament.* Translated and edited by M. E. J. Richardson. 5 vols. Leiden: Brill, 1994–1999.

Landes, George. *A Student's Vocabulary of Biblical Hebrew: Listed according to Frequency and Cognate.* 2d ed. SBLRBS 41. Atlanta: Society of Biblical Literature, 2001.

Merwe, Christo H. J. van der, Jackie A. Naudeg, and Jan H. Kroeze. *A Biblical Hebrew Reference Grammar.* Sheffield: Sheffield Academic Press, 1999.

Mitchel, Larry. *A Student's Vocabulary for Biblical Hebrew and Aramaic.* Grand Rapids, Mich.: Zondervan, 1984.

Owens, John Joseph. *Analytical Key to the Old Testament.* 4 vols. Grand Rapids, Mich.: Baker, 1989–1992.

Polzin, Robert. *Late Biblical Hebrew: Toward an Historical Typology of Biblical Hebrew Prose.* HSM 12. Missoula, Mont.: Scholars Press, 1976.

Putnam, Frederic C. *A Cumulative Index to the Grammar and Syntax of Biblical Hebrew.* Winona Lake, Ind.: Eisenbrauns, 1996.

Qimron, E. *The Hebrew of the Dead Sea Scrolls.* Atlanta: Scholars Press, 1986.

Robertson, David A. *Linguistic Evidence in Dating Early Hebrew Poetry.* SBLDS 3. Missoula, Mont.: Scholars Press, 1972.

Scott, William. *A Simplified Guide to BHS.* 3d ed. N. Richland Hills, Tex.: BIBAL, 1995.

Strong, James. *The Strongest Strong's Exhaustive Concordance of the Bible.* Revised by John R. Kohlenberger III and James A. Swanson. Grand Rapids, Mich.: Zondervan, 2001.

Tov, Emanuel. *Textual Criticism of the Hebrew Bible.* 2d ed. Minneapolis: Fortress, 2001.

Waltke, Bruce K., and Michael Patrick O'Connor. *An Introduction to Biblical Hebrew Syntax.* Winona Lake, Ind.: Eisenbrauns, 1990.

Wevers, John W. "Ḥeth in Classical Hebrew." Pp. 101–12 in *Essays on the Ancient Semitic World.* Edited by John W. Wevers and Donald B. Redford. Toronto: University of Toronto Press, 1982.

Williams, Ronald. *Hebrew Syntax: An Outline.* 2d ed. Toronto: University of Toronto Press, 1978.

Wonneberger, Reinhard. *Understanding BHS: A Manual for the Users of Biblica Hebraica Stuttgartensia.* 2d ed. Translated by Dwight R. Daniels. Rome: Biblical Institute Press, 1990.

Würthwein, Ernst. *The Text of the Old Testament: An Introduction to the Biblia Hebraica.* Rev. ed. Translated by Erroll F. Rhodes. Grand Rapids, Mich.: Eerdmans, 1995.

Yeivin, Israel. *Introduction to the Tiberian Masorah.* SBLMasS 5. Translated by E. J. Revell. Missoula, Mont.: Scholars Press, 1980.

HEBREW (POSTBIBLICAL)

Baruch A. Levine

1. THE LANGUAGE

Literature in the Hebrew language has been composed uninterruptedly from the biblical period until the present day, and virtually every phase of Hebrew creativity is relevant to biblical studies. It is necessary, therefore, to define how the term "postbiblical Hebrew" (PBH) is being employed so as to clarify the necessarily limited scope of this introduction. As used here, "postbiblical," in contrast to "biblical Hebrew" (BH), refers to that phase of the Hebrew language expressed in written sources from Palestine of the prerabbinic and rabbinic period; in chronological terms, from the late first century C.E. until approximately 400 C.E. Certain linguistic features that later became pronounced in PBH are earlier attested in late-biblical writings of the Persian period (538–312 B.C.E., e.g., Chronicles and Ezra-Nehemiah) and continue to appear increasingly in biblical writings of the early Hellenistic period (Ecclesiastes, Esther, and Song of Songs).

1.1. HISTORY

The most extensive repository of PBH consists of the Tannaitic writings: the Mishnah, Tosefta, the collections of halakic midrash (*Mekilta, Sipra,* and *Sipre*), and Tannaitic baraitot (talmudic passages that are "external" to the Mishnah). Also included are writings of the Palestinian Amoraim (who succeeded the Tannaim) preserved in the Jerusalem Talmud and the primary collections of haggadic midrash (the *Midrash Rabbah,* the *Pesiqta* collections, and the like). Surely, the basic passages of the Passover Haggadah, and certain early prayer texts, qualify as exemplars of PBH. In their canonical form, most of these sources do not antedate the early third century C.E., although much of their content was undoubtedly composed earlier. The Hebrew of these sources is referred to as *ləšôn ḥăkāmîm,* "the language of the sages," namely, rabbinic Hebrew.

As a result of intensive efforts at retrieval and study of early manuscripts of the rabbinic Hebrew texts, some of which are vocalized entirely or in part, it has been possible to correct many of the errors that were imbedded in printed editions (and even in poor handwritten copies), thereby allowing for a more accurate assessment of the orthography, phonology, and morphology of PBH and all that proceeds from such knowledge. In other words, it is now possible to have a better sense of how PBH sounded and to identify forms of the language with greater certainty. It has also been possible to take note of differences between the readings in Palestinian and in Babylonian manuscripts, suggesting that there may have been dialects of PBH.

The corpus of PBH has been augmented in recent decades by the discovery of texts in postbiblical epigraphic Hebrew (PBEH), consisting mostly of inscriptions, legal documents, and letters dating to the first two Christian centuries. These texts speak for Palestinian Jewish communities of the period immediately preceding the publication of the Mishnah and other Tannaitic writings. In addition to the independent value of their contents, they enable us to assess the realism of the language employed in the rabbinic writings themselves. The verdict is indisputable: rabbinic Hebrew is representative of prevalent forms of the contemporary written language. In fact, the epigraphic sources often make it possible to trace the formation of rabbinic Hebrew. As an example, a lease of arable land written in Hebrew during the years of the Bar Kokhba revolt (132–135+ c.e.) sounds remarkably like legal passages of the Mishnah dealing with similar matters (see below, §2.3).

For purposes of this discussion, writings in what has come to be known as "Qumran Hebrew" will not be included. Most scholars would classify the Hebrew of the sect's canonical writings, and of other literary and hermeneutic texts found at Qumran, as the "last branch" of biblical Hebrew. Qumran Hebrew had some impact on rabbinic Hebrew but not as much as might have been expected. Some examples of continuity will be noted.

Abba Bendavid authored a voluminous and meticulous work in Hebrew entitled *Biblical Hebrew and Mishnaic Hebrew*. In it he compared biblical and rabbinic Hebrew in exhaustive detail and was able to show that rabbinic Hebrew is a natural outgrowth of earlier phases of the language.[1] In fact, he proposed that it reflects the spoken Hebrew of Palestinian Jews, later adopted as the formal, written language by sages of the early Christian centuries. E. Y. Kutscher agreed with his assessment and further refined it in his valuable article in the *Encyclopaedia Judaica*.[2]

---

[1] Abba Bendavid, *Biblical Hebrew and Mishnaic Hebrew* (2 vols.; Tel Aviv: Dvir, 1967).

[2] E. Y. Kutscher, "Mishnaic Hebrew," *EncJud* 16:1590–1608. This article was later revised and published as chapter 6 in E. Y. Kutscher, *A History of the Hebrew Language* (ed. Raphael Kutscher; Jerusalem: Magnes, 1982). Those desiring in-depth

According to Kutscher's reconstruction, it was the destruction of the Second Temple that led to the demise of biblical Hebrew as a literary language and the rise of the current vernacular as the written language. Although the precise character of spoken Hebrew in that period is obscure, as is the nature of spoken Hebrew in earlier biblical times, it is possible in certain instances to trace the early development of specific PBH forms. It is Kutscher's view that spoken PBH flourished mostly in Judea, whereas in Galilee Aramaic had taken over. However, after the destruction of the Jerusalem temple, and following the later Bar Kokhba revolt (132–135+ C.E.), many Jews from the central and southern parts of the country, including the academic leadership, migrated to Galilee, bringing with them their version of Hebrew and the Tannaitic writings already composed in it. They still spoke Hebrew, but their children, growing up in an Aramaic-speaking environment, did not continue to do so. Consequently, PBH survived primarily as a written language.

Most modern research in PBH has been published in academic Hebrew, and in the past it has been a subject of interest primarily to Jewish scholars trained in reading Hebrew texts of all historical periods. Now that the importance of PBH for the study of the Hebrew Bible, as well as for the understanding of Judaism in late antiquity, is being increasingly realized by a wider scholarly audience, more studies in English and the European languages have begun to appear. At the same time, biblical scholars of all backgrounds are being motivated to gain competency in modern, academic Hebrew. In this connection, it bears mention that modern Hebrew itself owes much of its tone and vocabulary to PBH.

Jewish sources written in PBH constitute a vast and varied library of biblical interpretation, just as do those preserved in Aramaic. In fact, much of the haggadic midrash and the talmudic material (including the baraitot) preserved in PBH is interspersed with Aramaic passages and is often imbedded in Aramaic texts. The contents of such interpretation range in scope and character from precise lexicography to legal hermeneutic and from the semantics of diction to structural analysis of literary form. One who has not mastered PBH, like one who has not studied Aramaic, would find all of these sources, which reveal Jewish understandings of the

---

treatments of specific problems in PBH should consult the studies in M. Bar-Asher, ed., *Studies in Mishnaic Hebrew* (ScrHier 37; Jerusalem: Magnes, Hebrew University, 1998). Included are chapters on some aspects of PBH to be discussed here, including determination, purpose, and result clauses and the development of new conjugations from biblical roots. The collection opens with a review of previous studies of Mishnaic Hebrew grammar and an assessment of the available evidence.

Hebrew Bible at crucial periods in the history of religions, inaccessible in their original language.

Medieval Jewish luminaries such as Saadyah Gaon and Maimonides turned to rabbinic Hebrew for information on the direct meaning of biblical texts, finding it especially valuable for explaining biblical *hapax legomena*. It was their view that the sages preserved reliable traditions on the meaning of biblical Hebrew, deriving from the time when it was a living language. The semantics of biblical Hebrew are greatly illuminated in haggadic midrash, as an example, and, generally speaking, the intertextual method is basic to rabbinic interpretation. On the thematic level, once we leave philology and exegesis, rabbinic sources open a window into the later development of Judaism by dwelling on issues relating to the human-divine dialogue and the future of the Jewish people and their ongoing mandate to fulfill Mosaic law. One finds expansive discussions and disputations on Jewish self-definition, exile and restoration, this world and the next, virtue and faith, and suffering and divine justice.

Finally, the voluminous halakic materials preserved in PBH serve to reveal how Jewish communities in Palestine of the Roman period developed the requisite institutional structures and formulated legal and ritual procedures through a hermeneutic that enabled them to anchor their creativity in the text of the Hebrew Bible, principally in Torah literature. Quantitatively, most of what has been preserved in PBH consists of commentary on the text of the Hebrew Bible. Viewing the Hebrew Bible as the crystallization of a long process of formation has drawn scholars to the languages of the ancient Near East. Viewing the Hebrew Bible as the beginning of a continuous process of commentary and interpretation should recommend the study of PBH.

1.2. GRAMMATICAL FEATURES

Without a doubt, the most salient feature of PBH is the pervasive infusion of Aramaic, affecting phonology, morphology, tense system, syntax, and vocabulary. As an example, analysis of PBH shows that its tense system parallels that of Galilean Aramaic (largely preserved in Tannaitic writings) and also that of Christian-Palestinian and Samaritan Aramaic. The infusion of Aramaic is already apparent in PBEH and, as Kutscher intimates, might even allow us to classify PBH as a fusion language. Knowledge of ancient Aramaic is, therefore, prerequisite to a proper appreciation of PBH. It would be mistaken, however, to ignore other sources of input, such as Phoenician-Punic, early West Semitic, and dialects of Hebrew other than BH.

The grammatical outline that follows is intended merely to focus on some of the distinctive characteristics of PBH, drawing comparisons and, more often, contrasts with BH. It is based on Kutscher's treatments, cited above, using many of his illustrative examples and further elaborating on certain features of the language that he treated only cursorily. It hardly presumes to be comprehensive and is intended to facilitate the comprehension of PBH texts on the part of those whose competence lies primarily in the area of BH and the West Semitic languages, especially ancient Aramaic.

1.2.1. ORTHOGRAPHY

PBH demonstrates a marked tendency toward plene spelling, already noticeable in PBEH, while still retaining defective spelling in many instances. Such fluctuations occur to a lesser extent in BH, especially in late BH. Thus, in PBH, long *ū* and *ō* vowels are often spelled with *wāw*. Even short and half vowels may on occasion be signified with *wāw* and *yôd* (and even *ʾālep*), yielding forms such as *ʿômôrîm* "sheaves" (c.f. BH *ʿomārîm*) and *lîqrôt* "to read, call," where the short *i* vowel of the prefixed *lāmed* is written with *yôd*. Certain plene spellings found in Qumran Hebrew texts are also attested in PBH.

1.2.2. PHONOLOGY

Both the consonants and vowels of PBH are identical with those of BH, with some drifting and shifting discernible in the later phase. There was a degree of interchange between *ʾālep* and *hê*, and *ʾālep* and *ʿayin*. Laryngeals and pharyngeals, in general, were often confused, perhaps under the influence of Greek, but these did not completely lose their sound value. Spirantized *bêt* and *wāw* also merged at times. Other sound shifts are likewise known. Thus we find *ḥêt > ʿayin*, producing *ʿāg ʿûgâ* for *ḥāg ḥûgâ* "he drew a circle." Similarly, *qôp* and *kāp* were occasionally interchanged, and more frequently *bêt > pê*, so that a verbal form such as *ləhabqîaʿ* would be realized as *ləhapqîaʿ* "to break through." Final *mêm* in undeclined nouns often shifts to *nûn*, such as in *ʾādām > ʾādān* "person, man."

Most of these shifts are paralleled in Galilean Aramaic but were often hyper-corrected by copyists and printers of the rabbinic texts to conform to BH. A degree of shifting is also discernible with respect to vowels, as from *i* to *e* and from *ā* to *ō*, in line with Galilean Aramaic and with Septuagint transcriptions. We find metathesis and dissimilation, as from *rêš* to *lāmed* (e.g., *margārît > margālît* "pearl"). There are also clues in the rabbinic sources to different pronunciations in various regions of the country, akin to the *shibboleth* phenomenon. As a rule, these observable changes follow well-known sound shifts and need seldom obscure comprehension. Yet, it is likely that in its day PBH probably sounded considerably different from BH.

1.2.3. MORPHOLOGY

1.2.3.1. *Independent Personal Pronouns.* BH *ʾānōkî* "I" disappears from
PBH and is fully replaced by *ʾănî,* a process that had already begun in late
BH. Biblical Hebrew *ʾănaḥnû* (rarely *naḥnû*) "we" is replaced by *ʾānû,*
which represents an internal Hebrew development. Under the influence of
Aramaic *ʾant,* the second-person masculine singular independent pronoun
is often expressed as *ʾatt,* alongside *ʾattâ* "you." In the second- and third-
person plural, the casting of the independent pronouns is fluid, so that the
forms *ʾatten* and *ʾattem,* as well as *ḥēn* and *ḥēm,* can signify both masculine and feminine. As noted by Kutscher, the situation with respect to
independent personal pronouns is symptomatic of the character of PBH in
general and is the result of three forces: (1) the background of BH, (2) the
infusion of Aramaic, and (3) internal Hebrew developments.

1.2.3.2. *Pronominal Suffixes.* Vocalized manuscripts of the Mishnah reveal
that the second-person masculine singular suffix in PBH is realized as *-āk,*
not BH *-ekā,* and that the feminine is *-ik,* not BH *-ēk,* yielding forms such
as *dəbārāk* and *dəbārik,* respectively. In the plural, the casting of the suffixes is fluid, as between final *mêm* and *nûn,* just as it is in the
independent personal pronouns.

1.2.3.3. *Demonstrative Pronouns.* For the near deictic, PBH discards the
feminine *zōʾt* "this" and carries over late BH *zô* (also written *zōh* in BH),
which did not likely develop from *zōʾt* but rather represents a different
dialect of late BH. Instead of epicene BH *ʾēleh* "these" PBH has *ʾēlû* for
both masculine and feminine.
     For the distant deictic, PBH uses, in addition to *ḥaḥûʾ* (masculine)
and *ḥaḥîʾ* (feminine) "that," the forms *ḥallāz* (masculine) and *ḥallâ* (feminine) "that" and the plurals *ḥāʾēlû* and *ḥallālû* (*ḥēlêlû*) "those" (epicene).
PBEH attests the variation *ḥallāzô* "that." The function of the distant deictic can be expressed by declined forms of the particle *ʾt* plus a determined
noun form, such as *ʾôtô hayyôm* "that day." The reflexive pronominal
function can be expressed with *ʿeṣem* "bone" used in the sense of "self,"
such as in *ḥûʾ ʿaṣmô* "he, himself," or as an accusative: *qôneh ʾet ʾ ʿaṣmô*
"he acquires himself, secures his own freedom."

1.2.3.4. *Relative and Possessive Pronouns.* Instead of the predominant BH
relative *ʾăšer* "which, that," PBH employs prefixed *še,* already known in
late BH and which bears no relation to *ʾăšer,* whose basic meaning is
"where." It also generated an independent possessive pronoun by combining the relative *še* with possessive *lāmed,* resulting in *šel* (with
geminated *lāmed*) "of, belonging to," which is declined as *šellî* "mine," and
so on. The principal impact of these innovations is realized in the syntax

of PBH, where their origin and early development will be discussed against
the background of late BH.

1.2.3.5. *The Verb*. PBH generated the *a-b-a* consonantal pattern (e.g.,
kārôk "to wrap"), and it carries over from late BH reduplicative forms such
as *lənaʿănēaʿ* "to shake" and *ʿarbēb* "to mix." Significant changes appear
with respect to the verbal stems. The *puʿal* has virtually disappeared in
PBH, except for the participle (e.g., *məquddāš* "is sanctified"). The perfect
of the *hitpaʿel* has given way to a form *nitpaʿal* (this is the correct form),
which conveys similar force. Thus, *nitʿôrār* "he awakened" instead of
hitʿôrēr (see further). There are other developments also due to the influence of Aramaic. Thus, the *hipʿil* coexists with the *šapʿel*, whose role is
greatly expanded in PBH. There are rare traces of the internal *qal* passive,
especially in *primae nûn* roots.

There are differences in the force and functions of the verbal stems
between BH and PBH. In PBH, the *qal* can often express a denominative
function, such as in *pārāh ḥôlebet* "a milking cow." In intransitive and stative verbs, the *qal* may convey a more active sense than in BH. Thus, in
PBH *gādal* means "he grew, became great," whereas to express the state
of being one would say *hāyâ gādôl* "he was large." In PBH the *nipʿal* is
utilized extensively and lends itself to diverse functions (see below). It
tends to express reflexivity, not merely passivity, to a greater degree than
in BH and often signifies incipient (inchoate) action.

The functions of the *piʿel* are expansive in PBH. Apart from the intensive and causative functions, one notes many *piʿel* denominatives. The
piʿel can also have the force of an intransitive, signfiying inchoate action,
such as *bikkərû* (consonantal *bykrw*) "they began to ripen." It would
appear that the *piʿel* replaced the *qal* in some instances. The *hipʿil* retains
its earlier functions and, as noted, coexists with the the Aramaistic *šapʿel*,
which is conjugated like a *piʿel*. The *hopʿal* carries on, and the *nitpaʿel*,
which has all but replaced the perfect of the *hitpaʿel*, has several functions. These include inchoative: *ništaṭṭâ* "he went mad"; reciprocal:
ništaṭṭəpû "they became partners"; and passive: *nitgallâ* "it was uncov-
ered, it appeared." The *hitpaʿel* remains operative in participial,
imperfect, and imperative forms, where it often has virtually transitive
force. Thus, *hitqabbēl lî giṭṭî* means "receive my bill of divorce on my
behalf" (*m. Giṭ.* 6:2). Certain verb forms characteristic of BH disappeared,
like the cohortative, the short imperfect, and inverted forms with *wāw*-
consecutive. Of the infinitives, only the construction with prefixed *lāmed*
survived, and clusters composed with it, such as *millômar* (consonantal
mlwmr) "from saying."

Conjugation of the perfect differs from BH in two respects. The second-
person plural is the same for masculine and feminine, so that the forms

kətabtem and *kətabten* "you wrote," for example, are epicene. The second-person masculine singular is realized as *kātabtâ,* in the same long form as is found in Qumran Hebrew. As in Qumran Hebrew, there is a penchant in PBH for regularly employing the pausal form. The imperfect follows BH, except that the second- and third-person feminine plurals of BH have disappeared. The participle favors the *qôṭelet* form, although there are also instances of the *qôṭəlâ* form. The masculine plural alternates between the endings *-îm* and *-în,* under the influence of Aramaic. The plural feminine imperative of BH (*šəmôrnâ* "watch, guard") has disappeared. Kutscher notes that in PBH the participle can be negated by *lō',* not only by *'ên,* as in BH. The infinitive may be negated by *šallō'* plus the infinitive construct with prefixed *lāmed,* such as in *šallō' lišmôr* "not to watch."

Certain forms disappear from the written sources, whereas new vocalizations are generated. In the *qal* perfect of strong verbs, the *qāṭôl* form has disappeared, whereas the participial *qāṭôl* form has proliferated in the singular case of anomalous *yākôl* "to be able," yielding the feminine and plural forms *yəkôlâ, yəkôlîn,* and *yəkôlôt.* There is a general tendency to favor the *yiqṭôl* imperfect over the *yiqṭal,* even with respect to intransitive verbs. This pattern appears to be consistent in the case of *mediae ḥêt* verbs, such as in *yišḥôṭ* "he will slaughter" instead of BH *yišḥaṭ.* At times, the imperfect of the *hitpaʿel* is vocalized like Aramaic (e.g., *titḥabbār*). *Primae 'ālep* verbs may exhibit elision of the *'ālep,* yielding forms such as the infinitive *lômar* (consonantal *lwmr*) "to say" and *lôkal* (consonantal *lwkl*) "to eat." *Primae 'ayin* verbs in the *nipʿal* may be vocalized with *səgôl,* such as *neʿĕśâ* "it was done."

Third weak verbs show considerable change in PBH. *Tertiae 'ālep* verbs are usually treated as *tertiae yôd,* such as *qārînû* "we called, read," although the imperfect is still *yiqrā'* and infinitival *liqrôt* "to read" coexists with the less-frequent conflate form *liqrô't* (cf. Qumran Hebrew). The feminine ending with *tāw* is frequent in *nipʿal* perfect forms of third weak verbs, such as *niṭmêt* "she became impure" (*tertiae 'ālep*), *nikwêt* "she was burned," and *nišbêt* "she was taken captive" (*tertiae yôd*). Of considerable interest is the PBH form *hāyāt* "she/it was," the third feminine singular of the third weak verbal root *h-y-h,* which in BH appears as *hāyətâ.* Since the later form did not likely develop from the earlier, and since it cannot be traced to Aramaic influence, it probably derived from a different dialect of Hebrew. Aramaic influence accounts for forms such as *hĕwêh* (masculine) and *hĕwî* (feminine) imperative "be" and the plural imperative *hĕwû.* PBH also attests forms of this verb such as imperfect *yəhê'* instead of *yihyeh.* Also attested are participial forms with *qāmēṣ,* such as *zākeh* "he gains possession, merits" and *ḥāyeh* "he lives," alongside the more normal form, *qôneh* "he acquires." PBEH may well attest similar participial forms, even in strong verbs, perhaps under the influence of Aramaic.

The infinitive constructs of *primae yôd* and *primae nûn* verbs are patterned after the imperfect on the masculine model: *lêrēd* "to descend" rather than *lāredet,* and *lîtēn* "to give, pay" rather than *lātēt.* Also note the form *lîṭôl* "to take," with the assimilation of initial *nûn* and plene vocalization with *yôd.* Certain fluctuations are evident in the case of middle weak verbs, whereby *mediae yôd* verbs are often realized as *mediae wāw* and whereby the *nipʿal* participle and perfect of middle weak verbs coalesce, so that a form like *nîdôn* can mean both "he/it is judged" and "he/it was judged." We also encounter, for instance, a *hipʿil* participle *mēśîm* "he assigns," reflecting the *qal* imperfect *yāśîm* "he will put, place." PBH seems to favor geminate forms in the case of both transitive and intransitive verbs.

PBH exhibits a much more developed tense system than BH, undoubtedly due to the influence of Aramaic, as has been noted above. One finds the following tenses:

(a) The perfect, which also serves as a preterite.
(b) A modal imperfect, expressing intention or wish, or the imperative, or the negation of same. Thus, *ləʿôlām yōʾmār ʾādām* "A person ought always to say" or *lōʾ yōʾmār ʾādām* "A person ought not to say." The imperfect is not employed to convey the indicative future, that function having been appropriated by the participial present. This being the case, there was no longer need for the inverted perfect (*wəqāṭal*) or the inverted imperfect (*wayyiqṭōl*).
(c) Periphrastic tenses compounded with the verb *hāyâ* + the participle. Thus, we find a progressive perfect *hāyâ ʾômēr* (also *ʾômēr hāyâ*) "he used to say, was saying," a future *yəhēʾ yārēʾ* "he shall be in awe" (subjunctive), and an imperative *hĕwēh ʾômēr* "be saying, say."
(d) A true present tense conveyed by the participle, which also conveys the force of a present-future. Thus, hypothetically, *hûʾ nôsēaʿ* may mean "he is traveling" and also "he will be going away."
(e) The imperative, which carries on from BH.
(f) A new anticipatory future tense with *ʿātîd* ("expecting, in readiness") + infinitive construct with prefixed *lāmed: ʾattâ ʿātîd lîtēn* "You will be expected to give; you will ultimately give." Also note use of *sôp* "end," declined + infinitive construct *šessôpēnû libdôq* "that in the end, we will examine" (literally, "that our end is to examine").
(g) The passive participle, mainly of intransitive verbs, functioning as a present prefect, such as *məqubbāl ʾănî* "I am in receipt, I have received."

The overall effect of the above developments is to enable PBH to express more elaborate sequences of tenses and to place actions and situations in a punctive relation to each other, resulting in greater narrative freedom and an enhanced capacity for description. They also had an impact on the syntax of PBH, as will be shown below.

1.2.3.6. *The Noun and Verbal Nouns.* PBH exhibits considerable morphological creativity in generating or expanding usage of verbal nouns based on the *qal* and other stems. Kutscher counts about fifteen different forms based on the *qal* alone. Thus, the stative *qəṭîlâ* form is used extensively in PBH, such as *ʾăkîlâ* "eating" (130 attestations in the Mishnah alone). Other stative forms are recast as *qəṭîlâ*, so that we encounter a form such as *śərîpâ* "burning" for BH *śərēpâ*. We also find Aramaistic masculine forms such as *kəlāl* "general rule" and *pərāṭ* "specification" alongside feminine *qəṭālâ* "death, execution." New *qal* forms are *gāzēl* "robbery" and *ḥānēq* "strangulation." Finally, the *nomen agentis* of the *qal* comes into its own in PBH in such forms as *lāqôaḥ* "purchaser."

Turning to other stems, we find additional verbal noun forms. The *piʿel* yields forms such as *haddibbēr* "the logos" alongside *haddibbûr*, and feminine *kappārâ* "expiation," from Aramaic. There are also *piʿel*-based forms such as *wîddûy* "confession" (lit., "exposing oneself") that express the reflexive sense and *kārēt* "the penalty of being 'cut off,'" also expressed as *hikkārēt* in the *nipʿal*. The *hipʿil* yields both masculine and feminine verbal nouns configured like the infinitive, such as *heqṭēr* "burning" ("an offering on the altar") and *hôrāyâ/hôrāʾâ* "instruction." Verbal nouns based on the *qal* with affixes also occur, such as *gôzəlān* "robber" and *rôṣəḥān* "murderer" (in Babylonian sources *gazlān* and *raṣḥān*). These are Aramaistic forms, yet they hark back to the Akkadian affix *-ānu*. PBH developed new plurals in addition to masculine *-îm* and *-în* and feminine *-ôt*, such as *merḥăṣāʾôt* (in Babylonian sources) and *merḥăṣîyôt* (in Palestinian sources) "bath-houses." The plural of nouns ending in *-ût* is seen in *malkût, malkîyôt* "kingdom, kingdoms." PBH attests double plurals that yield combinations such as *rəʾšê šānîm* "New Years" and *bātê kənēsîyôt* "synagogues."

1.2.3.7. *Particles.* PBH exhibits some new particles, although as a rule the BH prepositions have remained. The following are noteworthy: *bintayim* "meanwhile, in the interim," *ʿakšāyw* "now," *kədê* "in order to, so as to," and *kêṣad* "how, in what manner." Prefixed *ʾālep* can function as prepositional *bêt*, such as in *ʾabayit* "in the house of, at the house of." There are cases where prefixed *lāmed* serves as the accusative particle, as in Aramaic, and the prepositions *ʿad* "up to, to" and *ʿal* "on, to" interchange, as they do in Galilean and Samaritan Aramaic. Negation is indicated by *ʾên*, which is declined as in *ʾênî* "I am not" and so forth, and the participle may also be negated by *lōʾ*, as already noted. We find constructions such as *ʾim lōʾ* (in PBEH *ʾîlōʾ*) "if not" and the shortened negative *ʾî* plus the independent pronoun, as in *ʾî ʾattâ* "you do not" or the interrogative "don't you?" We also find the affirmative *hēn* "yes" and *hēk* "how," taken from Aramaic. One notes a general fluidity in the use of prepositions.

1.2.4. SYNTAX

The distinctive character of PBH as a written language is perhaps determined more by syntax than by any other feature, with the possible exception of vocabulary. Before summarizing predominant syntactic features of PBH in some detail with a view to their background, a general observation is in order. In PBH the subject usually precedes the verb in the sentence. This is not consistently so, but is more of a prevalent pattern than in BH and is due to the influence of Aramaic syntax.

1.2.4.1. *Verbal Complements.* PBH favors various constructions, including the finite verb plus the participle as in *hitḥîl bôkeh* "he began crying," a combination only rarely attested in BH.

1.2.4.2. *Subordination.* The prominence in PBH of subordinate clauses, especially relative clauses, contrasts with the prevalence in BH of coordinate clauses joined by conjunctive *wāw*. A major consequence of this marked trend is seen in the manner of expressing possession, with subordination virtually replacing the declension of nouns with pronominal suffixes. Thus, instead of hypothetical *bêtî* "my house," we would find *habbayit šellî* (replacing *habbayit ʾăšer lî*). Although these marked changes are clearly due to the influence of Aramaic, it is curious that the actual way of signifying relative subordination in PBH (and PBEH) is with the particle (or prefix) *še* "that, which." As will be shown, this particle derives from contemporary Phoenician-Punic and is itself virtually unknown in Aramaic, where the particle *dî*, earlier *zî*, performs this function.

In fact, it would be practical to begin a discussion of the syntactic character of PBH as a whole by using the particle *še* as a probe, because its functions and utilization are so far reaching. B. A. Levine has traced the history of the particle in BH through Phoenician *ăše* (= prosthetic *ʾālep* + *še*) and prefixed *še* in Punic (rarely in Ammonite).[3] In an earlier study of spoken Hebrew in biblical times, Levine summarizes the utilization of relative *še* in late BH, most extensively in the Song of Songs and Ecclesiastes.[4] Noting that there is, of course, no etymological connection between *še* and *ʾăšer,* the relative pronoun in standard BH, Levine concludes that usage of

---

[3] B. A. Levine, "The Prefix *še* in Biblical Hebrew in the Light of Ancient Epigraphy," (Hebrew) *ErIsr* 18 (1985): 145–52.

[4] B. A. Levine, "Chapters in the History of Spoken Hebrew" (Hebrew), *ErIsr* 14 (1978): 155–60.

the particle *še* in Hebrew in late BH is due to the presence of Phoenician-speaking communities during the Persian period all along the Levantine coast, from Acco in the north, via Dor, to Ashdod in the south, and even reaching inland in some areas.

In Nehemiah 13:23–24 we read of contemporary Judeans speaking "Ashdodite" (*'ašdôdît*), a likely reference to Phoenician, and who no longer know how to speak Judean Hebrew (*yəhûdît*). It was about then that a form of the Phoenician-Punic relative pronoun began to be utilized in biblical writing. One notes that in the Lachish and Arad ostraca, which date to the very last decades of the period of the First Temple, the relative pronoun *'ăšer* still dominated, which helps to pinpoint the time when its replacement, the prefix *še,* was introduced. It is not necessary here to dwell on the one definitely early attestation of *še* in BH, in the Song of Deborah (Judg 5:7), which probably reflects Akkadian *ša.*

In earlier Phoenician inscriptions, we find the form *'š* (*separatim*), whereas in Punic the prefixed form *š* is attested, as in the Nora inscription from Sardinia, dated to the sixth century B.C.E. at the latest. There we have such constructions as *šh'* (‖ *šehû'*) "that he/it is, which is" and *šbn* (‖ *šeb-bānâ*) "which he built." In later Punic we find constructions with genitive *lāmed,* such as *h'š šlh* (‖ *hā'îš šellāh*) "her husband" and the Latin transcription in Poenilus, *syllohom* (cf. *šellāhem*) "which is theirs," with the *lāmed* geminated.

In summary, it can be stated that under Phoenician-Punic influence, late BH absorbed the relative particle *še* just as it was also coming under intense Aramaic influence. The result was that its syntax tended toward subordinate clauses, principally relative clauses, which were signified by prefixed *še.* Thus it was that the written Hebrew of the postexilic period, and the spoken Hebrew of the time, were affected in a way that laid the groundwork for the syntax of PBH. We now survey the workings of the particle *še* in PBH (and PBEH).

1.2.4.2.1. Syntactic Subordination. Before a possessive *lāmed,* the particle *še* expresses syntactic subordination. There are several possible constructions for this.

(a) When the subject and object are both determined: *hayyayin wəhahōmeṣ šellaggôyîm* "the wine and the vinegar of the Gentiles" (the prefix *še,* plus the geminated possessive *lāmed,* plus the noun with the definite article, which produces further gemination).
(b) When the subject and object are indeterminate: *lāšôn šellîzəhôrît* "a thread that is of crimson wool."
(c) Anticipatory genitive, with the independent possessive pronoun *šel* (*separatim*): *ribbônô šel hā'ôlām* "Its Master, (namely,) who is of the

world." A variant is the *junctim* construction: *ribbônô šellāʿôlām,* with the prefix *še* plus the possessive *lāmed,* geminated. This construction actually occurs in LBH, in Song 3:7: *hinnēh miṭṭātô šellišlōmōh* "Behold, his bed, (namely,) which is of Solomon." The tendency in PBH to imply determination without using the definite article has produced the construction: *ribbônô šel ʿôlām.* In PBEH and in early manuscripts of the Talmud we find, instead of gemination, plene renderings of prefixed *še* with *hê* and *ʾālep* plus possessive *lāmed.* Thus, in a Hebrew inscription from Dabbura in the Golan, dating to the late second or early third century C.E., incised on a basalt lintel, we read *zh byt mdrsw shlrby ʾlʿzr hqpr,* literally: "This is his House of Study, (namely,) of Rabbi ʾElʿazar Haqqappar." For the plene orthography itself, in differing syntactic roles, note the Ketib in Eccl 6:10 *ʿim šehattaqîp mimmennû* ("with one who is stronger than he" [Qere: *šettaqîp*]).[5] In P.Yadin 51:2, a Hebrew letter of Bar Kokhba (132–135 C.E.), we find the form *ša(h)tišlǝhû* "that you send.

(d) The independent possessive pronoun *šel* and its subject may be declined, producing possession through subordination. This already occurs in Song 1:6: *karmî šellî* "My vineyard, which is mine." It should be noted that Aramaic is the language that generated declined relative-genitives such as *dî lî/zî lî* "which is mine," combined as *dîlî/zîlî.*

1.2.4.2.2. Introducing a Relative Clause. The particle *še* may be prefixed to verbal and nominal forms, as well as to independent pronouns, to generate relative clauses. Following are illustrative passages, all coming from the very first chapter of the Mishnah, *Ber.* 1, translated literally for effect.

(a) *miššāʿâ šehakkôhănîm niknāsîm leʾĕkôl biṭărûmātān:* "From the time that/when the priests come in to partake of their offering" (participial present with temporal sense).
(b) *maʿăśeh šebbāʾû bānāyw mibbêt hammišteh:* "So it happened that his sons returned from a house of feasting"; *kol mah šeʾāmǝrû hăkāmîm:* "In every case that/where the sages said"; *happeh šeʾāmar hûʾ happeh šehittîr:* "The mouth that prohibited, it is the very mouth that permitted" (with the perfect).
(c) *šeʿābartā ʿal dibrê bêt hillēl:* "Because [literally, 'it is for the reason that'] you transgressed against the words of the House of Hillel."
(d) *šeneʾĕmar:* "That it is said (in Scripture)"—introduces biblical citation (with the *nipʿal* perfect).

---

[5] D. Urman, Jewish Inscriptions from Dabbura in the Golan," *IEJ* 22 (1972): 16–23.

It is to be noted that the particle *še* is often combined with prepositional elements, either independent or prefixed, as some of the above passages illustrate. Most of these combinations are modeled on Aramaic usage. Following are some further examples: *mippənê še-* "because, for the reason that"; *ʿal šûm še-* "because, for the reason that (also, *miššûm še-*); *kəšem še-* "in the same way that"; *kədê še-* "in order that." One could list scores of similar idiomatic constructions. Often the particle *še* clusters with prepositions prefixed to nouns, as in *śəʾōr šebbāʿîsâ* "the leaven that is in the dough."

1.2.4.2.3. *Prefixed to an Imperfect Verb.* When attached to a following verb in the imperfect, the particle *še* can function modally and as a virtual imperative or jussive.

> (a) In the modal function: *ʿad šeyyaʿăleh ʿamûd haššaḥar* "until it is that the pillar of dawn shall rise"; *miššeyyakkîr bên təkēlet ləlābān* "from (the time) that he could differentiate between royal blue and white." (Note the clustering of prepositions in the latter example.)
> (b) As a virtual imperative: In the example given above, from P.Yadin 51:2, a Bar Kokhba letter, the form *ša(h)tišləḥû* is best translated "that you send; you will send." This function is characteristic of Aramaic. Compare the following examples from the Mishnah: *šeyyəhēʾ* "that he/ it should be, let him/it be"; and *šellōʾ yihyu ʾēlû bənê bêtî* "Let these not be members of my household."

Before leaving the subject of subordinate clauses, note should be taken of the function of the definite article, prefixed *hê,* as a relative pronoun in the sense "the one who." This phenomenon is already attested in late BH. In Exod 16:17–18, we read *hammarbeh wəhammamʿîṭ* "the one who (gleaned) much and the one who (gleaned) little." It is much more frequent, however, in PBH, and often introduces general statements. Thus, *haššôḥēṭ ʾet happārâ* "The one who/whoever slaughters a cow"; *hammitkawwēn lômar tərûmâ wəʾāmar maʿăśēr* "The one who/ whoever intends to say 'priestly offering' but says 'tithe.'" Also note *kol hamməšallēm qeren wəḥōmeš* "Anyone who pays the principal, plus (the penalty of) one-fifth."

1.2.4.3. *Ellipsis.* PBH favors elliptical statements. This is one of the special nuances of the participle-present, especially the masculine plural participle functioning as a present-future tense. Thus, *pôdîn maʿăśēr šēnî kəšaʿar hazzôl* "They/we redeem (may redeem) the 'second tithe' according to the low price." Similarly, *mēʾēmātay ʾôkəlîn pērôt hāʾîlān?* "From what point do (may) they/we eat the fruit (of trees) that grew during the seventh year?" This works in the negative as well. Thus, *ʾên qôšrîn ʾet hassûs* "They/we do not hitch up the horse." The sense is that the participle is prescriptive, not merely descriptive, and that it is conveying what is customary, proper, or even required. Negatively, it can express what is improper or even forbidden. In the singular, we find statements such as *nôṭēaʿ ʾādām qiššût ûdəlaʿat* "A person 'plants' (may plant) cucumbers and pumpkins." For itself, ellipsis is also expressed by the third-person perfect plural, such as *gāzərû ʿāl yiḥûd happənûyâ* "They decreed against uniting with an unmarried woman." It is also seen in a limited way with the imperfect. Ellipsis is further expressed by the periphrastic tenses. An example of this is seen in *m. Sanh.* 4:5: *kêṣad məʾayyəmîn ʿāl ʿēdê nəpāšôt? maknîsîn ʾôtān ûməʾayyəmîn ʿălêhen* "How do they/we issue the charge to witnesses in a capital case? They/we would bring them in and issue the charge to them."

1.2.4.4. *Agreement.* Allowing for some fluidity, agreement as to number and gender is preserved in PBH, but there is less consistent agreement in respect of determination. Thus, we find constructions such as *kōhēn haggādôl* "the high priest" (instead of *hakkōhēn haggādôl*) and even virtual, or implied, agreement whereby the construction *kōhēn gādôl* would be rendered "the high priest." Thus, *m. Yoma* 1:1 reads *maprîšîn kōhēn gādôl* "They/we separate the high priest," and 1:3 has *ʾîšî kōhēn gādôl* "My sire, the high priest."

1.2.4.5. *Determination of the Direct Object.* In BH it is fairly consistent for the determined direct object of the transitive verb to be introduced by the accusative particle *ʾet* plus the definite article *hê*. Although this syntax is well attested in PBH, it is only one of several ways of signifying the determined direct object. Thus, *m. Bik.* 3:1: *kêṣad maprîšîn habbikkûrîm* "How do they/we set aside the offerings of firstfruits?" (without *ʾet*). But, see *m. ʾAbot* 2:9, *hārôʾeh ʾet hannôlād* "The one who sees what is being born [i.e., who is forward looking]." Normally, the accusative particle introduces the declined, direct object, which is, by definition, also determined. Thus, *hammôkēr ʾet śādēhû* "The one who/whoever sells his field." Also note usage of the accusative particle to introduce functional, determined direct objects, as in *məʿaśśēr ʾet šehûʾ nôtēn lâ* "He tithes that which he is giving her" (*m. Demai* 3:5). It is significant that PBH, more often than not, fails to signify determination in the direct object where we might expect it. To put it another way, determination is often implied with respect to the direct object, just as it is in some cases with respect to the subject. It has already been noted that declined forms of *ʾet* serve as distant demonstratives.

1.2.5. Lexicon and Diction

The following factors have figured in the formation of the lexicon of PBH and have affected its diction.

1.2.5.1. *Disuse and Replacement.* Certain BH words disappeared from
PBH, even terms for family relationships and body parts, semantic
areas that are usually regarded as being resistant to linguistic change.
Examples cited by Kutscher are BH *dôd* "uncle" and *beṭen* "belly." It is
inconceivable that even a single word occurring in the Hebrew Bible
was unknown in the PBH period, surely to those who wrote the canonical works in rabbinic Hebrew. Consequently, considerable weight
must be given to conscious replacement and responsiveness to new
vocabulary, coming primarily from spoken Hebrew and Aramaic. In
this connection, it is important to emphasize, as Kutscher does, that BH
does not represent the total repertoire of the Hebrew language, written and spoken, of the biblical period. Even the very sparse amount of
Hebrew epigraphy now available from the biblical period has revealed
vocabulary unknown from canonical sources, and one supposes there
was much more. Qumran Hebrew further endorses this conclusion.
Some of what is new in the vocabulary of PBH is, therefore, attributable to dialects other than BH. It has also been pointed out that
Phoenician and Punic may have contributed to the vocabulary of PBH
to some degree. In the same vein, it is also likely that PBH preserves
old West Semitic vocabulary, going back as early as Ugaritic, which is
absent from the BH lexicon.

1.2.5.2. *Changes in Meaning and Aspect.* At times, BH vocabulary persists
in PBH, but the meaning undergoes change. Kutscher points out the example of the Hebrew verb *n-h-g* "to lead," which is active-transitive in BH,
whereas in PBH it exhibits a stative-reflexive aspect, meaning "to conduct
oneself, to behave." To secure the force of the active-transitive in PBH one
would have to use the *piʿel,* such as *hammənahēg ʿôlāmô bəḥesed* "the one
[i.e., God] who conducts his world with kindness," or even the *hipʿil.* There
is also evidence of semantic progression. In this way, the BH verb *g-z-r* "to
cut" comes to convey in PBH the meaning "to decide, issue an edict," in
line with a well-known semantic syndrome. Connotations may become
specialized, so that the BH term *ʿăṣeret* "recessional, sacred convocation"
is used in PBH with special reference to the Pentecost festival. Similarly, a
term of wide connotations like BH *ṣədāqâ* comes, in PBH, to connote gifts
to the poor, specifically.

1.2.5.3. *Morphological Changes.* New lexemes were generated from
known Hebrew roots, as is generally true in the ongoing development of
agglutinated languages. In the case of PBH, many of these new mor-
phologies were appropriated from Aramaic, which had already developed
them. Some examples of this process have already been cited above, under
the heading "Morphology" (§1.2.3).

1.2.5.4. *Denominatives.* Aramaic is known for its extensive denominatives, and this undoubtedly affected PBH, along with other factors, in its proliferation of denominative forms. For example, late BH developed a secondary form, *tərûmâ* "levy, priestly offering" from the root *r-w-m* "to be high," with *tāw* preformative (Exod 25:2). Subsequently, PBH generated the denominative *tāram* "to donate."

1.2.5.5. *Borrowings from Aramaic and Other Languages.* There are many lexemes that are best known in Aramaic and that may be assumed to have entered PBH from that language. This process began, for the most part, in the late BH of the Persian period and accelerated with time. An example from late BH is consonantal *'sr* "binding agreement, edict" (vocalized both as Aramaic *'esar* and as late BH *'issar* in Num 30). Quite possibly, this Aramaic term is a calque of Akkadian *riksu* "contract, binding agreement" and related forms, from the Akkadian root *rakāsu* "to tie, bind." In fact, rabbinic sources are replete with legal and administrative terms that ultimately derive from Akkadian (sometimes even Sumerian). Consider such terms as the following: *dap* "tablet," from Akkadian *ṭ/duppu; taggār* "merchant," from Akkadian *tamkāru; 'ûmān* "artisan, craftsman," from Akkadian *ummānu.* A term like *šaṭār* "written document" resonates with the Akkadian verb *šaṭāru* "to write" but is itself an Aramaic creation, appropriated into Hebrew. Somewhat differently, the noun *kətāb* in the sense of "writ" enters PBH from Aramaic, although it is based on a common Semitic root. A typically Aramaic verb like *b-ṭ-l* "to cease, be idle," occurring once in Eccl 12:3, a late biblical book infused with Aramaisms, expands in PBH, generating various nominal and verbal forms.

There are surprisingly few Arabic words in PBH. Recent investigations have revealed a series of Arabic legal terms in PBEH, in the Judean Desert documents, some of which are written in Nabatean-Aramaic. A rare example is the Arabic verb *rahina* "to pledge," which, in the Judean Desert documents, is used in the simple stem and occurs in the Mishnah in the *hop'al* of the Hebrew: *'al hattînôqet šeḥûrḥănâ bə'ašqəlôn* "concerning the female infant who was pledged as security in Askelon" (*m. 'Ed.* 8:4).

There are quite a few Greek words appropriated into PBH. They are mostly administrative, mercantile, religious, and cultic terms and names of items from the material culture. Simply put, a type of building or gate, vessel, or the status of a person would often be expressed in Greek. Latin words in PBH lie mostly in the military or administrative spheres. Examples are *ligyôn* "legion," *liblār* "scribe," and the like. For purposes of recognition, it is important to note that many Greek and Latin loanwords underwent a degree of phonetic adjustment as they were appropriated into PBH and Aramaic. Thus, for example, a Greek term that began with a cluster of voiceless consonants would take on a prefixed, prosthetic *'ālep,* as in ʾisṭəraṭêgôs "commander," from strategós. In certain cases, Greek words became so much a part of the Hebrew language that they generated denominatives. A good `example is zîwwēg "to join," as in marriage, and nominal zîwwûg "match, pair," from the Greek zygón, "pair."

A number of Persian words entered PBH, usually via Aramaic. A classic example is gizbār "treasurer," frequently attested in Aramaic and ultimately deriving from Elamite and Old Persian ganza barra "bearer of the treasury."[6]

2. SELECTIONS FROM POSTBIBLICAL HEBREW

2.1. FROM *MISHNAH SANHEDRIN* 4:5

כיצד מאיימין על עדי נפשות? היו מכניסין אותן ומאיימין עליהן: שמא תאמרו
מאמד ,ומשמועה, עד מפי עד, ומפי אדם נאמן שמענו; או שמא אי אתם יודעין
שסופנו לבדוק אתכם בדרישה וחקירה. הוו יודעין, שלא כדיני ממונות דיני
נפשות: דיני ממונות־אדם נותן ממון ומתכפר לו; דיני נפשות־דמו ודם זרעיותיו
תלויין בו עד סוף העולם. שכן מצינו בקין שהרג את אחיו, שנאמר: 'דמי אחיך
צעקים'; אינו אומר 'דם אחיך' אלא 'דמי אחיך.' דמו ודם זרעיותיו ... לפיכך
נברא האדם יחידי, ללמדך, שכל המאבד נפש אחת מישראל מעלה עליו הכתוב,
כאילו אבד עולם מלא; וכל המקים נפש אחת מישראל כאילו קים עולם
מלא. ומפני שלום הבריות, שלא יאמר אדם אבא גדול מאביך; ושלא יהו מינין
אומרים: שתי רשויות בשמים. ולהגיד גדלתו שלהקדוש ברוך הוא: שאדם טובע
כמה מטבעות בחותם אחד, וכלן דומים זה לזה; ומלך מלכי המלכים הקדוש
ברוך הוא טבע כל אדם בחותמו שלאדם הראשון, ואין אחד מהן דומה לחברו.
לפיכך כל אחד ואחד חיב לומר: בשבילי נברא העולם...

2.1.1. TRANSLITERATION

kêṣad məʾayyəmîn ʿal ʿēdê nəpāšôt? hāyû maknîsîn ʾôtān ûməʾayyĕmîn ʿălêhen: šemmāʾ tōʾmərû mēʾōmed ûmiššemûʾâ; ʿēd mippî ʿēd ʿûmippî ʾādām neʾemān šāmaʿnû. ʾô šemmāʾ ʾî ʾattem yôdəʿîn šessôpēnû libdôq ʾetkem bidərîšâ waḥăqîrâ. hewû yôdəʿîn šellōʾ kədînê māmônôt dînê nəpāšôt. dînê māmônôt-ʾādām nôtēn māmôn ûmitkappēr lô. dînê nəpāšôt-damô wədam zarʿîyôtāyw təlûyîn bô ʿad sôp hāʿôlām. šekkēn māṣînû bəqayyin šehārag ʾet ʾāḥîw, šenneʾĕmar: "dəmê ʾăḥîkā ṣōʿăqîm." ʾênô ʾômēr

---

[6] The classic dictionary of Greek and Latin loanwords in rabbinic literature was published more than a century ago: Samuel Krauss, *Griechische und Lateinische Lehnwörter in Talmud, Midrasch und Targum* (Berlin: S. Calvary, 1898). An in-depth treatment, albeit of more limited scope, is Daniel Sperber, *A Dictionary of Greek and Latin Legal Terms in Rabbinic Literature* (Ramat-Gan: Bar Ilan University, 1984).

ʿdam ʾāḥîkā.' ʾella' ʿdəmê ʾāḥîkā'; dāmô wədam zarʿîyôtāyw. ləpîkāk nibrā'
hā'ādām yəḥîdî, ləlammədāk šekkol hammə'abbēd nepeš 'aḥat miyyiśrā'ēl
maʿăleh ʿālāyw hakkātûb kə'îlû 'ibbad ʿôlām mālē'; wəkol hamməqayyēm
nepeš 'aḥat miyyiśrā'ēl kə'îlû qiyyam ʿôlām mālē'. ûmippənê šəlôm
habbərîyôt, šellō' yō'mar 'ādām: "'abba' gādôl mē'ābîkā." wəšellō' yəḥû
mînîn 'ômərîm: "šətê rəšûyôt baššāmayim." ûləhaggîd gədūlatô šellhaqqādôš
bārûk hû'. še'ādām ṭôbēaʿ kammâ maṭbəʿôt bəḥôtām 'eḥād, wəkūllan
dômîm zeh lāzeh, ûmelek malkê hamməlākîm, haqqādôš bārûk hû', ṭābaʿ
kol 'ādām bəḥôtāmô šell'ādām hāri'šôn wə'ēn 'eḥād mēhen dômeh laḥăbērô.
ləpîkāk kol 'eḥād wə'eḥād ḥayyāb lômar: "bišbîlî nibrā' hāʿôlām."

2.1.2. TRANSLATION

How do they issue the charge to witnesses in capital cases? They
would bring them in and issue the charge to them: Perhaps you are making approximate statements, from hearsay, (that) one witness heard from
another, or (stating that), "We heard (this) from a trustworthy person," or
perhaps you do not know that in the end we will examine you with thorough interrogation. Be it known to you that capital cases are not like civil
cases. In civil cases a person makes monetary compensation and is exon-
erated. In capital cases the blood (of the victim) and the blood of his
descendants "are hanging" upon him (= the witness) to the end of time.
This is what we find (written) regarding Cain, who killed his brother, as it
is said (Genesis 4), "The bloods of your brother cry out." The (verse) does
not say the blood of your brother, but rather "the bloods of your brother,"
(both) his blood and the blood of his descendants. It is for this reason that
only a single human being was created, to teach you that anyone who
destroys one living soul from within Israel, Scripture weighs (the scales)
against him as if he had destroyed the entire human population. Whereas
anyone who preserves the life of one soul within Israel, it is as though he
had preserved the life of the entire human population. And to promote
harmony among people, so that one person will not be able to say, "My
father was greater than your father." And so that the sectarians will not be
able to say, "There are two authorities in heaven." And to relate the great-
ness of the Holy One, blessed be He. For when a person mints several
coins with one stamp, they are all alike. But the King of the Kings of Kings,
the Holy One, blessed be He, minted every person in the stamp of the first
human being, and yet not one of them is like the other! It is for this reason that every person should say: "It is for me that the world was created!"

2.1.3. NOTES

1. The opening sentence is elliptic, using the masculine plural
participle-present.

2. The plural masculine *piʿel* participle *məʾayyəmîn* "they charge" is a denominative from *ʾêmâ* "dread, fear" (Gen 15:12; Isa 33:18), adjectival *ʾāyōm* "awesome" (Hab 1:7). Note in this form that the masculine plural is signified by *nûn,* an Aramaistic feature common in PBH. The same thing is seen in the forms *yôdəʿîn* "know," *təlûyîn* "are hanging," and *mînîn* "sectarians." Yet other masculine plurals end in *mêm.*

3. In this selection, we find some of the periphrastic tenses characteristic of PBH. For example, *hāyû maknîsîn ʾôtān* "They would bring them in" (perfect of the verb *h-y-h* plus the participle); *hĕyû yôdəʿîn* "Be it known to you" (imperative of the verb *h-y-h* plus the participle).

4. To a considerable degree, the syntax is dominated by relative clauses introduced by prefixed *še.*

5. Other features reflected in this passage include: (a) double plurals, e.g., *dînê nəpāšôt* "capital cases" and *dînê māmônôt* "civil cases"; (b) fluctuations between plene and defective orthography; (c) repeated use of the definite article *hê* as a relative, e.g., *kol hamməqayyēm* "anyone who preserves"; (d) anticipatory genitive, e.g., *bəḥôtāmô šelʾādām hāriʾšôn* "in the stamp of the first human being." In the latter case, note that there is no agreement with respect to determination (it is not written *hāʾādām hāriʾšôn*) and also that the possessive pronoun is prefixed (*junctim*).

6. The conditional adverb *šemmāʾ* "if, perhaps" is Aramaic and is cognate with Akkadian *šumma.* At times it is negatively suggestive and best rendered "lest."

7. Note the convention of referring to the Hebrew Bible as *hakkātûb* "the written word, Scripture." This appellation is an active entity; it makes pronouncements and judgments!

2.2. SIPRA, *QEDÔŠÎM*, INTRODUCTION[7]

'וידבר ה' אל משה לאמר דבר אל בני ישראל ואמרת אליהם קדושים תהיו'
(ויקרא יט) מלמד שהפרשה נאמרה בהקהל. ומפני מה נאמרה בהקהל? מפני
שרוב גופי תורה תלוים בה. 'קדושים תהיו'־'פרושים היו. 'קדושים תהיו כי קדוש
אני ה' אלהיכם.' לומר: אם מקדישים אתם עצמיכם, מעלה אני עליכם כאילו
קידשתם אותי; ואם אין אתם מקדישים עצמיכם, מעלה אני עליכם כאילו לא
קידשתם אותי. או אינו אומר אלא: אם מקדישים אתם אותי, הריני מקודש; ואם
לאו־איני מקודש ת"ל (= תלמוד לומר) 'כי קדוש אני.' בקדושתי אני בין מקדשים
אותי ובין אין אין מקדשים אותי. אבא שאול אומר: פמליא למלך. ומה עליה להיות?
מחקה למלך.

---

[7] Isaac Hirsch Weiss, ed., *Sifrāʾ Dĕbê Rab, Qedôšîm* (Vienna: Schlossberg, 1857; repr., New York, Om, 1946), 86b, col. 1.

2.2.1. Transliteration

"wayyədabbēr ʾădônāy ʾel mōšeh lēʾmōr: dabbēr ʾēl bənê yiśrāʾēl wəʾāmartā ʾălêhem: qədôšîm tihyû" (wayyiqrāʾ 19). məlammēd šehappārāšâ neʾĕmrâ bəhaqhēl. ûmippənê mah neʾĕmĕrâ bəhaqəhēl? mippənē šerôb gûpē tôrâ təlûyîm bâ. "qədôšîm, tihyû"-pārôšîm hĕyû. "qədôšîm tihyû kî qādôšʾ ʾănî ʾădônāy ʾĕlōhêkem." lômar: ʾim maqdîšîm ʾattem ʿaṣmêkem maʿăleh ʾănî ʿălêkem kəʾîlû qîddaštem ʾôtî; wəʾim ʾên ʾattem maqdîšîm ʿaṣmêkem maʿăleh ʾănî ʿălêkem kəʾîlû lōʾ qîddaštem ʾôtî. ʾô ʾênô ʾômēr ʾellaʾ: ʾim maqdîšîm ʾattem ʾôtî hărênî mequddāš, wəʾim lōʾ- ʾênî mequddāš. tilmôd lômar: "kî qādôš ʾănî" biqədûšātî ʾănî, bên məqaddəšîm ʾôtî. ûbên ʾên məqaddəšîm ʾôtî. ʾabbāʾ šāʾûl ʾômēr: pammelyâ lammelek. ûmâ ʿālêhā lihyôt? məhaqqâ lammelek

2.2.2. Translation

Then YHWH spoke to Moses as follows: "Speak to the Israelite people and say to them, 'You shall be holy'" (Lev 19). It teaches that this parashah was spoken in the full assembly (of the people). And for what reason was it spoken in the full assembly (of the people)? Because most of the fundamental principles of the Torah "are hanging" upon it. "You shall be holy." Be separatists! "You shall be holy because I, YHWH, your God, am holy." That is to say, if you sanctify yourselves, I will weigh (the scales) in your favor as if you sanctified me, but if you do not sanctify yourselves, I will count it against you as if you had not sanctified me. Or is it that he is saying that (only) if you sanctify me am I sanctified, but if not—I am not sanctified? You should learn to say "for I am holy"—I am in my (state of) holiness whether they sanctify me, or whether they do not sanctify me. Abbaʾ Shaʾul says: "(It is like) the entourage (in relation) to the king. And what is it obliged to be (doing)? Emulating the king!"

2.2.3. Notes

1. Elliptical *məlammēd* "it teaches" often introduces commentary on a specific biblical verse (cf. infinitival *ləlammədāk* "to teach you" in the passage cited above from *m. Sanh.* 4:5). A further example of ellipsis, with virtual stative force, comes further on with *bēn ʾim maqdîšîm ʾôtî* "Whether they sanctify me," etc.

2. The form *təlûyîm* "are hanging" ("are contingent") reflects the widespread use of passive participles with stative force. The same locution occurs above in the selection from *m. Sanh.* 4:5.

3. The correct form is *pārôšîm* "separatists," which represents the *nomen agentis,* quite frequent in PBH, and has active force. It is also the name for the sect known as the Pharisees!

4. The phrase *tilmôd lômar* "You shall learn to say" is a formula that introduces biblical citations being adduced as proof texts.

5. The idiom *maʿăleh ʾănî ʿălêkem* "I will weigh (the scales) in your favor" is the positive reflex of the same idiom as appeared in the selection from *m. Sanh.* 4:5, where *ʿālāyw* meant "against him."

2.3. AN EXAMPLE OF PBEH: P.YADIN 46, LINES 1–12 (135 C.E.)[8]

בשנים לכסלו שנת שלוש לשמעון בן כוסבא נשיא ישראל בעין גדי ישוע קבי[ש]
בן שמעון מן עין גדי אמר לאלעזר בן חיטא ואליעזר בן שמואל שניהם
משם מודא אני לכם היום שחכרתי מכם תמקום שנקרה הסלם ותמקום שנקרה
הב*יר תללו חכרתי מכם תדקלים ותשאר האילן שבהם ותעפר הלבן ותדקל
הטוב ותחצד שבכפר תכול שההחזיק חנניה בן חיטא מלפני מזה שאזרע
תעפר הלבן ואנה תדקלים כנומוס ואכנוס לנפשי כל המה פירות והבאה
שיהיה שבמקום הלז עד זמן שישלם זמן הפירות של עין גדי של הירק
ושל האילן היך נומוס לעומת ככה אחכרתום לי בכסף זוזין מאה וששים
שהם סלעים ארבעין תללו אשקול לכם ואטול מכם קשרים אילא יתקבל לי
ועליכם לשפות לפני מן חרד ותגר עד ס[ורף] הזמן הלז ועליך אתה אלעזר
לקרב לי מן החכור הלז [ולשקו]ל [כסף] דינרין עשרה שהם סלעים שתים ושקל
חד וקים עלי לעמת ככה ישוע [בר] שמעון ענפשה

2.3.1. TRANSLITERATION

1. *bišənayim ləkislēw šənat šālôš ləšimʿôn ben kôsibbâ nəśîʾ yiśrāʾēl bəʾên gedî yēšûaʿ qby[š]*

2. *ben šimʿôn min ʿên geddî ʾāmar ləʾelʿāzār ben ḥayyāṭāʾ weʾĕlîʿezer ben šəmûʾēl, šənêhem*

3. *miššam: môdeʾ ʾănî lākem ḥayyôm šeḥākartî mikkem tammāqôm šenniqrâ hassulām wətammāqôm šenniqrâ*

4. *habbōr. tallālû ḥākartî mikkem; taddəqālîm wətaššəʾār bāʾîlān šebbāhem, wətaʿāpār ḥallābān wətaddeqel*

5. *haṭṭôb wətaḥăṣād šebbakkepar: takkol šeheḥĕzîq ḥănanyâ ben ḥayyāṭāʾ millipnê mizzeh. šeʾezraʿ*

6. *taʿāpār ḥallābān weʾaggeh taddəqālîm kənômôs wəʾeknôs lənapšî kol hammâ pêrôt wəhābāʾâ*

7. *šeyyihyeh šebbammāqôm hallāz ʿad zəman šeyyišlam zəman happêrôt šel ʿên gedî šel ḥayyārāq*

8. *wəšel bāʾîlān hêk nômôs ləʿummat kākâ ʾaḥkartûm lî bəkesep zûzîn mēʾah wəšiššîm*

---

[8] From Y. Yadin et al., eds., *The Documents from the Bar Kokhba Period in the Cave of Letters* (JDS 3; Jerusalem: Israel Exploration Society, 2002), 66.

9. *šebēm səlā'îm 'arbā'în tallālû 'ešqôl lākem wə'eṭṭôl mikkem qəšārîm 'îlō' yitqabbēl lî*

10. *wa'ălêkem ləšappôt ləpānay min ḥărār wətiggār 'ad s[ôp] hazzə man ḥallāz wə'ālêkā 'attâ 'el'āzār*

11. *ləqārēb lî min haḥăkôr ḥallāz [wəlišqô]l [kesep] dînārîn 'ăśārâ šebēm səlā'îm šəttayim wəšeqel*

12. *ḥad wəqayyām 'ālay lə'ummat kākâ yēšûa' [bar] šim'ôn 'annapšēh*

(three witnesses)

2.3.2. TRANSLATION

1. On the second of Kislev, year three of Shim'on, son of Kosiba, Premier of Israel, in Ein Gedi, Yeshu'a QBY[Š],

2. son of Shim'on, from Ein Gedi, stated to 'El'azar, son of 'El'azar, son of Ḥayyaṭa', and to 'Eli'ezer, son of Shemu'el, both of them

3. from there: I acknowledge to you this day that I have leased from you (both) the site that is called the *Sullam* and the site that is called

4. the *Bor.* Those have I leased from you (including) the date palms and the rest of the trees within them, as well as the cropland and the date palms

5. of first quality, and the (*ḥṣd*-date crop) that is in the village; all that Hananiah, son of Ḥayyaṭa' held prior to this. I (undertake) to sow

6. the cropland, and I will pick (or: prune) the date palms as is customary. And I shall gather in for my use all of those fruits and the crop

7. that will come into existence in that site, until such time as the fruit season at Ein Gedi will reach its end, both of vegetables

8. and of trees, as is customary. On this account, you have leased them to me for silver (in the sum of) 160 *zuz,*

9. which are (equivalent to) forty *sela'.* Those I shall count out to you (both), and I will take from you "ties." If not, (another) may be in receipt for me.

10. And it is incumbent upon you (or: [9] If it will not be received by me, [10] then it is incumbent upon you) to silence (all objections) before me (or: to provide clearance before me), against any grievance or contest, until the e[nd] of that season. And it is incumbent upon you, 'El'azar,

11. to deliver to me from (the amount of) that lease [and to weigh o]ut [silver] ten denarii, which are (equivalent to) two *sela',* plus [12] one [11] shekel.

12. I am legally bound on this account. Yeshu'a, [son of] Shim'on, on his own behalf.

(three witnesses)

2.3.3. NOTES

1. The determined accusative is affected by syncopation. Examples of this phenomenon are seen in *tammāqôm* "the site," reduced from *ʾet ham-māqôm,* and *tallālû* "those," from *ʾet hallālû.* This appears to represent how Hebrew was spoken.

2. Note the fluidity of *ʾālep* and *hê,* whereby we have participial *môdeʾ* (instead of *môdeh*) "(I) acknowledge," but *šenniqrâ* (instead of *šenniqrāʾ*) "that is called."

3. The text exhibits Aramaistic features. Examples are: (a) the verbal stem *ʾapʿel* instead of *hipʿil,* as in *ʾaḥkartûm* "you have leased them"; (b) Aramaic *ʾîlōʾ* "if not," *hêk* "how," and *taddeqel, taddaqālîm* "the palm tree, trees"; (c) the form *ʿannapšēh* (assimilated from *ʿal napšēh*) "on his own behalf," exhibits the Aramaic third masculine singular suffix, -*ēh.*

4. We find back-translations from Aramaic. Thus, *kol hammâ,* literally "all the what," reflecting Aramaic *kol mandaʿam,* and *laʿummat kākâ,* literally "facing this," reflecting Aramaic *loqŏbēl dāk.*

5. The term *nômôs* is Greek *nomos* "custom, law," often occurring in PBH as *nîmûs.* The construction *kĕnômôs* "like the custom" is often found.

6. Note the unusual *hipʿil* based form, *hăbāʾâ* "crop" in place of the expected form *tabûʾâ.*

3. ANCIENT SOURCES, MODERN RESOURCES

3.1. POSTBIBLICAL EPIGRAPHIC HEBREW

An excellent resource is Ada Yardeni's *Documentary Texts from the Judaean Desert, Parts A and B.* Part B contains an English section with translations of the texts and information on the script traditions. This compendium makes it possible to engage the overall corpus of epigraphic finds with the advantage of collated readings, an analysis of scripts, background information on various groups of texts, and reliable translations. Yardeni's hand drawings are an added benefit, enabling the reader to see an accurate image of a text as it was written in antiquity. Texts written in PBEH are usually executed in clear scripts that, in and of themselves, present few problems of decipherment, allowing for lacunae, fading ink, and the condition of the papyrus or other material on which the inscriptions are written.

3.2. POSTBIBLICAL HEBREW

The resources available to someone seeking to master PBH are plentiful in certain respects and yet lacking in others. There is as yet no scholarly grammar of rabbinic (or Mishnaic) Hebrew that is based on reliable manuscripts, nor is there yet a good dictionary of rabbinic Hebrew. The best talmudic dictionary, including both Hebrew and Aramaic, is that of

Jacob Levy, *Wörterbuch über die Talmudim und Midraschim*. The Academy of the Hebrew language in Jerusalem is preparing *The Historical Dictionary of the Hebrew Language* as a long-term project, and from time to time it issues computerized lexical materials that are very useful. Concordances of the Mishnah, Tosefta, Tannaitic literature, and the midrashic collections are also available.

The corpus of PBH is very extensive, and it is recommended that those new to the field acquaint themselves with its many collections before engaging the original sources. A good place to start is Jacob Neusner's article on the formative canon in rabbinic Judaism found in *The Encyclopedia of Judaism*. Unfortunately, no bibliography is provided for these entries, but they are succinctly formulated and highly informative. As a follow-up, see *Reader's Guide to Judaism,* a publication of the New York Public Library, under the appropriate topics, especially the "'Booklist Index." Although published several decades ago, and therefore not entirely up to date, the *Encyclopaedia Judaica* and its supplements contain authoritative articles on all of the rabbinic collections.

New translations of the rabbinic corpus are readily available, thanks mostly to the unprecedented efforts of Neusner and his associates. They have literally unlocked the vast body of rabbinic literature by providing multivolume English translations of both the Babylonian and Jerusalem Talmuds, the major midrashic texts, the Mishnah, and the Tosefta. All of these works contain valuable information on the contents and history of the relevant rabbinic collections.

The best study edition of the Mishnah is Hanoch Albeck, *Šiššāh Sidrê Mišnāh* (*The Six Orders of the Mishnah*). The text was vocalized by Hanoch Yalon, an eminent Semitist who pioneered the investigation of Mishnah manuscripts. This edition provides Hebrew introductions to each order and tractate, lists the relevant Torah passages, and includes a succinct Hebrew commentary to the text.

The Tosefta has been edited by the distinguished talmudist Saul Lieberman in *Tosefta Ki-fesutah: A Comprehensive Commentary on the Tosefta*. This is a multivolume work with a critical edition of the unvocalized text of the Tosefta based on the Erfurt manuscript with a short running commentary in Hebrew and an extensive, separate Hebrew commentary. There are many critical editions of the midrashic collections. A reliably vocalized edition of *Midrash Rabbah* with Hebrew commentary is that by Moshe Aryeh Mirkin.

4. BIBLIOGRAPHY

Albeck, Hanoch.*Šiššāh Sidrê Mišnāh*. 6 vols. Jerusalem: Bialik Institute and Dvir, 1958.

Bar-Asher, M. *Studies in Mishnaic Hebrew*. ScrHier 37. Jerusalem: Magnes, Hebrew University, 1998.

Bendavid, Abba. *Biblical Hebrew and Mishnaic Hebrew*. 2 vols. Tel Aviv: Dvir, 1967.

Krauss, Samuel. *Griechische und Lateinische Lehnwörter in Talmud, Mirdasch und Targum*. Berlin: S. Calvary, 1898.

Kutscher, E. Y. *A History of the Hebrew Language*. Edited by Raphael Kutscher. Jerusalem: Magnes, 1982.

———. "Mishnaic Hebrew." *EncJud* 16:1590–1608.

Leiberman, Saul, ed.. *Tosefta Ki-fesutah: A Comprehensive Commentary on the Tosefta*. 15 vols. New York: The Jewish Theological Seminary of America, 1955–1988.

Levine, B. A.. "Chapters in the History of Spoken Hebrew" (Hebrew). *ErIsr* 14 (1978): 155–60.

———. "The Prefix *še* in Biblical Hebrew in the Light of Ancient Epigraphy." (Hebrew) *ErIsr* 18 (1985): 145–52.

Levy, Jacob. *Wörterbuch über die Talmudim und Midraschim*. Berlin and Vienna: B. Harz, 1924.

Mirkin, Moshe Aryeh, ed. *Midraš Rabbāh*. 11 vols. Tel Aviv: Yavneh, 1967.

Neusner, Jacob. "Rabbinic Judaism: Formative Canon of." Pages 1132–75 in vol. 3 of *The Encyclopedia of Judaism*. Edited by Jacob Neusner, Alan J. Avery-Peck, and William S. Green. 3 vols. New York: Continuum, 1999.

Sperber, Daniel. *A Dictionary of Greek and Latin Legal Terms in Rabbinic Literature*. Ramat-Gan: Bar Ilan University, 1984.

Terry, Michael, ed. *Reader's Guide to Judaism*. Chicago: Fitzroy Dearborn, 2000.

Urman, D. "Jewish Inscriptions from Dabbura in the Golan." *IEJ* 22 (1972): 16–23.

Weiss, Isaac Hirsch, ed. *Sifrā' Děbê Rab, Qedôšîm*. Vienna: Schlossberg, 1857. Repr., New York: Om, 1946.

Yadin, Y., J. C. Greenfield, A. Yardeni, and B. A. Levine, eds. *The Documents from the Bar Kokhba Period in the Cave of Letters*. JDS 3. Jerusalem: Israel Exploration Society, 2002.

Yardeni, Ada. *Documentary Texts from the Judaean Desert*. Jerusalem: Dinur Center, Hebrew University, 2000.

HITTITE

Harry A. Hoffner Jr.

1. THE LANGUAGE

As recognized at the time of its decipherment, the Hittite language belongs to the Indo-European family of languages. It is a matter of controversy whether Hittite is a descendant of (Proto) Indo-European (abbreviated PIE) or belongs to a family parallel to it, both families descending from the parent language Indo-Hittite. One can show these two possible mappings of relationships in a "tree" or genealogical stemma as follows.

Possibility One: Hittite Descended from PIE

PIE
    Indo-Iranian
        Indian or Indo-Aryan (Sanskrit, etc.)
        Iranian (Avestan, Old Persian, etc.)
    Tocharian
    Armenian
    Anatolian
        Hittite (Nesite)
        Luwian (and Lycian)
        Palaic
        Lydian
    Balto-Slavic
        Slavic (Old Church Slavonic, Russian, etc.)
        Baltic (Lithuanian, Latvian)
    Greek
    Italic (Latin, etc.)
    Celtic
    Germanic

Possibility Two: Hittite and PIE Descended from Indo-Hittite

Indo-Hittite
    PIE
    Anatolian

183

At issue is whether one accounts for the simpler form of the Anatolian languages as to verbal modes and the like as a simplification of the more complex PIE or as a continuation of a simpler precursor (Indo-Hittite) prior to the development of greater complexity in PIE. It is an issue that students of Hittite should be aware of, but it has no significant bearing on how the Anatolian languages are studied and understood within their own historical period.[1]

The articulation of the derivative languages or "dialects" of Indo-European (or Indo-Hittite) is derived from considerations of historical linguistics, not from historical or geographical considerations. We cannot determine independently of these linguistic considerations that a given speech group lived together in a particular geographical area. It is not precluded that speakers of Common (or Proto) Anatolian lived outside the geographical limits of Anatolia. But the supposed descendant languages of Common Anatolia are all attested from written records found in Anatolia 3,500 years ago.

The development of the principal language groups (Hittite, Luwian, Palaic) from Common Anatolian from the viewpoint of phonology has been sketched by H. Craig Melchert.[2] Although the Luwian and Palaic languages have smaller surviving text corpora and have been less well understood, both grammatically and lexically, it is nevertheless possible to determine the broad lines of their linguistic interrelationship.

---

[1] An overview of the member languages of Indo-European can be found in Robert S. P. Beekes, *Comparative Indo-European Linguistics: An Introduction* (Amsterdam: Benjamins, 1995), 17–33. General orientation to the Indo-European languages can be found in several books in addition to Beekes: Heinz Kronasser, *Vergleichende Laut- und Formenlehre der Hethitischen* (Heidelberg: Winter, 1956); Bernhard Rosenkranz, *Vergleichende Untersuchungen der altanatolischen Sprachen* (ed. W. Winter; Trends in Linguistics, State-of-the-Art Report 8; The Hague: Mouton de Gruyter, 1978); Oswald J. L. Szemerényi, *Introduction to Indo-European Linguistics* (Oxford: Clarendon, 1996); Michael Meier-Brügger, *Indogermanische Sprachwissenschaft* (Berlin: de Gruyter, 2000). A resource center for textual materials in Indo-European languages can be found at the web site of the TITUS-Project at http://titus. uni-frankfurt.de/index.html. TITUS is an acronym for "Thesaurus Indogermanischer Text- und Sprachmaterialien."

[2] See the following works: H. Craig Melchert, "Historical Phonology of Anatolian," *Journal of Indo-European Studies* 21 (1993): 237–57; idem, *Anatolian Historical Phonology* (Leiden Studies in Indo-European 3; Amsterdam: Rodopi, 1994); idem, "Hittite Phonology," in *Phonologies of Asia and Africa* (ed. Alan S. Kay; Winona Lake, Ind.: Eisenbrauns, 1997), 555–67.

1.1. HISTORY

The story of the rediscovery of the Hittite writing system, language, and civilization has often been told. In its main lines it runs as follows. Hieroglyphic inscriptions chiseled into stone blocks found in Syria at the end of the nineteenth century were correctly connected to the people known from the Hebrew Bible and the Neo-Assyrian annals as the "Hittites." It could not be known at that time that the language of these inscriptions was not Hittite proper, but a dialect of Luwian. Yet the assumption that they related somehow to the ancient Hittites was correct. Similar inscriptions on rock reliefs in central Anatolia led explorers and archaeologists to the impressive ruins near the village of Boğazköy. Formal excavations begun there in 1906 under the direction of Hugo Winckler and Theodore Makridi revealed an impressive city dating from the time of the New Kingdom pharaohs of Egypt and the Kassite dynasty of Babylonia. Several huge archives of clay tablets inscribed in a variety of cuneiform writing very similar to the contemporary Amarna archives found in Egypt were discovered. Although many tablets were composed in Akkadian and could be read immediately, confirming the excavators' suspicion that they had found the capital of "Hatti," the vast majority were written in the native language of the Hittites.

Two tablets in this language had been found decades earlier in the Amarna archives, representing correspondence between the Egyptian pharaoh and the king of a land called "Arzawa" (later revealed to be located in southwestern Anatolia). A Danish scholar, Jürgen Knudtzon, had once claimed the two "Arzawa letters" were written in a previously unknown Indo-European language, but he subsequently retracted his claim under heavy criticism from specialists in Indo-European languages.[3] Working with a much larger corpus of well-preserved documents in the "Arzawa language" from Boğazköy, a Czech Assyriologist named Friedrich Hrozny demonstrated convincingly that Knudtzon's retracted theory was in fact correct and published the first adequate grammatical sketch of what henceforth became known as the "Hittite" language.[4]

---

[3] Jürgen Alexander Knudtzon, Sophus Bugge, and Alf Torp, *Die zwei Arzawa-briefe, die ältesten Urkunden in indogermanischer Sprache* (Leipzig: Hinrichs, 1902).

[4] On the decipherment of Hittite, see Friedrich Hrozny, "Die Lösung des hethitischen Problems," *Mitteilungen der Deutschen Orientgesellschaft zu Berlin* 56 (1915): 17–50; idem, *Die Sprache der Hethiter* (ed. Otto Weber; Boghazköi-Studien 1–2; Leipzig: Hinrichs, 1917); Emil Forrer, "Die acht Sprachen der Boghazköi-Inschriften," *SPAW* (1919): 1029–41; Gary M. Beckman, "The Hittite Language and its Decipherment," *Bulletin of the Canadian Society for Mesopotamian Studies* 31 (1996): 23–30.

1.2. WRITING SYSTEM

The principal writing system used for the Hittite language was cuneiform, inherited by the royal scribes of the Hittite capital from a branch of the cuneiform scribal tradition associated with northern Syria. The date and circumstances of its adoption are not uncontroversial, but the generally followed view is that the Old Kingdom monarch Hattušili I (c. 1650–1620) adopted it from scribes captured during his military campaigning in Syria.[5] These scribes adapted the phonetic values of some of the cuneiform signs to accommodate phonemes found in Hittite that were not found in Akkadian or Sumerian, the principal languages for which cuneiform was employed.

Hittite scribes did not use the separate series of signs employed for the writing of Akkadian that distinguished voiced and voiceless stops (b/p, g/k/, d/t). Nor did they need the signs developed in cuneiform to express the so-called "emphatic" stops of Semitic languages (principally the emphatic velar stop *q* in the cuneiform sign *qa*). For instance, for these scribes any of the signs *ga, ka,* and *qa* could be used for the sounds /ga/ or /ka/. To this day Hittitologists in their transcriptions arbitrarily follow the base value in cuneiform syllabary for the signs in question. This means one reads the variant writings of a word such as *ūgga* and *ūqqa* "I" or *šaqqaḫḫi* and *šaggaḫḫi* "I know" without prejudice as to the articulation of the internal velar. Beginning students are advised to look for all such words in alphabetical sequence under the voiceless, nonemphatic member of the class, in this case *k*.[6]

The royal scribes of Hatti also decided to combine three different ways of representing words in their own language. They could write them completely syllabically (e.g., *ša-ag-ga-aḫ-ḫi* "I know") with a logogram derived from the Akkadian language (*I-DI* from Akkadian *idû* "to know") or from the Sumerian language (LÚDUB.SAR "scribe"). Furthermore, they felt free to combine logograms from Sumerian and Akkadian

---

[5] Thomas V. Gamkrelidze, "The Akkado-Hittite Syllabary and the Problem of the Origins of the Hittite Script," *ArOr* 29 (1961): 406–18; J. David Hawkins, "The Origin and Dissemination of Writing in Western Asia," in *The Origins of Civilization* (ed. P. R. S. Moorey; Oxford: Clarendon, 1979), 128–66; idem, "Writing in Anatolia: Imported and Indigenous Systems," *World Archaeology* 17/3 (1986): 363–76. A different theory is proposed by Karl Hecker, "Zur Herkunft der hethitischen Keilschrift," in *Uluslararası 1. Hititoloji Kongresi Bildirileri (19–21 Temmuz 1990)* (Corum: Türk Kültür Bakanlığı, 1990), 53–63.

[6] For further discussion on these matters, see Johannes Friedrich, *Hethitisches Elementarbuch, 1. Teil: Kurzgefaßte Grammatik* (ed. Hans Krahe; 2d ed.; Indogermanische Bibliothek. 1. Reihe: Lehr- und Handbücher; Heidelberg: Winter, 1960), 21–25.

with Hittite syllabic writing, all in one word! DINGIR-*LIM-iš* consists of the Sumerian word DINGIR "god," the final syllable (in this case, genitive case, -*LIM*) of the Akkadian word *ilu* "god," and the stem vowel and nominative singular case ending -*š* of the underlying Hittite word *šiuniš* "god." There was no way in the cuneiform script to indicate which signs belonged to which of the three languages. But Hittitologists decided to use typographic distinctions in transcription to indicate this. Sumerograms are written in uppercase roman type, Akkadograms in uppercase italic type, and Hittite in lowercase italic.

Akkadian scribes already knew of and employed certain signs as semantic class markers (commonly known as "determinatives") for nouns indicating material (GIŠ "wood," NA_4 "stone," GAD "linen," SÍG "wool," URUDU "copper"), type of commodity (TÚG "textile," DUG "container"), features of terrain (ḪUR.SAG "mountain," ÍD "river"), geopolitically bounded areas (KUR "land," URU "city"), and categories of persons (DINGIR "god(dess)," LÚ "human male," MUNUS "human female"). Scribes prefixed (or in rare cases suffixed) these signs to nouns indicating the subcategory or individual example of persons or objects denoted. Hittite scribes took over the entire group of determinatives. Hittitologists follow the practice of Assyriologists in setting the transcriptions of these determinatives superscripted (e.g., ^{LÚ}SANGA "man (who is) a priest," ^{MUNUS}SANGA "woman (who is) a priest").

Although the span of time over which Hittite cuneiform was written (approximately five hundred years) is much shorter than Akkadian cuneiform, it is long enough to exhibit distinct styles of writing characteristic of the major historical periods: Old Hittite (ca. 1650–1500), Middle Hittite (ca. 1500–1350), and New Hittite (ca. 1350–1150). The characteristics of the cuneiform writing for each of these periods include (1) the specific shapes of the individual signs, (2) the manner in which all the signs were written, and (3) the manner of distributing the writing on the tablet. Issues in the *shapes of individual signs* include the number, type, and placement of the wedges to make up specific signs. The *manner of writing all signs* includes use of slant versus upright, deeply impressed versus shallow, and compact versus loosely grouped wedges in individual signs. It also involves the grouping of the individual signs in connected text, ligatures, and the like. The *manner of distributing the writing* on the surface of the tablets includes the use and size of vertical column dividers, beginning a text on the upper edge, and so forth.

Characteristics affecting only the individual signs are usually distinguished from those affecting entire lines or the entire tablet. The latter category is normally referred to as "ductus." Since scribes in the Middle and New Kingdom often had to make fresh copies of older tablets for the archives, scholars often have to distinguish a late copy of an old text from an early copy. Using sigla developed for the Chicago Hittite Dictionary, we designate a New Hittite copy (NS for New Script) of an Old Hittite (OH) text as "OH/NS." Since tablets in Old Hittite script can only be Old Hittite compositions, the notation "OS" is sufficient, as is "NH" for all New Hittite compositions.

Although the total number of distinct cuneiform signs attested in Hittite texts to date is 375, a working knowledge of only 130 suffices for serious productive study of Hittite cuneiform texts. Several of the common signs have simultaneously common syllabic, logographic, and determinative values.

Hittite scribes specialized in the drafting and copying of texts of specific genres. In particular, texts recording divination by liver inspection (extispicy) or the observation of bird flight (augury) were the specialty of a small group of expertly trained scribes. Their writing techniques often diverged from those of other scribes, not only in the ductus and forms of individual signs, but also in the common employment of abbreviations for specialized vocabulary. Thus the paleography of an oracle text inscribed during the Old Hittite period may not resemble that of other texts in the so-called "Old Script." The specialized vocabulary of mantic texts can also elude an inexperienced reader of Hittite.[7] Consequently, while students with minimal formal training in Hittite can usually read historical, diplomatic, mythological, and cultic texts with moderate effort, it requires special training to read Hittite oracle texts correctly.

1.3. GRAMMATICAL FEATURES

Like the other Indo-European languages, Hittite inflected its nouns and adjectives with a set of case endings. Its repertoire, however, was larger than that of the classical languages, Greek and Latin, containing eight cases: nominative, accusative, vocative, genitive, dative-locative, allative, instrumental, and ablative. Common Anatolian (and consequently all its descendant languages) was a "Split Ergative" language.[8] It developed an ergative case marker *-anti from the ablative-instrumental of neuter r/n-stems, which distinguished neuter nouns that were subjects of transitive verbs. Unlike most Indo-European languages, but like the other

---

[7] On the specialized vocabulary of these texts, see Emmanuel Laroche, "Lécanomancie hittite," *RA* 52 (1958): 150–62; idem, "Sur le vocabulaire de l'haruspicine hittite," *RA* 64 (1970): 127–39; Alfonso Archi, "Il sistema KIN della divinazione ittita," *OrAnt* 13 (1974): 113–44; idem, "L'ornitomanzia ittita," *SMEA* 16 (1975): 119–80.

[8] On this designation as it relates to Anatolian, see Andrew Garrett, "The Origin of NP Split Ergativity," *Lg* 66 (1990): 265–80, 287–91.

old Anatolian ones, Hittite possessed no feminine gender for nominals. Instead it had two "genders": animate and inanimate (traditionally called "common" and "neuter"), corresponding roughly to masculine-feminine versus neuter. Its nominals recognized a singular and plural, but no dual.

The verb had two tenses: a simple past (preterite) and a "nonpast" that usually corresponds to the modern English use of the present for habitual actions ("on Wednesdays he drives into the city") or our future tense ("next Wednesday I will accompany him"). The verb had two voices: active and middle, the latter having the same range of semantic options as the Greek middle. The equivalent of our passive voice was normally expressed by the (passive) participle of transitive verbs with an expressed or implied auxiliary verb "to be": *namma=ya kuieš* URU.DIDLI.ḪI.A BÀD *arḫa warnuwanteš ešir* "what fortified cities were [verb "to be" *ešir*] burned down [preverb + participle *arḫa warnuwanteš*]." The old Anatolian languages, including Hittite, lacked the subjunctive and optative modes of the other Indo-European languages. They expressed the force of the subjunctive ("would, could, might") and optative ("should, ought to") with the use of various independent adverbs and modal particles (e.g., *man*).

Personal and demonstrative pronouns could be independent, accented words (*ug, zig, apaš, weš, šumeš, apē*) or clitic elements (*-mu, -ta, -aš, -naš, -šmaš*) attached to accented nouns or verbs. In their clitic forms they were attached to the first word of the clause. Hittite possessed and used a wide variety of clitic particles in addition to the above-mentioned clitic pronouns. Like the latter, these were attached to the first word of the clause and always appeared in a fixed sequence. Among them were particles indicating reflexivity (*-z*), quoted speech (*-wa*), and local aspects of the predicate of the clause (*-ašta, -apa, -kan, -šan*).

In prose texts word order was regular, with the finite verb customarily occupying the final position in the clause. In Old Hittite there were three nonenclitic clause-connecting particles: *šu, ta,* and *nu.* The first two disappeared in post–Old Hittite, leaving only *nu* to assume the roles of the others. The particle *nu* became ubiquitous as a clause connective in Middle and New Hittite, virtually obligatory in all clauses, both main clauses and subordinate ones. Suppression of *nu* or a corresponding clitic connective such as *-ma* created asyndesis, which had a special significance in New Hittite syntax. Only in cultic texts was asyndesis fairly common and with no implication of a special meaning.

2. SIGNIFICANCE FOR THE BIBLE

Although the rediscovery of the Hittites was historically a direct outgrowth of biblical studies during the last decades of the nineteenth century, throughout the twentieth century Hittitologists paid scant attention to the

bearing of Hittite texts upon the interpretation of the Hebrew Bible. Similarly, scholars trained in biblical studies have generally failed to appreciate
the value of consulting Hittite texts and have lacked the tools and teach-
ers to provide training in the language and writing system of the Hittites.
Furthermore, easily available editions of Hittite texts and chrestomathies
(i.e., readers) were unavailable. As a result, both Hittitologists and biblicists
were denied help from each other's fields of inquiry. A small compensation of this relative lack of interest was that it kept biblical scholars from
being inundated with premature and inaccurate citations of Hittite texts.
There was, however, not a total lack of interest in comparative study. Articles have been written on specific points of comparison[9] and on the
possibility of some direct contact between the Israelites and Hittites;[10] and
rare articles or books have sought to give a broader, more systematic presentation of the situation.[11]

---

[9] Among works studying points of comparison, see F. Charles Fensham, "Maledictions and Benedictions in Ancient Near Eastern Vassal Treaties and the Old
Testament," *ZAW* 74 (1962): 1–9; idem, "Salt and Curse in the Old Testament and
the Ancient Near East," *BA* 25 (1962): 48–50; idem, "Clauses of Protection in Hittite Vassal Treaties and the Old Testament," *VT* 13 (1963): 133–43; H. Hänsler, "Der
historische Hintergrund von Richter 3, 8–10," *Bib* 11 (1930): 391–418; 12 (1931):
3–26, 271–96, 395–410; M. W. Hauschild, "Die kleinasiatischen Völker und ihre
Beziehungen zu den Juden," *ZfE* 53 (1921): 518–28; Harry A. Hoffner Jr., "Symbols
for Masculinity and Feminity: Their Use in Ancient Near Eastern Sympathetic Magic
Rituals," *JBL* 85 (1966): 326–34; idem, "Second Millennium Antecedents to the
Hebrew *'ÔB*," *JBL* 86 (1967): 385–401; idem, "A Hittite Analogue to the David and
Goliath Contest of Champions?" *CBQ* 30 (1968): 220–25; idem, "Hittite *tarpis* and
Hebrew *teraphim*," *JNES* 27 (1968): 61–69; Abraham Malamat, "Doctrines of
Causality in Hittite and Biblical Historiography: A Parallel," *VT* 5 (1955): 1–12;
George E. Mendenhall, *Law and Covenant in Israel and the Ancient Near East*
(Pittsburgh: Biblical Colloquium, 1955); Heinrich Otten, "Kampf von König und
Göttheit in einem hethitischen Ritualtext," *BaghM* 7 (1968): 139–42; Archibald
Henry Sayce, "Hittite and Mittannian Elements in the Old Testament," *JTS* 29
(1928): 401–6; H. M. Wolf, *The Apology of Hattusilis Compared with Other Politi-
cal Self-Justifications of the Ancient Near East* (Ann Arbor, Mich.: University
Microfilms, 1967).

[10] See, e.g., F. M. Th. Böhl, "Tudḫalia I, Zeitgenosse Abrahams, um 1650 v. Chr,"
ZAW 42 = NS 1 (1924): 148–53; Emil Forrer, "The Hittites in Palestine: I," *PEQ* 68
(1936): 190–203; idem, "The Hittites in Palestine: II," *PEQ* 69 (1937): 100–15.

[11] Harry A. Hoffner Jr., "Some Contributions of Hittitology to Old Testament
Study: The Tyndale Archaeology Lecture, 1968," *TynBul* 20 (1969): 27–55; H. R.
Kaplan, "Anatolian Elements in the EB III Culture of Palestine," *ZDPV* 97 (1981):
18–35; Aharon Kempinski, "Hittites in the Bible—What Does Archaeology Say?"
BAR 5/4 (1979): 20–45; Ruth Mayer-Opificius, "Die Hethiter und das Alte Testament,"

Most important applications of insights from Hittite textual material to the interpretation of the Hebrew Bible do not require a thorough knowledge of the Hittite lexicon or grammar. Valid comparisons can often be derived from existing editions and translations. But a wide familiarity with edited texts is a minimal necessity for biblical scholars seeking to benefit from Hittite textual material. And this in itself usually requires a formal classroom introduction that extends beyond the elements of grammar and vocabulary to orientation in tools and methods of Hittitological research. Where knowledge of the language becomes helpful, and even essential, is in the evaluation of loanwords or loan translations. Sometimes such words occur in only one passage of the Hebrew Bible and Hittite texts. For example, the term *spsg* occurs only once in the Hebrew Bible (Prov 26:23; see *BHS* textual apparatus), but several times in Ugaritic texts, and fairly often (as *zapzagi*) in Hittite rituals. Finding and evaluating these occurrences is not easy for an outsider to the discipline, especially since no complete dictionary (as opposed to glossaries) of Hittite yet exists that has covered words beginning with *z*. Similarly, it has been suggested that the Hebrew (originally Philistine?) term for a helmet, written either *kōbaᶜ* or *qōbaᶜ*, is related to Hittite *kubaḫi,* and the Hebrew (originally Canaanite?) term for a non-Israelite (i.e., "pagan") priest, *kōmer,* is found not only in Old Assyrian *kumru* but also in Hittite *kumra.*

It would be exaggerating the yield of Hittite-Hebrew comparative studies to claim that they equal in importance the comparative studies derived from Egyptian, Assyro-Babylonian, or Ugaritic texts. The last-named in particular will probably always remain the richest comparative source for the Hebrew Bible. It should be noted, however, that the value of Hittite texts consists not only in the native Hittite material. There are, for example, a number of West Semitic compositions translated into Hittite that are only known from that source and from a rich body of Hurrian material both in the Hurrian language albeit embedded in Hittite-language compositions, and in unilingual Hurrian texts found only at Boğazköy. Therefore, although it is often the case that the connection with the Hebrew Bible runs through Hurrian population groups resident in Syria and Palestine

---

in *Mysterium der Gnade: Festscrhift für Joh. Auer* (ed. H. Rossmann; Regensburg: Pustet, 1975), 65–73; James C. Moyer, "Hittite and Israelite Cultic Practices: A Selected Comparison," in *Scripture in Context II: More Essays on the Comparative Method* (ed. William H. Hallo; Winona Lake, Ind.: Eisenbrauns, 1983), 19–38; Moshe Weinfeld, "Social and Cultic Institutions in the Priestly Source against Their Ancient Near Eastern Background," in *Eighth World Congress of Jewish Studies: Panel Sessions, Bible Studies and Hebrew Language* (Jerusalem: Hebrew University Press: 1983), 95–129; idem, *Justice and Righteousness in Israel and the Nations* (Hebrew) (Jerusalem: Magnes, 1985).

rather than direct Hittite contact, the access to these important textual materials only comes through a familiarity with the Hittite corpus and an ability to evaluate it in its Hittite context.

The main error committed by those who wrongly draw parallels is the failure to understand the data in the contexts of both the Hittite and Israelite cultures. Hittitologists need a thorough training in Israelite history and culture, in Hebrew (and ideally Canaanite, i.e., Ugaritic) language, and in the principles and methods of biblical exegesis. Biblicists need a thorough grounding in Hittite language, writing systems, text corpora, history, and culture. Contemplating the necessary expertise can deter individuals from even attempting cross-cultural comparative studies. But solid preparation can yield valuable insights. My own study included thorough training in Hebrew language and literature, principles of exegesis and textual criticism, history and archaeology of Syro-Palestine in seminary. This was followed by thorough training in Akkadian, Egyptian, and Ugaritic in graduate school, self-study in graduate school of the Hittite language (no specialist in Hittite was available to offer instruction at my institution), and many years of subsequent study and data collection in Hittite and Luwian text corpora.

Study of Hittite texts yields benefits for the study of Hebrew law, cultic procedures, covenant terminology, historiography, and wisdom literature. Relatively little has emerged directly affecting the interpretation of prophetic literature as a genre, although individual literary motifs in the prophetic literature have been clarified and their understanding deepened. The main source for the concepts and categories of Hittite legal thought remains the text popularly called the "Hittite code" or "the Hittite laws." This now exists in a new edition helpfully annotated and provided with glossary and indices, as well as in a separate recent English translation. Cultic procedures are known from the massive body of Hittite rituals and festival texts, as well as from an extremely valuable text called the "Instructions for Priests and Temple Officials," also available in a relatively recent critical edition and English translation. Understanding of Israelite covenant concepts and terminology can be enriched from study of Hittite state treaties, of which only the major ones are available in one publication in a somewhat dated edition, but handily collected in a recent and highly competent English translation. The primary sources for the study of Hittite historiography are the royal edicts, military annals, and historical prologue sections of state treaties. Secondary sources consist of several good, lengthy articles on the subject. Comparative studies are few in number, but what ones exist are quite useful.

The most recently published text that has a significant bearing on the Hebrew Bible and ancient Israelite culture is the so-called "Song of Release." The text is a bilingual, whose original version is Hurrian. Since its text is unknown outside of Boğazköy, it has been speculated that it was composed there. It exists in several copies, a few quite well preserved. It was discovered in 1984 and first reported with provisional German translation of the best understood parts in the same year. All existing copies date from the Middle Hittite period (ca. 1500–1400).[12] Although the component sections of the long narrative are reasonably well preserved, their sequence is still controversial. The overall subject of the composition is the fall of the city-state of Ebla. The text seems to attribute that fall to a divine judgment on Ebla for failing to release prisoners. The prisoners seem to be debt slaves, and the release demanded by the god Teššub is the Hurrian equivalent of the Israelite sabbatical release or the Jubilee (Hebrew *dərôr*). The narrative parts of the text portray a banquet in the palace of the goddess of the netherworld, Hurrian Allani, and several scenes in Ebla in which the king, who bears the West Semitic title *meki* (for *melki?*), seeks to persuade his council to proclaim a general release of the prisoners, but meets with opposition chiefly in the form of an eloquent councilman named Zazalla. Another part of the text contains a large number of vignettes (sometimes called "parables") that relate the ungrateful and unwise behavior of persons, animals, or inanimate objects, which then meet with disaster. After each of these stories the author compares the behavior to that of a human being. Each implies a kind of moral to the story. Among these vignettes are several that can be related to biblical *topoi,* such as the ungrateful copper vessel that turns against its maker (cf. the potter and his vessel in Jer 18:6; Isa 29:16; 45:9; Rom 9:20–21).

3. ANCIENT SOURCES, MODERN RESOURCES

Tablets and fragments of Hittite cuneiform tablets found at the capital city number well over thirty thousand. Of these, the lion's share have been published as careful drawings in sixty volumes in the *Keilschrifturkunden aus Boghazköi* (*KUB*) series, forty-one volumes in the *Keilschrifttexte aus Boghazköi* (*KBo*) series, and ten other volumes not part of a lengthy series. In addition, 116 tablets or large fragments from Maşat Höyük were published, and a smaller number from Kušakli, together with scattered individual tablets from Alalakh, Ugarit, and Amarna. The largest corpus of tablets outside of Boğazköy has been found at Ortaköy (ancient Šapinuwa) in the Turkish province of Corum. But it will be many years before these many texts (estimates run to ten thousand) are copied and edited. Most known Hittite

---

[12] The critical edition and definitive study of the text is Erich Neu, *Das hurritische Epos der Freilassung I: Untersuchungen zu einem hurritisch-hetischen Textensemble aus Ḫattuša* (Studien zu den Boğazköy-Texten 32; Wiesbaden: Harrassowitz, 1996). A recent English translation of the complete text is Harry Hoffner Jr., *Hittite Myths* (2d ed.; SBLWAW 2; Atlanta: Scholars Press, 1998), 65–80.

cuneiform texts have been found at sites in central Turkey. A much smaller number have been found in the archives of peoples of the Mediterranean littoral (Syria, Palestine, Egypt) having diplomatic relations with the Hittites.

3.1. HITTITE COMPOSITIONS

The following are the most important Hittite compositions for comparative study with the Hebrew Bible. They are listed in the order in which their entries occur in the standard catalogue of Hittite texts, *Catalogue des textes hittites* (*CTH*)[13] and each marked with its entry number, where information can be found as to the text sources and edition.

CTH 1: *Proclamation of Anitta.* Valuable for comparative historiography and cultural practices such as the sowing of the ruins of a sacked city with salt and weeds (cf. Judg 9:45).

CTH 3: *Zalpa Text* (to which add text source *KBo* 22.2). Important for comparative historiography as an example of a mythological prologue added to an authentic historical narrative, so that the prologue may give a moral basis for the events in the historical narrative. Also has a story of abandoning children in baskets in the river, similar on the surface to the Exodus narrative on the birth of Moses, but with an opposite intent of the mother.

CTH 6: *Political Testament of Hattušili I.* Disinheritance of unworthy sons and adoption of grandson Muršili I. The evil sister of Hattušili connives and is characterized by the metaphor "the Snake."

CTH 40: *Deeds of Šuppiluliuma I.* Reports of military activities of Šuppiluliuma before and after his accession. Includes military engagements with confederations of "tribal troops" similar to the groupings of Israelite tribes during the era of the judges.

CTH 61: *Annals of Muršili II.* Useful for comparative historiography, especially the reporting of divine intervention on behalf of the Hittite king and the king's presentation of a legal complaint to the enemy before engagement, much as in Judg 11:12–27. In both texts the "case" is to be tried by the gods and the verdict rendered by the outcome of the battle.

CTH 81: *Apology of Hattušili III.* Broadly comparable to the "apology" of David in the biblical narrative, which justifies his assuming the throne of Saul. Also appears to contain an allusion to a single combat of champions to avoid a general engagement of rival armies, comparable to the story of David and Goliath.[14]

---

[13] Emmanuel Laroche, *Catalogue des textes hittites* (Études et Commentaires 75; Paris: Klincksieck, 1971).

[14] On the genre of apology, see P. K. McCarter, "The Apology of David," *JBL* 99 (1980): 489–504; Wolf, *Apology of Hattusilis.* On the David and Goliath parallel, see Hoffner, "A Hittite Analogue."

CTH 106 and the more recently published *Bronze Tablet Treaty*. Parallel to the biblical oath of mutual loyalty between the young David and the heir presumptive, Prince Jonathan.[15]

CTH 264: *Instructions for Priests*. Numerous parallels to Israel's cultic provisions, its tabernacle and temple, and the organization and duties of priests.[16]

CTH 291: Two Tablets of the *Hittite Laws*. Numerous parallels to Israelite laws, including levirate marriage, measuring to the nearest town to determine liability for an unknown manslayer, terms of indentured servitude that are comparable to term of service of the ʿebed ʿibrî in Exod 21:2, and laws against sexual relations with domestic animals (the act being called ḫurkel in Hittite, compared to Lev 18–20 and Deut 22:9–11).[17]

CTH 324: *Myth of the Absconding of the God Telipinu*. Provides mythological background to Elijah's taunting words to the priests of Baal in 1 Kgs 18:27.[18]

CTH 446, 449, 475, 481, 492. Rituals with sacrifices at the *a-a-bi* pits. Important background to the use of the ʾôb in the Hebrew Bible to consult the dead, as seen, for example, in 1 Sam 28 and in prophetic taunts such as Isa 8:19 and 29:4.[19]

---

[15] The critical edition of the *Bronze Tablet Treaty* is Heinrich Otten, *Die Bronzetafel aus Boğazköy: Ein Staatsvertrag Tuthalijas IV* (Studien zu den Boğazköy-Texten 1; Wiesbaden: Harrassowitz, 1988). Translations and discussions of the text can be found in Gary Beckman, *Hittite Diplomatic Texts* (2d ed.; SLBWAW 7; Atlanta: Scholars Press, 1999); Oliver R. Gurney, "The Treaty with Ulmi- Tešub," *AnSt* 43 (1993): 13–28; Susanne Heinhold-Krahmer, "Zur Bronzetafel aus Boğazköy und ihrem historischen Inhalt," *AfO* 38–39 (1991–1992): 138–58; Philo H. J. Houwink ten Cate, "The Bronze Tablet of Tudhaliyas IV and Its Geographical and Historical Relations," *ZA* 82 (1992): 233–70.

[16] Jacob Milgrom, "The Shared Custody of the Tabernacle and a Hittite Analogy," *JAOS* 90 (1970): 204–9; idem, "The Concept of Maʿal in the Bible and the Ancient Near East," *JAOS* 96 (1976): 236–47; idem, "Hittite ḫuelpi," *JAOS* 96 (1976): 575–76.

[17] For translations and discussions of this legal material, see Harry A. Hoffner Jr., "Incest, Sodomy and Bestiality in the Ancient Near East," in *Orient and Occident: Essays Presented to Cyrus H. Gordon on the Occasion of His Sixty-Fifth Birthday* (ed. Harry A. Hoffner Jr.; Neukirchen-Vluyn: Neukirchener Verlag, 1973), 81–91; idem, "The Hittite Laws," in *Law Collections from Mesopotamia and Asia Minor* (ed. Martha T. Roth; 2d ed.; Atlanta: Scholars Press, 1997), 211–47; idem, *The Laws of the Hittites: A Critical Edition* (Documenta et Monumenta Orientis Antiqui 23; Leiden: Brill, 1997).

[18] A translation of this text can be found in Hoffner, *Hittite Myths*, 2d ed., 14–15.

[19] Billie Jean Collins, "Necromancy, Fertility and the Dark Earth: The Use of Ritual Pits in Hittite Cult," in *Proceedings of the Conference on Magic in the Ancient*

CTH 342: *Myth of Ba'al and Ašertu*. A Canaanite myth unknown outside of Boğazköy that contains thematic similarities with the encounter between Joseph and Potiphar's wife in Gen 39. Traces of the West Semitic *parallelismus membrorum* remain even in the Hittite translation.

CTH 360: *Tale of Appu*. Moralistic prologue about the gods vindicating a just person against evil opponents followed by the narrative of Appu to illustrate it. Similar in structure to the book of Job, with its prologue and epilogue framing narrative.[20]

CTH 378: *Plague Prayers of Muršili II*. Used by scholars to show doctrines of causality in Hittite and biblical historiography.[21]

CTH 406, 427, 450. Rituals in which symbols of masculinity (bow and arrows) and femininity (spindle and distaff) are exchanged in order to deprive enemy males of their virility.[22]

3.2. GRAMMARS, DICTIONARIES, CONCORDANCES, AND OTHER TOOLS

3.2.1. SIGN LEXICON

The authoritative sign lexicon for Hittite texts is C. Rüster and E. Neu's *Hethitisches Zeichenlexikon: Inventar und Interpretation der Keilschriftzeichen aus den Boğazköy-Texten* (*HZL*). Christel Rüster assisted Heinrich Otten for many years in producing excellent hand copies for the *KBo* series. Erich Neu has produced some of the standard analyses of the criteria for dating Hittite cuneiform texts by paleography. The volume contains not only the complete known repertory of signs but virtually all known variants in the appearance of signs, arranged under each entry in roughly chronological order. Under each sign entry are listed all known examples of multisign logograms (Sumerograms and Akkadograms) and proper names that contain the sign in question. Of particular value to beginners are the tables at the back of *HZL* of common CV, VC, and CVC signs and of easily confused signs.

3.2.2. GRAMMARS

Still the best instructional grammar of Hittite is J. Friedrich's *Hethitisches Elementarbuch*. Less satisfactory, but written in English, is W. H. Held

---

World, August 1998, Orange, California (Leiden: Brill, 1999); Harry A. Hoffner Jr., "Second Millennium Antecedents."

[20] Translations of the text are in Harry A. Hoffner Jr., *Hittite Myths* (ed. Burke Long; SBLWAW 2; Atlanta: Scholars Press, 1990), 82–85; idem, *Laws of the Hittites*.

[21] See, for example, Abraham Malamat, "Doctrines of Causality."

[22] These texts were studied in Hoffner, "Symbols for Masculinity and Femininity," with parallels drawn to biblical motifs.

et al., *Beginning Hittite.* A new elementary grammar co-authored by H. Hoffner and H. C. Melchert is in preparation. The best concise grammar of Cuneiform Luwian is E. Laroche, *Dictionnaire de la langue louvite.* A larger grammatical study of the Luwian noun formations is F. Starke, *Untersuchung zur Stammbildung des keilschrift-luwischen Nomens,* and the same author has studied the case endings in his essay "Die Kasusendungen der luwischen Sprachen." Hieroglyphic Luwian grammar can be surveyed briefly in R. Werner and B. Lüscher, *Kleine Einführung ins Hieroglyphen-Luwische,* but the most complete and authoritative treatment forms a part of the newly published *Corpus of Hieroglyphic Luwian Inscriptions* by J. D. Hawkins.

3.2.3. HITTITE LANGUAGE

Still the best concise coverage of the entire Hittite vocabulary is the glossary by J. Friedrich, *Hethitisches Wörterbuch* with its three supplements, recently reprinted under one cover as *Kurzgefasstes Hethitisches Wörterbuch.* Although this work was last updated (in the third supplement) in 1966, it is marked by a careful, cautious, and accurate approach and is a model of conciseness. It provides a German translation of all words whose meanings were known to Friedrich, a selection of inflected forms, a brief bibliography of studies of the word's meaning, and sometimes a proposed etymology. A more recent Hittite-German word list that covers the entire alphabet is J. Tischler's *Hethitisch-deutsches Wörterverzeichnis.* Although this is more up to date, it lacks many useful features of Friedrich's earlier work, such as the inflected forms and the bibliographies.

Two projects have been underway since the 1970s to produce complete dictionaries of Hittite on the scale of W. von Soden's *Akkadisches Wörterbuch* and the *Assyrian Dictionary of the Oriental Institute of the University of Chicago.* The first is the revised and augmented second edition of J. Friedrich's *Hethitisches Wörterbuch,* begun under the direction of Annelies Kammenhuber of the University of Munich and continued now by one of her students, Inge Hofmann. This dictionary began its coverage with A and has now reached the word *ḫarka-* in volume 3. The second project is *The Hittite Dictionary of the Oriental Institute of the University of Chicago* (*CHD*). Work began in Chicago in 1974 under the joint direction of Hans Güterbock and Harry Hoffner on the basis of lexical files collected over a period of ten years by Hoffner and augmented by *CHD* staff over the following years. In order to avoid immediate overlap with the Munich project, the *CHD* began its published coverage with L. To date, volumes covering words beginning with L, M, N, and P have been published, and the first installment of S is due to appear imminently. The *CHD* is currently implementing plans to place published volumes online so articles can be consulted over the Internet with the use of browser software. Both of these projects attempt to include treatments of all known words appearing in published texts, whether or not their meanings have been determined, and to reproduce together with context notations and full translations representative occurrences of these words. This enables users with limited access to the original sources to appreciate and weigh the evidence for determining the meaning. The *CHD* also includes notations indicating the best guess as to the date of original composition and of the copy of many cited sources. By means of this documentation a user can see the chronological development in the various meanings and grammatical usages.

3.2.4. LUWIAN LANGUAGE

The latest glossary of the Cuneiform Luwian texts is C. Melchert, *Cuneiform Luvian Lexicon,* which is concise, cautious, and accurate. All attested words are cited, whether or not a translation can be ventured. Some Hieroglyphic Luwian words are listed and glossed in Friedrich's *Hethitisches Wörterbuch* and its three supplements under the appendix "Nachbarsprachen." But the usefulness of glossaries and word lists for Hieroglyphic Luwian published prior to J. D. Hawkins et al. in *Hieroglyphs and Luwian: New Evidence for the Connection* is quite limited. Hawkins's work changed the readings of several high-frequency signs and thus revocalized many words. Among these earlier works is P. Meriggi's *Hieroglyphisch-hethitisches Glossar,* which was once a standard tool. Even E. Laroche's *Les Hiéroglyphes Hittites,* which in many respects still remains a crucial tool, suffers in this respect.

3.2.5. HURRIAN LANGUAGE

A truly current Hurrian glossary is badly needed in view of the many texts newly available. At present the latest complete glossary is that of E. Laroche, *Glossaire de la langue hourrite,* which must be supplemented by tabulations and lists in new publications such as E. Neu, *Das hurritische Epos der Freilassung I.* Neu's death in 1999 deprived us of his projected companion volume, which would have contained a complete glossary of this extremely valuable text. It remains to be seen if this work can be finished by someone else in the near future. Other valuable sources include the essays by B. André-Salvini and M. Salvini, "A New Trilingual Vocabulary from Ras Shamra and the Relationship between Hurrian and Urartian"; D. Owen and G. Wilhelm, "Lexical Index"; and the three articles published by Wilhelm in 1992 listed in the bibliography.

3.2.6. SUMEROGRAMS AND AKKADOGRAMS

An older listing of Sumerograms and Akkadograms in Hittite texts can be found in Friedrich's *Hethitisches Wörterbuch* and its three supplements.

This is now seriously incomplete and inaccurate in the rendering of Sumerian words. An up-to-date replacement is found in Rüster and Neu's *HZL*, in which each logogram is accompanied by the number of the sign in the repertoire under which it is catalogued with a German and a Turkish translation.

3.2.7. HITTITE CUNEIFORM TEXTS

No one can adequately keep up with Hittite textual evidence without a catalogue of known text compositions. This is particularly so because one not only has to identify and locate all the known compositions but also to reconstruct their texts from a myriad of joins and duplicates. In the 1950s, 1960s, and 1970s the leading authority in this field was the French linguist Emmanuel Laroche, whose *magnum opus* was his catalogue of Hittite texts. This material was published originally in installments in the journal *Revue hittite et asianique* and subsequently produced in a revised and enlarged second edition as *Catalogue des textes hittites* in 1971 and 1972. But almost thirty years have passed since the last update of this work, and Laroche is long dead. There have been recent indications that a team of Italian Hittitologists may attempt to produce a digital version of a new catalogue. But in the meantime the best work in identifying new joins and duplicates is being done by the German researcher Detlav Groddek, whose publications in *AoF* are listed in the bibliography. For the beginning student it is enough to utilize Laroche's catalogue and consult the online additions at the web sites of B. J. Collins named "Hittite Home Page" (http://www.asor.org/HITTITE/HittiteHP.html), and the "Hethitologie Portal Mainz (http://www.orient.uni-wuerzburg.de).

3.2.8. TOPONYMS

The great Tübingen Atlas of ancient Western Asia has produced a series of valuable volumes cataloguing toponyms from the major text corpora and time periods. The 1978 volume covering the Hittite Empire is *Répertoire Géographique des Textes Cunéiformes* by G. F. del Monte and J. Tischler with a later supplement by del Monte in 1992. Here will be found not only the textual references but also translations of the immediate context of the more significant ones and a relatively complete bibliography of studies positing a location for the toponym in question.

3.2.9. PERSONAL NAMES

The first comprehensive collection and study of the personal names of the Hittite texts was E. Laroche's 1955 article "Onomastique hittite: additions et corrections." He published a revised and much-augmented second edition in 1966 with the title *Les noms des Hittites*. Additions to this second

edition can be found in G. M. Beckman's "A Contribution to Hittite Onomastic Studies."

3.2.10. Divine Names

For many years the only systematic and comprehensive collection of
divine names was E. Laroche, *Recherches sur les noms des dieux hittites.*
Although he published supplements and eventually revised editions of his
collection of personal names, Laroche never attempted this with his collection of divine names. Recently there has appeared a new
comprehensive collection: B. H. L. van Gessel's *Onomasticon of the Hittite Pantheon.* This has the advantage of completeness and great detail.
Every attested occurrence is listed together with bibliography on the deity
so designated. But unlike Laroche's work, van Gessel's does not group the
various deities according to their ethnic provenience, nor is there much
discussion of the deities whose names are catalogued. Perhaps he felt this
was being done in the recent comprehensive volumes on Hittite religion
by V. Haas, *Geschichte der hethitischen Religion,* and M. Popko, *Religions
of Asia Minor.*

3.2.11. Mythology

An abbreviated but helpful dictionary of Hittite mythology was pub-
lished in E. von Schuler, "Kleinasien: Die Mythologie der Hethiter und
Hurriter." Comprehensive collections of Hittite myths in translation have
recently appeared in A. Bernabé, *Textos literarios hetitas;* H. A. Hoffner,
Hittite Myths and the augmented second edition of *Hittite Myths;* and
F. Pecchioli Daddi and A. M. Polvani, *La mitologia ittita.*

3.2.12. Royal Seals

The first comprehensive corpus of hieroglyphic seals of Hittite monarchs was H. G. Güterbock's two-volume set *Siegel aus Boğazköy,*
published in 1940 and 1942. A more recent attempt was begun in
N. Boysan-Dietrich et al., *Sammlung hieroglyphischer Siegel, I.* For those
interested in surveying the royal seals chronologically and observing the
visual arrangement of their motifs and characteristic legends, H. Gonnet's
Catalogue des documents royaux hittites du IIe millénaire avant J.-C. is
indispensable and convenient.

3.2.13. Royal Titulary

Much can be learned about the trends in royal ideology through the
succession of Hittite kings by using the information compiled by Gonnet
in his study "La titulature royale hittite au IIe millénaire avant J.-C." This

handy little work extracts the sequence of titles following the royal names of all known Hittite kings.

3.2.14. CLASSIFIED BIBLIOGRAPHY

Bibliography on Hittite text, language, and civilization that has appeared during the period of 1915–1995 was collected and arranged in the three volumes by Souček and Siegelová listed in the bibliography.

4. BIBLIOGRAPHY

André-Salvini, Béatrice, and Mirjo Salvini. "A New Trilingual Vocabulary from Ras Shamra and the Relationship between Hurrian and Urartian." Pages 267–76 in *Nuzi at Seventy-Five*. Edited by David I. Owen and Gernot Wilhelm. Bethesda, Md.: CDL, 1999.

Archi, Alfonso. "Il sistema KIN della divinazione ittita." *OrAnt* 13 (1974): 113–44.

———. "L' ornitomanzia ittita." *Studi Micenei et Egeo-Anatolici* 16 (1975): 119–80.

Beckman, Gary M. "A Contribution to Hittite Onomastic Studies." *JAOS* 103 (1983): 623–27.

———. *Hittite Diplomatic Texts*. 2d ed. SBLWAW 7. Atlanta: Scholars Press, 1999.

———. "The Hittite Language and Its Decipherment." *Bulletin of the Canadian Society for Mesopotamian Studies* 31 (1996): 23–30.

Beekes, Robert S. P. *Comparative Indo-European Linguistics: An Introduction*. Amsterdam: Benjamins, 1995.

Bernabé, Alberto. *Textos literarios hetitas*. Madrid: Alianza Editorial, 1987.

Böhl, F. M. Th. "Tudhhalia I, Zeitgenosse Abrahams, um 1650 v. Chr." *ZAW* 42 = NS 1 (1924): 148–53.

Boysan-Dietrich, Nilüfer, Massimiliano Marazzi, and Helmuth Nowicki. *Sammlung hieroglyphischer Siegel, I*. Würzburg: Königshausen/ Neumann, 1983.

Collins, Billie Jean. "Necromancy, Fertility and the Dark Earth: The Use of Ritual Pits in Hittite Cult." In *Proceedings of the Conference on Magic in the Ancient World, August 1998, Orange, California*. Leiden: Brill, 1999.

del Monte, Giuseppe F. *Die Orts- und Gewässernamen der hethitischen Texte: Supplement*. Repertoire géographique des textes cunéiformes 6.2. Beihefte zum Tübinger Atlas des Vorderen Orients B/7.6. Wiesbaden: Reichert, 1992.

del Monte, Giuseppe F., and Johann Tischler. *Die Orts- und Gewässernamen der hethitischen Texte*. Edited by Wolfgang Röllig. Repertoire géographique des textes cunéiformes 6. Beihefte zum Tübinger Atlas des Vorderen Orients B/7. Wiesbaden: Reichert, 1978.

Fensham, F. Charles. "Clauses of Protection in Hittite Vassal Treaties and the Old Testament." *VT* 13 (1963): 133–43.

―――. "Maledictions and Benedictions in Ancient Near Eastern Vassal Treaties and the Old Testament." *ZAW* 74 (1962): 1–9.

―――. "Salt and Curse in the Old Testament and the Ancient Near East." *BA* 25 (1962): 48–50.

Forrer, Emil. "Die acht Sprachen der Boghazköi-Inschriften." *SPAW* (1919): 1029–41.

―――. "The Hittites in Palestine." *PEQ* 68 (1936): 190–203; (1937): 100–115.

Friedrich, Johannes. *Hethitisches Elementarbuch, 1. Teil: Kurzgefaßte Grammatik.* Edited by Hans Krahe. 2d ed. Indogermanische Bibliothek. 1. Reihe: Lehr- und Handbücher. Heidelberg: Winter, 1960.

―――. *Hethitisches Wörterbuch: Kurzgefaßte kritische Sammlung der Deutungen hethitischer Wörter.* Heidelberg: Winter, 1952.

―――. *Kurzgefasstes Hethitisches Wörterbuch: kurzgefasste kritische Sammlung der Deutungen hethitischer Wörter.* Indogermanische Bibliothek. 2. Reihe: Wörterbucher. Heidelberg: Winter, 1991.

Gamkrelidze, Thomas V. "The Akkado-Hittite Syllabary and the Problem of the Origins of the Hittite Script." *ArOr* 29 (1961): 406–18.

Garrett, Andrew. "The Origin of NP Split Ergativity." *Lg* 66 (1990): 261–96.

Gessel, B. H. L. van. *Onomasticon of the Hittite Pantheon.* 3 vols. HO 1/33:1–3. Leiden: Brill, 1998–2001.

Gonnet, Hatice. *Catalogue des documents royaux hittites du IIe millénaire avant J.-C., Langues et Civilizations orientales.* Paris: Éditions du Centre National de la Recherche Scientifique, 1975.

―――. "La titulature royale hittite au IIe millénaire avant J.-C." *Hethitica* 3 (1979): 3–108.

Groddek, Detlev. "Fragmenta Hethitica dispersa I." *AoF* 21 (1994): 328–38.

―――. "Fragmenta Hethitica dispersa III." *AoF* 23 (1996): 101–10.

―――. "Fragmenta Hethitica dispersa IV." *AoF* 23 (1996): 298–307.

―――. "Fragmenta Hethitica dispersa V/VI." *AoF* 25 (1998): 227–46.

Gurney, Oliver R. "The Treaty with Ulmi-Tešub." *AnSt* 43 (1993): 13–28.

Güterbock, Hans Gustav. *Die Königssiegel der Grabungen bis 1938.* Vol. 1 of *Siegel aus Boğazköy.* Edited by Ernst F. Weidner. AfOB 5. Berlin: Im Selbstverlag des Herausgebers, 1940.

―――. *Die Königssiegel von 1939 und die übrigen Hieroglyphensiegel.* Vol. 2 of *Siegel aus Boğazköy.* Edited by Ernst F. Weidner. AfOB 7. Berlin: Im Selbstverlag des Herausgebers, 1942.

Haas, Volkert. *Geschichte der hethitischen Religion.* HO 1/15. Leiden: Brill, 1994.

Hänsler, H. "Der historische Hintergrund von Richter 3, 8–10." *Bib* 11 (1930): 391–418; 12 (1931): 3–26, 271–96, 395–410.

Hauschild, M. W. "Die kleinasiatischen Völker und ihre Beziehungen zu den Juden." *ZfE* 53 (1921): 518–28.

Hawkins, J. David. *Corpus of Hieroglyphic Luwian Inscriptions.* Berlin: de Gruyter, 2000.

———. "The Origin and Dissemination of Writing in Western Asia." Pages 128–66 in *The Origins of Civilization.* Edited by P. R. S. Moorey. Oxford: Clarendon, 1979.

———. "Writing in Anatolia: Imported and Indigenous Systems." *World Archaeology* 17/3 (1986): 363–76.

Hawkins, J. David, Anna Morpurgo Davies, and Günter Neumann. *Hittite Hieroglyphs and Luwian: New Evidence for the Connection.* NAWG, Philologisch-historische Klasse 73/6. Göttingen: Vandenhoeck & Ruprecht, 1974.

Hecker, Karl. "Zur Herkunft der hethitischen Keilschrift." Pages 53–63 in *Uluslararas 1: Hititoloji Kongresi Bildirileri (19–21 Temmuz 1990).* Corum: Türk Kültür Bakanlığı, 1990.

Heinhold-Krahmer, Susanne. "Zur Bronzetafel aus Boğazköy und ihrem historischen Inhalt." *AfO* 38–39 (1991–1992): 138–58.

Held, Warren H., Jr., William R. Schmalstieg, and Janet E. Gertz. *Beginning Hittite.* Columbus, Ohio: Slavica Publishers, 1987.

Hoffner, Harry A., Jr. "Appu and His Two Sons." Pages 153–55 in *Canonical Compositions from the Biblical World.* Vol. 1 of *The Context of Scripture.* Edited by William W. Hallo and K. Lawson Younger Jr. Leiden: Brill, 1997.

———. "A Hittite Analogue to the David and Goliath Contest of Champions?" *CBQ* 30 (1968): 220–25.

———. "The Hittite Laws." Pages 211–47 in *Law Collections from Mesopotamia and Asia Minor.* Edited by Martha T. Roth. 2d. ed. SBLWAW 6. Atlanta: Scholars Press, 1997.

———. *Hittite Myths.* Edited by Burke Long. SBLWAW 2. Atlanta: Scholars Press, 1990.

———. *Hittite Myths.* Edited by Gary M. Beckman. 2d. ed. SBLWAW 2. Atlanta: Scholars Press, 1998.

———. "Hittite *tarpis* and Hebrew *teraphim*." *JNES* 27 (1968): 61–69.

———. "Incest, Sodomy and Bestiality in the Ancient Near East." Pages 81–90 in *Orient and Occident: Essays Presented to Cyrus H. Gordon on the Occasion of his Sixty-Fifth Birthday.* Edited by Harry A. Hoffner Jr. Neukirchen-Vluyn: Neukirchener Verlag, 1973.

———. *The Laws of the Hittites. A Critical Edition.* Documenta et Monumenta Orientis Antiqui 23. Leiden: Brill, 1997.

———. "Second Millennium Antecedents to the Hebrew ʾÔḆ." *JBL* 86 (1967): 385–401.

———. "Some Contributions of Hittitology to Old Testament Study: The Tyndale Archaeology Lecture, 1968." *TynBul* 20 (1969): 27–55.

_____. "Symbols for Masculinity and Femininity: Their Use in Ancient Near Eastern Sympathetic Magic Rituals." *JBL* 85 (1966): 326–34.

Houwink ten Cate, Philo H. J. "The Bronze Tablet of Tudhaliyas IV and its Geographical and Historical Relations." *ZA* 82 (1992): 233–70.

Hrozny, Friedrich. "Die Lösung des hethitischen Problems." *Mitteilungen der Deutschen Orientgesellschaft zu Berlin* 56 (1915): 17–50.

_____. *Die Sprache der Hethiter.* Edited by Otto Weber. Boghazköi-Studien 1–2. Leipzig: Hinrichs, 1917.

Kaplan, H. R. "Anatolian Elements in the EB III Culture of Palestine." *ZDPV* 97 (1981): 18–35.

Kempinski, Aharon, "Hittites in the Bible—What Does Archaeology Say?" *BAR* 5/4 (1979): 20–45.

Knudtzon, Jürgen Alexander, Sophus Bugge, and Alf Torp. *Die zwei Arzawa-briefe, die ältesten Urkunden in indogermanischer Sprache.* Leipzig: Hinrichs, 1902.

Kronasser, Heinz. *Vergleichende Laut- und Formenlehre der Hethitischen.* Heidelberg: Winter, 1956.

Laroche, Emmanuel. *Catalogue des textes hittites.* Études et Commentaires 75. Paris: Klincksieck, 1971.

_____. "Catalogue des textes hittites, premier supplément." *RHA* 30 (1972): 94–133.

_____. *Dictionnaire de la langue louvite.* Bibliothèque archéologique et historique de l'institut français d'archéologie d'Istanbul 6. Paris: Adrien-Maisonneuve, 1959.

_____. *Glossaire de la langue hourrite.* 2 vols. Paris: Klincksieck, 1978–1979.

_____. "Lécanomancie hittite." *RA* 52 (1958): 150–62.

_____. *Les Hiéroglyphes Hittites, I.* Paris: CNRS, 1960.

_____. *Les noms des Hittites.* Paris: Klincksieck, 1966.

_____. "Onomastique hittite: additions et corrections." *RHA* 13 (1955): 41–58.

_____. *Recherches sur les noms des dieux hittites* (= *Revue hittite et asiatique* 7 [1947]). Paris: Maisonneuve, 1947.

_____. "Sur le vocabulaire de l'haruspicine hittite." *RA* 64 (1970): 127–39.

Malamat, Abraham. "Doctrines of Causality in Hittite and Biblical Historiography: A Parallel." *VT* 5 (1955): 1–12.

Mayer-Opificius, Ruth. "Die Hethiter und das Alte Testament." Pages 65–73 in *Mysterium der Gnade: Festschrift für Joh. Auer.* Edited by H. Rossmann. Regensburg: Pustet, 1975.

McCarter, P. K. "The Apology of David." *JBL* 99 (1980): 489–504.

Meier-Brügger, Michael. *Indogermanische Sprachwissenschaft.* Berlin and New York: de Gruyter, 2000.

Melchert, H. Craig. *Anatolian Historical Phonology.* Leiden Studies in Indo-European 3. Amsterdam and Atlanta: Rodopi, 1994.

———. *Cuneiform Luvian Lexicon*. Lexica Anatolica 2. Chapel Hill, N. C.: Self-published, 1993.

———. "Historical Phonology of Anatolian." *Journal of Indo-European Studies* 21 (1993): 237–57.

———. "Hittite Phonology." Pages 555–67 in *Phonologies of Asia and Africa*. Edited by Alan S. Kaye. Winona Lake, Ind.: Eisenbrauns, 1997.

Mendenhall, George E. *Law and Covenant in Israel and the Ancient Near East*. Pittsburgh: Biblical Colloquium, 1955.

Meriggi, Piero. *Hieroglyphisch-hethitisches Glossar*. Wiesbaden: Harrassowitz, 1962.

Milgrom, Jacob. "The Concept of Maꜥal in the Bible and the Ancient Near East." *JAOS* 96 (1976): 236–47.

———. "Hittite ḫuelpi." *JAOS* 96 (1976): 575–76.

———. "The Shared Custody of the Tabernacle and a Hittite Analogy." *JAOS* 90 (1970): 204–9.

Moyer, James C. "Hittite and Israelite Cultic Practices: A Selected Comparison." Pages 19–38 in *Scripture in Context II: More Essays on the Comparative Method*. Edited by William W. Hallo. Winona Lake, Ind.: Eisenbrauns, 1983.

Neu, Erich. *Das hurritische Epos der Freilassung I: Untersuchungen zu einem hurritisch-hethitischen Textensemble aus Ḫattuša*. Studien zu den Boğazköy-Texten 32. Wiesbaden: Harrassowitz, 1996.

Otten, Heinrich. *Die Bronzetafel aus Boğazköy: Ein Staatsvertrag Tuthalijas IV*. Studien zu den Boğazköy-Texten 1. Wiesbaden: Harrassowitz, 1988.

———. "Kampf von König und Gottheit in einem hethitischen Ritualtext." *BaghM* 7 (1968): 139–42.

Owen, David I., and Gernot Wilhelm. "Lexical Index." Pages 439–51 in *Nuzi at Seventy-Five*. Edited by David I. Owen and Gernot Wilhelm. Bethesda, Md.: CDL, 1999.

Pecchioli Daddi, Franca, and Anna Maria Polvani. *La mitologia ittita*. Testi del Vicino Oriente antico 4.1. Brescia: Paideia Editrice, 1990.

Popko, Maciej. *Religions of Asia Minor*. Translated by Iwona Zych. Warsaw: Academic Publications Dialog, 1995.

Rosenkranz, Bernhard. *Vergleichende Untersuchungen der altanatolischen Sprachen*. Edited by W. Winter. Trends in Linguistics, State-of-the-Art Reports 8. The Hague: Mouton de Gruyter, 1978.

Rüster, Christel, and Erich Neu. *Hethitisches Zeichenlexikon: Inventar und Interpretation der Keilschriftzeichen aus den Boğazköy-Texten*. Studien zu den Boğazköy-Texten Beiheft 2. Wiesbaden: Harrassowitz, 1989.

Sayce, Archibald Henry. "Hittite and Mittannian Elements in the Old Testament." *JTS* 29 (1928): 401–6.

Schuler, Einar von. "Kleinasien: Die Mythologie der Hethiter und Hurriter."
    Pages 141–215 in *Wörterbuch der Mythologie*. Edited by H. W. Haus-
    sig. Stuttgart: Ernst Klett Verlag, 1965.

Souček, Vladimir, and Jana Siegelová. *Systematische Bibliographie der Het-
    hitologie 1915–1995*. 3 vols. Praha: Národní Muzeum, 1996.

Starke, Frank. "Die Kasusendungen der luwischen Sprachen." Pages
    407–25 in *Serta Indogermanica: Festschrift für Günter Neumann zum
    60. Geburtstag*. Edited by Johann Tischler. Innsbruck: Institut für
    Sprachwissenschaft der Universität Innsbruck, 1982.

———. *Untersuchung zur Stammbildung des keilschrift-luwischen Nomens.*
    Studien zu den Boğazköy-Texten 31. Wiesbaden: Harrassowitz, 1990.

Szemerényi, Oswald J. L. *Introduction to Indo-European Linguistics.*
    Oxford: Clarendon, 1996.

Tischler, Johann. *Hethitisch-deutsches Wörterverzeichnis*. Innsbrucker
    Beiträge zur Sprachwissenschaft 39. Innsbruck: Institut für Sprachwis-
    senschaft der Universität Innsbruck, 1982.

Weinfeld, Moshe. *Justice and Righteousness in Israel and the Nations*
    (Hebrew). Jerusalem: Magnes, 1985.

———. "Social and Cultic Institutions in the Priestly Source against Their
    Ancient Near Eastern Background." Pages 95–129 in *Eighth World Con-
    gress of Jewish Studies: Panel Sessions, Bible Studies and Hebrew
    Language*. Jerusalem: Hebrew University Press, 1983.

Werner, Rudolph, and Barbara Lüscher. *Kleine Einführung ins Hiero-
    glyphen-Luwische*. OBO 106. Freiburg: Universitätsverlag, 1991.

Wilhelm, Gernot. "Hurritische Lexikographie und Grammatik: Die hurri-
    tisch-hethitische Bilingue aus Boğazköy." *Or* 61 (1992): 122–41.

———. "Notizen zum hurritischen Wörterbuch." *Studi Micenei et Egeo-
    Anatolici* 29 (1992): 245–48.

———. "Zum viersprachigen Vokabular aus Ugarit." *Studi Micenei et Egeo-
    Anatolici* 29 (1992): 249–54.

Wolf, H. M. *The Apology of Hattusilis Compared with Other Political Self-
    Justifications of the Ancient Near East*. Ann Arbor, Mich.: University
    Microfilms, 1967.

PHOENICIAN

Charles R. Krahmalkov

1. THE LANGUAGE

Phoenician, in the broadest sense, was a group of related Canaanite dialects (regional forms) spoken in ancient Lebanon and Palestine. In the narrower and stricter sense, the term denotes the dialect of the *Ponnīm,* the inhabitants of the region of Sidon-Tyre-Acco (ancient *Pūt*); this dialect, called *Ponnīm* by its speakers, was used by all inhabitants of Lebanon-Palestine as a quasi national language. The word *Phoenician,* as well as Latin *Poenus* and *punicus,* derive from the term *Ponnīm.*[1] Here it is important to observe that in classical antiquity, the terms *Phoenicia* and *Phoenician* were also synonymous and essentially conterminous with the native terms *Canaan* and *Canaanites.*

Two dialects of Lebanese Phoenician are epigraphically attested: (1) Byblian, the language of the city of Byblos; and (2) *Ponnīm* (Tyro-Sidonian). These were quite different from one another, particularly with regard to the pronouns. Byblian, known from thirteen inscriptions, spanning the period 1000 to 400 B.C.E., was always confined to its own region, playing little or no part in the history of Phoenician expansion and colonization in the course of the first millennium B.C.E. In marked contrast, Tyro-Sidonian, which had emerged as the primary of the Phoenician dialects already at the beginning of the first millennium B.C.E. with the rise to power of the city-states of Tyre and Sidon, became a world-class language: the dialect first came to be used as a common standard language by all Phoenicians; then, for a brief moment in history (ninth-eighth centuries B.C.E.), acquired the status of a lingua franca in parts of the Middle East; and later, in the western Mediterranean, became the rival of Greek and Latin.

In Palestine, Phoenician dialects were spoken along the coast, in the Shephelah (lowlands) and in the valleys. Best attested of these is the language

---

[1] On the geographical term *Pūt* and the ethno-linguistic term *Ponnīm,* see Charles R. Krahmalkov, *Phoenician-Punic Dictionary* (OLA 90; Studia Phoenicia 15; Leuven: Peeters, 2000), 10–13; and idem, *Phoenician-Punic Grammar* (Handbook of Oriental Studies Section One 54; Leiden: Brill, 2001), 1–7.

of the city of Lachish, known from several inscriptions but also from Num 1:4, a single line of Lachishite or closely related Palestinian Phoenician preserved by chance in the Bible. This language is not to be confused with the Judean Canaanite (Hebrew), the national language of the Israelites, used in the so-called Lachish letters of the early sixth century B.C.E.[2]

The importance of Phoenician in antiquity is related directly to the prestige of the Western dialect (Punic) spoken in North Africa, southern Spain, Malta, Sardinia, and western Sicily. This form of Phoenician was brought to the western Mediterranean in the course of Tyro-Sidonian exploration and colonization, beginning in the thirteenth century B.C.E., of which the most significant date and event was the founding of the great city of Carthage (near Tunis in present-day Tunisia) in the year 825 or 814 B.C.E. Western Phoenician, called Punic by scholars in order to differentiate it from Phoenician (Eastern Phoenician, the dialect of Lebanon, Cyprus, and Palestine), was the language of the Carthaginian Empire. Similar to but not the same as Phoenician, Punic appears to have been based on the dialect of Palestine; it is the language of the major part of the corpus of "Phoenician" inscriptions and the more important part of this corpus.

Phoenician was written in an alphabet of twenty-two letters reflecting its repertory of twenty-two consonantal phonemes. This alphabet was not, as often mistakenly asserted, invented by the Phoenicians but, rather, was an adaptation of the early West Semitic alphabet to the needs of their own language. It was this twenty-two-letter Phoenician adaptation of the West Semitic alphabet that was adopted by the Israelites and later by the Greeks, who acknowledged the borrowing by calling their own alphabet *ta Phoinikeia grammata,* "the Phoenician letters." Furthermore, the historical character of the borrowing is evident from the fact that the letters of the Greek and Hebrew alphabets bear the same names, all purely Phoenician.

1.1. THE CONSONANTS

The Phoenician (consonantal) alphabet and the probable manner of articulation of the consonants are as follows: ʾ (ʾ), B (b), G (g), D (d), H (h), W (w), Z (zd, dz), Ḥ (ḥ), Ṭ (ṭ), Y (y), K (k), L (l), M (m), N (n), S (s), ʿ (ʿ), P (p), Ṣ (ts), Q (q), R (r), Š (ś, pronounced s), T (t).

Although outwardly similar to Hebrew (Judean Canaanite), Phoenician was quite different from Hebrew in morphophonology, syntax, and lexicon. For the Bible scholar, it is therefore most useful to speak of the major differences of Phoenician from Hebrew and, at the same time, provide a

---

[2] For a brief discussion of Lachishite Phoenician and the passage in Num 1:4, in which two instances of the Phoenician relative pronoun occur, see Krahmalkov, *Phoenician-Punic Grammar,* 94.

brief outline of Phoenician grammar as a general introduction to the language for the nonspecialist. In the following discussion, Phoenician and Hebrew words are written in italics, but vocalized Phoenician cited from Latin-letter inscriptions of the Late Roman period or from ancient transcriptions is set in small caps. Our knowledge of the pronunciation of Phoenician is derived largely from Latin-letter Punic of the Roman period.

Phoenician did not possess the sound *sh*. That is why Saint Augustine, a native speaker of Punic, was able to play on the coincidence of Punic *salūs* "three, Trinity" (Heb. *šālōš*) and Latin *salus* "salvation." Ephraimite, the Canaanite dialect of the northern part of ancient Israel, shared this feature of phonology with Phoenician, as we know from the biblical story (Judg 12:4–6) of the Ephraimites' inability to pronounce correctly the Judean Canaanite word *šibbōlet*. Asked to pronounce the word, the Ephraimite, although able to hear the sound *sh,* was unable to produce (articulate) it, pronouncing *sibbōlet* instead.

Phoenician, unlike Masoretic Hebrew, did not know the double (plosive versus fricative pronunciation) of the consonant series B (b-v), G (g-gh), D (d-dh), K (k-kh), P (p-f), T (t-th). In Punic however, *b* was pronounced *v* before a consonant: MYNTSYFTH (*mintsivt*) "stela" (Heb. *maṣṣēbâ*); and *p* in late Punic was pronounced *f* in all positions: FEL "he made," FELA "she made," FELU "they made," FELIOTH "something made."

1.2. THE VOWELS

The vowel *a* was generally pronounced *i* in a closed unstressed syllable but generally as *o* in a stressed syllable: hence, Punic IDDIR ("great," Hebrew *'addîr*) and YMACOM (*im-maqom*) "the place" (Hebrew *ham-māqôm*); Punic CAROTHI "I called" (Hebrew *qārā'tî*) and NASOTHI "I carry" (Heb. *naśá'tî*). The long vowel *ō* in an open and/or unstressed syllable was generally pronounced *ū:* Punic DUBER "says" (Hebrew *dōbēr*). To illustrate the difference between Hebrew and Phoenician pronunciation, compare Hebrew *māh 'āmar hakkōhēn* ("What did the priest say?") and its Phoenician realization *mū 'amor hik-kūhen*.

1.3. MORPHOLOGY

Independent personal pronouns: *'anī* (rare) and *'anīki* "I"; *'atta* "you" (masc.) and *'atti* (fem.); *hū* "he" and *hī* "she"; *'anaḥnu* and *naḥnu* "we"; *'attim* "ye"; *hmt* "they" (masc. and fem., pronunciation unknown).

Suffix pronouns (possessive) with the noun: *sūsī* "my horse"; *sūska* "your [masc.] horse"; *sūski* "your [fem.] horse"; *sūso* "his horse" but *sūsi* in the genitive case and *sūsêyo* "his horses"; *sūsa* "her horse" but *sūsi* in the genitive case and *sūsêya* "her horses"; *sūson* "our horse" but *sūsen* in the genitive case; *sūskom* "your horse"; *sūsom* "their horse" but *sūsnom* in the genitive case and *sūsênom* "their horses." The genitive case is governed by (1) a construct noun, (2) a preposition, (3) the so-called accusative particle *'et*.

Demonstrative pronouns, with the noun: *sūs ᵉzdê* "this horse"; *sūsot ᵉzdō* "this mare"; *sūsīm 'ille* "these horses." The use of the definite article with the noun was optional. Normally, the demonstrative pronoun does not receive the definite article, but there are two instances of the latter use in Phoenician. The definite article is *ha-* before a word beginning with *'*, *ḥ, ḫ,* or *ʿ*, but *hiC-* (C = doubling of the initial consonant of the word following) in all other cases, such as *hissūs* "the horse," but *ha'īś* "the man."

The interrogative pronouns: *mī* "who?" and *mū* "what?" The indefinite pronoun "one" was expressed by *'adom* or *'īś*. Phoenician possessed, aside from the suffixal possessive pronouns, an independent possessive pronoun *'īś lo* "his": *hibbêt 'īś lo* "his house." The reflexive possessive "his own" was expressed by the word *binati* (or *bitti*) following a suffixal pronoun, such as *bêto binati* "his own house." Pronominal direct objects were expressed either by suffixal pronouns or by the independent direct object pronoun *ʿaltêyo* "him" (in Punic, *'oto* was used).

Relative pronoun: One archaic relative pronoun was *zū-*, known from Old Byblian of the tenth to ninth centuries B.C.E. In the archaic Phoenician dialect of Lachish (thirteenth century B.C.E.), the relative pronoun was *še-*. Early in the first millenium, the relative pronoun *'īś* came into use in all forms of Phoenician and Punic. In Neo-Punic, one also finds the relative pronouns *mū* and *mū 'īś*.

Nouns: The feminine ending of the noun in the singular is *-ot* (but *-at-*, untressed, before suffixal pronouns) or *-t*. The masculine plural ending is *-īm*, and in the construct *-ê*. The feminine plural ending is *-ūt*.

The verb: The verbal system is essentially the same as that of Classical Hebrew, having the following "forms": (1) prefixing A (Old West Semitic *yaqṭulu*); (2) prefixing B (Old West Semitic *yaqṭul*); (3) suffixing (Old West Semitic *qaṭala*); (4) active participle and passive participle; (5) imperative; (6) infinitive absolute and infinite construct. The forms in themselves were not marked for tense or aspect but received their tense and aspect reference from the syntactic structure in which they are imbedded and from the position they occupied within the structure. So, for instance, the suffixing verb (Phoenician *qaṭol*) was *not* a past perfective form but rather, depending on the type of clause and position within the clause, may be past perfective (non clause-initial); present perfective; future (in result clause of a temporal or conditional sentence); jussive/optative; or consecutive (following a main verb and assuming the tense and aspect reference of that verb).

The stems attested are (1) *qal,* including the *qal* inner passive (*gunebte* "I have been robbed!"); (2) *nipʿal;* (3) *piʿel* and its passive *puʿal;* (4) *yipʿil*

(Punic *ip^ʿil*), corresponding to Hebrew *hip^ʿil;* (5) *hitpe^ʿel.* Byblian Phoenician also has *hipta^ʿal,* used to express the intransitive of a transitive verb.

Past perfective action is expressed in one dialect by obligatory clause-initial prefixing verb B (*ya^ʿal higgeber ^ezde* "this man went up") but in another dialect by the obligatory clause-initial infinite absolute (*śakōr ʾanīki* "I hired"). In both dialects, the past perfective must be expressed by the suffixing verb if the verb is non clause-initial (*hiddelt ^ezdō samarti biqqīr* "I nailed this plaque on to the wall"). The infinitive absolute is extensively used, expressing future tense, jussive/optative, subjunctive, and imperative.

Noticeable and different from the Hebrew verbal system, the Phoenician uses the infinitive construct extensively to express periphrastic tenses and moods: future indicative; jussive/optative; subjunctive; imperative.

1.4. IDENTIFYING A PHOENICIAN TEXT

Notwithstanding the linguistic similarity of Phoenician and Hebrew (Judean), the languages differed, as observed earlier, in numerous matters of phonology, morphology, syntax, and lexicon. One can readily distinguish a Phoenician from a Hebrew text, even if little content survives, by such salient differences. Here, in addition, is a concise list of lexical differences to look for.

(1) Nouns: *pa^ʿam* "foot, leg" (Heb. *regel,* not attested in Phoenician); *r^ʿt* "resolution, decision." Plurals often differ from Hebrew, such as Phoenician *ʾīśīm* (Heb. *ʾănāšīm*); *ʾiśśūt* (Heb. *nāšīm*); *milkayūt* (Heb. *məlākôt*); *delahūt* (Heb. *dəlātôt*); *maqōmīm* (Heb. *məqômôt*).

(2) Verbs: *ʾ-r-ś* "ask" alongside *ś-ʾ-l;* *b-q-y* "tarry, remain" (not attested in Heb.); *d-l-y* "possess, own" (rare in Heb., only in poetry); *h-w-y* "live" (Heb. *h-y-y*); *h-z-y* "see" (Heb. *r-ʾ-y,* not attested in Phoenician); *k-w-n* "to be" in the *qal* (Heb. *h-y-y,* unknown in Phoenician); *k-r-m* "honor" (*yip^ʿil* stem, not attested in Heb.); *p-^ʿ-l* "do, make" (Heb. *^ʿ-ś-y,* rare in Phoenician).

(3) Adjectives: *ʾiddīr* and *kibbīr* "big, large" (Heb. *gādôl,* not attested in Phoenician); *ṣā^ʿīr* "small" (Heb. *qāṭōn,* not attested in Phoenician); *śippīr* "beautiful" (Heb. *yāpeh,* attested in Phoenician with the meaning "proper").

(4) Prepositions: *ʾet* "to, for, with" (Hebrew *^ʿim* is not attested in Phoenician); *bod* "by," expressing agency; *limin* "from" is more common than simple *min; limibbi-* "in," a common compound preposition equivalent to simple *bi-.* The preposition *ʾel* is rarely attested and only in Byblian and Egypto-Palestinian Phoenician.

(6) Adverbs and Conjunctions: *biribbīm* "very, much" (Heb. *mə^ʾōd,* not attested in Phoenician); *ʾim* "or" (Heb. *ʾô* is not attested in Phoenician); *likūn* "in order that"; *lima* or *lamma* "lest" (Heb. *pen,* not attested in Phoenician); *kemū ʾīś* "when" (Heb. *ka^ʾăšer*).

(7) Particles: *'ammā* "as for." The particles negating the verb are (1) *bal,* (2) *'ī,* and (3) *'ībal.* Phoenician did not possess the negative particle *lō'.* The particles expressing existence were *'iś* "there is/are" (Heb. *yēś*) and *bal* "there is/are not"; the negative particle *'ēn* was unknown in Phoenician. Phoenician possessed two particles used before a determined noun that was the direct object of an active transitive verb: (1) *'et* and its predictable alternate *'ōt,* the latter used immediately before a noun carrying a possessive pronoun; and (2) the preposition *'alt.* Both particles were nonobligatory.

2. SIGNIFICANCE FOR THE BIBLE

Many literary genres are represented in the inscriptional corpus, some of these not instanced in the Israelite tradition, perhaps because they did not exist or were not preserved or are not yet discovered. This broader sampling than found in Hebrew, if sparse in itself, affords a generous view of Phoenician-Punic society and culture in its many forms and variations. For the scholar of the Bible and biblical civilization, Phoenician literature is a key to the richness and complexity of the culture and society to which the ancient Israelites belonged and in which they participated. In the following discussion, the abbreviation *KAI* stands for the text-collection *Kanaanäische und aramäische Inschriften,* and the abbreviation *CIS* is for *Corpus Inscriptionum Semiticarum.*[3]

2.1. ROYAL INSCRIPTIONS

The royal inscriptions are the longest specimens of classical Phoenician prose. For this reason alone, they are of extreme importance; they are also among the earliest Phoenician texts. To this group belong such inscriptions as those of the Sidonian kings Esmunazor (*KAI* 14) and Tibnit (*KAI* 13), the earlier Sidonian-language inscription of King Kilamuwa (*KAI* 24), and the Byblian inscription of King Yehawmilk (*KAI* 10). Especially noteworthy is the long eighth-century B.C.E. inscription of Aztwadda, king of the Danunians (*KAI* 26), which appears in three contemporaneous examplars at the same site. While the three "versions" are essentially identical, they are not the same with regard to certain specific matters of content and syntax, indicating that to some extent the lapidary scribe responsible for all three exemplars exercised personal discretion in phrasing each. This serves as a caution to those Bible scholars who argue uncritically for the necessary existence of a single *Vorlage* underlying differing manuscript traditions.

---

[3] Bibliographical details for both collections are found in the final section of this article.

2.2. HISTORICAL INSCRIPTIONS

Numerous historical inscriptions chronicle events in Phoenician history that are immediately relevant to the biblical history. For instance, in the Israelite literary tradition, one finds frequent mention of the remote Phoenician region of Tarshish, which late Alexandrine Jewish tradition identified as Carthage and occasionally rendered it as such in the Septuagint. Tarshish was the distant port to which Jonah, embarking by ship from the Phoenician Joppa (Yafo), sought to flee far from God. (Note that in the Phoenician inscription of King Esmunazor, Joppa and Dor are Phoenician cities.) It was to Tarshish, in the year 701 B.C.E., that Isaiah (chap. 23) bade the Sidonians, defeated by Assyria, to sail in search of refuge. From Tarshish itself, identifying the site as Nora in Sardinia, just across the Mediterranean from Carthage, we actually have the foundation stela (*KAI* 46) of the colony, composed in the ninth to eighth century B.C.E. It reads:

> [Refounded here is the colo]ny of Tarshish. It was driven out from Sardinia. May the people of the colony prosper! Its mother-city is Kition. The founder is ŠBN. Its leader is Pumay.

The inscription twice gives the Phoenician word for "colony" as *maṣṣab,* in Hebrew used of a military outpost, thus providing the important datum that the first Phoenician colonies were outpost forts, much like those on the American frontier, that were the nuclei of the later cities. The inscription further confirms this by designating the colony's leader as *nagīd,* the word used in Hebrew of the commandant of a fortified city. Moreover, the first epigraphically and historically attested Carthaginian, Yadaʿmilk bin Paday, identifies himself as "a soldier whom Pygmalion equipped for military service,"[4] that is, as a member of the garrison that manned the outpost fort at primitive Carthage.

Yadaʿmilk bin Paday is known to us from a tiny gold medallion from Carthage that was kept and deposited as a family heirloom in the tomb of his son or grandson in the Douimes necropolis at Carthage. Perhaps the greatest significance of the medallion and its inscription is that it confirms that Pygmalion (*Pgmlyn*), the king of Tyre in whose seventh year (825 or 814 B.C.E.) Carthage was founded according to legend, was the historical founder of the city. The medallion-inscription is of further interest for its opening formula, a traditional Canaanite oath of fealty to God and king: "For Astarte, for Pygmalion!" We find this same formula in the Israelite tradition in the oath of fealty, "For Yahweh, and for Gideon!"

---

[4] *KAI* 73.1/6.

(Judg 7:18), and yet again in a recently discovered text from Eqron: "For Baal, and for Padi!"[5]

No less interesting and important to the Bible scholar is an early fifth-century B.C.E. Carthaginian inscription (*CIS* I 5632) dated "in the twentieth year of the Carthaginian Republic."[6] From this text we learn the Phoenician expression for the Republic of Carthage: "The Rule of the *Šofṭīm* in Carthage" or, in Punic, *šefōṭ hiššōfṭīm biQarthadašt*. This is comparable to the designation of the premonarchic period in ancient Israel as *yəmê šəpōṭ haššōpəṭîm* in Ruth 1:1.

2.3. HISTORIOGRAPHY

Authentic Phoenician historiographic prose is attested in the form of the closing portion of a full Carthaginian report of the campaign of 406 B.C.E. against the Siceliote Greek city of Akragas (Agrigentum). The extant segment, appearing at the end of the inscription (*CIS* I 5510) and serving to date the text, relates the final Carthaginian assault and seizure of Agrigentum in late December 406, on the morning following the flight of many of the citizens to the nearby city of Gela:

> The generals Idnibal son of Gisco the Great and Himilco son of Hanno the Great, proceeding at dawn, seized Agrigentum; and they (the Agrigentines), including those who fled, made peace.[7]

It is possible that Carthaginian inscription *CIS* I 5511, very similar paleographically to 5510, speaks of "a time of peace and prosperity," perhaps an allusion to the outcome of the great victory in Sicily.

2.4. GENEALOGIES

Several inscriptions are extant that beautifully evidence the tradition of preserving lengthy family genealogies. Of special interest is the genealogy of the Carthaginian Baalay (*KAI* 78), which lists seventeen generations

---

[5] On the Carthage inscription and its relevance to Judg 7:18, see Charles R. Krahmalkov, "The Foundation Date of Carthage: The Douimes Pendant Inscription," *JSS* 26 (1981): 177–91. For the Eqron inscription, see S. Gitin and Mordechai Cogan, "A New Type of Dedicatory Inscription from Ekron," *IEJ* 49 (1999): 193–202. Gitin and Cogan did not take into consideration the evidence of the Douimes Phoenician inscription for this oath of fealty and dedication.

[6] See Charles R. Krahmalkov, "Notes on the Rule of the Softim in Carthage," *RSF* 4 (1976): 155–57.

[7] See Charles R. Krahmalkov, "A Carthaginian Report of the Battle of Agrigentum, 406 B.C.," *RSF* 2 (1974): 171–77.

back to his ancestor Miṣry "the Egyptian," evidently one of the founding fathers or earliest settlers of Carthage. Another seventeen-generation genealogy is recorded in Carthaginian inscription *KAI* 68. From a Neo-Punic inscription from Lepcis Magna (*KAI* 124) we learn that families preserved their genealogies in documents called individually "family chronicle" (*kitōbit dibrê ibbêt*), in which were recorded general events in the history of the family, including adoptions and slave holdings.

2.5. TEMPLE DEDICATIONS, INAUGURATIONS, AND LISTS

A large number of texts are temple dedications, detailing the building, repair, and financing of sanctuaries and temples, large and small. These texts provide invaluable information about the structure and infrastructure of the Phoenician temple: the temple, although of three constituent rooms, was perceived by the Phoenicians as bipartite, consisting of (1) a foreroom (*ʿurpot*) and (2) the sanctuary (*miqdas ḥibbêt* or simply *miqdas*), being (a) a main room and (b) a holy of holies (*taw*). We also learn that associated with the temple was a depository (*mifqad*) where divine statues and other holy objects were stored.

Several texts are associated with the ceremony of delivering a newly built temple to its divine owner, the god, on "the day the god entered the temple" and the delivery of objects necessary for the inception of the divine liturgy to the god's servants, the priests of the temple. The inauguration of the sanctuaries of Baal and Thinnith-Phanebal in Thinnisut, North Africa, is described as follows (*KAI* 137.4–7):

> These gods entered these sanctuaries on the seventeenth of the month of First Mufa of this year. Four metal vessels were made for these sanctuaries —two *sippim* and two *zaborim*—and were delivered to <the priests> Aris bin ANKN and Bostar bin YPS.

On the inauguration day, we learn from a Carthage inscription (*KAI* 81) that all property belonging to the temple "was brought into the custody of the sanctuaries and the temple mount was put off limits to the public."

As the Phoenician and Punic inscriptions also make clear, the founding, building, maintenance, repair, and equipment of sanctuaries and temples was the responsibility of city-government bureaus such as "those in charge of temples." It was always regarded as an act of great public service on the part of private individuals and sodalities to assist in this work.

Among the inscriptions relating to Phoenician religion, one of the most interesting is a list of payments made over two months to persons who had rendered service for the liturgy of the Astarte temple of Kition, Cyprus (*KAI* 37). The list includes the bakers who had baked the shewbread of the goddess, the barbers who shaved the cult statue, the temple servitor boys, and many other functionaries, great and small. The information provided by this great inscription, together with that in others, permits the scholar to reconstruct with some certainty the actual daily holy liturgy (*ml'kt qdšt*) of a Phoenician temple.

2.6. NETHERWORLD AND AFTERLIFE

The Punic netherworld was ruled by the goddess *Ḥwt,* the Eve of the biblical tradition, who, like her Israelite counterpart, was also called *'Amma* "Mother" (biblical *'ēm kol ḥāy* "the mother of everyone living"). Eve, as mistress of the netherworld, bore the titles *'ilot mūlekit (h)imiske* "Goddess Who Rules the Dead" (*KAI* 89) and *ba'alt (h)aḥadarūt* "Mistress of the Chambers <of the Netherworld>" (*KAI* 83). As in Israelite religion, the dead attained the status of gods, becoming *'allōnīm rafa'īm* (or simply *rafa'īm*) "the deified dead"; the righteous dead are declared those who have earned *miskab 'et rafa'īm* "<eternal> sleep among the deified dead." A special class among the deified dead were those children who had been sacrificed by their parents according to the *molk*-rite; they were designated *'ilīm zəbūḥīm* "the sacrificed ones who are gods."[8]

2.7. CHILD SACRIFICE EPIGRAPHS

Western Phoenicia's "peculiar institution" was child sacrifice, an ancient and arcane rite that had for the most part become obsolete in the Levantine homeland. Why the rite flourished in the West is not yet fully understood, but so-called "relict areas," where institutions abandoned in the motherland continued, are not uncommon. Written testimony to the rite is attested from the seventh century in Carthage and Malta right down into the Christian period in North Africa. The rite itself was called *molk* or, more fully, *molk 'adom* "human sacrifice" or *molk Ba'al* "a sacrifice to Baal," the Baal here being the god Baalhammon. In the period after approximately 400 B.C.E., the goddess Thinnith-Phanebal is paired with Baalhammon as divine recipient of the sacrifice. The child sacrificial victim was called an *'izrim,* a obscure word that is actually defined in the Sidonian Esmunazor inscription as "one snatched away before one's time, at the age of a few days." The sex of the *'izrim* is often designated by the phrase *'izrim 'īš* "a male child sacrificial victim" or *'izrim 'issat* "a female sacrificial victim." Thus, in a sacrificial inscription from the Roman period written in Latin letters we read: Lymyth Icsina Micebal ysrim ys au Mylthe,

---

[8] J. M. Reynolds and J. B. Ward Perkins, *Inscriptions of Roman Tripolitania* (Rome and London: British School at Rome, 1952), 893.4/5.

"<This is the stela> of the deceased Icsina Micebal, male child sacrificial victim, the brother of Mylthe."[9] Parents are recorded as having delivered both a male and female child to the gods.

Inasmuch as the child was "brought" or "carried" by the priest to the pyre, he or she was also called *naśī lilīm* "one brought to the god," which term appears in Latin transcription as *nasi lilim*. Indeed, the etiquette of infant sacrifice in the pre-Roman period required the lie that the child was not sacrificed but merely brought and presented to the gods. Thus, we find the standard euphemisms that a parent "brought" (*naśoʾ*) the child or "gave" (*śom, yaton*) the child. It is only in the late Roman period that the society allowed the honest statement that the parent had "sacrificed" (*zaboḥ*) the child. Most telling is the clothing of the sacrificial rite itself under the euphemism *yūm naʿīm webarīk* "the good and happy day!" The child was delivered up to Baalhammon and Thinnith-Phanebal by its parents in fulfillment of a vow (*nidir*) made to these gods in a moment or time of personal difficulty (*nidir bimeṣarrīm*), stipulating that if the gods would "hear their voice" and answer their prayers, they (the parents) would make the ultimate sacrifice of one or more of their own children.

The ex-voto stela was placed at the site where the incinerary urn containing cremated remains of the child was placed. Such sites often contain thousands of such urns and associated inscribed funerary stelae. In the earliest sacrificial inscriptions, it was Baalhammon alone to whom the sacrifice was made: "<This is> a stela <commemorating> a sacrifice to Baal that PN son of PN gave to Baalhammon, his Lord; because He heard the sound of his words (prayers)." Later, the sacrifice was made to Baalhammon and his female consort, the powerful goddess, Thinnith-Phanebal. Because many parents refused to deliver their own child to the pyre, instead purchasing another's infant to sacrifice, the religious authorities required the parent to affirm in the inscription that the child was *biśeʾrī bitti* "of his own flesh" or, as stated in Israelite descriptions of the rite, *mizzarʿô* "of his own seed."

2.8. SACRIFICIAL TARIFFS

A common type of inscription was the temple tariff (*biʿot*). These tariffs, posted at the temple, provided information to the sacrificer, whether individuals, families, or sodalities. They detailed such matters as the cost of each kind of animal, what part of the sacrificed animal belonged to the sacrificer and what part to the priest, what obligations lay upon the priests and the public, and what fines were to be levied against priests for noncompliance with the tariff. The stone-inscribed temple tariff was a

---

[9] Ibid., 827.1/3.

shortened version of a fuller and more detailed document kept by the public bureau in charge of sacrifices. This document, as clearly stated in the temple tariff version, was available for consultation by the general public. The tariffs make clear that sacrifice in all its aspects was scrupulously controlled by the state.

2.9. SOCIETY AND SODALITY

Many Phoenician and Punic texts relate to the centerpiece of Phoenician life and society, the active pursuit of "service on behalf of one's community" (*miśrat 'et penê gaw* or simply *miśrat*) on the part of the individual and the collective. Preserved in a late Phoenician inscription from Athens is the text of a resolution passed by the Sidonian community assembly of that city to reward one of its members for having fulfilled his charge to supervise and see to the completion of the building of the court of the temple of the god Baal of Sidon (*KAI* 60). The inscription is, moreover, a specimen of elegant Phoenician prose.

The pursuit of public service was also an important part of the mission of the Phoenician men's sodalities or social clubs. Of these, the *mirzaḥ* and the *mizraḥ* are attested in inscriptions. The sodalities were tightly organized clubs, headed by a "convenor" (*kūneś*), fiscally run by a "comptroller" (*meḥeśśeb*), and boasting a large membership of "fellows" (*ḥaberīm*). In several inscriptions the names of the entire membership are listed, and the reader of the inscription is asked to "Read what is set down from top to bottom!" (*KAI* 145). The sodalities undertook to build and repair the temples of the gods to whose cult they were devoted, and they proudly honored those of their members who had accomplished notable public service. We learn also that the members of sodalities as a group "prayed opposite Heaven" beseeching, "May the God grant us of his blessings!" (*KAI* 147). The members of the sodalities also sacrificed together at the temple (*KAI* 69; 159).

2.10. BELLES-LETTRES

Specimens of both traditional Canaanite and Hellenistic (Greek) belles-lettres are attested in the inscriptions. An example of traditional Phoenician poetry, imitating form and style going back to late second millennium B.C.E., is a three-verse Punic poem, composed about 350 C.E. by Iulius Nasif, a soldier of a Tripolitanian (Western Libyan) frontier zone colonial militia. The work was preserved as his epitaph on his gravestone. The poem is of interest because of its use of the ancient rhetorical adornment of *parallelismus membrorum* ("From Adnim I expelled the wicked fellow / From the Syrtis, him of ill repute"), but also because it is composed in perfect rhythmic iambic trimeters (BADNÍM GARÁSTH IS ÓN // MYSÝGRTHIM BÁL SCM RÁ). The rhythm (meter) speaks to the much-debated question as to whether biblical Hebrew poetry was composed metrically. We know the meter of the Nasif poem because the composition, written in Latin letters, is fully vocalized.[10]

The use of *parallelismus membrorum* is again encountered in a Punic-letter religious hymn (*KAI* 145) to the god HTR-Meskar:

> Exalt the name of the holy god:
> HTR, ruler of the dry land,
> Meskar, ruler of the sea,
> He who commands fear because of his might!

In this work, we find the so-called "break-up" of the binomial HTR-Meskar in the manner of Ugaritic and Hebrew poetry, as well as the use of end-rhyme, a feature of Punic poetry and poetic prose attested elsewhere.

Hellenistic belletristic literature in Punic comes down to us in the form of entrance monologues, dialogue and single lines belonging to several Punic-language comedies. These were excerpted from their original sources and reused by the Roman playwright T. Maccius Plautus in his comedy *Poenulus,* a translation of the Attic play *Carchedonius.* Some of these Punic passages derive in fact from the Punic version of the same Attic comedy. Punic is unique among the West Semitic languages in having been the vehicle for classical Greek drama in the vernacular. The Western Phoenicians had embraced Greek literary culture centuries before the Hellenistic age. For a brief introduction to these fragments of drama in Punic, see the introductions to my books *Phoenician-Punic Dictionary* and *Phoenician-Punic Grammar* cited in the closing section of this chapter.

2.11. ISRAELITES AND ISRAELITE RELIGION IN PHOENICIA

In Israelite literary and historical tradition, the influence of Phoenicia, especially of Phoenician cults, on Israelite society is portrayed as a matter of grave national concern. In contrast, the Phoenician inscriptions show no such hostility toward Israel, Israelites, and Israelite religion but, rather, tolerance. No more dramatic attestation to the presence, acceptance, and importance of Israelites in Phoenicia is the fact that the chief of scribes in the great Cypriote Phoenician city of Kition was a member of an Israelite family. The family's integration into Phoenician life and society is consistent with the Phoenician view that "Phoencian" was not a racial but a cultural term: a Phoenician was one who spoke Phoenician and participated in

---

[10] For the text of this poem, see C. R. Krahmalkov, "'When He Drove Out Yrirachan': A Phoenician (Punic) Poem, ca. A.D. 350," *BASOR* 294 (1994): 69–82.

Phoenician culture. This view persisted to the very end of Phoenician civilization: in the Punic inscriptions of Roman Tripolitania of the early Christian period, the term *Sorim,* "Tyrians" or "Phoenicians," does not connote race but culture, for the "Tyrians" in this part of the African interior were Phoenician-speakers but racially Libyans (Berbers).

Regarding the impact of Israelite religion upon the Phoenicians, we find in a fourth-century B.C.E. Phoenician inscription from Egypt (*KAI* 48) a Phoenician worshiper of the goddess [ʾš]*rt šmrn* "Samarian Ashrata (Asherah)" known from the cult *yhwh šmrn wʾšrth* "Samarian Yahweh and Ashrata" attested in Hebrew inscriptions from Kuntillet ʿAjrûd and Khirbet el-Qom in the ninth to eighth centuries B.C.E.

3. TOOLS FOR THE RESEARCHER AND SCHOLAR

In one's study of Phoenician, the Bible scholar will want to consult reference works that provide accurate descriptions of the language and its lexicon. The following is a concise, selective bibliography of available grammars and dictionaries, with some observations that may be useful to the nonspecialist in Phoenician and Punic.

3.1. PHOENICIAN GRAMMARS

Harris, Zellig Shabbetai. *A Grammar of the Phoenician Language.* AOS 8. New Haven, Conn.: American Oriental Society, 1936. The first modern grammar of Phoenician and Punic. A masterpiece by the great American linguist, written as a doctoral dissertation at the University of Pennsylvania. The grammatical description of Phoenician and Punic is outdated, but the splendid glossary (71–156) remains ever useful.

Segert, Stanislav. *A Grammar of Phoenician and Punic.* Munich: Beck, 1976. An excellent grammar. Similar in content and grammatical description of the language to the first (1951) and second (1970) editions of Johannes Friedrich's *Phönizisch-Punische Grammatik* discussed below. The bibliography is especially useful.

Friedrich, Johannes, and Wolfgang Röllig, *Phönizisch-Punische Grammatik.* 3d ed. Revised by Maria Giulia Amadasi Guzzo and Werner R. Mayer. AnOr 55. Rome: Biblical Institute Press, 1999. A completely and fundamentally revised version of Johannes Friedrich's classic *Phönizisch-punische Grammatik* (AnOr 32; Rome: Pontifical Biblical Institute, 1951), which also appeared in a second revised edition (AnOr 46) in 1970. The Bible scholar should use this third edition, for it contains a fuller and accurate description of the language.

Krahmalkov, Charles R. *A Phoenician-Punic Grammar.* Handbook of Oriental Studies Section One 54. Leiden: Brill, 2001. Presents a new and original description of the grammar of the Phoenician-Punic language based on and including new data for phonology, morphology, and syntax. The introduction will be informative to the nonspecialist.

3.2. DICTIONARIES

Harris, Zellig Shabbetai. "Glossary of Phoenician." Pages 71–156 in *Grammar of the Phoenician Language.* AOS 8. New Haven, Conn.: American Oriental Society, 1936. See the comments on this work above. The glossary, if somewhat outdated, is still useful to the researcher.

Tomback, Richard S. *A Comparative Lexicon of the Phoenician and Punic Languages.* SBLDS 32. Missoula, Mont.: Scholars Press, 1978. This comprehensive dictionary, written as a doctoral dissertation at New York University under the direction of Professor Baruch Levine, is an eminently useful resource, particularly for its etymological and comparative Semitics orientation.

Fuentes-Estañol, María-José. *Vocabulario Fenicio.* Biblioteca Fenicia. Barcelona: Consejo Superior de Investigaciones Científicas, 1980.

Hoftijzer, Jan, and Karel Jongeling. *Dictionary of the North-West Semitic Inscriptions.* 2 vols. Leiden: Brill, 1995. This great work, an updated version of the *Dictionnaire des inscriptions sémitiques de l'Ouest* (Leiden: Brill, 1965) by Ch.-F. Jean and Jan Hoftijzer, is an indispensable tool to the researcher. Phoenician and Punic items are all clearly marked, and, most important, the authors provide for each item a select overview of scholarly opinions as well as references.

Krahmalkov, Charles R. *Phoenician-Punic Dictionary.* OLA 90. Studia Phoenicia 15. Leuven: Peeters, 2000. This work presents much new vocabulary, especially items that appear in Latin letters in the late Neo-Punic texts of Roman Tripolitania and in the literary fragments of Punic drama preserved by the Roman playwright T. Maccius Plautus in his comedy *Poenulus.* The introduction to the dictionary has comments on Phoenician-Punic literature that may be of interest to the researcher and scholar.

3.3. BASIC TEXT COLLECTIONS

The standard publication of the corpus of Phoenician, Punic and Neo-Punic inscriptions is *Corpus Inscriptionum Semiticarum.* Pars Prima: Inscriptiones Phoenicia continens. Paris: E Reipublicae Typographeo, 1881–. This work, commonly abbreviated *CIS* I, now contains almost seven thousand inscriptions. These large folio volumes are to be found in the holdings of only a few large universities. Since access to these volumes is difficult, the researcher may wish to consult the smaller collections of Phoenician-Punic texts that are readily available. The following is a selective list of such collections.

Cooke, George Albert. *A Text-Book of North-Semitic Inscriptions: Moabite, Hebrew, Phoenician, Aramaic, Nabataean, Palmyrene, Jewish.* Oxford: Clarendon, 1903. This classic work contains a small number of texts but ones representative of all periods and dialects: Phoenician, Punic, and Neo-Punic. The technical apparatus and scholarship are superb.

Donner, Herbert, and Wolfgang Rollig, *Kanaanäische und aramäische Inschriften.* Wiesbaden: Harrassowitz, 1966–1968. The standard handbook-collection of Phoenician and Punic texts, known by its familiar abbreviation *KAI*. It is the single most indispensable work in the study of Phoenician and Punic inscriptions by reason of its broad collection of texts from all regions and periods and for the quality of its critical apparatus and scholarship.

Gibson, John C. L. *Phoenician Inscriptions.* Vol. 3 of *Textbook of Syrian Semitic Inscriptions.* Oxford: Clarendon, 1983. This volume contains Phoenician texts only. Gibson provides extensive discussion of epigraphic matters as well as detailed specific commentary on each text, which provides the best available general introduction to Phoenician epigraphy.

Magnanini, Pietro. *Le iscrizioni fenicie dell'Oriente: Testi, traduzioni, glossari.* Rome: Istituto di Studi del Vicino Oriente, Universita degli Studi di Roma, 1973. The most complete collection of Phoenician texts from the Levant, Cyprus, Egypt, and the Sidonian communities in Greece. No Punic texts are represented. Translations and vocabulary are presented but no critical commentary on the texts.

Amadasi, Maria Giulia Guzzo. *Le iscrizioni fenicie e puniche delle colonie in Occidente.* Studi Semitici 28. Rome: Istituto di Studi del Vicino Oriente, Universita di Roma, 1967. The most complete collection of Phoenician, Punic, and Neo-Punic texts from the Western Mediterranean: Sardinia, Malta, Sicily, Spain, including the Punic dedication of the Astarte temple in Pyrgi, Etruria. Superb commentary. No texts from North Africa, however, are included.

UGARITIC

Peggy L. Day

1. THE LANGUAGE

Ugaritic is the name that modern scholars have given to the West Semitic language, written in an alphabetic cuneiform utilizing thirty signs, that was indigenous to the city-state of Ugarit approximately 1360 to 1180 B.C.E. The signs have purely consonantal values, with the exception of the Ugaritic equivalent of *ʾālep,* which is represented by three signs, *ʾu, ʾi,* and *ʾa.* Tell Ras Shamra, the ancient city of Ugarit, is located about twelve kilometers north of modern-day Latakia, Syria. It is about eight hundred meters inland from a small Mediterranean bay named Minet el-Beida, "White Harbor," so called because of the white rocks at the bay's entrance. These rocks served in antiquity as a navigational landmark for seafarers. As it was the port city on the Levantine coast that was closest to Cyprus, with overland routes connecting it to the northern and eastern interior and sea routes connecting it to the south, Ugarit was a major commercial center that linked the ancient Near East to the Aegean. Ugarit is named in documents found at Ebla, Mari, Alalakh, Boğazköy, Tell Aphek, and Amarna, while documents from Ugarit evidence the city's political and commercial relations with Crete, Cyprus, Hatti, Egypt, and various Syro-Palestinian city-states. Written communication between Ugarit and places external to the city-state was carried on in Akkadian, the lingua franca of the time. Ugaritic was used for matters of concern internal to the city-state.

1.1. HISTORY OF DECIPHERMENT

In March of 1928, as the story goes, a local laborer (unnamed in scholarly reports of the event, as is typical of the "local resident stumbles on archaeological treasure" genre) plowing near Minet el-Beida dislodged a stone slab that covered a passageway leading to a vaulted tomb. At that time, however, Syria and Lebanon were being governed under the French Mandate, and article 14 of the Mandate prohibited unauthorized persons from digging for antiquities, so the plowing story may well have been a necessary fiction, as the nearby townspeople had been gleaning artifacts from the site prior to the alleged plowing incident. Be that as it may, article 14 also provided monetary incentives for those reporting the discovery of antiquities to the proper authorities, and the department of the French High Commission responsible for antiquities was the Service des antiquités, headquartered in Beirut and under the direction of the Assyriologist Charles Virolleaud. When Virolleaud was informed of the find, he dispatched a colleague to visit the site and was sufficiently impressed by the colleague's report to visit the site twice himself. The tomb was clearly part of an extensive necropolis, presumably associated with the mound the locals called Ras Shamra. The tomb type, as well as pottery finds in and around it, proved to be Cypriot, with some pottery fragments exhibiting Mycenaean influence. Virolleaud also found an inscribed cylinder seal that demonstrated that the ancient city had links to Anatolia as well. These preliminary findings were published in *Syria,* a journal founded by René Dussaud expressly for the purpose of reporting on archaeological discoveries made in Syria under the French Mandate.

In addition to being the founder and current editor of *Syria,* in 1928 René Dussaud was also a Near Eastern antiquities conservator at the Louvre and a member of the Académie des Inscriptions et Belles-Lettres. Both of these institutions sponsored and funded excavations. Dussaud at this time was particularly interested in connections between preclassical and oriental cultures, an interest that he and others were beginning to frame by the notion of syncretism. The preliminary finds in the Ras Shamra area led him to speculate that the as yet anonymous ancient city was a Cypriot outpost that imported and traded goods from as far away as the Aegean, thus making it a site especially relevant to his intellectual interests. He initiated and succeeded in securing funding from both of the above-named bodies for one season of excavation, and he chose Claude Schaeffer to head the expedition. Digging commenced in early April of 1929, and on May 14 the first cuneiform tablets were unearthed, followed two days later by a hoard of mint-condition tools and weapons that included five axeheads inscribed with cuneiform signs. When Virolleaud arrived at the site to examine the cuneiform inscriptions he quickly realized that some of them, including those on the axeheads, were of a type theretofore unknown, as the signs themselves were simplified and the repertoire of signs was far less in number than that required for syllabic cuneiform writing. Virolleaud's position as Director of the Service des antiquités gave him the authority to instruct Schaeffer to hand over to him all of the inscribed texts, which Schaeffer reluctantly did, and the two agreed that Virolleaud would publish the texts by year's end.

Though Virolleaud could justify retaining all of the texts according to a section of article 14 of the Mandate that permitted such action for scientific reasons, this move contravened normal practice regarding the distribution of archaeological proceeds between the Service and the excavation's sponsor(s). It also thwarted Dussaud, who, in his role of conservator at the Louvre, had a vested interest in obtaining artifacts for the museum's collection and who, to a large extent, controlled the funding for further excavation. Approximately six weeks after Virolleaud gained possession of the inscribed texts, Henri Seyrig was appointed as the new Director of the Service and Virolleaud relocated to Paris. The inscribed tablets and axeheads came into the possession of the Louvre, but Virolleaud retained publication rights.

Virolleaud evidently continued to be influenced by Dussaud's interpretation of the site. Even though he recognized that the cuneiform of the inscriptions was alphabetic and, on the basis of the brevity of words established by the presence of word dividers in the texts, that vowels most probably were not represented, he nevertheless suggested looking toward Cyprus and the Aegean as the most likely key to determining the language of the inscriptions. He maintained this position into April of 1930, when the appearance of his *editio princeps,* published in *Syria* 10, permitted other scholars access to this as yet undeciphered language.

Within a week of receiving his copy of the publication, Hans Bauer, a German Semitic linguist and epigrapher, had deciphered enough of the language to aver that it was a dialect of Phoenician and, in a series of communications to Dussaud that included illustrative examples, had convinced him by mid-May that he had essentially succeeded in deciphering the language. The presence of word dividers permitted Bauer to categorize certain signs as prefixes, suffixes, and prepositions. Then, on the basis of his notion of the relative frequency among a repertoire of consonants to express these values in a West Semitic language, he tentatively began assigning possible values to signs. He combined this approach with following up on certain purely formal observations that Virolleaud had made in his *editio princeps* and with his own search for common Semitic words that he hypothesized would be present in a West Semitic text. In this manner he determined what he believed to be the correct values of twenty signs. A selection of Bauer's preliminary results was first published in the June 4, 1930, issue of *Vossische Zeitung,* a Berlin newspaper. The article included a number of words that Bauer believed he had discerned, but because he did not refer to tablet and line numbers, the only proposal that could be traced back to specific signs in the inscriptional material was *grzn,* a four-sign word that appeared on one of the five axeheads.

Bauer was not the only one endeavoring to decipher the language. Édouard (Paul) Dhorme, director of the École Biblique in Jerusalem, was not only an accomplished Semitic linguist and epigrapher like Bauer, but he had also been decorated for his cryptological work in World War I. Positing that the language was West Semitic, he too followed up on a formal observation Virolleaud had made in his *editio princeps* and began looking for common West Semitic words. He found *b'l* and *mlk* but was then thrown off course until, in mid-June of 1930, W. F. Albright showed him Bauer's *Vossische Zeitung* article. Dhorme accepted Bauer's values for the four-sign word on one of the axeheads being *grzn*, understood as a word meaning "axe," and with that additional information proceeded correctly to identify, by August 15, 1930, at least eighteen and possibly nineteen signs.

On August 20, 1930, a short article by Bauer appeared in *Forschungen und Fortschritte* and included references to specific tablets and lines as well as drawings of selected sign groups along with Bauer's transliteration and translation of them. Dussaud sent Dhorme a copy of this publication, which he received just after he had finished proofing the article that contained his results to August 15. Now able to discern more of the specifics of Bauer's alphabet, but still not having seen it in its entirety, Dhorme added a September 14 postscript to his own article to the effect that he and Bauer differed on the identification of three very frequent and therefore important signs. He then sent off a proofed but not yet published copy of his article to Bauer, which Bauer received toward the end of September. At this juncture Bauer was awaiting the imminent appearance of his *Entzifferung der Keilschrifttafeln von Ras Schamra,* a monograph that contained the first publication of his entire alphabet. He received Dhorme's proof copy too late to revise his own publication, and as a result it is clear exactly how far Bauer had progressed essentially independently. Of the twenty-five signs to which Bauer assigned values, fourteen would prove to be essentially correct. Though Bauer could not incorporate Dhorme's results into his monograph, he did append a postscript acknowledging receipt of Dhorme's results and expressing his realization on that basis that his monograph contained several mistakes. By October 5, 1930, having had the benefit of consulting Dhorme's results, Bauer produced a revised alphabet: twenty-five of the twenty-six signs to which he assigned values would prove to be essentially correct.

In early October of 1930, over six months after the appearance of his *editio princeps,* Virolleaud once again entered the written record. In an October 1 letter addressed to Dussaud in his capacity as president of the Académie, Virolleaud announced that he had succeeded in deciphering the Ras Shamra alphabet. At this juncture Virolleaud was definitely aware of Bauer's unquestionably flawed results as published in *Forschungen und Fortschritte* and of Dhorme's superior but nonetheless still flawed results, which had appeared in *Revue Biblique* in the latter part of September. Also at this juncture, Virolleaud was the only one of the three who had had access to important new texts unearthed in the 1930 campaign. In his letter, Virolleaud briefly described having been able to identify in the 1929 texts some number of words that seemed to be Semitic, but he did not divulge when he had made these identifications. He then went on to say that the 1930 texts were necessary in order to resolve difficulties that had not been solved (and, by implication, could not be solved) on the basis of the 1929 texts alone. He stated that, of the twenty-eight signs he had isolated, he had definitively identified twenty-six, but his letter does not include a list of signs with corresponding values. His letter closed by offering to make a presentation to the Académie that would delineate his method and communicate his principal results.

Virolleaud made his presentation on October 24, 1930. In the prefaced and slightly supplemented version in which his presentation was published, Virolleaud insisted more forcefully that the 1930 texts were necessary to accomplish complete decipherment and laid claim to having definitively identified twenty-seven out of twenty-eight signs, but once again no sign list was included. In the text of the article Virolleaud assigned values to twenty-six signs, of which twenty-four were essentially correct. Thus by October 24, and giving Virolleaud the benefit of the doubt, the most signs he could have correctly discerned was twenty-five, and while his degree of dependence on the work of Bauer and Dhorme remains murky, it is clear that he did not achieve that result independently. It is also clear that Virolleaud's (oft-repeated) claim that the Ras Shamra alphabet could not be deciphered on the basis of the 1929 texts alone was a false one as, together, Bauer and Dhorme had discerned twenty-five signs without the 1930 texts—the same number as the most generous allotment attributable to Virolleaud at approximately the same time—and Virolleaud had the advantage of the 1930 texts. In any event, with the appearance in print of Virolleaud's sign list in January of 1932, decipherment of the language was essentially (though not entirely) complete and in the public domain. The language itself still had not been named Ugaritic (Bauer, for instance, called it Saphonic), as the name of the ancient city remained to be definitively established.

1.2. HISTORICAL DEVELOPMENT

Given Ugarit's destruction in the early twelfth century B.C.E., there were no direct ties between it and the ancient state of Israel. Ugarit did have commercial relations with various Palestinian city-states, mostly in coastal areas outside the later political control of Israel, though one text mentions a commercial relationship with Hazor. Van Soldt points to literary evidence linking Ugarit closely to the Bashan area. Exemplars of alphabetic cuneiform writing have been found elsewhere in the Levant, though these exemplars diverge from the standard Ugaritic alphabet in that they exhibit a smaller range of phonemes/signs. A very limited number of Ugaritic texts also employ this short cuneiform alphabet.

Due to the relatively short time span of the written record, little can be said about the historical development of the language. One can observe, however, that the mythological and epic texts evidence certain archaic features not found in the administrative texts, and the administrative texts demonstrate that certain phonemic mergers were in process. Scholars concur that Ugaritic is a Northwest (also called Syro-Palestinian) Semitic language, the subgrouping of ancient Semitic languages of which Classical Hebrew was a member. Scholars disagree, however, on whether Ugaritic should be classified along with Hebrew as a Canaanite Northwest language or belongs to a separate and otherwise unexampled branch of the Northwest Semitic language family. Since understanding the arguments put forward in support of these respective positions requires detailed knowledge of the various Semitic languages themselves as well as advanced training in historical linguistics, only a few remarks will be offered here.

Proponents of the opposing positions differ over theoretical models and therefore over what counts as evidence as well as the weight to assign to various pieces of evidence. For example, the Amarna letters, which date to the mid-fourteenth century B.C.E. and therefore are basically contemporary with the earliest of the Ugaritic documents, contain vocalized pronominal, nominal, and verbal forms that diverge from Akkadian, which is the ostensible language of these letters. Since the relevant letters were sent to the Egyptian court from city-states in the Levant, the divergent forms have been generally understood to be Canaanite, and, on that premise, these divergent forms constitute the earliest body of significant evidence relevant to the Canaanite language family. Proceeding on the basis of shared innovation as the key diagnostic feature for determining language groups, John Huehnergard has pointed out that certain of the divergent forms differ in significant and developmentally complex ways from their Ugaritic counterparts, and thus he judges Ugaritic to represent a separate branch of Northwest Semitic. Josef Tropper disputes Huehnergard's criteria and gives the Amarna evidence much less weight, focusing instead on features that (his reconstruction of) proto-Canaanite and Ugaritic have in common, regardless of whether these features are a result of shared innovation. Tropper classes Ugaritic as a Canaanite language. In short, the classification of Ugaritic remains a topic of scholarly debate but one that, for the purposes at hand, need not detain us. While Huehnergard's position is overall the more convincing, this does not detract from the enormous contribution the Ugaritic texts have made to understanding various facets of both the Hebrew of the Hebrew Bible as well as the conceptual context of many Hebrew Bible texts.

2. SIGNIFICANCE FOR THE BIBLE

Although Ugaritic is not a direct ancestor of Hebrew and may not even be a member of the Canaanite language family, it has nevertheless made an important contribution to better understanding the language of the

Hebrew Bible. As the Hebrew language itself changed during the centuries in which what eventually would become the Hebrew Bible was being written, and as that material continued to be transmitted by persons progressively more removed from the earlier phases of the language, knowledge of certain archaic features of the language became lost. Ugaritic has aided in recovering some of this lost knowledge. Before turning to specific examples, methodological cautions must be expressed. Ugaritic is *not* Hebrew, and so the existence of specific morphological and syntactical features in Ugaritic is not in itself reason enough to posit the existence of these features in Hebrew. The same holds true for lexical issues. Simply because a word has a certain meaning in Ugaritic (and the methodology of assigning meaning to Ugaritic words also requires close scrutiny and will receive further comment below) is not reason enough to presume that meaning for the word's Hebrew cognate. The scholarship of Mitchell Dahood and the Rome school has often been singled out for censure in these two regards. Dahood was what one might call a consonantal fundamentalist when it came to the text of the Hebrew Bible. His position was that the Masoretic vocalization of the text and its division into words was open to challenge and emendation, but the consonantal portion of the text was virtually unassailable. He imported features of Ugaritic into Hebrew as a means of demonstrating the alleged veracity of the consonantal text. While a few of his proposals have gained general acceptance, the majority remain highly debatable or have been rejected on the grounds of insufficient proof. What constitutes sufficient proof will be articulated in the process of illustrating the contributions Ugaritic has made to better understanding Hebrew, the topic to which we now turn.

The complexity of the Hebrew verbal system continues to evoke frustration on the part of students and grammarians alike. Especially vexing is the apparent use of the prefix conjugation (*yqtl,* as opposed to the suffix conjugation *qtl,* the former often referred to as the imperfect and the latter as the perfect), *without* the so-called *wāw*-conversive, to signify past punctual (as opposed to past iterative or durative) time. While this evidently can occur in both prose and poetry, the relevant Ugaritic material is poetic, and so this discussion will focus on instances of the phenomenon in Hebrew poetry. Ugaritic poetry employs prefix-conjugation verbs with a past punctual meaning in compositions concerning the mythic or epic past. Is this datum relevant to better understanding verbal usages in Hebrew poetry? Placing this question within the broader context of a historical and comparative approach to the Semitic languages is a methodological necessity for determining the answer to it. Viewed from this broader perspective, it can be observed that languages such as Akkadian and Arabic have not one but two prefix conjugations, one of which can signify past punctual time. The Amarna letters also distinguish between a prefix form *yaqtulu,* used to signify a range of meanings consistent with the Hebrew imperfect, and a second prefix form, *yaqtul,* that can be used to denote past punctual time. The Akkadian and Arabic evidence indicates that the phenomenon of more than one prefix conjugation is not limited to the Canaanite group of languages and so in theory could be relevant to both Hebrew and Ugaritic, even if Ugaritic is not a Canaanite language. In Classical Hebrew final short vowels have been lost, and, positing that earlier Hebrew shared the phenomenon evinced by the Amarna letters, this loss would have eradicated the formal distinction in Hebrew between **yaqtul* and **yaqtulu.* The resultant falling together of previously distinct prefix conjugations would explain the past punctual usage of the prefix conjugation in Hebrew. Furthermore, if this is the correct explanation for the phenomenon in Hebrew, the Ugaritic instances of a past punctual prefix conjugation are relevant because the Ugaritic situation is not simply superficially comparable, but rather the respective phenomena are historically related.

In Ugaritic, the verbal paradigm corresponding to the Hebrew *qal* (= G or *Grundform*) has an internal passive. Again, this phenomenon is attested in non-Canaanite languages such as Arabic. The Ugaritic (and Amarna) evidence for G passives has reinforced the contention that Hebrew passive forms that are problematic in their Masoretic vocalizations as *puʿal* or *hopʿal* should be understood as *qal* forms, so that the existence of an archaic *qal* passive in Hebrew is now generally accepted.

The Ugaritic poetic texts also evidence the use of a particle that scholars call the enclitic *mêm,* which can be attached to virtually any part of speech. Its precise meaning remains debated, though in certain contexts it appears to denote emphasis. The discovery of this enclitic *mêm* in Ugaritic prompted investigation of the biblical text for evidence of the particle. It is now generally agreed that enclitic *mêm* existed in classical Hebrew poetry, but because the particle itself and its meaning were lost in the course of the transmission of the Hebrew Bible, it has been confused with other morphemes formed with *mêm* (such as the masculine plural suffix *-îm,* the pronominal suffix *-ām,* etc.) in the Masoretic vocalization of the text. The evidence for the existence of enclitic *mêm* is convincing for several reasons. First, there are enough instances of *mêm* being problematic when understood according to Masoretic vocalization to comprise a relatively large pool of test cases. Secondly, positing enclitic *mêm* provides a consistent solution to multiple instances of the same type of problem. For example, there are numerous instances of nouns vocalized by the Masoretes as masculine plurals appearing, with their *-îm* endings intact, as the first member of a construct chain, contrary to the rules of Hebrew grammar. Positing that the Masoretes misunderstood enclitic *mêm* attached to the first member of a construct chain provides a consistent resolution to this type of problem. Thirdly, positing an enclitic *mêm* provides an excellent explanation for resolving variant readings in parallel texts, such as 2 Sam 22:16 compared with Ps 18:16. MT reads *'ăpîqê yām* in the former and *'ăpîqê mayim* in the latter. In this instance, conjecturing that the Masoretes did not recognize enclitic *mêm* and so read it as the first consonant of the word *mayim* resolves the differing readings of the parallel texts. Finally, enclitic *mêm* may explain anomalies such as *lāmô* as an alternate form of *lô* for the preposition *l* with the third-person masculine singular suffix.

Space constraints preclude discussion of the various other individual features of Ugaritic that have been proposed as having relevance for a better understanding of Hebrew, such as vocative *lāmed,* double-duty suffixes, alternate prefixes and suffixes to mark certain finite verb forms, the presence of case endings, and the range of meaning of various prepositions. The merits of these proposals must be considered on a case-by-case basis.

The Ugaritic texts have often been employed in an effort to date various Hebrew Bible poetic compositions. This approach is most closely associated with the Albright school of biblical studies, especially with the work of Frank Moore Cross, David Noel Freedman, and several of their students. Given that the Ugaritic corpus dates from the fourteenth to the early twelfth centuries B.C.E. and therefore predates any composition found in the Hebrew Bible, this approach uses the Ugaritic poetic texts to argue that certain poems in the Hebrew Bible date to an early period in the formation of Israel's religious traditions. The argument entails noting a multiplicity of grammatical, syntactical, lexical, and stylistic features that characterize Ugaritic poetry and then examining Hebrew Bible compositions to see to what extent they exhibit these same characteristics. The presence of one or two features is not considered sufficient evidence of early composition. Rather, biblical texts must exhibit numerous characteristics of Ugaritic poetry to be judged truly archaic. Proceeding in this manner, Cross, Freedman, and other members of the Albright school have advocated the relative antiquity of compositions such as Exod 15:1b–18 and Judg 5:2–30. Dating poems such as these as early has had a significant effect on subsequent reconstructions of Israelite history and tradition, as the texts judged archaic have then been given greater weight by some scholars as evidence for what "actually happened" or for the early stages of a particular tradition. Great care must be exercised in evaluating these reconstructions, as the biblical texts in question are mythological or epic in nature and not early exemplars of history writing.

Analysis of the compositional style of the Ugaritic poetic texts has led to the observation that they exhibit traits indicative of oral traditional narrative. This analysis is indebted to the work of Albert Lord and other folklorists who have articulated the differences between traditional stories generated and transmitted orally and narratives composed by writing. Key characteristics of oral traditional composition in the Ugaritic texts include the employment of stock words, phrases, and formulae to describe oft-repeated scenes, actions, themes, and motifs, as well as the pervasive use of what many scholars call parallelism. Parallelism can refer to words frequently found paired in the same or adjoining cola of poetry (i.e., parallel pairs) and also to common semantic and syntactic features shared most prevalently by two or three cola. The following example illustrates both usages of the term parallelism:

> Let me tell you, Prince Baal,
> let me repeat, Rider of the Clouds:
>
> Behold your enemy, Baal
> behold, you will kill your enemy,
> behold, you will annihilate your foe.
>
> You will take your eternal kingship,
> your dominion forever and ever.

This example consists of a bicolon, a tricolon, and a second bicolon. Word pairs such as "enemy" and "foe," "kill" and "annihilate," and "kingship" and "dominion" appear frequently in Ugaritic poetry and thus may be considered traditional parallel pairs. The persistent pairing of synonymous, complementary, and (though not present in the example) antithetic terms as well as the syntactic parallels between and among groups of cola characterize the compositional technique. The pervasive use of parallelism, in both senses of the word, also characterizes Hebrew Bible poems such as Exod 15:1b–18, the oracles of Balaam in Num 23–24, and Deut 32:1–43, among others. That Ugaritic and Hebrew poetry share both this fundamental compositional technique as well as numerous specific parallel pairs, type-scenes, themes, and motifs significantly enhances the argument for viewing ancient Israel as participating in a Levantine cultural continuum dating back at least to the Late Bronze Age. Before turning to a sampling of these specific shared features, methodological cautions must once again be offered.

The Ugaritic texts have not been unearthed in pristine condition. Numerous lacunae and partially preserved lines, words, and letters occur in the texts, and their state of preservation is steadily deteriorating. In some cases the formulaic nature of the compositional style, such as the proclivity for describing scenes that occur in multiple narrative situations (e.g., setting out on a journey, reacting to good and bad news, commission and delivery of a message) identically or nearly identically, can greatly aid in the reconstruction of lacunae and of poorly preserved words and lines. Unfortunately, the lacunae and broken words and lines have sometimes been filled by scholars in conformity with preconceived notions, and this has impeded rather than aided understanding the texts. Further difficulties issue from the fact that we do not possess anything resembling an indigenous dictionary of Ugaritic. Syllabically written lexical texts listing equivalent words in Sumerian, Akkadian, Hurrian, and Ugaritic provide meanings for over one hundred Ugaritic words, but the meaning of the bulk of Ugaritic words has been adduced on the basis of cognate evidence drawn from the various Semitic languages coupled with contextual coherence. Frequently occurring words in clear contexts have, for the most part, been assigned generally accepted meanings. But the assignation of meaning to rare words, words preserved in broken contexts, and words without an evident cognate can be heavily conditioned by a particular scholar's interpretation of a particular text. Mark Smith has ably documented these phenomena with respect to the major schools of interpretation of the Baal cycle.

A glaring example of how preconceived notions have adversely affected understanding the texts concerns the goddess Anat. Presuming sexuality and reproduction to be the interpretive keys to understanding female deities, and encumbered by a probiblical bias that assumes the inferiority (and often, the moral reprehensibility) of all other ancient Near Eastern religions, numerous scholars have posited that Anat's relationship with Baal included a sexual component, even though there is no clear reference in the Ugaritic texts to Anat engaging in sexual intercourse. Rather, this alleged sexual activity has been read into available lacunae, and *hapax legomena* and other cryptic words and episodes have then been invested with appropriately supportive meanings. The problem has been further compounded by interpreting this alleged sexual behavior as the mythological expression of the so-called sacred marriage rite, otherwise known as ritual (or sacred) prostitution, itself a highly questionable scholarly construct. Interpreted in this way, the Ugaritic texts have then been cited as evidence relevant to understanding the Deuteronomistic and prophetic critique of improper cultic practice in ancient Israel. As this example illustrates, it is necessary to examine very carefully claims made on the basis of the Ugaritic texts to ensure that they are well grounded in the texts and are not the product of eisegesis. Arguments hinging on the alleged meaning of rare words or episodes in broken contexts are particularly suspect. Also highly problematic are interpretations that presume a necessary link between myth and ritual.

The Ugaritic texts dubbed the Baal (or Baal and Anat) cycle have had a profound impact on understanding numerous Hebrew Bible texts. "Baal (and Anat) cycle" is the term used by many scholars for six tablets and various fragments (*CAT* 1.1–1.6) arranged in a particular order and considered as a group. The relationship of these tablets and tablet fragments to one another is debated, due in part to the often extensive lacunae. Do all six tablets actually belong together? *CAT* 1.1 is very fragmentary and its relationship to the others especially difficult to judge, and the six tablets and tablet fragments were not all found in the same place. *CAT* 1.2 contains a clear description of the warrior and storm god Baal vanquishing (Prince) Sea, yet in *CAT* 1.3 the deity Anat equally as clearly affirms that she finished off Sea. While contradictions such as this one can be plausibly explained by traditional narrative theory as alloforms (or variant tellings) of "the same" story, some scholars have argued that it is doubtful that variant tellings of this nature would coexist in a single, continuous narrative. This and other problems of coherence, coupled with the issue of find spots, suggest that the six tablets may not be a continuous narrative but a group of separate narratives focusing on Baal (and, to a lesser extent, on Anat). Narrative continuity between the end of 1.5 and the beginning of 1.6 indicates that at least these two tablets do tell a continuous tale.

In terms of how the Baal cycle has contributed to better understanding Hebrew Bible texts, space constraints prohibit an exhaustive treatment. However, in the Baal cycle, Baal is clearly presented as a storm deity. He is called Cloudrider (e.g., 1.1 IV 8); his voice sounds in the clouds, and he flashes lightning (e.g., 1.4 V 8–9); and his rains water the earth (e.g., 1.4 V 6-7; cf. 1.5 V 6–8). These features also characterize Yahweh, who is called Rider on the Clouds (Ps 68:5) and who, in passages such as 2 Sam 22 (par. Ps 18), is enveloped by thick clouds (v. 12), with thunder as his voice (v. 14) and lightning as his arrows (v. 15). In 1.2 of the Baal cycle, Baal defeats in combat the deity known by the names (Prince) Sea and (Judge) River, names that typically appear in parallel construction. Recognizing Sea/River as an enemy of the storm god Baal has led to a deeper appreciation of texts such as Hab 3:8, where River and Sea are paired as the object of Yahweh's anger. Like Baal, the warrior Yahweh in Hab 3 is overtly described by phenomena associated with storms, such as clouds pouring down water (v. 10) and lightning functioning as a mythological spear (v. 11). In 1.2 of the Baal cycle, Baal's victory over Sea/River entails assuming eternal kingship, called everlasting dominion in the second colon of the bicolon (1.2 IV 10). This parallel pairing is applied to Yahweh in Ps 145:13, and he is described as enthroned forever over the primordial waters in, for example, Ps 29:10, a psalm that many have argued is a thinly veiled adaptation of an earlier paean to Baal. The association between victory over Sea/River and eternal rule is extended to ground the Davidic dynasty in Ps 89:26, where Yahweh, by virtue of his ruling over the raging of (the) Sea, establishes

David's power over Sea/River(s). (A variation of this theme appears in
Mari text A.1968, in which the storm god is depicted as giving the
weapons he used to defeat the primordial waters to a newly enthroned
king.) The association between the storm god's power over the primordial deeps and eternal rule is present, albeit arguably in modified form,
in Exod 15, where the blast of warrior Yahweh's nostrils creates a storm
at sea that discomfits the enemy and results in the proclamation of Yahweh's eternal reign.

In 1.3, the claim to have routed Sea/River is extended to include
assertions of conquest over a serpent/dragon, described as twisting and
seven-headed (1.3 III 38–42). In Ps 74:13, Yahweh's conquest of Sea is
described in the parallel colon as a victory over a many-headed dragon
(understanding MT's pluralization of "dragon" as an instance of a misunderstood enclitic *mêm*). Yahweh's serpent foe is described as twisting in
Isa 27:1 and is called Leviathan, a name that is cognate with Ugaritic
Lotan, found elsewhere in the Baal cycle (1.5 I 1–3) as the name of the
twisting, seven-headed dragon. Additional passages, such as Isa 51:9 and
Ps 89:11, celebrate Yahweh's defeat of the serpent/dragon. The principal
concern, however, of 1.3, is Baal's request for a "house," a concern that
also dominates 1.4. Comparison with the Mesopotamian *Enuma Elish* suggests that the house/temple-building theme is intended to function as a
recognition of Baal's victory over the primordial waters and his ensuing
kingship, hence the placement of 1.3 and 1.4 after 1.2 (i.e., the sequenc-
ing of the tablets, indicated by their numbering, is a scholarly construction
influenced by the order of events in *Enuma Elish*). This house-building
theme, following a (modified) description of Yahweh's power over the
deeps and in association with proclamation of his kingship, is found in
Exod 15. Baal's house is built on Mount Sapan, described as the holy
mountain of his heritage and his hill of might (1.3 III 29–31; cf. *CAT* 1.101
1–3). Yahweh's mountain is described similarly in Ps 78:54 and Exod
15:17, and in Ps 48:3 Zion is essentially equated with Mount Sapan. In the
biblical material, Yahweh's defeat of the Sea (dragon) is clearly associated
with cosmogony (e.g., Pss 74:12–17; 89:10–13) and the "creation" (e.g.,
Exod 15:1b–18) or repatriation (Isa 51:9–11) of his people. Though cosmogony likewise proceeds from the conquest of the primordial deeps in
Enuma Elish, scholars debate whether this theme is evident in the Baal
cycle. Some indication of this theme may be inferred from 1.4 V 6–7,
where the building of Baal's house is linked with his provision of life-giving rains, a prerequisite for ordering and sustaining life in the Levant. It
has been argued that the "when … then" syntactical construction of 1.5 I
1–5, which describes the drooping of the heavens as a consequence of the
defeat of the dragon, is a formulaic expression of cosmogony. It has also
been argued that the dismemberment of Sea (1.1 IV 27), if that is the correct

translation, may tersely express the motif of Yahweh's (and Marduk's) dividing up of the primordial waters as a prelude to ordering earth and skies (cf. Gen 1:6–9).

The last two columns of 1.4 and all of 1.5 and 1.6 are primarily concerned with Baal's relationship to Mot, the Ugaritic deity whose name means death. Mot's realm, for example in 1.4 VIII 7–9, is described by the Ugaritic cognate of Hebrew *'ereṣ,* a common word for earth or land. The usage of the Ugaritic cognate to describe Mot's realm launched a search for netherworldly connotations of Hebrew *'ereṣ,* a search that produced positive and enlightening results. Positing this connotation in Exod 15:12, for example, yields a fuller appreciation of the meaning of the passage, which tells of the demise of the Egyptian troops in the waters of the Reed Sea. Exodus 15:12's use of the verb "to swallow" (*blʿ*) in this context (cf., e.g., Num 16:32) is consistent with the Ugaritic metaphor of Mot's devouring appetite, found for example in 1.4 VIII 17–20 and 1.5 I 14–22. Sheol is credited with widening its throat and eating voluminously in Isa 5:14, and Jonah 2:3 talks of Sheol's belly. That Baal and his entourage, including his life-giving rains (1.5 V 6–11), descend into Mot's belly (1.5 II 2–6) is a mythological explanation of drought and/or the dry season, and this theme may provide background information for a fuller understanding of 1 Kgs 18.

When Baal's death (1.5 VI 8–10) and descent into Mot's realm is made known to El, he immediately performs acts of mourning, falling to the ground, pouring dirt on his head, and donning special clothing (1.5 VI 14–17). These acts connoted mourning in ancient Israel as well (e.g., Josh 7:6; Lam 2:10), thus once again illustrating some degree of cultural continuity (cf. Ezek 27:30). The Ugaritic text goes on to describe El gashing and cutting himself (1.5 VI 17–22; cf. 1.6 I 2–5), acts attributed to the prophets of Baal in 1 Kgs 18:28 when their petition to him to send fire went unanswered. Deuteronomy 14:1, for example, prohibits self-laceration in mourning for the dead.

CAT 1.6 continues to narrate mourning and lamentation for Baal. Baal's return to the realm of life later in the tablet (1.6 V; cf. 1.6 III 20–21) has occasioned interpretations of Baal as a dying and rising god akin to Adonis and Tammuz. But the language of death and life is better understood as expressing the presence or absence of the storm god's rains. *CAT* 1.6 VI 45–49 mentions the rule of the sun goddess over a group called the *rpʾum,* who, in subsequent cola, are described as gods and the dead. This group appears in *CAT* 1.161 as dead ancestors of the royal line of Ugarit. The Ugaritic term is cognate with the Hebrew *rəpāʾîm,* which was a poorly understood term prior to the discovery of the Ugaritic texts. The *rəpāʾîm* and the dead appear in parallel construction in Ps 88:11 and Isa 26:14, 19. Isaiah 14:9 portrays the Rephaim as deceased royalty, not limited to the Ugaritic royal line. The Ugaritic data also aid in understanding texts such as Gen 14:5, in which the Rephaim are said to be among the pre-Israelite inhabitants of the land.

3. ANCIENT SOURCES, MODERN RESOURCES

The corpus of published and unpublished tablets and tablet fragments written in the Ugaritic language is approximately thirteen hundred, of which the vast majority are administrative. Internal correspondence and texts dealing with local legal matters are two additional genres. Tablets produced by scribes in training (including abecedaries) are also in evidence, and there are four exemplars of so-called hippiatric texts, which deal with treatments for ailing horses. The Baal cycle comprises six of the approximately 150 tablets and tablet fragments found at Ugarit and the associated tell Ras Ibn Hani that can be categorized as literary or religious (i.e., mythological, paramythological, epic, or cultic), and it is this group of texts that has been of principal interest to Hebrew Bible scholars. The multitablet narratives titled by the names of their central characters, Keret and Aqhat, have received attention on par with that paid to the Baal cycle, and a number of single-tablet texts have received significant, though lesser, attention. A complete bibliography of important works pertinent to this group of texts simply cannot be presented here, as it is voluminous.

One of the most frustrating aspects of working with the Ugaritic texts is the fact that the respective tablets are referred to by different notation systems. Virolleaud, who published the *editio princeps* of numerous texts, frequently used (except for the texts found in 1929) a system of Roman numerals combined with title abbreviations (e.g., III AB) or simply title abbreviations. Other scholars working on the texts in the 1930s and into the 1950s essentially, though not always precisely, followed Virolleaud. The principal published collections (in transliteration) of the texts employ different systems, referred to in the literature as:

UT plus number = C. H. Gordon, *Ugaritic Textbook*. Rome: Pontifical Biblical Institute, 1965.
CTA plus number = A. Herdner, *Corpus des tablettes en cunéiformes alphabétiques découvertes à Ras Shamra-Ugarit de 1929 à 1939*, volume 1. Paris: Imprimerie Nationale, 1963.
KTU plus number.number = M. Dietrich, O. Loretz, and J. Sanmartín, *Die keilalphabetischen Texte aus Ugarit*, volume 1. Neukirchen-Vluyn: Neukirchener Verlag, 1976.
CAT plus number.number = M. Dietrich, O. Loretz, and J. Sanmartín, *The Cuneiform Alphabetic Texts from Ugarit, Ras Ibn Hani and Other Places*. Münster: Ugarit-Verlag, 1995.

The last of these collections is a second edition of *KTU* that includes texts
not published in *KTU*. For *CAT* texts that appeared in *KTU* the numbers
remain the same. However, on the basis of collation and critical study subsequent to 1976, *CAT* sometimes diverges from *KTU* in the readings it
proposes. The first number in the *KTU/CAT* system represents the editors'
classification of the texts into genres, with the number 1 denoting literary
and religious texts, the group of principal interest to biblical scholars. In
an attempt to rectify the problem of multiple notation systems, Bordreuil
and Pardee proposed numbering the tablets according to the campaign
during which they were discovered plus their inventory numbers, preceded by RS (denoting Ras Shamra) or RIH (denoting Ras Ibn Hani). From
1929 through 1974 the campaigns are numbered 1–35 (i.e., 1 is the 1929
campaign, 2 is the 1930 campaign, etc., with excavations suspended 1940–
1947 inclusive), and the campaigns beginning in 1975 are numbered by the
year itself, minus indication of the century (i.e., the 1975 campaign is 75,
the 1976 campaign is 76, etc.). Thus:

> RS or RIH plus number.number = P. Bordreuil and D. Pardee, *La trou-
> vaille épigraphique l'Ougarit,* volume 1: *Concordance.* Paris: Éditions
> Recherche sur les civilisations, 1989.

This work is not a concordance in the usual sense. Rather, it catalogues all
inscribed items according to the campaign in which the item was found
and includes information on find spots, the museum holding the item (the
vast majority of items are in the national museums of Damascus, Aleppo,
or the Louvre), where the *editio princeps* was published, and in which (if
any) collection (*UT, KTU,* etc.) the item appears. All of the above works
provide some cross-referencing to notation systems other than their own.
An online collection of the Ugaritic texts (based on *KTU*) is available at
http://www.labherm.filol.csic.es, accessed by clicking on GSRC-Internet.
This is the website of the Banco de datos filológicos semíticos nordocci-
dentales (BDFSN) Project, based in Madrid and headed by J.-L. Cunchillos.
The texts and accompanying concordance are also available on CD-ROM
(see below).

That the various collections sometimes differ in their readings under-
scores the need for accessible, high-quality photographs of the texts.
Three projects are addressing that need: the Ugaritic Tablets Digital Edition Project (UTDE), the Edinburgh Ras Shamra Project (ERSP), and
BDFSN. Photographs produced by ERSP were used in the preparation of
CAT. A very limited selection of images of Ugaritic tablets is available on
the ERSP website, http://www.ed.ac.uk/~ugarit/home.htm. Information
about UTDE is available on the West Semitic Research Project home page,
http://www.usc.edu/dept/LAS/wsrp/. As of September 2000, this site did

not include a catalogue of available photographs. Providing an online database of high resolution images is one of the project's goals. Online images are also a goal of BDFSN but are not currently on their website.

The most up-to-date concordances of Ugaritic are:

Cunchillos, J.-L., and J.-P. Vita. *Banco de datos filológicos semíticos noroccidentales II Concordancia de palabras ugaríticas.* 3 vols. Madrid: Institución Fernando el Católico, 1995. (updated version integrated with the *KTU* database online at http://www.labherm.filol.csic.es, click on GSRC-Internet)

Del Olmo Lete, G., and Joaquín Sanmartín. *Diccionario de la lengua ugarítica.* 2 vols. Barcelona: Editorial AUSA, 1996, 2000.

Dietrich, Manfred, and Oswald Loretz. *Word-List of the Cuneiform Alphabetic Texts from Ugarit, Ras Ibn Hani and Other Places.* Münster: Ugarit-Verlag, 1996.

Kottsieper, I. "Indizes und Korrekturen zur 'Word-List of the Cuneiform Alphabetic Texts.'" *UF* 29 (1997): 243–383.

Zemánek, P. *Ugaritischer Wortformenindex.* Hamburg: Helmut Buske, 1995.

Three Ugaritic grammars are:

Segert, Stanislav. *A Basic Grammar of the Ugaritic Language.* Berkeley and Los Angeles: University of California Press, 1984.

Sivan, Daniel. *A Grammar of the Ugaritic Language.* Leiden: Brill, 1997.

Tropper, J. *Ugaritische Grammatik.* Münster: Ugarit-Verlag, 2000.

Bibliographies of Ugaritic studies are:

Cunchillos, J.-L. *La Trouvaille épigraphique de l'Ougarit 2: Bibliographie.* Paris: Éditions Recherche sur les civilisations, 1990.

Dietrich, Manfred, and Oswald Loretz. *Ugaritic Bibliography 1928–1966.* Neukirchen-Vluyn: Neukirchener Verlag, 1973.

———. *Analytic Ugaritic Bibliography 1967–1971.* Neukirchen-Vluyn: Neukirchener Verlag, 1986.

———. *Analytic Ugaritic Bibliography 1972–1988.* Neukirchen-Vluyn: Neukirchener Verlag, 1996.

Pardee, Dennis. "Ugaritic Bibliography." *AfO* 34 (1987): 366–471. (organized by Ugaritic words)

Translations of major Ugaritic texts (including citations of earlier/other translations) are:

Caquot, André, Maurice Sznycer, and Andrée Herdner, A. *Mythes et légendes.* Vol. 1 of *Textes ougaritiques.* Paris: Cerf, 1974.

Caquot, André, J.-M. de Tarragon, and J.-L. Cunchillos. *Textes religieux, rituels, correspondance.* Vol. 2 of *Textes ougaritiques.* Paris: Cerf, 1989.

Hallo, William, ed. *Canonical Compositions from the Biblical World.* Vol. 1 of *The Context of Scripture.* Leiden: Brill, 1997.

Parker, Simon B., ed. *Ugaritic Narrative Poetry.* SBLWAW 9. Atlanta: Scholars Press, 1997.

Smith, Mark S. *Introduction with Text, Translation and Commentary of KTU 1.1–1.2.* Vol. 1 of *The Ugaritic Baal Cycle.* Leiden: Brill, 1994.

Wyatt, Nick. *Religious Texts from Ugarit: The Words of Ilimilku and His Colleagues.* Sheffield: Sheffield Academic Press, 1998.

Selected foundational studies that apply Ugaritic materials to the study of the Hebrew Bible are:

Clifford, Richard J. *The Cosmic Mountain in Canaan and the Old Testament.* HSM 4. Cambridge, Mass.: Harvard University Press, 1972.

Cross, Frank M. *Canaanite Myth and Hebrew Epic.* Cambridge, Mass.: Harvard University Press, 1973.

Cross, Frank M., and David Noel Freedman. *Studies in Ancient Yahwistic Poetry.* Missoula, Mont.: Scholars Press, 1975.

Fisher, Loren R., ed. *Ras Shamra Parallels: The Texts from Ugarit and the Hebrew Bible.* 2 vols. Rome: Biblical Institute Press, 1972, 1975.

Miller, Patrick D. *The Divine Warrior in Early Israel.* HSM 5. Cambridge, Mass.: Harvard University Press, 1973.

Mullen, E. Theodore. *The Assembly of the Gods: The Divine Council in Canaanite and Early Hebrew Literature.* HSM 24. Chico, Calif.: Scholars Press, 1980.

Robertson, D. A. *Linguistic Evidence in Dating Early Hebrew Poetry.* SBLDS 3. Missoula, Mont.: Scholars Press, 1972.

Tromp, N. J. *Primitive Conceptions of Death and the Nether World in the Old Testament.* Rome: Biblical Institute Press, 1969.

Selected more recent works (starred items indicate those with substantial bibliographies):

*Brooke, G. J., A. H. W. Curtis, and J. F. Healey, eds. *Ugarit and the Bible: Proceedings of the International Symposium on Ugarit and the Bible, Manchester, September 1992.* Münster: Ugarit-Verlag, 1994.

Hackett, Jo Ann. "Can a Sexist Model Liberate Us? Ancient Near Eastern Fertility Goddesses." *JFSR* 5 (1989): 65–76.

*Hendel, Ronald S. *The Epic of the Patriarch: The Jacob Cycle and the Narrative Traditions of Canaan and Israel.* HSM 42. Atlanta: Scholars Press, 1987.

Hillers, Delbert R. "Analyzing the Abominable: Our Understanding of Canaanite Religion." *JQR* 75 (1985): 253–69.

*Lewis, Theodore J. *Cults of the Dead in Ancient Israel and Ugarit.* HSM 39. Atlanta: Scholars Press, 1989.

Oden, Robert A. *The Bible without Theology*. San Francisco: Harper & Row, 1987.

*Parker, Simon B. *The Pre-Biblical Narrative Tradition: Essays on the Ugaritic Poems Keret and Aqhat*. SBLRBS 24. Atlanta: Scholars Press, 1989.

*Smith, Mark S. *The Early History of God: Yahweh and Other Deities in Ancient Israel*. San Francisco: Harper & Row, 1990.

*van der Toorn, Karel, Bob Becking, and Pieter W. van der Horst, eds. *Dictionary of Deities and Demons in the Bible*. 2d ed. Leiden: Brill, 1999.

*Watson, W. G. E., and N. Wyatt, eds. *Handbook of Ugaritic Studies*. Leiden: Brill, 1999.

*Wyatt, N., et al., eds. *Ugarit, Religion and Culture: Proceedings of the International Colloquium on Ugarit, Religion and Culture, Edinburgh, July 1994*. Münster: Ugarit-Verlag, 1996.